The Red Bridge Reader

SECOND EDITION

Sharon J. Gerson and James K. Norman

And the DeVry - Kansas City English Faculty

SIMON & SCHUSTER CUSTOM PUBLISHING

Printed in the United States of America

10 9 8 7 6 5 4 3 2 1

Please visit our website at www.sscp.com

ISBN 0–536–01773-5

BA 98531

SIMON & SCHUSTER CUSTOM PUBLISHING
160 Gould Street/Needham Heights, MA 02194
Simon & Schuster Higher Education Publishing Group

Copyright Acknowledgments

For our children,
Reed,
Stacy and Stefani

Contents

CHAPTER 6

Comparison / Contrast: Discovering Similarities and Differences

CHAPTER 7

Cause / Effect: Tracing Reasons and Results

CHAPTER 10

Documented Essays:
Reading and Writing from Sources

Introduction

In this second edition we have made numerous changes. As well as the new cover design with the more appropriate color and the picture of the Red Bridge, we have altered the reader in the following ways:

1. Removed essays that students and teachers found uninteresting.

2. Added essays to all chapters.

3. Included end-of-chapter writing-topic suggestions. Some of these suggestions are keyed to specific chapter readings, and others are more open-ended.

4. Provided checklists at the end of each chapter to help students self-evaluate their papers before other students or their teachers read them.

We hope that students and teachers alike continue to find this reader as useful in the English 110 and 125 classes as we have found it to be.

We would like to thank all of our DeVry-Kansas City English colleagues and students for their input. Also, we want to thank our editor, Terry Brennan, for his invaluable assistance.

We look forward to receiving any ideas you have about our text. You can reach us via e-mail at Sgerson@Kc.devry.edu and Knorman@Kc.devry.edu. Please contact us with any comments or suggestions.

James K. Norman and Sharon J. Gerson

CHAPTER 1

Description

Exploring Through the Senses

Using Description

All of us use description in our daily lives. We might, for example, try to convey the horrors of a recent history exam to our parents, or help a friend visualize someone we met on vacation, or describe an automobile accident for a police report. Whatever our specific purpose, description is fundamental to the act of communication: We give and receive descriptions constantly, and our lives are continually affected by this simple yet important rhetorical technique.

Defining Description

Description may be defined as the act of capturing people, places, events, objects, and feelings in words so that a reader (or listener) can visualize and respond to them. Unlike narration, which traditionally presents events in a clear time sequence, description essentially suspends its objects in time, making them exempt from such limits of chronology. Description is one of our primary forms of self-expression; it paints a verbal picture that helps the reader understand or share a sensory experience through the process of "showing" rather than "telling." Telling your friends, for example, that "the campgrounds were filled with friendly, happy activities" is not as engaging as *showing* them by saying, "The campgrounds were alive with the smell of spicy baked beans, the sound of high-pitched laughter, and the sight of happy families sharing the warmth of a fire."

Descriptions range between two broad types: (1) totally objective reports, which we might find in a dictionary or an encyclopedia, and (2) very subjective accounts, which focus almost exclusively on personal impressions. The same horse, for instance, might be described by one writer as "a large, solid-hoofed herbivorous mammal having a long mane and a tail" and by another as "a magnificent and spirited beast flaring its nostrils in search of adventure." Most descriptive writing, however, falls somewhere between these two extremes: "a large, four-legged beast in search of adventure."

Objective description is principally characterized by its impartial, precise, and emotionless tone. Found most prominently in technical and scientific writing, such accounts might include a description of equipment to be used in a chemistry experiment, the results of a market survey for a particular consumer product, or a medical appraisal of a heart patient's physical symptoms. In situations like these, accurate, unbiased, and easily understandable accounts are of the utmost importance.

Subjective description, in contrast, is intentionally created to produce a particular response in the reader or listener. Focusing on feelings rather than on raw data, it tries to activate as many senses as possible, thereby leading the audience to a specific conclusion or state of mind. Examples of subjective descriptions could involve a parent's disapproving comments about one of your friends, a professor's glowing analysis of your most recent "A" paper, or a basketball coach's critique of his team's losing effort in last night's big game.

In most situations, the degree of subjectivity or objectivity in a descriptive passage depends to a large extent upon the writer's purpose and intended audience. In the case of the heart patient mentioned above, the person's physician might present the case in a formal, scientific way to a group of medical colleagues; in a personal, sympathetic way to the invalid's spouse; and in financial terms to a number of potential contributors in order to solicit funds for heart disease research.

The following paragraph describes one student's fond memories of visiting "the farm." As you read it, notice the writer's use of subjective description to communicate to her readers the multitude of contradictory feelings she connects with this rural retreat.

The shrill scream of the alarm shatters a dream. This is the last day of my visit to the place I call "the farm," an old ramshackle house in the country owned by one of my aunts. I want to go out once more in the peace of the early morning, walk in the crisp and chilly hour, and breathe the sweet air. My body feels jarred as my feet hit the hard-packed clay dirt. I tune out my stiff muscles and cold arms and legs and instead focus on two herons playing hopscotch on the canal bank. Every few yards I walk towards them; they fly one over the other, an almost equal distance away from me. A killdeer with its piercing crystalline cry dips its body as it flies low over the water, the tip of its wing leaving a ring to reverberate outward. The damp earth has a strong, rich, musky scent. To the east, dust rises, and for the first time I hear the clanking and straining of a tractor as it harrows smooth the soil before planting. A crop duster rises close by just as it cuts off its release of spray, the acrid taste of chemical filtering down through the air. As the birds chatter and peck at the fields, I turn to escape to my life in the city.

Reading and Writing Descriptive Essays

All good descriptions share four fundamental qualities: (1) an accurate sense of audience and purpose, (2) a clear vision of the object being described, (3) a careful selection of details, and (4) a consistent point of view or perspective from which a writer composes. The dominant impression or main effect the writer wishes to leave with a specific audience dictates virtually all of the verbal choices in a descriptive essay. Although description is featured in this chapter, you should also pay close attention to how other rhetorical strategies (such as example, division/classification, and cause/effect) can effectively support the dominant impression.

How to Write a Descriptive Essay

Preparing to Write. Before you choose a writing assignment, discover your own ideas and opinions about the general topic of the essay. Then, just as you do when you read an essay, you should determine the audience and purpose for your description (if these are not specified for you in the assignment). To whom are you writing? And why? Will an impartial, objective report be appropriate, or should you present a more emotional, subjective account to accomplish your task? In assessing your audience, you need to determine what they do and do not know about your topic. This information will help you make decisions about what you are going to say and how you will say it. Your purpose will be defined by what you intend your audience to know, think, or believe after they have read your descriptive essay. Do you want them to make up their own minds about summer rituals or old age, for example, based on an objective presentation of data, or do you hope to sway their opinion through a more subjective display of information? Or perhaps you will decide to blend the two techniques in order to achieve the impression of personal certainty based on objective evidence. What dominant impression do you want to leave with your audience? As you might suspect, decisions regarding audience and purpose are as important to writing descriptions as they are to reading descriptions and will shape your descriptive essay from start to finish.

The second quality of good description concerns the object of your analysis and the clarity with which you present it to the reader. Whenever possible, you should thoroughly investigate the person, place, moment, or feeling you wish to describe, paying particular attention to its effect upon each of your five senses. What can you see, smell, hear, taste, and touch as you examine it? If you want to describe your house, for example, begin by asking yourself a series of pertinent questions: How big is the house? What color is it? How many exterior doors does the house have? How many interior? Are any of the rooms wallpapered? If so, what is the color and texture of that wallpaper? How many different shades of paint cover the walls? Which rooms have constant noises (from clocks and other mechanical devices)? Are the kitchen appliances hot or cold to the touch? What is the quietest room in the house? the noisiest? What smells do you notice in the laundry? In the kitchen? In the basement? Most important, do any of these sensory questions trigger particular childhood memories? Although you will probably not use all of these details in your descriptive essay, the process of generating and answering such detailed questions will help reacquaint you with the object of your description as it also assists you in designing and focusing your paper.

Writing. As you write, you must select the details of your description with great care and precision so that you leave your reader with a specific impression. If, for instance, you want your audience to feel the warmth and comfort of your home, you might concentrate on describing the plush carpets, the big upholstered chairs, the inviting scent of hot apple cider, and the crackling fire. If, on the other hand, you want to gain your audience's sympathy, you might prefer to focus on the sparse austerity of your home environment: the bare walls, the quietness, the lack of color and decoration, the dim lighting, and the frigid temperature. Your careful choice of details will help control your audience's reaction.

To make your impression even more vivid, you could use figurative language to fill out your descriptions. Using words "figuratively" means using them imaginatively rather than literally. The two most popular forms of figurative language are *simile* and *metaphor.* A *simile* is a comparison between two dissimilar objects or ideas introduced by *like* or *as*: "The rocking chairs sounded like crickets" (Bradbury). A metaphor is an implied comparison between two dissimilar objects or ideas that is not introduced by *like* or *as*: "Life for younger persons is still a battle royal of each against each." Besides enlivening your writing, figurative language helps your readers understand objects, feeling, and ideas that are complex or obscure by comparing them with things that are more familiar.

The last important quality of an effective descriptive essay is point of view, your physical perspective on your subject. Because the organization of your essay depends on your point of view, you need to choose a specific angle from which to approach your description. If you verbally jump around your home, referring first to a picture on the wall in your bedroom, next to the microwave in the kitchen, and then to the quilt on your bed, no reasonable audience will be able to follow your description. Nor will they want to. If, however, you move from room to room in some logical, sequential way, always focusing on the details you want your readers to know, you will be helping your audience form a clear, memorable impression of your home. Your vision will become their vision. In other words, your point of view plays a part in determining the organization of your description. Working spatially, you could move from side to side (from one wall to another in the rooms we have discussed), from top to bottom (from ceiling to floor), from near to far (from farthest to closest point in a room), or you might progress from large to small objects, from uninteresting to interesting, or from funny to serious. Whatever plan you choose should help you accomplish your purpose with your particular audience.

Rewriting. As you reread each of your descriptive essays, play the role of your audience and try to determine what dominant impression you revive by the end of your reading. Is this the impression you were trying to convey? How does the essay make you feel? What does it make you think about? Which sense does it stimulate? Are you "showing" rather than "telling" in your description? Which sections of the essay are most effective? What could you do to make the weaker sections more effective? Could you, for example, add more detailed information, reorganize some of the essay, or omit irrelevant material?

Student Essay: Description at Work

In the following essay, a student relives some of her childhood memories through a subjective description of her grandmother's house. As you read it, pay particular attention to the different types of sensual details the student writer chooses in order to communicate to readers her dominant impression of her grandmother's home. Notice also her use of carefully chosen details to "show" rather than "tell" us about her childhood reminiscences.

Grandma's House

Writer's point of view or perspective   <u>My most vivid childhood memories</u> are set in my Grandma Goodlink's house, a curious blend of familiar and mysterious treasures. Grandma lived at the end of a dead-end street, in the same house she had lived in since the first day of her marriage. That was half a century and thirteen children ago. A set of crumbly steps made of concrete mixed with gravel led up to her front door. I remember a big gap between the house and the steps, <u>as if someone had not pushed them up close enough to the house.</u> Anyone who looked into the gap could see <u>old toys and books</u> that had fallen into the crack behind the steps and had remained there, forever irretrievable. *(Dominant impression) (Comparison simile) (Sight)*

    Only a hook-type lock on the front door protected Grandma's many beautiful antiques. Her living room was set up <u>like a church or schoolroom,</u> with an <u>old purple velvet couch</u> against the far wall and two chairs immediately in front of the couch facing the same direction. <u>One-half of the couch was always buried in old clothes, magazines, and newspapers, and</u> <u>a lone shoe sat atop the pile, a finishing touch to some bazaar modern sculpture.</u> To one side was an aged and <u>tuneless</u> upright piano with <u>yellowed keys.</u> The ivory *(Comparison simile) (Sight) (Sight) (Comparison metaphor) (Sound) (Sight)*

overlay was missing so that the wood underneath Sight
showed through, and many of them made only a muf-
Sound fled and frustrating thump, no matter how hard I
pressed them. On the wall facing the piano was the
room's only window, draped with yellowed lace cur- Sight
tains. Grandma always left that window open. I
Smell remember sitting near it, smelling the rain while the
curtains tickled on my face. Touch

For no apparent reason, an old curtain hung in the
door between the kitchen and the living room. In the
kitchen, a large formica-topped table always held at
least a half-dozen varieties of homemade jelly, as well Taste
as a loaf of bread, gooseberry pies or cherry pies with
the pits left in, boxes of cereal, and anything else not
Comparison requiring refrigeration, as if the table served as a small,
(simile) portable pantry. Grandma's kitchen always smelled of Smell
toast, and I often wondered—and still do—if she lived
entirely on toast. A hole had eaten through the kitchen Sight
floor, not just the warped yellow linoleum, but all the
way through the floor itself. My sisters and I never
wanted to take a bath at Grandma's house, because we
discovered that anyone who lay on the floor on his
stomach and put one eye to the hole could see the Sight
bathtub, which was kept in the musty basement Smell
because the upstairs bathroom was too small.

The back bedroom was near the kitchen and adjacent to the basement stairs. I once heard one of my
aunts call that room a firetrap, and indeed it was. The
room was wallpapered with the old newspapers Sight
Grandma liked to collect, and the bed was stacked
high with my mother's and aunt's old clothes. There
was no space between the furniture in that room, only
a narrow path against one wall leading to the bed. A
sideboard was shoved against the opposite wall; a
sewing table was pushed up against the sideboard; a
short chest of drawers lay against the sewing table;
and so on. But no one could identify these pieces of
forgotten furniture unless he dug through the sewing
patterns, half-made dresses, dishes, and books. Any
outsider would just think this was a part of the room
where the floor had been raised to about waist-level,
so thoroughly was the mass of furniture hidden.

Stepping off Grandma's sloping back porch was
Comparison like stepping into an enchanted forest. The grass and
(simile) weeds were hip-level, with a tiny dirt path leading to
nowhere, as if it had lost its way in the jungle. A fancy Comparison
white fence, courtesy of the neighbors, bordered the (simile)

Sight yard in back and vainly attempted to hold the goose-berries, raspberries, and blackberries that grew wildly along the side of Grandma's yard. Huge crabapple, cherry, and walnut trees shaded the house and hid the sky. I used to stand under them and look up, pretending to be deep in a magic forest. The ground was <u>cool and damp</u> under my bare feet, even in the middle of Touch the day, and my head would fill with the <u>sweet fragrance of mixed spring flowers</u> and <u>throaty cooing of</u> Smell <u>doves</u> I could never find but could always hear. But, Sound before long, the wind would shift, and the <u>musty aroma of petroleum</u> from a nearby refinery would jerk Smell me back to reality.

Grandma's house is indeed a place for memories. Just as her decaying concrete steps store the treasures of many lost childhoods, <u>her house still stands, guarding the memories of generations of children and grandchildren.</u>

Dominant impression rephrased

Student Writer's Comments

Writing this descriptive essay was easy and enjoyable for me. I just picked a place I know well and brainstormed about it, being sure to think of images from all five senses. After I had plenty of images, I organized my essay as if I were walking through Grandma's house. I devoted one paragraph to each room, plus one for the yard. In my rewriting, I looked for opportunities to use comparisons and found plenty. My biggest problem was that I had too many memories and thus had to be selective. I hated leaving out anything!

Some Final Thoughts on Description

Because description is one of the most basic forms of verbal communication, you will find descriptive passages in most of the reading selections throughout this textbook. Description provides us with the means to capture our audience's attention and clarify certain points in all of our writing. The examples chosen for the following section, however, are predominantly descriptive—the main purpose in each being to involve the readers' senses as vividly as possible. As you read through each of these essays, try to determine its intended audience and purpose, the object of the description, the extent to which details are included or excluded, and the author's point of view. Equipped with these four areas of reference, you can become an increasingly sophisticated reader and writer of descriptive prose.

A Guard's First Night on the Job

William Recktenwald

When I arrived for my first shift, 3 to 11 P.M., I had not had a minute of training except for a one-hour orientation lecture the previous day. I was a "fish," a rookie guard, and very much out of my depth.

A veteran officer welcomed the "fish" and told us: "Remember, these guys don't have anything to do all day, 24 hours a day, but think of ways to make you mad. No matter what happens, don't lose your cool. Don't lose your cool!"

I had been assigned to the segregation unit, containing 215 inmates who are the most trouble. It was an assignment nobody wanted.

To get there, I passed through seven sets of bars. My uniform was my only ticket through each of them. Even on my first day, I was not asked for any identification, searched, or sent through a metal detector. I could have been carrying weapons, drugs, or any other contraband. I couldn't believe this was what's meant by a maximum-security institution. In the week I worked at Pontiac, I was subjected to only one check, and that one was cursory.

The segregation unit consists of five tiers, or galleries. Each is about 300 feet long and has 44 cells. The walkways are about 3 1/2 feet wide, with the cells on one side and a rail and cyclone fencing on the other. As I walked along one gallery, I noticed that my elbows could touch cell bars and fencing at the same time. That made me easy pickings for anybody reaching out of a cell.

The first thing they told me was that a guard must never go out on a gallery by himself. You've got no weapons with which to defend yourself, not even a radio to summon help. All you've got is the man with whom you're working.

My partner that first night was Bill Hill, a soft-spoken six-year veteran who immediately told me to take the cigarettes out of my shirt pocket because the inmates would steal them. Same for my pen, he said—or "They'll grab it and stab you."

We were told to serve dinner on the third tier, and Hill quickly tried to fill me in on the facts of prison life. That's when I learned about cookies and the importance they have to the inmates.

"They're going to try and grab them, they're going to try and steal them any way they can," he said. "Remember, you only have enough cookies for the gallery, and if you let them get away, you'll have to explain to the guys at the end why there weren't any for them."

Hill then checked out the meal, groaning when he saw the drippy ravioli and stewed tomatoes. "We're going to be wearing this," he remarked, before deciding to simply discard the tomatoes. We served nothing to drink. In my first six days at Pontiac, I never saw an inmate served a beverage.

Hill instructed me to put on plastic gloves before we served the meal. In view of the trash and waste through which we'd be wheeling the food cart. I thought he was joking. He wasn't.

"Some inmates don't like white hands touching their food," he explained.

Everything went routinely as we served the first 20 cells, and I wasn't surprised when every inmate asked for extra cookies.

Suddenly, a huge arm shot through the bars of one cell and began swinging a metal rod at Hill. As he ducked away, the inmate snared the cookie box.

From the other side of the cart, I lunged to grab the cookies and was grabbed in turn. A powerful hand from the cell behind me was pulling my arm. As I jerked away, objects began crashing about, and a metal can struck me in the back.

Until that moment I had been apprehensive. Now I was scared. The food cart virtually trapped me, blocking my retreat.

Whirling around, I noticed that mirrors were being held out of every cell so the inmates could watch the ruckus. I didn't realize the mirrors were plastic and became terrified that the inmates would start smashing them to cut me up.

The ordinary din of the cell house had turned into a deafening roar. For the length of the tier, arms stretched into the walkway, making grabbing motions. Some of the inmates swung brooms about.

"Let's get out of here—now!" Hill barked. Wheeling the food cart between us, we made a hasty retreat.

Downstairs, we reported what had happened. My heart was thumping, my legs felt weak. Inside the plastic gloves, my hands were soaked with sweat. Yet the attack on us wasn't considered unusual by the other guards, especially in segregation. That was strictly routine, and we didn't even file a report.

What was more shocking was to be sent immediately back to the same tier to pass out medication. But as I passed the cells from which we'd been attacked, the men in them simply requested their medicine. It was as if what had happened minutes before was already ancient history. From another cell, however, an inmate began raging at us. "Get my medication," he said. "Get it now, or I'm going to kill you." I was learning that whatever you're handing out, everybody wants it, and those who don't get it frequently respond by threatening to kill or maim you. Another fact of prison life.

Passing cell no. 632, I saw that a prisoner I had helped take to the hospital before dinner was back in his cell. When we took him out, he had been disabled by mace and was very wobbly. Hill and I had been extremely gentle, handcuffing him carefully, then practically carrying him down the stairs. As we went by his cell this time, he tossed a cup of liquid on us.

Back downstairs, I learned I would be going back to that tier for a third time, to finish serving dinner. This time, we planned to slip in the other side of the tier so we wouldn't have to pass the trouble cells. The plates were already prepared.

"Just get in there and give them their food and get out,' Hill said. I could see he was nervous, which made me even more so. "Don't stop for anything. If you get hit, just back off, 'cause if they snare you or hook you some way and get you against the bars, they'll hurt you real bad."

Everything went smoothly. Inmates in the three most troublesome cells were not getting dinner, so they hurled some garbage at us. But that's something else I had learned; getting no worse than garbage thrown at you is the prison equivalent of everything going smoothly.

Take This Fish and
Look at It

Sam Scudder

It was more than fifteen years ago that I entered the laboratory of Professor Agassiz, and told him I had enrolled my name in the Scientific School as a student of natural history. He asked me a few questions about my object in coming, my antecedents generally, the mode in which I afterwards proposed to use the knowledge I might acquire, and, finally, whether I wished to study any special branch. To the latter I replied that, while I wished to be well grounded in all departments of zoology, I purposed to devote myself specially to insects. (1)

"When do you wish to begin?" he asked. (2)

"Now," I replied. (3)

This seemed to please him, and with an energetic "Very well!" he reached from a shelf a huge jar of specimens in yellow alcohol. "Take this fish," he said, "and look at it; we call it a haemulon; by and by I will ask what you have seen." (4)

With that he left me, but in a moment returned with explicit instructions as to the care of the object entrusted to me. (5)

"No man is fit to be a naturalist," said he, "who does not know how to take care of specimens." (6)

I was to keep the fish before me in a tin tray, and occasionally moisten the surface with alcohol from the jar, always taking care to replace the stopper tightly. Those were not the days of ground-glass stoppers and elegantly shaped exhibition jars; all the old students will recall the huge necklace glass bottles with their leaky, wax-besmeared corks, half eaten by insects, and begrimed with cellar dust. Entomology was a cleaner science than ichthyology, but the example of the Professor, who had unhesitatingly plunged to the bottom of the jar to produce the fish, was infectious; and though this alcohol had a "very ancient and fishlike smell," I really dared not show any aversion within these sacred precincts, and treated the alcohol as though it were pure water. Still I was conscious of a passing feeling of disappointment, for gazing at a fish did not commend itself to an ardent entomologist. My friends at home, too, were annoyed when they discovered that no amount of eau-de-Cologne would drown the perfume which haunted me like a shadow. (7)

In ten minutes I had seen all that could be seen in that fish, and started in search of the Professor—who had, however, left the Museum; and when I returned, after lingering over some of the odd animals stored in the upper apartment, my specimen was dry all over. I dashed the fluid over the fish as if to resuscitate the beast from a fainting fit, and looked with anxiety for a return of the normal sloppy appearance. This little excitement over, nothing was to be done but to return to a steadfast gaze at my mute companion. Half an hour passed—an hour—another hour; the fish began to look loathsome. I turned it over and around; looked it in the face—ghastly; from behind, beneath, above, sideways, at three-quarters' view—just as ghastly. I was in despair; at an early hour I concluded that lunch was necessary; so, with infinite relief, the fish was carefully replaced in the jar, and for an hour I was free. (8)

On my return, I learned that Professor Agassiz had been at the Museum, but had gone, and would not return for several hours. My fellow-students were too busy to be disturbed by continued conversation. Slowly I drew forth that hideous fish, and with a feeling of desperation again looked at it. I might not use a magnifying-glass; instruments of all kinds were interdicted. My two hands, my two eyes, and the fish: it seemed a most limited field. I pushed my finger down its throat to feel how sharp the teeth were. I began to count the scales in the different rows, until I was convinced that was nonsense. At last a happy thought struck me—I would draw the fish; and now with surprise I began to discover new features in the creature. Just then the Professor returned. (9)

"That is right," said he; "a pencil is one of the best of eyes. I am glad to notice, too, that you keep your specimen wet, and your bottle corked." (10)

With these encouraging words, he added: "Well, what is it like?" (11)

He listened attentively to my brief rehearsal of the structure of parts whose names were still unknown to me: the fringed gill-arches and movable operculum; the pores of the head, fleshy lips and lidless eyes; the lateral line, the spinous fins and forked tail; the compressed and arched body. When I finished, he waited as if expecting more, and then with an air of disappointment: "You have not looked very carefully; why," he continued more earnestly, "you haven't even seen one of the most conspicuous features of the animal, which is plainly before your eyes as the fish itself; look again, look again!" and he left me to my misery. (12)

I was piqued; I was mortified. Still more of that wretched fish! But now I set myself to my task with a will, and discovered one new thing after another, until I saw how just the Professor's criticism had been. The afternoon passed quickly; and when, towards its close, the Professor inquired: "Do you see it yet?" (13)

"No," I replied, "I am certain I do not, but I see how little I saw before." (14)

"That is next best," said he, earnestly, "but I won't hear you now; put away your fish and go home; perhaps you will be ready with a better answer in the morning. I will examine you before you look at the fish." (15)

This was disconcerting. Not only must I think of my fish all night, studying, without the object before me, what this unknown but most visible feature might be; but also, without reviewing my discoveries, I must give an exact account of them the next day. I had a bad memory; so I walked home by Charles River in a distracted state, with my two perplexities.(16)

The cordial greeting from the Professor the next morning was reassuring; here was a man who seemed to be quite as anxious as I that I should see for myself what he saw. (17)

"Do you perhaps mean," I asked, "that the fish has symmetrical sides with paired organs?" (18)

His thoroughly pleased "Of course! of course!" repaid the wakeful hours of the previous night. After he had discoursed most happily and enthusiastically— as he always did—upon the importance of this point, I ventured to ask what I should do next. (19)

Oh, look at your fish!" he said, and left me again to my own devices. In a little more than an hour he returned, and heard my new catalogue. (20)

"That is good, that is good!" he repeated; "but that is not all; go on"; and so for three long days he placed that fish before my eyes, forbidding me to look at anything else, or to use any artificial aid. "Look, look, look," was his repeated injunction. (21)

This was the best entomological lesson I ever had—a lesson whose influence has extended to the details of every subsequent study; a legacy the Professor had left to me, as he has left it to so many others, of inestimable value, which we could not buy, with which we cannot part. (22)

A year afterward, some of us were amusing ourselves with chalking outlandish beasts on the Museum blackboard. We drew prancing starfishes; frogs in mortal combat; hydra-headed worms; stately crawfishes, standing on their tails, bearing aloft umbrellas; and grotesque fishes with gaping mouths and staring eyes. The Professor came in shortly after, and was as amused as any at our experiments. He looked at the fishes. (23)

"Haermulons, every one of them," he said; Mr.—drew them." (24)

True; and to this day, if I attempt a fish, I can draw nothing but haemulons. (25)

The fourth day, a second fish of the same group was placed beside the first, and I was bidden to point out the resemblances and differences between the two; another and another followed, until the entire family lay before me, and a whole legion of jars covered the table and surrounding shelves; the odor had become a pleasant perfume; and even now, the sight of an old, six-inch worm-eaten cork brings fragrant memories. (26)

The whole group of haemulons was thus brought in review; and, whether engaged upon the dissection of the internal organs, the preparation and examination of the bony framework, or the description of the various parts, Agassiz's training in the method of observing facts and their orderly arrangement was ever accompanied by the urgent exhortation not to be content with them. (27)

"Facts are stupid things," he would say, "until brought into connection with some general law." (28)

At the end of eight months, it was almost with reluctance that I left these friends and turned to insects; but what I had gained by this outside experience has been of greater value than years of later investigation in my favorite groups. (29)

Graduation

Maya Angelou

The children in Stamps trembled visibly with anticipation. Some adults were excited too, but to be certain the whole young population had come down with graduation epidemic. Large classes were graduating from both the grammar school and the high school. Even those who were years removed from their own day of glorious release were anxious to help with preparations as a kind of dry run. The junior students who were moving into the vacating classes' chairs were tradition-bound to show their talents for leadership and management. They strutted through the school and around the campus exerting pressure on the lower grades. Their authority was so new that occasionally if they pressed a little too hard it had to be overlooked. After all, next term was coming, and it never hurt a sixth grader to have a play sister in the eighth grade, or a tenth-year student to be able to call a twelfth grader Bubba. So all was endured in a spirit of shared understanding. But the graduating classes themselves were the nobility. Like travelers with exotic destinations on their minds, the graduates were remarkably forgetful. They came to school without their books, or tablets or even pencils. Volunteers fell over themselves to secure replacements for the missing equipment. When accepted, the willing workers might or might not be thanked, and it was of no importance to the pregraduation rites. Even teachers were respectful of the now quiet and aging seniors, and tended to speak to them, if not as equals, as beings only slightly lower than themselves. After tests were returned and grades given, the student body, which acted like an extended family, knew who did well, who excelled, and what piteous ones had failed.

Unlike the white high school, Lafayette County Training School distinguished itself by having neither lawn, nor hedges, nor tennis court, nor climbing ivy. Its two buildings (main classrooms, the grade school and home economics) were set on a dirt hill with no fence to limit either its boundaries or those of bordering farms. There was a large expanse to the left of the school which was used alternately as a baseball diamond or basketball court. Rusty hoops on swaying poles represented the permanent recreational equipment, although bats and balls could be borrowed from the P.E. teacher if the borrower was qualified and if the diamond wasn't occupied.

Over this rocky area relieved by a few shady tall persimmon trees the graduating class walked. The girls often held hands and no longer bothered to speak to the lower students. There was a sadness about them, as if this old world was not their home and they were bound for higher ground. The boys, on the other hand, had become more friendly, more outgoing. A decided change from the closed attitude they projected while studying for finals. Now they seemed not ready to give up the old school, the familiar paths and classrooms. Only a small percentage would be continuing on to college—one of the South's A & M (agricultural and mechanical) schools, which trained Negro youths to be carpenters, farmers, handymen, masons, maids, cooks and baby nurses. Their future rode heavily on their shoulders, and blinded them to the collective joy that had pervaded the lives of the boys and girls in the grammar school graduating class.

Parents who could afford it had ordered new shoes and ready-made clothes for themselves from Sears and Roebuck or Montgomery Ward. They also engaged the best seamstresses to make the floating graduating dresses and to cut down second-hand pants which would be pressed to a military slickness for the important event.

Oh, it was important, all right. Whitefolks would attend the ceremony, and two or three would speak of God and home, and the Southern way of life, and Mrs. Parsons, the principal's wife, would play the graduation march while the lower-grade graduates paraded down the aisles and took their seats below the platform. The high school seniors would wait in empty classrooms to make their dramatic entrance.

In the Store I was the person of the moment. The birthday girl. The center. Bailey had graduated the year before, although to do so he had had to forfeit all pleasures to make up for his time lost in Baton Rouge.

My class was wearing butter-yellow piqué dresses, and Momma launched out on mine. She smocked the yoke into tiny crisscrossing puckers, then shirred the rest of the bodice. Her dark fingers ducked in and out of the lemony cloth as she embroidered raised daisies around the hem. Before she considered herself finished she had added a crocheted cuff on the puff sleeves, and a pointy crocheted collar.

I was going to be lovely. A walking model of all the various styles of fine hand sewing and it didn't worry me that I was only twelve years old and merely graduating from the eighth grade. Besides, many teachers in Arkansas Negro schools had only that diploma and were licensed to impart wisdom.

The days had become longer and more noticeable. The faded beige of former times had been replaced with strong and sure colors. I began to see my classmates' clothes, their skin tones, and the dust that waved off pussy willows. Clouds that lazed across the sky were objects of great concern to me. Their shiftier shapes might have held a message that in my new happiness and with a little bit of time I'd soon decipher. During that period I looked at the arch of heaven so religiously my neck kept a steady ache. I had taken to smiling more often, and my jaws hurt from the unaccustomed activity. Between the two physical sore spots, I suppose I could have been uncomfortable, but that was not the case. As a member of the winning team (the graduating class of 1940) I had outdistanced unpleasant sensations by miles. I was headed for the freedom of open fields.

Youth and social approval allied themselves with me and we trammeled memories of slights and insults. The wind of our swift passage remodeled my features. Lost tears were pounded to mud and then to dust. Years of withdrawal were brushed aside and left behind, as hanging ropes of parasitic moss.

My work alone had awarded me a top place and I was going to be one of the first called in the graduating ceremonies. On the classroom blackboard, as well as on the bulletin board in the auditorium, there were blue stars and white stars and red stars. No absences, no tardiness, and my academic work was among the best of the year. I could say the preamble to the Constitution even faster than Bailey. We timed ourselves often: "We the people of the Unlted States in order to form a more perfect union. . . ." I had memorized the Presidents of the United States from Washington to Roosevelt in chronological as well as alphabetical order.

My hair pleased me too. Gradually the black mass had lengthened and thickened, so that it kept at last to its braided pattern, and I didn't have to yank my scalp off when I tried to comb it.

Louise and I had rehearsed the exercises until we tired out ourselves. Henry Reed was class valedictorian. He was a small, very black boy with hooded eyes, a long, broad nose and an oddly shaped head. I had admired him for years because each term he and I vied for the best grades in our class. Most often he bested me, but instead of being disappointed I was pleased that we shared top places between us. Like many Southern Black children, he lived with his grandmother, who was as strict as Momma and as kind as she knew how to be. He was courteous, respectful and soft-spoken to elders, but on the playground he chose to play the roughest games. I admired him. Anyone, I reckoned, sufficiently afraid or sufficiently dull could be polite. But to be able to operate at a top level with both adults and children was admirable.

His valedictory speech was entitled "To Be or Not to Be." The rigid tenth-grade teacher had helped him write it. He'd been working on the dramatic stresses for months.

The weeks until graduation were filled with heady activities. A group of small children were to be presented in a play about buttercups and daisies and bunny rabbits. They could be heard throughout the building practicing their hops and their little songs that sounded like silver bells. The older girls (nongraduates, of course) were assigned the task of making refreshments for the night's festivities. A tangy scent of ginger, cinnamon, nutmeg and chocolate wafted around the home economics building as the budding cooks made samples for themselves and their teachers.

In every corner of the workshop, axes and saws split fresh timber as the woodshop boys made sets and stage scenery. Only the graduates were left out of the general bustle. We were free to sit in the library at the back of the building or look in quite detachedly, naturally, on the measures being taken for our event.

Even the minister preached on graduation the Sunday before. His subject was, "Let your light so shine that men will see your good works and praise your Father, who is in Heaven." Although the sermon was purported to be addressed to us, he used the occasion to speak to backsliders, gamblers, and general ne'er-do-wells. But since he had called our names at the beginning of the service we were mollified.

Among Negroes the tradition was to give presents to children going only from one grade to another. How much more important this was when the person was graduating at the top of the class. Uncle Willie and Momma had sent away for a Mickey Mouse watch like Bailey's. Louise gave me four embroidered hand-kerchiefs. (I gave her crocheted doilies.) Mrs. Sneed, the minister's wife, made me an undershirt to wear for graduation, and nearly every customer gave me a nick-el or maybe even a dime with the instruction "Keep on moving to higher ground," or some such encouragement.

Amazingly the great day finally dawned and I was out of bed before I knew it. I threw open the back door to see it more clearly, but Momma said, "Sister, come away from that door and put your robe on."

I hoped the memory of that morning would never leave me. Sunlight was itself young, and the day had none of the insistence maturity would bring it in a few hours. In my robe and barefoot in the backyard, under cover of going to see about my new beans, I gave myself up to the gentle warmth and thanked God that no matter what evil I had done in my life He had allowed me to live to see this day. Somewhere in my fatalism I had expected to die, accidentally, and never have the chance to walk up the stairs in the auditorium and gracefully receive my hard-earned diploma. Out of God's merciful bosom I had won reprieve.

Bailey came out in his robe and gave me a box wrapped in Christmas paper. He said he had saved his money for months to pay for it. It felt like a box of chocolates, but I knew Bailey wouldn't save money to buy candy when we had all we could want under our noses.

He was as proud of the gift as I. It was a soft-leather-bound copy of a col-lection of poems by Edgar Allan Poe, or, as Bailey and I called him, "Eap." I turned to "Annabel Lee" and we walked up and down the garden rows, the cool dirt between our toes, reciting the beautifully sad lines.

Momma made a Sunday breakfast although it was only Friday. After we fin-ished the blessing, I opened my eyes to find the watch on my plate. It was a dream of a day. Everything went smoothly and to my credit, I didn't have to be remind-ed or scolded for anything. Near evening I was too jittery to attend to chores, so Bailey volunteered to do all before his bath.

Days before, we had made a sign for the Store, and as we turned out the lights Momma hung the cardboard over the doorknob. It read clearly: CLOSED, GRADUATION.

My dress fitted perfectly and everyone said that I looked like a sunbeam in it. On the hill, going toward the school, Bailey walked behind with Uncle Willie, who muttered, "Go on, Ju." He wanted him to walk ahead with us because it embarrassed him to have to walk so slowly. Bailey said he'd let the ladies walk together, and the men would bring up the rear. We all laughed, nicely.

Little children dashed by out of the dark like fireflies. Their crepe-paper dresses and butterfly wings were not made for running and we heard more than one rip, dryly, and the regretful "uh uh" that followed.

The school blazed without gaiety. The windows seemed cold and unfriendly from the lower hill. A sense of ill-fated timing crept over me, and if Momma hadn't reached for my hand I would have drifted back to Bailey and Uncle Willie, and possibly beyond. She made a few slow jokes about my feet getting cold, and tugged me along to the now-strange building.

Around the front steps, assurance came back. There were my fellow "greats," the graduating class. Hair brushed back, legs oiled, new dresses and pressed pleats, fresh pocket handkerchiefs and little handbags, all homesewn. Oh, we were up to snuff, all right. I joined my comrades and didn't even see my family go in to find seats in the crowded auditorium.

The school band struck up a march and all classes filed in as had been rehearsed. We stood in front of our seats, as assigned, and on a signal from the choir director, we sat. No sooner had this been accomplished than the band started to play the national anthem. We rose again and sang the song, after which we recited the pledge of allegiance. We remained standing for a brief minute before the choir director and the principal signaled to us, rather desperately I thought, to take our seats. The command was so unusual that our carefully rehearsed and smooth-running machine was thrown off. For a full minute we fumbled for our chairs and bumped into each other awkwardly. Habits change or solidify under pressure, so in our state of nervous tension we had been ready to follow our usual assembly pattern: the American national anthem, then the pledge of allegiance, then the song every Black person I knew called the Negro National Anthem. All done in the same key, with the same passion and most often standing on the same foot.

Finding my seat at last, I was overcome with a presentiment of worse things to come. Something unrehearsed, unplanned, was going to happen, and we were going to be made to look bad. I distinctly remember being explicit in the choice of pronoun. It was "we," the graduating class, the unit, that concerned me then.

The principal welcomed "parents and friends" and asked the Baptist minister to lead us in prayer. His invocation was brief and punchy, and for a second I thought we were getting on the high road to right action. When the principal came back to the dais, however, his voice had changed. Sounds always affected me profoundly and the principal's voice was one of my favorites. During assembly it melted and lowed weakly into the audience. It had not been in my plan to listen to him, but my curiosity was piqued and I straightened up to give him my attention.

He was talking about Booker T. Washington, our "late great leader," who said we can be as close as the fingers on the hand, etc. . . . Then he said a few vague things about friendship and the friendship of kindly people to those less fortunate than themselves. With that his voice nearly faded, thin, away. Like a river diminishing to a stream and then to a trickle. But he cleared his throat and said, "Our speaker tonight, who is also our friend, came from Texarkana to deliver the commencement address, but due to the irregularity of the train schedule, he's going to, as they say, 'speak and run.'" He said that we understood and wanted the man to know that we were most grateful for the time he was able to give us and then something about how we were willing always to adjust to another's program, and without more ado—"I give you Mr. Edward Donleavy."

Not one but two white men came through the door offstage. The shorter one walked to the speaker's platform, and the tall one moved to the center seat and sat down. But that was our principal's seat, and already occupied. The dislodged gentleman bounced around for a long breath or two before the Baptist minister gave him his chair, then with more dignity than the situation deserved, the minister walked off the stage.

Donleavy looked at the audience once (on reflection, I'm sure that he wanted only to reassure himself that we were really there), adjusted his glasses and began to read from a sheaf of papers.

He was glad "to be here and to see the work going on just as it was in the other schools."

At the first "Amen" from the audience I willed the offender to immediate death by choking on the word. But Amens and Yes, sir's began to fall around the room like rain through a ragged umbrella.

He told us of the wonderful changes we children in Stamps had in store. The Central School (naturally, the white school was Central) had already been granted improvements that would be in use in the fall. A well-known artist was coming from Little Rock to teach art to them. They were going to have the newest microscopes and chemistry equipment for their laboratory. Mr. Donleavy didn't leave us long in the dark over who made these improvements available to Central High. Nor were we to be ignored in the general betterment scheme he had in mind.

He said that he had pointed out to people at a very high level that one of the first-line football tackles at Arkansas Agricultural and Mechanical College had graduated from good old Lafayette County Training School. Here fewer Amen's were heard. Those few that did break through lay dully in the air with the heaviness of habit.

He went on to praise us. He went on to say how he had bragged that "one of the best basketball players at Fisk sank his first ball right here at Lafayette County Training School."

The white kids were going to have a chance to become Galileos and Madame Curies and Edisons and Gauguins, and our boys (the girls weren't even in on it) would try to be Jesse Owenses and Joe Louises.

Owens and the Brown Bomber were great heroes in our world, but what school official in the white-goddom of Little Rock had the right to decide that those two men must be our only heroes? Who decided that for Henry Reed to become a scientist he had to work like George Washington Carver, as a bootblack, to buy a lousy microscope? Bailey was obviously always going to be too small to be an athlete, so which concrete angel glued to what country seat had decided that if my brother wanted to become a lawyer he had to first pay penance for his skin by picking cotton and hoeing corn and studying correspondence books at night for twenty years?

The man's dead words fell like bricks around the auditorium and too many settled in my belly. Constrained by hard-learned manners I couldn't look behind me, but to my left and right the proud graduating class of 1940 had dropped their heads. Every girl in my row had found something new to do with her handkerchief. Some folded the tiny squares into love knots, some into triangles, but most were wadding them, then pressing them flat on their yellow laps.

On the dais, the ancient tragedy was being replayed. Professor Parsons sat, a sculptor's reject, rigid. His large, heavy body seemed devoid of will or willingness, and his eyes said he was no longer with us. The other teachers examined the flag (which was draped stage right) or their notes, or the windows which opened on our now-famous playing diamond.

Graduation, the hush-hush magic time of frills and gifts and congratulations and diplomas, was finished for me before my name was called. The accomplishment was nothing. The meticulous maps, drawn in three colors of ink, learning and spelling decasyllabic words, memorizing the whole of *The Rape of Lucrece*—it was for nothing. Donleavy had exposed us.

We were maids and farmers, handymen and washerwomen, and anything higher that we aspired to was farcical and presumptuous.

Then I wished that Gabriel Proser and Nat Turner had killed all whitefolks in their beds and that Abraham Lincoln had been assassinated before the signing of the Emancipation Proclamation, and that Harriet Tubman had been killed by that blow on her head and Christopher Columbus had drowned in the *Santa Maria*.

It was awful to be a Negro and have no control over my life. It was brutal to be young and already trained to sit quietly and listen to charges brought against my color with no chance of defense. We should all be dead. I thought I should like to see us all dead, one on top of the other. A pyramid of flesh with the whitefolks on the bottom, as the broad base, then the Indians with their silly tomahawks and teepees and wigwams and treaties, the Negroes with their mops and recipes and cotton sacks and spirituals sticking out of their mouths. The Dutch children should all stumble in their wooden shoes and break their necks. The French should choke to death on the Louisiana Purchase (1803) while silkworms ate all the Chinese with their stupid pigtails. As a species, we were an abomination. All of us.

Donleavy was running for election, and assured our parents that if he won we could count on having the only colored paved playing field in that part of Arkansas. Also—he never looked up to acknowledge the grunts of acceptance— also, we were bound to get some new equipment for the home economics building and the workshop.

He finished, and since there was no need to give any more than the most perfunctory thank-you's, he nodded to the men on the stage, and the tall white man who was never introduced joined him at the door. They left with the attitude that now they were off to something really important. (The graduation ceremonies at Lafayette County Training School had been a mere preliminary.)

The ugliness they left was palpable. An uninvited guest who wouldn't leave. The choir was summoned and sang a modern arrangement of "Onward, Christian Soldiers," with new words pertaining to graduates seeking their place in the world. But it didn't work. Elouise, the daughter of the Baptist minister, recited "Invictus," and I could have cried at the impertinence of "I am the master of my fate, I am the captain of my soul."

My name had lost its ring of familiarity and I had to be nudged to go and receive my diploma. All my preparations had fled. I neither marched up to the stage like a conquering Amazon, nor did I look in the audience for Bailey's nod of approval. Marguerite Johnson, I heard the name again, my honors were read, there were noises in the audience of appreciation, and I took my place on the stage as rehearsed.

I thought about colors I hated: ecru, puce, lavender, beige and black.

There was shuffling and rushing around me, then Henry Reed was giving his valedictory address, "To Be or Not to Be." Hadn't he heard the whitefolks? We couldn't be, so the question was a waste of time. Henry's voice came out clear and strong. I feared to look at him. Hadn't he got the message? There was no "nobler in the mind" for Negroes because the world didn't think we had minds, and they let us know it. "Outrageous fortune"? Now, that was a joke. When the ceremony was over I had to tell Henry Reed some things. That is, if I still cared. Not "rub," Henry, "erase." "Ah, there's the erase." Us.

Henry had been a good student in elocution. His voice rose on tides of promise and fell on waves of warnings, The English teacher had helped him to create a sermon winging through Hamlet's soliloquy. To be a man, a doer, a builder, a leader, or to be a tool, an unfunny joke, a crusher of funky toadstools. I marveled that Henry could go through with the speech as if we had a choice.

I had been listening and silently rebutting each sentence with my eyes closed; then there was a hush, which in an audience warns that something unplanned is happening. I looked up and saw Henry Reed, the conservative, the proper, the A student, turn his back to the audience and turn to us (the proud graduating class of 1940) and sing, nearly speaking,

> *"Lift ev'ry voice and sing*
> *Till earth and heaven ring*
> *Ring with the harmonies of Liberty . . ."*

It was the poem written by James Weldon Johnson. It was the music composed by J. Rosamond Johnson. It was the Negro national anthem. Out of habit we were singing it.

Our mothers and fathers stood in the dark hall and joined the hymn of encouragement. A kindergarten teacher led the small children onto the stage and the buttercups and daisies and bunny rabbits marked time and tried to follow:

> *"Stony the road we trod*
> *Bitter the chastening rod*
> *Felt in the days when hope, unborn, had died.*
> *Yet with a steady beat*
> *Have not our weary feet*
> *Come to the place for which our fathers sighed?"*

Each child I knew had learned that song with his ABC's and along with "Jesus Loves Me This I Know." But I personally had never heard it before. Never heard the words, despite the thousands of times I had sung them. Never thought they had anything to do with me.

On the other hand, the words of Patrick Henry had made such an impression on me that I had been able to stretch myself tall and trembling and say, "I know not what course others may take, but as for me, give me liberty or give me death."

And now I heard, really for the first time:

> *"We have come over a way that with tears*
> *has been watered,*
> *We have come, treading our path through*
> *the blood of the slaughtered."*

While echoes of the song shivered in the air, Henry Reed bowed his head, said "Thank you," and returned to his place in the line. The tears that slipped down many faces were not wiped away in shame.

We were on top again. As always, again. We survived. The depths had been icy and dark, but now a bright sun spoke to our souls. I was no longer simply a member of the proud graduating class of 1940; I was a proud member of the wonderful, beautiful Negro race.

Oh, Black known and unknown poets, how often have your auctioned pains sustained us? Who will compute the lonely nights made less lonely by your songs, or the empty pots made less tragic by your tales?

If we were a people much given to revealing secrets, we might raise monuments and sacrifice to the memories of our poets, but slavery cured us of that weakness. It may be enough, however, to have it said that we survive in exact relationship to the dedication of our poets (including preachers, musicians and blues singers).

Summer Rituals

Ray Bradbury

Yes, summer was rituals, each with its natural time and place. The ritual of lemonade or ice-tea making, the ritual of wine, shoes, or no shoes, and at last, swiftly following the others, with quiet dignity, the ritual of the front-porch swing.

On the third day of summer in the late afternoon Grandfather reappeared from the front door to gaze serenely at the two empty eye rings in the ceiling of the porch. Moving to the geranium-pot-lined rail like Ahab surveying the mild day and the mild-looking sky, he wet his finger to test the wind, and shucked his coat to see how shirt sleeves felt in the westering hours. He acknowledged the salutes of other captains on yet other flowered porches, out themselves to discern the gentle ground swell of weather, oblivious to their wives chirping or snapping like fuzzball hand dogs hidden behind black porch screens.

"All right, Douglas, let's let it up."

In the garage they found, dusted, and carried forth the howdah, as it were, for the quiet summer-night festivals, the swing chair which Grandpa chained to the porch-ceiling eyelets.

Douglas, being lighter, was first to sit in the swing. Then, after a moment, Grandfather gingerly settled his pontifical weight beside the boy. Thus they sat, smiling at each other, nodding, as they swung silently back and forth, back and forth.

Ten minutes later Grandma appeared with water buckets and brooms to wash down and sweep off the porch. Other chairs, rockers and straight-backs, were summoned from the house.

"Always like to start sitting early in the season," said Grandpa, "before the mosquitoes thicken."

About seven o'clock you could hear the chairs scraping back from the tables, someone experimenting with a yellow-toothed piano, if you stood outside the dining-room window and listened. Matches being struck, the first dishes bubbling in the suds and tinkling on the wall racks, somewhere, faintly, a phonograph playing. And then as the evening changed the hour, at house after house on

23

the twilight streets, under the immense oaks and elms, on shady porches, people would begin to appear, like those figures who tell good or bad weather in rain-or-shine clocks.

Uncle Bert, perhaps Grandfather, then Father, and some of the cousins; the men all coming out first into the syrupy evening, blowing smoke, leaving the women's voices behind in the cooling-warm kitchen to set their universe alight. Then the first male voices under the porch brim, the feet up, the boys fringed on the worn steps or wooden rails where sometime during the evening something, a boy or a geranium pot, would fall off.

At last, like ghosts hovering momentarily behind the door screen, Grandma, Great-grandma, and Mother would appear, and the men would shift, move, and offer seats. The women carried varieties of fans with them, folded newspapers, bamboo whisks, or perfumed kerchiefs, to start the air moving about their faces as they talked.

What they talked of all evening long, no one remembered next day. It wasn't important to anyone what the adults talked about; it was only important that the sounds came and went over the delicate ferns that bordered the porch on three sides; it was only important that the darkness filled the town like black water being poured over the houses, and that the cigars glowed and that the conversations went on, and on. The female gossip moved out, disturbing the first mosquitoes so they danced in frenzies on the air. The male voices invaded the old house timbers; if you closed your eyes and put your head down against the floor boards you could hear the men's voices rumbling like a distant, political earthquake, constant, unceasing, rising or falling a pitch.

Douglas sprawled back on the dry porch planks, completely contented and reassured by these voices, which would speak on through eternity, flow in a stream of murmurings over his body, over his closed eyelids, into his drowsy ears, for all time. The rocking chairs sounded like crickets, the crickets sounded like rocking chairs, and the moss-covered rain barrel by the dining-room window produced another generation of mosquitoes to provide a topic of conversation through endless summers ahead.

Sitting on the summer-night porch was so good, so easy and so reassuring that it could never be done away with. These were rituals that were right and lasting; the lighting of pipes, the pale hands that moved knitting needles in the dimness, the eating of foil-wrapped, chill Eskimo Pies, the coming and going of all the people. For at some time or other during the evening, everyone visited here; the neighbors down the way, the people across the street; Miss Fern and Miss Roberta humming by in their electric runabout, giving Tom or Douglas a ride around the block and then coming up to sit down and fan away the fever in their cheeks; or Mr. Jonas, the junkman, having left his horse and wagon hidden in the alley, and ripe to bursting with words, would come up the steps looking as fresh as if his talk had never been said before, and somehow it never had. And last of all, the children, who had been off squinting their way through a last hide-and-seek or kick-the-can, panting, glowing, would sickle quietly back like boomerangs along the soundless lawn, to sink beneath the talking of the porch voices which would weigh and gentle them down.

Oh, the luxury of lying in the fern night and the grass night and the night of susurrant, slumbrous voices weaving the dark together. The grownups had forgotten he was there, so still, so quiet Douglas lay, noting the plans they were making for his and their own futures. And the voices chanted, drifted, in moon-lit clouds of cigarette smoke while the moths, like late appleblossoms come alive, tapped faintly about the far street lights, and the voices moved on into the coming years. . . .

Marrying Absurd

Joan Didion

To be married in Las Vegas, Clark County, Nevada, a bride must swear that she is eighteen or has parental permission and a bridegroom that he is twenty-one or has parental permission. Someone must put up five dollars for the license. (On Sundays and holidays, fifteen dollars. The Clark County Courthouse issues marriage licenses at any time of the day or night except between noon and one in the afternoon, between eight and nine in the evening, and between four and five in the morning.) Nothing else is required. The State of Nevada, alone among these United States, demands neither a premarital blood test nor a waiting period before or after the issuance of a marriage license. Driving in across the Mojave from Los Angeles, one sees the signs way out on the desert, looming up from that moonscape of rattlesnakes and mesquite, even before the Las Vegas lights appear like a mirage on the horizon: "GETTING MARRIED? Free License Information First Strip Exit." Perhaps the Las Vegas wedding industry achieved its peak operational efficiency between 9:00 p.m. and midnight of August 26, 1965, an otherwise unremarkable Thursday which happened to be, by Presidential order, the last day on which anyone could improve his draft status merely by getting married. One hundred and seventy-one couples were pronounced man and wife in the name of Clark County and the State of Nevada that night, sixty-seven of them by a single justice of the peace, Mr. James A. Brennan. Mr. Brennan did one wedding at the Dunes and the other sixty-six in his office, and charged each couple eight dollars. One bride lent her veil to six others. "I got it down from five to three minutes," Mr. Brennan said later of his feat. "I could've married them en masse, but they're people, not cattle. People expect more when they get married."

What people who get married in Las Vegas actually do expect—what, in the largest sense, their "expectations" are—strikes one as a curious and self-contradictory business. Las Vegas is the most extreme and allegorical of American settlements, bizarre and beautiful in its venality and in its devotion to immediate gratification, a place the tone of which is set by mobsters and call girls and ladies' room attendants with amyl nitrite poppers in their uniform pockets. Almost everyone notes that there is no "time" in Las Vegas, no night and no day and no past and no future (no Las Vegas casino, however, has taken the obliteration of the ordinary time sense quite so far as Harold's Club in Reno, which for a while issued, at odd intervals in the day and night, mimeographed "bulletins" carrying news from the world outside); neither is there any logical sense of where one is. One is standing on a highway in the middle of a vast hostile desert looking at an eighty-foot sign which blinks "STARDUST" or "CAESAR'S PALACE." Yes, but what does that explain? This geographical implausibility reinforces the sense that what happens there has no connection with "real" life; Nevada cities like Reno and Carson are ranch towns, Western towns, places behind which there is some historical imperative. But Las Vegas seems to exist only in the eye of the beholder: All of which makes it an extraordinarily stimulating and interesting place, but an odd one in which to want to wear a candlelight satin Priscilla of Boston wedding dress with Chantilly lace insets, tapered sleeves and a detachable modified train.

And yet the Las Vegas wedding business seems to appeal to precisely that impulse. "Sincere and Dignified Since 1954," one wedding chapel advertises. There are nineteen such wedding chapels in Las Vegas, intensely competitive, each offering better, faster, and, by implication, more sincere services than the next: Our Photos Best Anywhere, Your Wedding on a Phonograph Record, Candlelight with Your Ceremony, Honeymoon Accommodations, Free Transportation from Your Motel to Courthouse to Chapel and Return to Motel, Religious or Civil Ceremonies, Dressing Rooms, Flowers, Rings, Announcements, Witnesses Available, and Ample Parking. All of these services, like most others in Las Vegas (sauna baths, payroll-check cashing, chinchilla coats for sale or rent) are offered twenty-four hours a day, seven days a week, presumably on the premise that marriage, like craps, is a game to be played when the table seems hot.

But what strikes one most about the Strip chapels, with their wishing wells and stained-glass paper windows and their artificial bouvardia, is that so much of their business is by no means a matter of simple convenience, of late-night liaisons between show girls and baby Crosbys. Of course there is some of that. (One night about eleven o'clock in Las Vegas I watched a bride in an orange minidress and masses of flame-colored hair stumble from a Strip chapel on the arm of her bridegroom, who looked the part of the expendable nephew in movies like *Miami Syndicate.* "I gotta get the kids," the bride whimpered. "I gotta pick up the sitter, I gotta get to the midnight show." "What you gotta get," the bride-groom said, opening the door of a Cadillac Coupe de Ville and watching her crumple on the seat, "is sober.") But Las Vegas seems to offer something other than "convenience"; it is merchandising "niceness," the facsimile of proper ritual, to children who do not know how else to find it, how to make the arrangements, how to do it "right." All day and evening long on the Strip, one sees actual wedding parties, waiting under the harsh lights at a crosswalk, standing uneasily in the parking lot of the Frontier while the photographer hired by The Little Church of the West ("Wedding Place of the Stars") certifies the occasion, takes the picture: the bride in a veil and white satin pumps, the bridegroom usually in a white dinner jacket, and even an attendant or two, a sister or a best friend in hot-pink *peau de soie*, a flirtation veil, a carnation nosegay. "When I Fall in Love It Will Be Forever," the organist plays, and then a few bars of Lohengrin.

The mother cries; the stepfather, awkward in his role, invites the chapel hostess to join them for a drink at the Sands. The hostess declines with a professional smile; she has already transferred her interest to the group waiting outside. One bride out, another in, and again the sign goes up on the chapel door: "One moment please—Wedding."

I sat next to one such wedding party in a Strip restaurant the last time I was in Las Vegas. The marriage had just taken place; the bride still wore her dress, the mother her corsage. A bored waiter poured out a few swallows of pink champagne ("on the house") for everyone but the bride, who was too young to be served. "You'll need something with more kick than that," the bride's father said with heavy jocularity to his new son-in-law; the ritual jokes about the wedding night had a certain Panglossian character, since the bride was clearly several months pregnant. Another round of pink champagne, this time not on the house, and the bride began to cry. "It was just as nice," she sobbed, "as I hoped and dreamed it would be."

An Athlete's Locker Room

Student

One of the most distinctive, and perhaps most easily recognizable, atmospheres is that of an athlete's locker room. As you enter, the unmistakable odor of perspiring bodies, damp leather, and dirty clothes hits your nostrils; it is a familiar one for the athlete, but sometimes unbearable for others. The room is usually large, and dim, and long enough to be lined with rows of army-green lockers. The dryers hum in the background while the steam from the showers settles and penetrates every nook and cranny, making the floor and walls seem damp and wet. We bring our emotions into this sanctuary, away from prying eyes and ears, to release our jubilation, disappointments and discouragements, and sometimes our tears. The language would make an English professor cringe, yet nothing could ever change it. It may sound offensive in many respects, but to an athlete it is part of his life that he cherishes and never forgets when those days are set aside for a different kind of life.

My Grandma

Student

Monday through Friday my Grandma was a hard working woman with little time for fun. However, staying at Grandma's house on a Saturday night was something my cousins and I looked forward to; with no other adults around, Grandma's personality sparkled and she would cast aside her inhibitions in the desire to show us a good time. At times, we would laugh as she would dance around the room with a fringed tablecloth thrown dramatically around her shoulders, a flower clenched in her teeth, henna colored hair tossing to and fro. Other nights she would drag out her beat-up banjo and teach us the bluegrass and gospel music she learned as a girl in the hills of Arkansas. Grandma's twangy voice fit right in with the rhythm of toe tappin' and banjo pickin', and every part of her being would be caught up in her music. She would always encourage us to join in, but we could only be a pale imitation of her vibrancy. When arthritis bent her fingers and it became too painful to play the banjo, she got a player piano and had us do the pumping, leaving her free to demonstrate a Charleston or jitterbug. Arthritis finally took its toll and she could no longer play an instrument or dance around a room. Some of the magic went out of her life then; I know a very special part of my childhood was taken from me. I will never forget the laughter, song, and fun of spending Saturday night at Grandma's house.

An Urban Legend

Student

Many cities around the country have their own versions of a similar story, that is not true, but assumed true. This is called an urban legend. More than likely we have all heard them; sometimes you believe them. The one urban legend that sticks out in my mind is the buried treasure. It was told to me about fifteen years ago. This story was about an old man who lived in my neighborhood, who had just lost his wife in a car accident. The man was a wealthy real estate agent, and owned thirty acres of woods that was behind his house. There were always scary stories about the wooded lot, so I had never explored them much. The old man slowly lost his sanity and could no longer trust anyone, so he never left his house anymore. Now he was the subject of rumors, and it made the man all the more interesting to talk about. The next door neighbor claims to have seen the old man walk into the woods with a cigar box and a shovel, coming out empty handed. She said he repeated this ritual at least twice a week. One year later the man passed on, but his family could not find the money he had saved up in his savings account, leaving the whereabouts of the money a mystery. This story was told to me and my friends by older kids who said they thought the money was in the woods. They had decided enough was enough, and became tired of looking. My friends and I were bored anyway, so we started the search. This search would last four years before we had any clues! There were holes dug all over the woods where we tried to find the cigar boxes. One of my friend's found an empty cigar box near an old pond in the woods. My friends and I dug fiercely around the old pond, but to our dismay we came up empty handed. That was when we decided to quit, and pass on the legend to my friends little brother. Years have passed now and the legend is still out there, and so are the holes that we dug in the earth embedding our memories into the mysterious wooded lot.

Learning Experience
Student

It was eight years ago, and I can still remember how my friends coerced me into joining the National Guard. I was sitting around at a party with some of my older friends when they started talking about the fun things they did when they were at guard camp. I was 17 years old and about 5 years younger than the youngest of them. All the maneuvers and such sounded like a lot of fun, the way they explained it. There was just one catch. I would have to go to boot camp for 13 weeks. So the summer in between my junior and senior year came, and I was on a plane to Fort Benning, Georgia. Here I was, 17 years old, spending my summer under the supervision of Drill Sergeant Remmington while all of my friends were back home partying away.

I'll never forget the first morning when the Drill Sergeant walked in at 4:45 with a tin trash can in one hand and his night stick in the other hand. It made for a really unpleasant alarm clock, but it was very effective. I was 5 feet 9 inches tall, and I weighed about 120 pounds soaking wet. The only thing that I ever heard out of the Drill Sergeant's mouth was screaming and yelling. My underwear had to be folded a certain way, my socks had to be folded just right and my tee shirts had to look like my battle buddies. For the first week I threw up at least once a day, so the doctor put me on some nerve pills. The whole time I would think back to my friends that told me how fun guard camp was, and wonder how I could be so gullible.

That was eight years ago, and to this day I still reflect a lot of my present accomplishments to the training that I received that summer. It has definitely made me a better husband and father. Today, I can control my temper much better than when I was a young teenager. Whenever someone starts to get on my nerves or something, I know that the best thing to do is to walk away or ignore them. This, I learned from ignoring the Drill Sergeant as he was yelling at me. Sometimes my wife gets upset with me because I try to keep things too squared away, but in the end she forgives me because she knows what I have been through. Over all, the experience that I endured while at Fort Benning, Georgia, was one that will continue to help me for years to come.

Ch. 1: Description

Suggestions for writing:

Remember that a topic for a descriptive paper will probably be more effective if you write about a person, place, or thing that has had a profound effect on you.

1. Write an essay or paragraph describing your first day or night on a new job. This wouldn't have to be as negative an experience as the one described in "A Guard's First Night on the Job" (p. 8), but sometimes negative experiences give you more material to work with than positive ones.

2. Describe a teacher or professor who greatly influenced you in some way, perhaps an influence that you did not notice until months or years later.

3. Write a descriptive essay or paragraph on one of the following topics or a similar topic:

    a rock concert
    your most or least favorite holiday
    your most or least favorite relative
    your first boyfriend/girlfriend
    the worst web site you've seen

    your most or least favorite actor
    a job interview
    registering for college
    a favorite vacation spot
    your favorite web site

Description checklist:

1. Does your essay or paragraph begin with a focus statement (or a thesis sentence)?

2. Did you structure your description effectively? Did you use a spatial pattern of organization? Chronological? Least to most important?

3. What dominant impression does your paper create for the reader?

4. Do you appeal specifically to the reader's senses? Which ones?

5. Did you use an effective vantage point? Is your perspective fixed or moving?

6. Are your word choices effective? Are they precise, colorful, descriptive, emotional? Are they appropriate for your topic and audience?

7. Is your writing coherent and unified?

8. Did you vary your sentence patterns?

9. Did you check for correctness of grammar, punctuation and spelling?

CHAPTER 2

Narration

Telling a Story

Using Narration

A good story is a powerful method of getting someone's attention. The excitement that accompanies a suspenseful ghost story, a lively anecdote, or a vivid joke easily attests to this effect. In fact, narration is one of the easiest verbal skills we all learn as children, providing us with a convenient, logical, and easily understood means of sharing our thoughts with other people. Storytelling is powerful because it offers us a way of dramatizing our ideas so that others can identify with them.

Defining Narration

Narration involves telling a story that is often based on personal experience. Stories can be oral or written, real or imaginary, short or long. A good story, however, always has a point or purpose. It can be the dominant mode (as in a novel or short story), supported by other rhetorical strategies, or it can serve the purpose of another rhetorical mode (as in a persuasive essay, a historical survey, or a scientific report).

In its subordinate role, narration can provide examples or explain ideas. If asked why you are attending college, for example, you might turn to narration to make your answer clear, beginning with a story about your family's hardships in the past. The purpose of telling such a story would be to help your listeners appreciate your need for higher education by encouraging them to understand and identify with your family history.

Unlike description, which generally portrays people, places, and objects in *space*, narration asks the reader to follow a series of actions through a particular *time* sequence. Description often complements the movement of narration, though. People must be depicted, for instance, along with their relationships to one another, before their actions can have any real meaning for us; similarly, places must be described so that we can picture the setting and understand the activities in a specific scene. The organization of the action and the time spent on each episode in a story should be based principally on a writer's analysis of the interests and needs of his or her audience.

To be most effective, narration should prolong the exciting parts of a story and shorten the routine facts that simply move the reader from one episode to another. If you were robbed on your way to work, for example, a good narrative describing the incident would concentrate on the traumatic event itself rather than on such mundane and boring details as what you had for breakfast and what clothes you had put on prior to the attack. Finally, just like description, narration *shows* rather than *tells* its purpose to the audience. The factual statement "I was robbed this morning" could be made much more vivid and dramatic through the addition of some simple narration: "As I was walking to work at 7:30 a.m., a huge and angry-looking man ran up to me, thrust a gun into the middle of my stomach, and took my money, my new wristwatch, all my credit cards, and my pants—leaving me penniless and embarrassed."

The following paragraph written by a student recounts a recent parachuting experience. As you read this narrative, notice especially the writer's use of vivid detail to *show* rather than *tell* her message to the readers.

> *I have always needed occasional "fixes" of excitement in my life, so when I realized one spring day that I was more than ordinarily bored, I made up my mind to take more than ordinary steps to relieve that boredom. I decided to go parachuting. The next thing I knew, I was stuffed into a claustrophobically small plane with five other terrified people, rolling down a bumpy, rural runway, droning my way to 3,500 feet and an exhilarating experience. Once over the jump area, I waited my turn, stepped onto the strut, held my breath, and then kicked off into the cold, rushing air as my heart pounded heavily. All I could think was, "I hope this damn parachute opens!" The sensation of falling backwards through space was unfamiliar and disconcerting till my chute opened with a loud "pop," momentarily pulling me upwards toward the distant sky. After several minutes of floating downward, I landed rudely on the hard ground. Life, I remembered happily, could be awfully exciting. And a month later, when my tailbone had stopped throbbing, I still felt that way.*

How to Write a Narrative Essay

Preparing to Write. First, you should answer the prewriting questions to help you generate thoughts on the subject at hand. Next, as in all writing, you should explore your subject matter and discover as many specific details as possible. Some writers rely on the familiar journalistic check-list of Who, What, When, Where, Why, and How to make sure they cover all aspects of their narrative. If you were using the story of a bas-ketball game at your college to demonstrate the team spirit of your school, for example, you might want to consider telling your readers *who* played in the game and/or *who* attended; *what* happened before, during, and after the game; *when* and *where* it took place; *why* it was being played (or *why* these particular teams were playing each other or *why* the game was especially important); and *how* the winning basket was shot. Once you have generated these ideas, you should always let your purpose and audience ultimately guide your selection of details, but the process of gathering such journalistic information gives you some material from which to choose. You will also need to decide whether or not to include dialogue in your narrative. Again, the dif-ference here is between *showing* and *telling*: Will your audience bene-fit from reading what was actually said, word for word, during a dis-cussion, or will a brief description of the conversation be sufficiently effective? In fact, all the choices you make at this stage of the com-posing process will give you material with which to create emphasis, suspense, conflict, and interest in your subject.

Next, you must decide upon the point of view that will most readily help you achieve your purpose with your specific audience. Point of view includes the (1) person, (2) vantage point, and (3) atti-tude of your narrator. Person refers to who will tell the story: an unin-volved observer, a character in the narrative, or an omniscient (all-see-ing) narrator. This initial decision will guide your thoughts on vantage point, which is the frame of reference of the narrator: close to the action, far from the action, looking back on the past, or reporting on the present. Finally, your narrator will naturally have an attitude or personal feeling about the subject: accepting, hostile, sarcastic, indif-ferent, angry, pleased, or any of a number of similar emotions. Once you adopt a certain perspective in a story, you must follow it for the duration of the narrative. This consistency will bring focus and coher-ence to the story.

Writing. After you have explored your topic and adopted a particular point of view, you need to write a thesis statement and select and arrange the details of your story coherently so that the narrative has a clear beginning, middle, and end. The most natural way to organize the events of a narrative, of course, is chronologically. In your story about the school basketball game, you would probably narrate the relevant details in the order they occurred (i.e., sequentially, from the beginning of the game to its conclusion). More experienced writers may elect to use flashbacks: An athlete might recall a significant event that happened during the game, or a coach might recollect the contest's turning point. Your most important consideration is that the elements of a story must follow some sort of time sequence aided by the use of clear and logical transition (e.g., "then," "next," "at this point," "suddenly") that help the reader move smoothly from one event to the next.

Rewriting. As you reread the narrative you have written, pretend you are a reader and make sure you have told the story from the most effective point of view, considering both your purpose and your audience. Will your readers identify with your narrator? To what extent does this narrator help you achieve your purpose? Is the narrator's attitude appropriate to your subject?

Further, as you reread, make certain you can follow the events of the story as they are related. Does one event lead naturally to the next? Are all the events relevant to your purpose? Will these events interest your audience? Have you chosen appropriate details to enhance the story? Do you show rather than tell your message?

Student Essay: Narration at Work

The following essay characterizes the writer's mother by telling a story about an unusual family vacation. As you read it, notice how the student writer states her purpose clearly and succinctly in the first paragraph. She then becomes an integral part of her story as she carefully selects examples and details that help convey the passage of time.

A Vacation with My Mother

First person narrator — <u>I had an interesting childhood</u>—not because of where I grew up and not because I ever did anything particularly adventuresome or thrilling. In fact, I don't think my life seemed especially interesting to me at the time. But now, telling friends about my supposedly ordinary childhood, I notice an array of responses ranging from astonishment to hilarity. <u>The source of their surprise and amusement is my mother</u>—gracious, charming, sweet, and totally out of synchronization with the rest of the world. <u>One strange family trip we took when I was eleven captures the essence of her zaniness.</u> (*General subject*, *Focused subject*, *Thesis statement*)

My two sets of grandparents lived in Colorado and North Dakota, respectively, and my parents decided we would spend a few weeks driving to those states and seeing all the sights along the relaxed and rambling way. <u>My eight-year-old brother, David, and I had some serious reservations.</u> If Dad had ever had Mom drive him to school, we reasoned, he'd never even consider letting her help drive us anywhere out of town, let alone one of California. If we weren't paying attention, we were as likely to end up at her office or the golf course as we were to arrive at school. Sometimes (*Narrator's attitude*, *Examples*) she'd drop us off at a friend's house to play and then forget where she'd left us. The notion of going on a long trip with her was really unnerving.

Transition How can I explain my mother to a stranger? Have you ever watched reruns of the old "I Love Lucy" with Lucille Ball? I did as a child, and I thought Lucy Ricardo was normal. I lived with somebody a lot like her. Now, Mom wasn't a redhead (not usually, anyway), and Dad wasn't a Cuban nightclub owner, but at

Narrator's home we had the same situation of a loving but vantage bemused husband trying to deal with the off-the-wall point logic and enthusiasm of a frequently exasperating wife. We all adored her, but we had to admit it: Mom was a flaky, absent-minded, genuine eccentric.

Transition As the first day of our trip approached, David and I reluctantly said goodbye to all of our friends. Who knew if we'd ever see any of them again? Finally, the moment of our departure arrived, and we loaded suitcases, books, games, some packing gear, and a Careful tent into the car and bravely drove off. We bravely selection drove off again two hours later after we'd returned of details home to get the purse and traveler's checks that Mom had forgotten.

David and I were always a little nervous when using gas station bathrooms if Mom was driving while Use of Dad napped. "You stand outside the door and play dialogue lookout while I go, and I'll stand outside the door and play lookout while you go." I had terrible visions: "Honey, where are the kids?" "What?! Oh, gosh . . . I Examples thought they were being awfully quiet. Uh . . . Idaho?" We were never actually abandoned in a strange city, but we weren't about to take any chances.

Transition On the fourth or fifth night of the trip, we had trouble finding a motel with a vacancy. After driving futilely for an hour, Mom suddenly had a great idea: Why didn't we find a house with a likely-looking back Example yard and ask if we could pitch our tent there? To her, the scheme was eminently reasonable. Vowing quietly to each other to hide in the back seat if she did it, David and I groaned in anticipation mortification. To our profound relief, Dad vetoed the idea. Mom never could understand our objections. If a strange family showed up on her front doorstep, Mom would have been delighted. She thinks everyone in the world is as nice as she is. We finally found a vacancy in the next town. David and I were thrilled—the place featured bungalows in the shape of Native-American teepees.

Transition   The Native-American motif must have reminded my parents that we had not as yet used the brand-new tent, Coleman stove, portable mattress, and other camping gear we had brought. We headed to a national park the next day and found a campsite by a lake. It took hours to figure out how to get the tent up—it was one of those deluxe models with mosquito-net Careful windows, canvas floors, and enough room for three selection large families to sleep in. It was after dark before we of details finally got it erected, and the night had turned quite cold. We fixed a hurried campfire dinner (chicken burned on the outside and raw in the middle) and prepared to go to sleep. That was when we realized that Mom had forgotten to bring along some important pieces of equipment—our sleeping bags. The four of us huddled together on our thin mattresses under the carpet from the station-wagon floor. That ended our camping days. Give me a stucco teepee any time.

We drove through several states and saw lots of great sights along the way: the Grand Canyon, Examples Carlsbad Caverns, caves, mountains, waterfalls, even a (spatial haunted house. David and I were excited and amazed order) at all the wonders we found, and Mom was just as enthralled as we were. Her constant pleasure and sense of the world as a beautiful, magical place was infectious. I never realized until I grew up how really childlike—in the best sense of the word—my mother actually is. She is innocent, optimistic, and always ready to be entertained.

Transition   Looking back on that long-past family vacation, I Narrator's now realize that my childhood was more special attitude because I grew up with a mother who wasn't afraid to try anything and who taught me to look at the world as a series of marvelous opportunities to be explored. What did it matter that she thought England was bordered by Germany? We were never going to try to drive there. So what if she was always leaving her car keys in Examples the refrigerator or some other equally inexplicable Concluding place? In the end, we always got where we were going— remark and we generally had a grand time along the way.

Student Writer's Comments

The hardest thing about writing this narrative was trying to decide what material to use and what to leave out. I enjoyed writing about this childhood vacation because of all the memories it brought back. I soon realized, though, that I could not include everything that came to mind. I learned how important careful, judicious editing really is. I took the raw material of a very lengthy first draft and forced myself to choose the story that best captured my mother and what life was like growing up under the care of such a lovely but daffy individual. I made myself ruthlessly eliminate anything that interfered with the overall effect I was trying to create, including any unnecessary words and phrases.

Some Final Thoughts on Narration

Just as with other modes of writing, all decisions regarding narration should be made with a specific purpose and an intended audience constantly in mind. As you will see, each narrative in this section is directly at a clearly defined audience. Notice, as you read them, how each writer manipulates the various features of narration so that the readers are simultaneously caught up in the plot and deeply moved to feel, act, think, and believe the writer's personal options.

Mind Your Tongue, Young Man

Sandra Flahive Maurer

It was one of those days filled with the little vexations of life. In the morning, insult was added to injury when I got a speeding ticket after having a root canal. At work, the computer fouled me up by going down. By noon, the banana I'd brought for lunch had turned black and squishy, and finally, as I sped for home at the end of the day, the needle on the car's fuel indicator shook convulsively in its demand for a thirst–quenching gulp of gas.

Although I don't remember that I uttered any profanities upon encountering the day's irritations, in all likelihood I did. Like most people, I've never been known to have a lily-white mouth.

On that particular evening, I was eager to get home because I was giving a dinner party. However, my main concern was that I couldn't make it without first obliging the car's needs. I whipped off the freeway and headed for the nearest convenience store, only to find all eight pumps taken.

"Damn," I remember exclaiming as I impatiently waited my turn. But I soon found myself using another expletive when a cheeky woman in a Volvo tried to nudge ahead of me and cheat me of my already established territorial rights.

Eventually I was able to sidle up to a pump and fill the tank. Then I darted inside to pay—only to have to wait in line for the privilege of forking over money. As I stood, swearing under my breath about another delay in my life, I was only vaguely aware of a young man in front of me. He had plunked a Pepsi on the counter and was reaching into his pockets for money.

"Ninety-four cents, please," declared the middle-aged clerk. "Oh, and I'll take this pack of cigarettes, too," the young man stated matter-of-factly, as he pitched his selection on the counter.

"ID," countered the clerk, in a tone that suggested he had made this request many times before. The casual command caused me to focus on the person ahead of me. He was extremely slight with delicate features and a face as smooth as a baby's heel. I silently agreed with the clerk's decision to question his age. He could have been 21—or he could have been 15. It was impossible to tell.

"ID," said the clerk a second time, after the customer failed to respond with anything but a surly look.

Apparently the question about his age was more than he could stand, and upon being asked twice, the young man burst forth with a string of verbal garbage. "Goddam it! I don't have any f—ing identification with me. I don't haul the f—ing thing everywhere I go!" To which the clerk calmly remarked, "Then, it will be 94 cents for the Pepsi. No ID, no cigarettes."

With that rejection, the angry young man spewed a stream of obscenities that have become part of today's vocabulary. "I just ain't got my f—ing ID with me today. I told you."

I'd been observing the exchange more out of a sense of indifference than anything. All I wanted was to pay for my gas and get on my way. But my indifference vanished when the clerk, reacting to the profanity, suddenly reached across the counter with both arms, grabbed the fellow by the collar and literally plucked him off the floor. With fire in his eyes and passion in his voice, he growled, "That is enough! You watch what you say in here, do you understand? There's a lady present!" Then he shoved the guy away with obvious contempt.

The foulmouthed offender was stunned. So was I! Instinctively, I looked around to see where the "lady" was. I glanced up and down the nearby aisles and peered high into the corners where mirrors reveal all activity in the store. I had an image of some little old woman in a housedress, shuffling along in sturdy orthopedic shoes, her white hair done up in a bun, her purse dangling from her arm. I didn't see her anywhere.

All I saw in the mirror was the reflection of the two combatants—and my own. The obvious hit me hard. *I* was the "lady." I was flabbergasted by the clerk's stern admonition on my behalf. No one had tried to protect me from offensive language before.

With considerable speed the astonished young man paid for his drink and scurried from the store. I did likewise, still so startled by the clerk's actions that I didn't respond to his gallantry.

It was only after I began driving from the convenience store that I realized the significance of the episode. Profanity seems to be one of those problems about which almost everyone agrees something should be done. Yet few of us ever do anything about it. On the contrary, most of us contribute, if not to its proliferation, at least to its continuation, by swearing ourselves or making no attempt to curb it in others.

I recalled with guilt all the less-than-delicate language that had rolled off my tongue through the years—when I was mad, when I was glad, when I was trying to be dramatic and, yes, even when I had to wait in line for a few seconds. But nothing as crass as what I'd just heard.

And now, in an act of omission myself, I had failed to respond. Why hadn't *I* told the culprit to knock it off when his first raunchy words foamed out of his mouth? Why hadn't I given so much as a second's thought to rebuking him about his language? It's so familiar that it passes unnoticed, just runs off our backs. At the very least, why hadn't I thanked the clerk for taking a stand against offensive language in his store?

Recently I read a newspaper article that stated although Americans do have a concern about all the unbridled profanity around us every day, the reality is that we are swearing more, hearing it less.

Unfortunately, there must be some truth to the story—as shown by my experience in the convenience store. Granted it seems only natural that someone might be in shock after being subjected to a string of raw expressions while waiting to pay for gas. What surprises me is how much more astonished I was by the store clerk's gallant intervention and stand against vulgarity in his establishment than by the cussing of an angry young punk denied a pack of cigarettes.

A Total Eclipse

Annie Dillard

It began with no ado. It was odd that such a well-advertised public event should have no starting gun, no overture, no introductory speaker. I should have known right then that I was out of my depth. Without pause or preamble, silent as orbits, a piece of the sun went away. We looked at it through welders' goggles. A piece of the sun was missing; in its place we saw empty sky.

I had seen a partial eclipse in 1970. A partial eclipse is very interesting. It bears almost no relation to a total eclipse. Seeing a partial eclipse bears the same relation to seeing a total eclipse as kissing a man does to marrying him, or as flying in an airplane does to falling out of an airplane. Although the one experience precedes the other, it in no way prepares you for it. During a partial eclipse the sky does not darken—not even when 94 percent of the sun is hidden. Nor does the sun, seen colorless through protective devices, seem terribly strange. We have all seen a sliver of light in the sky; we have all seen the crescent moon by day. However, during a partial eclipse the air does indeed get cold, precisely as if someone were standing between you and the fire. And blackbirds do fly back to their roosts. I had seen a partial eclipse before, and here was another.

What you see in an eclipse is entirely different from what you know. It is especially different for those of us whose grasp of astronomy is so frail that, given a flashlight, a grapefruit, two oranges, and fifteen years, we still could not figure out which way to set the clocks for Daylight Saving Time. Usually it is a bit of a trick to keep your knowledge from blinding you. But during an eclipse it is easy. What you see is much more convincing than any wild-eyed theory you may know.

You may read that the moon has something to do with eclipses. I have never seen the moon yet. You do not see the moon. So near the sun, it is as completely invisible as the stars are by day. What you see before your eyes is the sun going through phases. It gets narrower and narrower, as the waning moon does, and, like the ordinary moon, it travels alone in the simple sky. The sky is of course background. It does not appear to eat the sun; it is far behind the sun, The sun simply shaves away; gradually, you see less sun and more sky.

The sky's blue was deepening, but there was no darkness. The sun was a wide crescent, like a segment of tangerine. The wind freshened and blew steadily over the hill. The eastern hill across the highway grew dusky and sharp. The towns and orchards in the valley to the south were dissolving into the blue light. Only the thin river held a trickle of sun.

Now the sky to the west deepened to indigo, a color never seen. A dark sky usually loses color. This was a saturated, deep indigo, up in the air. Stuck up into that unworldly sky was the cone of Mount Adams, and the alpenglow was upon it. The alpenglow is that red light of sunset which holds out on snowy mountaintops long after the valleys and tablelands are dimmed. "Look at Mount Adams," I said, and that was the last sane moment I remember.

I turned back to the sun. It was going. The sun was going, and the world was wrong. The grasses were wrong: they were platinum. Their every detail of stem, head, and blade shone lightless and artificially distinct as an art photographer's platinum print. This color has never been seen on earth. The hues were metallic: their finish was matte. The hillside was a nineteenth-century tinted photograph from which the tints had faded. All the people you see in the photograph, distinct and detailed as their faces look, are now dead. The sky was navy blue. My hands were silver. All the distant hills' grasses were fine-spun metal which the wind laid down. I was watching a faded color print of a movie filmed in the Middle Ages; I was standing in it, by some mistake. I was standing in a movie of hillside grasses filmed in the Middle Ages. I missed my own century, the people I knew, and the real light of day.

I looked at Gary [her husband]. He was in the film. Everything was lost. He was a platinum print, a dead artist's version of life. I saw on his skull the darkness of night mixed with the colors of day. My mind was going out, my eyes were receding the way galaxies recede to the rim of space. Gary was light-years away, gesturing inside a circle of darkness, down the wrong end of a telescope. He smiled as if he saw me; the stringy crinkles around his eyes moved. The sight of him, familiar and wrong, was something I was remembering from centuries hence, from the other side of death: yes, *that* is the way he used to look, when we were living. When it was our generation's turn to be alive. I could not hear him: the wind was too loud. Behind him the sun was going. We had all started down a chute of time. At first it was pleasant: now there was no stopping it. Gary was chuting away across space, moving and talking and catching my eye, chuting down the long corridor of separation. The skin on his face moved like thin bronze plating that would peel.

The grass at our feet was wild barley. It was the wild einkorn wheat which grew on the hilly flanks of the Zagros Mountains, above the Euphrates valley, above the valley of the river we called *River*. We harvested the grass with stone sickles. I remember. We found the grasses on the hillsides; we built our shelter beside them and cut them down. That is how he used to look then, that one, moving and living and catching my eye, with the sky so dark behind him, and the wind blowing. God save our life.

From all the hills came screams. A piece of sky beside the crescent sun was detaching. It was a loosened circle of evening sky, suddenly lighted from the back. It was an abrupt black body out of nowhere; it was a flat disk; it was almost over the sun. That is when there were screams. At once this disk of sky slid over the sun like a lid. The sky snapped over the sun like a lens cover. The hatch in the brain slammed. Abruptly it was dark night, on the land and in the sky. In the night sky was a tiny ring of light. The hole where the sun belongs is very small. A thin ring of light marked its place. There was no sound. The eyes dried, the arteries drained, the lungs hushed. There was no world. We were the world's dead people rotating and orbiting around and around, embedded in the planet's crust, while the earth rolled down. Our minds were light-years distant, forgetful of almost everything. Only an extraordinary act of will could recall to us our former, living selves and our contexts in matter and time. We had, it seems, loved the planet and loved our lives. But could no longer remember the way of them. We got the light wrong. In the sky was something that should not be there. In the black sky was a ring of light. It was a thin ring, an old, thin silver wedding band, an old, worn ring. It was an old wedding band in the sky, or a morsel of bone. There were stars. It was all over.

Passport to Knowledge

Mark Mathabane

When my mother began dropping hints that I would soon be going to school, I vowed never to go because school was a waste of time. She laughed and said, "We'll see. You don't know what you're talking about." My philosophy on school was that of a gang of ten-, eleven- and twelve-year-olds whom I so revered that their every word seemed that of an oracle.

These boys had long left their homes and were now living in various neighborhood junkyards, making it on their own. They slept in abandoned cars, smoked glue and benzene, ate pilchards and brown bread, sneaked into the white world to caddy and, if unsuccessful, came back to the township to steal beer and soda bottles from shebeens, or goods from the Indian traders on First Avenue. Their life-style was exciting, adventurous and full of surprises; and I was attracted to it. My mother told me that they were no-gooders, that they would amount to nothing, that I should not associate with them, but I paid no heed. What does she know? I used to tell myself. One thing she did not know was that the gang's way of life had captivated me wholly, particularly their philosophy on school: they hated it and considered an education a waste of time.

They, like myself, had grown up in an environment where the value of an education was never emphasized, where the first thing a child learned was not how to read and write and spell, but how to fight and steal and rebel; where the money to send children to school was grossly lacking, for survival was first priority. I kept my membership in the gang, knowing that for as long as I was under its influence, I would never go to school.

One day my mother woke me up at four in the morning.

"Are they here? I didn't hear any noises," I asked in the usual way.

"No," my mother said. "I want you to get into that washtub over there."

"What," I balked, upon hearing the word *washtub*. I feared taking baths like one feared the plague. Throughout seven years of hectic living the number of baths I had taken could be counted on one hand with several fingers missing. I simply had no natural inclination for water; cleanliness was a trait I still had to acquire. Besides, we had only one bathtub in the house, and it constantly sprung a leak.

"I said get into that tub!" My mother shook a finger in my face.

Reluctantly, I obeyed, yet wondered why all of a sudden I had to take a bath. My mother, armed with a scrub brush and a piece of Lifebuoy soap, purged me of years and years of grime till I ached and bled. As I howled, feeling pain shoot through my limbs as the thistles of the brush encountered stubborn callouses, there was a loud knock at the door.

Instantly my mother leaped away from the tub and headed, on tiptoe, toward the bedroom. Fear seized me as I, too, thought of the police. I sat frozen in the bathtub, not knowing what to do.

"Open up, Mujaji [my mother's maiden name]," Granny's voice came shrilling through the door. "It's me."

My mother heaved a sigh of relief, her tense limbs relaxed. She turned and headed to the kitchen door, unlatched it and in came Granny and Aunt Bushy.

"You scared me half to death," my mother said to Granny. "I had forgotten all about your coming."

"Are you ready?" Granny asked my mother.

"Yes—just about," my mother said, beckoning me to get out of the washtub.

She handed me a piece of cloth to dry myself. As I dried myself, questions raced through my mind: What's going on? What's Granny doing at our house this ungodly hour of the morning? And why did she ask my mother, "Are you ready?" While I stood debating, my mother went into the bedroom and came out with a stained white shirt and a pair of faded black shorts.

"Here," she said, handing me the togs, "put these on."

"Why?" I asked.

"Put them on I said!"

I put the shirt on; it was grossly loose-fitting. It reached all the way down to my ankles. Then I saw the reason why: it was my father's shirt!

"But this is Papa's shirt," I complained. "It don't fit me."

"Put it on," my mother insisted. "I'll make it fit."

"The pants don't fit me either," I said. "Whose are they anyway?"

"Put them on," my mother said. "I'll make them fit."

Moments later I had the garments on; I looked ridiculous. My mother started working on the pants and shirt to make them fit. She folded the shirt in so many intricate ways and stashed it inside the pants, they too having been folded several times at the waist. She then choked the pants at the waist with a piece of sisal rope to hold them up. She then lavishly smeared my face, arms and legs with a mixture of pig's fat and vaseline. "This will insulate you from the cold," she said. My skin gleamed like the morning star and I felt as hot as the center of the sun and I smelled God knows like what. After embalming me, she headed to the bedroom.

"Where are we going, Gran'ma?" I said, hoping that she would tell me what my mother refused to tell me. I still had no idea I was about to be taken to school.

"Didn't your mother tell you?" Granny said with a smile. "You're going to start school."

"What!" I gasped, leaping from the chair where I was sitting as if it were made of hot lead. "I am not going to school!" I blurted out and raced toward the kitchen door.

My mother had just reappeared from the bedroom and guessing what I was up to, she yelled, "Someone get the door!"

Aunt Bushy immediately barred the door. I turned and headed for the window. As I leaped for the windowsill, my mother lunged at me and brought me down. I tussled, "Let go of me! I don't want to go to school! Let me go!" but my mother held fast onto me.

"It's no use now," she said, grinning triumphantly as she pinned me down. Turning her head in Granny's direction, she shouted, "Granny! Get a rope quickly!"

Granny grabbed a piece of rope nearby and came to my mother's aid. I bit and clawed every hand that grabbed me, and howled protestations against going to school; however, I was no match for the two determined matriarchs. In a jiffy they had me bound, hands and feet.

"What's the matter with him?" Granny, bewildered, asked my mother. "Why did he suddenly turn into an imp when I told him you're taking him to school?"

"You shouldn't have told him that he's being taken to school," my mother said. "He doesn't want to go there. That's why I requested you come today, to help me take him there. Those boys in the streets have been a bad influence on him."

As the two matriarchs hauled me through the door, they told Aunt Bushy not to go to school but stay behind and mind the house and the children.

The sun was beginning to rise from beyond the veld when Granny and my mother dragged me to school. The streets were beginning to fill with their everyday traffic: old men and women, wizened, bent and ragged, were beginning their rambling; workless men and women were beginning to assemble in their usual coteries and head for shebeens in the backyards where they discussed how they escaped the morning pass raids and contemplated the conditions of life amidst intense beer drinking and vacant, uneasy laughter, young boys and girls, some as young as myself, were beginning their aimless wanderings along the narrow, dusty streets in search of food, carrying bawling infants piggyback.

As we went along some of the streets, boys and girls who shared the same fears about school as I were making their feelings known in a variety of ways. They were howling their protests and trying to escape. A few managed to break loose and make a mad dash for freedom, only to be recaptured in no time, admonished or whipped, or both, and ordered to march again.

As we made a turn into Sixteenth Avenue, the street leading to the tribal school I was being taken to, a short, chubby black woman came along from the opposite direction. She had a scuttle overflowing with coal on her *doek*-covered (cloth-covered) head. An infant, bawling deafeningly, was loosely swathed with a piece of sheepskin onto her back. Following closely behind the woman, and picking up pieces of coal as they fell from the scuttle and placing them in a small plastic bag, was a half naked, potbellied and thumb-sucking boy of about four. The woman stopped abreast. For some reason we stopped too.

"I wish I had done the same to my oldest son," the strange woman said in a regretful voice, gazing at me. I was confounded by her stopping and offering her unsolicited opinion.

"I wish I had done that to my oldest son," she repeated, and suddenly burst into tears; amidst sobs, she continued, "before . . . the street claimed him . . . and . . . turned him into a *tsotsi*."

Granny and my mother offered consolatory remarks to the strange woman.

"But it's too late now," the strange woman continued, tears now streaming freely down her puffy cheeks. She made no attempt to dry them. "It's too late now," she said for the second time, "he's beyond any help. I can't help him even if I wanted to. *Uswile* [He is dead]."

"How did he die?" my mother asked in a sympathetic voice.

"He shunned school and, instead, grew up to live by the knife. And the same knife he lived by ended his life. That's why whenever I see a boy-child refuse to go to school, I stop and tell the story of my dear little *mbitsini* [heartbreak]."

Having said that, the strange woman left as mysteriously as she had arrived.

"Did you hear what that woman said!" my mother screamed into my ears. "Do you want the same to happen to you?"

I dropped my eyes. I was confused.

"Poor woman," Granny said ruefully. "She must have truly loved her son."

Finally, we reached the school and I was ushered into the principal's office, a tiny cubicle facing a row of privies and a patch of yellowed grass.

"So this is the rascal we'd been talking about," the principal, a tall, wiry man, foppishly dressed in a black pin-striped suit, said to my mother as we entered. His austere, shiny face, inscrutable and imposing, reminded me of my father. He was sitting behind a brown table upon which stood piles of dust and cobweb-covered books and papers. In one upper pocket of his jacket was arrayed a variety of pens and pencils; in the other nestled a lily-white handkerchief whose presence was more decorative than utilitarian. Alongside him stood a disproportionately portly black woman, fashionably dressed in a black skirt and a white blouse. She had but one pen, and this she held in her hand. The room was hot and stuffy and buzzing with flies.

"Yes, Principal," my mother answered, "this is he."

"I see he's living up to his notoriety," remarked the principal, noticing that I had been bound. "Did he give you too much trouble?"

"Trouble, Principal," my mother sighed. "He was like an imp."

"He's just like the rest of them, Principal," Granny sighed. "Once they get out into the streets, they become wild. They take to the many vices of the streets like an infant takes to its mother's milk. They begin to think that there's no other life but the one shown them by the *tsotsis*. They come to hate school and forget about the future."

"Well," the principal said. "We'll soon remedy all that. Untie him."

"He'll run away," my mother cried.

"I don't think he's that foolish to attempt that with all of us here."

"He *is* that foolish, Principal," my mother said as she and Granny began untying me. "He's tried it before. Getting him here was an ordeal in itself."

The principal rose from his seat, took two steps to the door and closed it. As the door swung closed, I spotted a row of canes of different lengths and thicknesses hanging behind it. The principal, seeing me staring at the canes, grinned and said, in a manner suggesting that he had wanted me to see them, "As long as you behave, I won't have to use any of those on you."

Use those canes on me? I gasped. I stared at my mother—she smiled, at Granny—she smiled too. That made me abandon any inkling of escaping.

"So they finally gave you the birth certificate and the papers," the principal addressed my mother as he returned to his chair.

"Yes, Principal," my mother said, "they finally did. But what a battle it was. It took me nearly a year to get all them papers together." She took out of her handbag a neatly wrapped package and handed it to the principal. "They've been running us around for so long that there were times when I thought he would never attend school, Principal," she said.

"That's pretty much standard procedure, Mrs. Mathabane," the principal said, unwrapping the package. "But you now have the papers and that's what's important.

"As long as we have the papers," he continued, minutely perusing the contents of the package, "we won't be breaking the law in admitting your son to this school, for we'll be in full compliance with the requirements set by the authorities in Pretoria."

"Sometimes I don't understand the laws from Pitori," Granny said. "They did the same to me with my Piet and Bushy. Why, Principal, should our children not be allowed to learn because of some piece of paper?"

"The piece of paper you're referring to, Mrs. Mabaso [Granny's maiden name]," the principal said to Granny, "is as important to our children as a pass is to us adults. We all hate passes; therefore, it's only natural we should hate the regulations our children are subjected to. But as we have to live with passes, so our children have to live with the regulations, Mrs. Mabaso. I hope you understand, that is the law of the country. We would have admitted your grandson a long time ago, as you well know, had it not been for the papers. I hope you understand."

"I understand, Principal," Granny said, "but I don't understand," she added paradoxically.

One of the papers caught the principal's eye and he turned to my mother and asked, "Is your husband a Shangaan, Mathabane?"

"No, he's not, Principal," my mother said. "Is there anything wrong? He's Venda and I'm Shangaan."

The principal reflected for a moment or so and then said, concernedly, "No, there's nothing seriously wrong. Nothing that we can't take care of. You see, Mrs. Mathabane, technically, the fact that your child's father is a Venda makes him ineligible to attend this tribal school because it is only for children whose parents are of the Shangaan tribe. May I ask what language the children speak at home?"

"Both languages," my mother said worriedly, "Venda and Shangaan. Is there anything wrong?"

The principal coughed, clearing his throat, then said, "I mean which language do they speak more?"

"It depends, Principal," my mother said, swallowing hard. "When their father is around, he wants them to speak only Venda. And when he's not, they speak Shangaan. And when they are out at play, they speak Zulu and Sisotho."

"Well," the principal said, heaving a sigh of relief. "In that case, I think an exception can be made. The reason for such an exception is that there's currently no school for Vendas in Alexandra. And should the authorities come asking why we took in your son, we can tell them that. Anyway, your child is half-half."

Everyone broke into a nervous laugh, except me. I was bewildered by the whole thing. I looked at my mother, and she seemed greatly relieved as she watched the principal register me; a broad smile broke across her face. It was as if some enormously heavy burden had finally been lifted from her shoulders and her conscience.

"Bring him back two weeks from today," the principal said as he saw us to the door. "There're so many children registering today that classes won't begin until two weeks hence. Also, the school needs repair and cleaning up after the holidays. If he refuses to come, simply notify us, and we'll send a couple of big boys to come fetch him, and he'll be very sorry if it ever comes to that."

As we left the principal's office and headed home, my mind was still against going to school. I was thinking of running away from home and joining my friends in the junkyard.

I didn't want to go to school for three reasons: I was reluctant to surrender my freedom and independence over to what I heard every school-going child call "tyrannous discipline." I had heard many bad things about life in tribal school—from daily beatings by teachers and mistresses who worked you like a mule to long school hours—and the sight of those canes in the principal's office gave ample credence to rumors that school was nothing but a torture chamber. And there was my allegiance to the gang.

But the thought of the strange woman's lamentations over her dead son presented a somewhat strong case for going to school: I didn't want to end up dead in the streets. A more compelling argument for going to school, however, was the vivid recollection of all that humiliation and pain my mother had gone through to get me the papers and the birth certificate so I could enroll in school, What should I do? I was torn between two worlds.

But later that evening something happened to force me to go to school.

I was returning home from playing soccer when a neighbor accosted me by the gate and told me that there had been a bloody fight at my home.

"Your mother and father have been at it again," the neighbor, a woman, said. "And your mother left."

I was stunned.

"Was she hurt badly?"

"A little bit," the woman said. "But she'll be all right. We took her to your grandma's place."

I became hot with anger.

"Is anyone in the house?" I stammered, trying to control my rage.

"Yes, your father is. But I don't think you should go near the house. He's raving mad. He's armed with a meat cleaver. He's chased out your brother and sisters, also. And some of the neighbors who tried to intervene he's threatened to carve them to pieces. I have never seen him this mad before."

I brushed aside the woman's warnings and went. Shattered windows convinced me that there had indeed been a skirmish of some sort. Several pieces of broken bricks, evidently broken after being thrown at the door, were lying about the door. I tried opening the door; it was locked from the inside. I knocked. No one answered. I knocked again. Still no one answered, until, as I turned to leave:

"Who's out there?" my father's voice came growling from inside.

"It's me, Johannes," I said.

"Go away, you bastard!" he bellowed. "I don't want you or that whore mother of yours setting foot in this house. Go away before I come out there and kill you!"

"Let me in!" I cried. "Dammit, let me in! I want my things!"

"What things? Go away, you black swine!"

I went to the broken window and screamed obscenities at my father, daring him to come out, hoping that if he as much as ever stuck his black face out, I would pelt him with the half-a-loaf brick in my hand. He didn't come out. He continued launching a tirade of obscenities at my mother and her mother, calling them whores and bitches and so on. He was drunk, but I wondered where he had gotten the money to buy beer because it was still the middle of the week and he was dead broke. He had lost his entire wage for the past week in dice and had had to borrow bus fare.

"I'll kill you someday for all you're doing to my mother," I threatened him, overwhelmed with rage. Several nosey neighbors were beginning to congregate by open windows and doors. Not wanting to make a spectacle of myself, which was something many of our neighbors seemed to always expect from our family, I backtracked away from the door and vanished into the dark street. I ran, without stopping, all the way to the other end of the township where Granny lived. There I found my mother, her face swollen and bruised and her eyes puffed up to the point where she could scarcely see.

"What happened, Mama?" I asked, fighting to hold back the tears at the sight of her disfigured face.

"Nothing, child, nothing," she mumbled, almost apologetically, between swollen lips. "Your papa simply lost his temper, that's all."

"But why did he beat you up like this, Mama?" Tears came down my face. "He's never beaten you like this before."

My mother appeared reluctant to answer me. She looked searchingly at Granny, who was pounding millet with pestle and mortar and mixing it with sorghum and nuts for an African delicacy. Granny said, "Tell him, child, tell him. He's got a right to know. Anyway, he's the cause of it all."

"Your father and I fought because I took you to school this morning," my mother began. "He had told me not to, and when I told him that I had, he became very upset. He was drunk. We started arguing, and one thing led to another."

"Why doesn't he want me to go to school?"

"He says he doesn't have money to waste paying for you to get what he calls a useless white man's education," my mother replied. "But I told him that if he won't pay for your schooling, I would try and look for a job and pay, but he didn't want to hear that, also. 'There are better things for you to work for,' he said. 'Besides, I don't want you to work. How would I look to other men if you, a woman I owned, were to start working?' When I asked him why shouldn't I take you to school, seeing that you were now of age, he replied that he doesn't believe in schools. I told him that school would keep you off the streets and out of trouble, but still he was belligerent."

"Is that why he beat you up?"

"Yes, he said I disobeyed his orders."

"He's right, child," Granny interjected. "He paid *lobola* [bride price] for you. And your father ate it all up before he left me."

To which my mother replied, "But I desperately want to leave this beast of a man. But with his *lobola* gone I can't do it. That worthless thing you call your husband shouldn't have sold Jackson's scrawny cattle and left you penniless."

"Don't talk like that about your father, child," Granny said. "Despite all, he's still your father, you know. Anyway, he asked for *lobola* only because he had to get back what he spent raising you. And you know it would have been taboo for him to let you or any of your sisters go without asking for *lobola*."

"You and Papa seemed to forget that my sisters and I have minds of our own," my mother said. "We didn't need you to tell us whom to marry, and why, and how. If it hadn't been for your interference, I could have married that schoolteacher."

Granny did not reply; she knew well not to. When it came to the act of "selling" women as marriage partners, my mother was vehemently opposed to it. Not only was she opposed to this one aspect of tribal culture, but to others as well, particularly those involving relations between men and women and the upbringing of children. But my mother's sharply differing opinion was an exception rather than the rule among tribal women. Most times, many tribal women questioned her sanity in daring to question well-established mores. But my mother did not seem to care; she would always scoff at her opponents and call them fools in letting their husbands enslave them completely.

Though I disliked school, largely because I knew nothing about what actually went on there, and the little I knew had painted a dreadful picture, the fact that a father would not want his son to go to school, especially a father who didn't go to school, seemed hard to understand.

"Why do you want me to go to school, Mama?" I asked, hoping that she might, somehow, clear up some of the confusion that was building in my mind.

"I want you to have a future, child," my mother said. "And, contrary to what your father says, school is the only means to a future. I don't want you growing up to be like your father."

The latter statement hit me like a bolt of lightning. It just about shattered every defense mechanism and every pretext I had against going to school.

"Your father didn't go to school," she continued, dabbing her puffed eyes to reduce the swelling with a piece of cloth dipped in warm water, "that's why he's doing some of the bad things he's doing. Things like drinking, gambling and neglecting his family. He didn't learn how to read and write; therefore, he can't find a decent job. Lack of any education has narrowly focused his life. He sees nothing beyond himself. He still thinks in the old, tribal way, and still believes that things should be as they were back in the old days when he was growing up as a tribal boy in Louis Trichardt. Though he's my husband, and your father, he doesn't see any of that."

"Why didn't he go to school, Mama?"

"He refused to go to school because his father led him to believe that an education was a tool through which white people were going to take things away from him, like they did black people in the old days. And that a white man's education was worthless insofar as black people were concerned because it prepared them for jobs they can't have. But I know it isn't totally so, child, because times have changed somewhat. Though our lot isn't any better today, an education will get you a decent job. If you can read or write you'll be better off than those of us who can't. Take my situation: I can't find a job because I don't have papers, and I can't get papers because white people mainly want to register people who can read and write. But I want things to be different for you, child. For you and your brother and sisters. I want you to go to school, because I believe that an education is the key you need to open up a new world and a new life for yourself, a world and life different from that of either your father's or mine. It is the only key that can do that, and only those who seek it earnestly and perseveringly will get anywhere in the white man's world. Education will open doors where none seem to exist. It'll make people talk to you, listen to you and help you; people who otherwise wouldn't bother. It will make you soar, like a bird lifting up into the endless blue sky, and leave poverty, hunger and suffering behind. It'll teach you to learn to embrace what's good and shun what's bad and evil. Above all, it'll make you a somebody in this world. It'll make you grow up to be a good and proud person. That's why I want you to go to school, child, so that education can do all that, and more, or you."

A long, awkward silence followed, during which I reflected upon the significance of my mother's lengthy speech. I looked at my mother; she looked at me.

Finally, I asked, "How come you know so much about school, Mama? You didn't go to school, did you?"

"No, child," my mother replied. "Just like your father, I never went to school." For the second time that evening, a mere statement of fact had a thunderous impact on me. All the confusion I had about school seemed to leave my mind, like darkness giving way to light. And what had previously been a dark, yawning void in my mind was suddenly transformed into a beacon of light that began to grow larger and larger, until it had swallowed up, blotted out, all the blackness. That beacon of light seemed to reveal things and facts, which, though they must have always existed in me, I hadn't been aware of up until now.

"But unlike your father," my mother went on, "I've always wanted to go to school, but couldn't because my father, under the sway of tribal traditions, thought it unnecessary to educate females. That's why I so much want you to go, child, for if you do, I know that someday I too would come to go, old as I would be then. Promise me, therefore, that no matter what, you'll go back to school. And I, in turn, promise that I'll do everything in my power to keep you there."

With tears streaming down my cheeks and falling upon my mother's bosom, I promised her that I would go to school "forever." That night, at seven and a half years of my life, the battlelines in the family were drawn. My mother on the one side, illiterate but determined to have me drink, for better or for worse, from the well of knowledge. On the other side, my father, he too illiterate, yet determined to have me drink from the well of ignorance. Scarcely aware of the magnitude of the decision I was making or, rather, the decision which was being emotionally thrusted upon me, I chose to fight on my mother's side, and thus my destiny was forever altered.

The Perfect Picture

James Alexander Thom

It was early in the spring about 15 years ago—a day of pale sunlight and trees just beginning to bud. I was a young police reporter, driving to a scene I didn't want to see. A man, the police-dispatcher's broadcast said, had accidentally backed his pickup truck over his baby granddaughter in the driveway of the family home. It was a fatality.

As I parked among police cars and TV-news cruisers, I saw a stocky white-haired man in cotton work clothes standing near a pickup. Cameras were trained on him, and reporters were sticking microphones in his face. Looking totally bewildered, he was trying to answer their questions. Mostly he was only moving his lips, blinking and choking up.

After a while the reporters gave up on him and followed the police into the small white house. I can still see in my mind's eye that devastated old man looking down at the place in the driveway where the child had been. Beside the house was a freshly spaded flower bed, and nearby a pile of dark, rich earth.

"I was just backing up there to spread that good dirt," he said to me, though I had not asked him anything. "I didn't even know she was outdoors." He stretched his hand toward the flower bed, then let it flop to his side. He lapsed back into his thoughts, and I, like a good reporter, went into the house to find someone who could provide a recent photo of the toddler.

A few minutes later, with all the details in my notebook and a three-by-five studio portrait of the cherubic child tucked in my jacket pocket, I went toward the kitchen where the police had said the body was.

I had brought a camera in with me—the big, bulky Speed Graphic which used to be the newspaper reporter's trademark. Everybody had drifted back out of the house together—family, police, reporters and photographers. Entering the kitchen, I came upon this scene:

On a Formica-topped table, backlighted by a frilly curtained window, lay the tiny body, wrapped in a clean white sheet. Somehow the grandfather had managed to stay away from the crowd. He was sitting on a chair beside the table, in profile to me and unaware of my presence, looking uncomprehendingly at the swaddled corpse.

The house was very quiet. A clock ticked. As I watched, the grandfather slowly leaned forward, curved his arms like parentheses around the head and feet of the little form, then pressed his face to the shroud and remained motionless.

In that hushed moment I recognized the makings of a prize-winning news photograph. I appraised the light, adjusted the lens setting and distance, locked a bulb in the flashgun, raised the camera and composed the scene in the view finder.

Every element of the picture was perfect: the grandfather in his plain work clothes, his white hair backlighted by sunshine, the child's form wrapped in the sheet, the atmosphere of the simple home suggested by black iron trivets and World's Fair souvenir plates on the walls flanking the window. Outside, the police could be seen inspecting the fatal rear wheel of the pickup while the child's mother and father leaned in each other's arms.

I don't know how many seconds I stood there, unable to snap that shutter. I was keenly aware of the powerful story-telling value that photo could have, and my professional conscience told me to take it. Yet I couldn't make my hand fire that flashbulb and intrude on the poor man's island of grief.

At length I lowered the camera and crept away, shaken with doubt about my suitability for the journalistic profession. Of course I never told the city editor or any fellow reporters about that missed opportunity for a perfect news picture.

Everyday on the newscasts and in the papers, we see pictures of people in extreme conditions of grief and despair. Human suffering has become a spectator sport. And sometimes, as I'm watching news film, I remember that day.

I still feel right about what I did.

My Experience with Hunting

Student

When I was seven, my father and a few of his friends took me on my first hunting trip. I excitedly thought of stalking wild prey through the forest, like Daniel Boone facing the untold dangers of the wild. But for me, the sport of hunting did not give the satisfaction I had expected. In most sports, we tend to think of the thrill of victory and the agony of defeat. For me, however, hunting involved the thrill of defeat and the agony of victory. The thrill of defeat is the feeling that I experienced when my father missed a shot at a deer and the deer ran off unharmed. The agony of victory is the guilt feelings experienced when one has taken a life.

During the beginning of the trip I could not wait to get out into the forest. While we unpacked the truck and set up camp, all I did was brag about the giant buck I was going to bag. Once out in the field I wanted to be the first to bag a deer and show my father and his friends that I was no longer a child. I walked ahead of them, stalking through the forest with my rifle in hand, imagining myself as the seasoned combat veteran searching the jungles for enemy patrols. I didn't spot any enemy patrols; I didn't spot any deer either.

My father's friend Jim was the first to see any deer. He called us over to use his binoculars: we saw a small herd of maybe ten deer. As we stalked closer to the herd, we stumbled upon a large doe. Everyone decided since this was my first trip, I should be the one to take the first shot. I suddenly felt nervous and I wanted someone else to take the shot, but I couldn't let my father or any of his friends know this. As I drew down and brought the deer into focus, I could see her big brown eye's staring at me. This caused me to hesitate, feeling the conflict of not wanting to take the animal's life and not wanting to let my father down in front of his friends. I forced myself to squeeze the trigger and the shot rang out. The deer ran about thirty feet and fell. My father and friends all cheered and congratulated me on my first kill.

To me, being congratulated for killing the animal did not seem quite appropriate, especially at the sight of the shivering fawn I spotted only twenty feet from its now dead mother. I never imagined the amount of intense guilt that could be felt by one person. I felt as if I was in a state of limbo and extremely disappointed with myself. I never thought I would take a life because I was afraid to disappoint someone. The deer that I killed was an innocent creature that did not deserve to die in the name of sport. To me, the premeditated killing of defenseless animals is not a sport.

It might sound strange, but I still enjoy hunting. I love being outdoors in the country, the fresh air, the trees, streams, animals and birds. The excitement felt when out in the wilderness stalking a wild animal is one of the most intense feelings I have ever felt. But now when I hunt and get an animal in my sights, I squeeze a shutter release instead of a trigger. This still gives me all the excitement of the hunt, without having to take a life. I still get to bring home a trophy of my prey, but I leave the animal alive and unharmed in its home. This is my idea of a successful hunt.

An Eventful Flight
Student

It is two A.M., and our mission briefing has been completed as I walk toward the flight line. The flood lights glow dimly on the aircraft, as the sweet smell of the sea breeze gently awakens the senses. I go through the ritual of preparing myself for the flight. I have no thoughts, except for those which guide me through my routine. I don the smooth Nomex flight suit, my leather boots and finally my issue flight vest. I check for my ID tags, that my collar is up and that my helmet is on and visor is down. "Clear on the 'P'?" shouts the pilot. "Clear," I respond. The sound of ignitors ticking fills the air as the small starting engine surges and comes to life.

The pilots go through their pre-flight check list as I walk around the helicopter one last time to insure that everything is in proper order, or at least appears that way. With the radio checks finished, flight control checks complete, and navigation settings entered, we begin to fire up the aircraft. "Clear on '1' and '2'?" bursts through my helmet. "'1' and '2' are clear sir," I garble back. The low painful moaning of the two turbo-shaft engines is felt throughout my body. Slowly and begrudgingly, the engines respond with obvious protest. Rotor blades begin to turn and the bitter sweet smell of jet fuel fills the air. In less than two minutes, we will be skating along the wave tops at 175 miles per hour, with a full load to bring across the pond to the waiting personnel in need of our goods. The rotors are now turning at full flight speed, and the helicopter is begging to fly. I take one last look around and satisfied I climb in and we become airborne.

This is my thirty-second trip across. With a fifty-five minute flight time, the opportunity for one's mind to wander is great. Our destination, once known as "The Paris of the Middle East," now resembles a scene from "Escape from New York." The oil refinery to the south still smolders from a Syrian rocket launched more than a week ago. I think of previous missions and our importance here. I recall all the events which brought me to this alien place. I wonder about my family and loved ones, and how I wish I could tell them exactly where I am. Yet always in the back of my mind the question remains, "Will I be back at the block at the end of this day or end up fish-bait?"

My introspection is suddenly interrupted by the announcement that we're ten minutes out. I pass out our Kevlar vests and sit on the extra one. The pilots arm the chaff dispenser and warm up the radar jamming equipment. The moon's reflection casts an eerie green hue through my PVS-6 night vision goggles. I notice the color of the water has changed from crystal blue to the brown-green produced by the pollution of the city and the trash carelessly discarded into the sea. The lights of the city seem to be inching ever closer and I can see the revolving light from the forbidden international airport eight kilometers to the south.

Standard procedure for this mission call for only one ship at the target landing zone at a time. With this in mind, we make a standard break, and continue heading for the shoreline. Ninety seconds later, we make the radio call "Feet Dry," indicating we have made landfall. Once splendid destination resorts lay in ruins below us, along with relics of exotic playgrounds. Every time I see this version of hell, I am amazed at the destructive power of the human race. We execute a hard cyclic climb, which is followed by a one hundred and eighty degree pedal turn. Then finally we drop the collective and plant the Lz.

Cargo and personnel are rapidly removed from the aircraft. The one hundred and twenty seconds we spend at the landing zone, always seems like one hundred and twenty hours. The missile lock indicator glows a devilish red, and we occasionally receive stray small arms fire. With the new cargo for the return trip loaded, I inform the pilots we are ready for take off. After a jerk of power and a rush of gravity we become airborne once again. Thirty seconds later, we are 'Feet Wet' and heading for the holding point.

Our sister ship passes us on her way inbound in complete darkness. I try to relax. Though we had been in and out the threat was still present and we were by no means out of danger. Waiting for the other helicopter is always the worst part of this mission. Finally we got the call "Feet Wet." With this, we leave our holding pattern and turn away from the coast, heading for home. Relief slowly starts to overcome me and the adrenaline rush begins to subside. Ten minutes out, the Kevlar is removed and stowed and the chaff dispenser is returned to the safe position. With the hard part of the mission accomplished, I settle back for the trip home and start to consider what I will have for breakfast.

Suddenly, the pitch of the engine increases dramatically, followed by a sharp cracking sound. I glance toward the cockpit and see the starboard side engine fire light illuminated. Before the pilots can ask, I lean out the window as far as my harness will allow. Heavy black smoke is now pouring out the exhaust duct. I confirm the engine fire and emergency shut down procedures are initiated. Before the engine can be shut down, it decides to go south. This leaves us in a very precarious position. With only one engine left operating and a full load of cargo that cannot be dumped overboard due to its sensitive nature, our choices are limited. I begin to recall the weekend of water egress training I received before being accepted for this mission. I try to step through in my mind all the things I need to remember, find a reference point, secure all loose items, remain calm, remain calm, and most importantly remain calm. The pilots are also in a very difficult position. Either we try to make it home on one engine over eighty miles of open water, return to the landing zone or ditch the aircraft and swim. None of the aforementioned options appeals to me all that much.

Thoughts of my family and friends rush through my head. I consider the very real possibility I will never see them again. An eternity seems to pass until the pilots make the decision to return to the landing zone. The original Lz has already been vacated and the evidence of our arrival removed. With only one engine, now severely over torqued, we need a runway to land on. With this in mind, we have only one choice. An old highway turned runway is located ten kilometers to the north; this will be our destination.

We make the radio calls to our sister ship, flight following service and ground control radio, to inform them of our condition and our intentions. Now the fun begins.

As we turn to the north and begin preparations for landing, we are notified that another aircraft has been scrambled to fly cover for us. Unfortunately, it will not be on station for an hour and by that time we will be down and en route to the embassy complex. We turn to heading zero-nine-zero and begin our base leg to the "runway", call "Feet Dry" and prepare for what will be the most important landing of our lives. The second helicopter of our flight is no longer holding off shore. She is now approximately sixty feet above and to our starboard side flying cover. Turning to heading one-eight-zero, we begin our final approach with the air thick with anticipation. The runway comes into sight and we begin to decrease the air speed. The customary ease to the ground is now replaced with a sharp drop and increased anxieties. Now over the threshold of the runway, the power is decreased even more and we land with an abrupt jolt to everything in the aircraft. The helicopter rolls to a stop and we shut it down. Our flying cover informs us they must continue back to base, due to an ever decreasing fuel level.

In this city of bedlam, it is virtually impossible to distinguish the friendlies from the non-friendlies. This is officially a humanitarian mission, so we carry absolutely no weapons. As the rotor blades coast to a stop a pair of jeeps, a cargo truck and an armored personnel carrier rush toward the aircraft. We have no idea as to who is driving these vehicles. To our relief, this is our guard unit and they inform us we have thirty minutes to prepare to leave.

Thirty minutes is not nearly enough time for us to accomplish all the tasks needed to abandon the aircraft. I concentrate on the secure radios, avionics, and sensitive electronics, while the pilots remove the contents we loaded at the original landing zone. I work with abandon, while the minutes fly by like never before in my life. All the equipment is loaded into the cargo truck. Then, in turn, we climb into the APC and head for the embassy. As we drive away, I turn to peek through the rifle slot to get one last look at my helicopter. I wonder if I will ever see her again.

The seven kilometer trip to the embassy complex is thankfully uneventful. We arrive to a flurry of activity and are immediately herded into a briefing room. We are informed that a fifteen man guard squad has been sent to secure the airfield and protect the aircraft. Through a window, I can see the sun beginning its ascent above the distant horizon. The adrenaline flow from the previous hour's events is starting to subside. I then realize how truly lucky we had been.

Several of the embassy staff enter the room, with coffee and some danishes. Even though we have been up for ten hours already, it is breakfast time. I was thankful for the chance to try to smooth out the knots in my stomach. Half way through my coffee, the Chief Liaison Officer enters the room and quickly begins briefing us on the situation and the plan for our removal from this place. We are informed that all non-essential equipment will be removed from the helicopter and we will be flying it back to the base. The plan calls for us to join up with a Lebanese Army gunship at nine o'clock. The gunship will escort us to a rendezvous point. Once there, we will join a flight of a helicopters from our base and two marine super cobra attack helicopters. The only other option is to destroy the aircraft in its place. There is no possible way to replace or repair the broken engine, on this side of the pond.

Two hours later we are back inside the APC and heading for the air strip. When we arrive, we notice a large crowd gathered outside the airfield fence. If I didn't know better, I would think the circus was in town. The mood of the crowd is one of excitement and curiosity. We perform our standard preflight checks, except we do not need to check the starboard engine. The pilots climb in. I remain outside to observe the starting procedures. The engine is started and the rotor blades begin to turn. I am filled with doubt concerning our return trip.

With the rotors turning at full flight speed, we wait for the radio call from our Lebanese companion. Finally, it comes and we begin to roll forward. We travel down the rough runway and once at eighty knots the helicopter lifts off. The rest of the trip goes exactly as planned. We meet our next escort and follow them home. The events of this day have made me very aware of the uncertainties in life. Before this event, I thought I would be ready for anything that might arise. However, now I merely hope that when put in another position like this one, my luck will remain as it was that eventful day in September.

Ch. 2: Narration

Suggestions for writing:

1. Write a narrative about a disturbing occurrence or event that you witnessed but didn't get involved in. How did you feel later about not getting involved? (See "Mind Your Tongue, Young Man," p. 42.)

2. Write a narrative about a sports or academic achievement that you worked very hard to accomplish.

3. Write a narrative about the first time you were ever treated as an adult.

4. Write a narrative about a time you got away with something that you should have been punished for (or vice versa).

5. Write a narrative about one of the following topics or a similar topic:

the worst date you ever had	the birth of your child
a funeral	your wedding day
a surprise party you gave or received	your worst day on the job

Narration checklist:

1. Is the paper organized chronologically?

2. Is there a conflict or an element of dissonance at the center of your narrative?

3. If the action in your narrative does result from a conflict, do you resolve this conflict for the reader?

4. Have you used appropriate transitional words and phrases so that your reader can easily follow the sequence of events?

5. Did you develop your ideas fully and in a variety of ways? Did you use examples? Physical descriptions? Illustrations?

6. Did you appeal to your reader's senses? Which ones?

7. Did you employ any dialogue in your narrative? If so, did you punctuate it clearly and correctly?

8. Did you vary the length and type of sentences in your narrative?

9. Did you check for correctness of grammar, punctuation and spelling?

CHAPTER 3

Example

Illustrating Ideas

Using Examples

Citing an example to help make a point is one of the most instinctive techniques we use in communication. If, for instance, you state that being an internationally ranked tennis player requires constant practice, a friend might challenge that assertion and ask what you mean by "constant practice." When you respond "about three hours a day," your friend might ask for more specific proof. At this stage in the discussion, you could offer the following illustration to support your statement: When not on tour, Steffi Graf practices three hours per day; Monica Seles, four hours; and Andre Agassi, two hours. Your friend's doubt will have been answered through your use of examples.

Defining Examples

Well-chosen examples and illustrations are an essay's building blocks. They are drawn from your experience, your observations, and your reading. They help you *show* rather than *tell* what you mean, usually by supplying concrete details (references to what we can see, smell, taste, hear, or touch) to support abstract ideas (such as faith, hope, understanding, love), by providing specifics (I like chocolate) to explain generalizations (I like sweets), and by giving definite references (turn left at the second stoplight) to clarify vague statements (turn in a few blocks). Though illustrations take many forms, writers often find themselves indebted to description or narration (or some combination of the two) in order to supply enough relevant examples to achieve their rhetorical intent.

As you might suspect, examples are important ingredients in producing exciting, vivid prose. Just as crucial is the fact that carefully chosen examples can often encourage your readers to feel one way or another about an issue being discussed. If you tell your parents, for instance, that living in a college dormitory is not conductive to academic success, they may doubt your word, perhaps thinking that you are simply attempting to coerce money out of them for an apartment. You can help dispel this notion, however, by giving them specific examples of the chaotic nature of dorm life: the party down the hall that broke up at 2:00 A.M. when you had a chemistry exam that same morning at 8 o'clock; the stereo next door that seems to be stuck on its highest decibel level all hours of the day and night; and the new "friend" you recently acquired who thinks you are the best listener in the world—especially when everyone else has the good sense to be asleep. After such a detailed and well-documented explanation, your parents could hardly deny the strain of this difficult environment on your studies. Examples can be very persuasive.

The following paragraphs written by a student use examples to explain how he reacts to boredom in his life. As you read this excerpt, notice how the writer shows rather than tells the readers how he copes with boredom by providing exciting details that are concrete, specific, and definite.

> We all deal with boredom in our own ways. Unfortunately, most of us have to deal with it far too often. Some people actually seek boredom. Being bored means that they are not required to do anything; being boring means that no one wants anything from them. In short, these people equate boredom with peace and relaxation. But for the rest of us, boredom is not peaceful. It produces anxiety.
>
> Most people deal with boredom by trying to distract themselves from boring circumstances. Myself, I'm a reader. At the breakfast table over a boring bowl of cereal, I read the cereal box, the milk carton, the wrapper on the bread. (Have you ever noticed how many of those ingredients are unpronounceable?) Waiting in a doctor's office, I will gladly read weekly news magazines of three years ago, a book for five-year-olds, advertisements for drugs, and even the physician's odd-looking diplomas on the walls. Have you ever been so bored you were reduced to reading through all the business cards in your wallet? Searching for names similar to yours in the phone book? Browsing through the National Enquirer while waiting in the grocery line? At any rate, that's my receipt for beating boredom. What's yours?

—— *Example* ———————————————————————— *69*

How to Write an Essay that Uses Examples

Preparing to Write. Before you can use examples in an essay, you must first think of some. One good way to generate ideas is to use some of the prewriting techniques. You should then consider these thoughts in conjunction with the purpose and audience specified in your chosen writing assignments.

Writing. In an example essay, a thesis statement or controlling idea will help you begin to organize your paper. The examples you use should always be relevant to the thesis and purpose of your essay. If, for instance, the person talking tennis players cited the practice schedules of only unknown players, her friend certainly would not be convinced of the truth of her statement about how hard internationally ranked athletes work at their games. To develop a topic principally with examples, you can use one extended example or several shorter examples, depending on the nature and purpose of your assertion. If you are attempting to prove that Americans are more health-conscious now than they were twenty years ago, citing a few examples from your own neighborhood will not provide enough evidence to be convincing. If, however, you are simply commenting on a neighborhood health trend, you can legitimately refer to these local cases. Furthermore, always try to find examples with which your audience can identify so that they can follow your line of reasoning. If you want your parents to help finance an apartment, citing instances from the lives of current rock stars will probably not prove your point, because your parents may not sympathize with these particular role models.

The examples you choose must also be arranged as effectively as possible in order to encourage audience interest and identification. If you are using examples to explain the imaginative quality of Disneyland, for instance, the most logical approach would probably be to organize your essay by degrees (i.e., from least to most imaginative or most to least original). But if your essay uses examples to help readers visualize your bedroom, a spatial arrangement of the details (moving from one item to the next) might be easiest for your readers to follow. If the subject concerned a series of important events, like graduation weekend, the illustrations might most effectively be organized chronologically. As you will learn from reading the selections that follow, careful organization of examples can lead quite easily to unity (a sense of wholeness or interrelatedness) and coherence (clear, logical development) in your essays. Unity and coherence produce good writing—and that, of course, helps foster confidence and accomplishment in school and in your professional life.

Rewriting. As you reread your example essay, look closely at the choice and arrangement of details in relation to your purpose and audience. Have you included enough examples to develop each of your topics adequately? Are the examples you have chosen relevant to your thesis? Have you selected examples that your readers can easily understand? Have you arranged these examples in a logical manner that your audience can follow?

Student Essay: Examples at Work

In the following essay, a student uses examples to explain and analyze her parent's behavior as they prepare for and enjoy their grandchildren during the Christmas holidays. As you read it, study the various examples the student writer uses to convince us that her parents truly undergo a transformation each winter.

Mom and Dad's Holiday Disappearing Act

General topic · Often during the winter holidays, people find surprises: Children discover the secret contents of brightly wrapped packages that have teased them for weeks; cooks are astonished by the wealth of smells and memories their busy kitchens can bring about; workaholics stumble upon the true joy of a few days' rest. *(Details to capture holiday spirit)*

Background information · My surprise over the past few winters has been the personality transformation my parents go through around mid-December as they change from Dad and Mom into Poppa and Granny. Yes, they become grandparents and are completely different people from the people I know the other eleven and a half months of the year. *(Thesis statement)*

First point · The first sign of my parents' metamorphosis is the delight they take in visiting toy and children's clothing stores. These two people, who usually despise anything having to do with shopping malls, become crazed consumers. While they tell me to budget my money and shop wisely, they are buying every doll, dump truck, and velvet outfit in sight. And this is only the beginning of the holidays! *(Examples relevant to thesis)*

Transition · When my brother's children arrive, Poppa and Granny come into full form. First they throw out all ideas about the balanced diet for their grandkids. While we were raised in a house where everyone had to take two bites of broccoli, beets, or liver (foods that appeared quite often on our table despite constant groaning), the grandchildren never have to eat anything that does not appeal to them. Granny carries marshmallows in her pockets to bribe the littlest ones into following her around the house, while Poppa offers "surprises" of candy and cake to them all day *(Second point)* *(Humorous examples (organized from most to least healthy))*

Example 71

long. Boxes of chocolate-covered cherries disappear while the bran muffins get hard and stale. The kids love all the sweets, and when the sugar revs up their energy level, Granny and Poppa can always decide to leave and do a bit more shopping or go to bed while my brother and sister-in-law try to deal with their supercharged, hyperactive kids.

Transition   Once the grandchildren have arrived, Granny and Poppa also seem to forget all of the responsibility lec- Third point tures I so often hear in my daily life. If little Tommy throws a fit at a friend's house, he is "overwhelmed by the number of adults"; if Mickey screams at his sister during dinner, he is "developing his own personality"; if Nancy breaks Granny's vanity mirror (after being told twice to put it down), she is "just a curious child." But, Examples if I track mud into the house while helping to unload in the form groceries, I become "careless"; if I scold one of the sons grandkids for tearing pages out of my calculus book, I am "impatient." If a grandchild talks back to her mother, Granny and Poppa chuckle at her spirit. If I mumble one word about all of this dotage, Mom and Dad reappear to have a talk with me about petty jealousies.

     When my nieces and nephews first started appear- Transition ing at our home for the holidays a few years ago, I to conclu- probably was jealous, and I complained a lot. But now I spend more time simply sitting back and watching Mom and Dad change into what we call the "Incredible Huggers." They enjoy their time with these Writer's grandchildren so much that I easily forgive them their attitude Granny and Poppa faults.

     I believe their personality change is due to the lack Writer's of responsibility they feel for the grandkids: In their analysis of role as grandparents, they don't have to worry about situation sugar causing cavities or temporary failures of self-discipline turned into lifetime faults. Those problems are up to my brother and sister-in-law. All Granny and Poppa have to do is enjoy and love their grandchildren. They have all the fun of being parents without any of the attendant obligations. And you know what? Specific reference Concluding I think they've earned the right to make this transfor- to intro- remark mation—at least once a year. duction

Student Writer's Comments

To begin this essay, I scratched out an outline by first listing examples of my parents' behavior, then figured out how they fit together. Once I sat down to write, I was stumped. I wanted the introduction to be humorous, but I also wanted to maintain a respectable tone (so I wouldn't sound like a whiny kid!). Finally, I just decided to write down *anything* to get started and come back to the beginning later on. All those examples and anecdotes were swimming around in my head wanting to be committed to paper. I found I needed my thesaurus and dictionary from the very beginning; they helped to take the pressure off coming up with the perfect word every time I was stuck. As I neared the middle of the paper, the introduction popped into my head, so I jotted down my thoughts and continued with the flow of ideas I needed for the body of my paper. Writing my conclusion helped me put my experiences with my parents into perspective. I had never really tried to analyze how I felt toward them or why they acted as they do during the Christmas holidays. They were glad to hear I had figured them out!

Some Final Thoughts on Examples

Although examples are often used to supplement and support other methods of development—such as cause/effect, comparison/contrast, and process analysis—the essays in this section are focused principally on examples. A main idea is expressed in the introduction of each, and the rest of the essay provides examples to bolster that contention. As you read these essays, pay close attention to each author's choice and arrangement of examples; then try to determine which organizational techniques are most persuasive for each specific audience.

Civil Rites

Caroline Miller

I was taking my kids to school not long ago when I had one of those experiences particular to parents—a moment that nobody else notices, but that we replay over and over because in it we see something new about our children.

On this morning the bus was standing-room-only as we squeezed on at our regular stop. Several blocks later my son, Nick, found a free seat halfway back on one side of the bus and his little sister, Elizabeth, and I took seats on the other.

I was listening to Lizzie chatter on about something when I was surprised to see Nick get up. I watched as he said something quietly to an older, not quite grandmotherly woman who didn't look familiar to me. Suddenly I understood: He was offering her his seat.

A little thing, but still I was flooded with gratitude. For all the times we have talked about what to do and what not to do on the bus—say "Excuse me," cover your mouth when you cough, don't point, don't stare at people who are unusual looking—this wasn't something I had trained him to do. It was a small act of gallantry, and it was entirely his idea.

For all we try to show our kids and tell them how we believe people should act, how we hope *they* will act, it still comes as a shock and a pleasure—a relief, frankly—when they do something that suggests they understand. All the more so because in the world in which Nick is growing up, the rules that govern social interaction are so much more ambiguous than they were when we were his age. Kids are exposed to a free-for-all of competing signals about what's acceptable, let alone what's admirable. It's a world, after all, in which *in your face* is the style of the moment. Civility has become a more or less elusive proposition.

I was reminded of this incident on the train the other day, on another crowded morning, as I watched a young man in an expensive suit slip into an open seat without so much as losing his place in *The New York Times*, smoothly beating out a silver-haired gentleman and a gaggle of young women in spike heels.

My first thought was that his mother would be ashamed of him. And then I thought, with some amusement, that I am hopelessly behind the times. For all I know, the older man would've been insulted to be offered a seat by someone two or three decades his junior. And the women, I suppose, might consider chivalry a sexist custom. Besides, our young executive or investment banker probably had to compete with women for the job that's keeping him in Italian loafers; why would he want to offer a potential competitor a seat?

Of course, this sort of confusion is about much more than etiquette on public transportation. It's about what we should do for each other, and expect of each other, now that our roles are no longer closely dictated by whether we are male or female, young or old.

Not for a minute do I mourn the demise of the social contract that gave men most of the power and opportunity, and women most of the seats on the bus. But operating without a contract can be uncomfortable, too. It's as if nobody quite knows how to behave anymore; the lack of predictability on all fronts has left all our nerve endings exposed. And the confusion extends to everything from deciding who goes through the door first to who initiates sex.

Under the circumstances, civility requires a good deal more imagination than it once did, if only because it's so much harder to know what the person sitting across from you—whether stranger or spouse—expects, needs, wants from you. When you don't have an official rulebook, you have to listen harder, be more sensitive, be ready to improvise.

But of course improvising is just what Americans do best. And unlike the European model, our particular form of civility here in the former colonies aims to be democratic, to bridge our diverse histories with empathy and respect. At a moment when so many people are clamoring for attention, and so many others are nursing their wounds, the need for empathy and respect is rather acute.

And so, as we encourage our children to define themselves actively, to express themselves with confidence, we hope they will also learn to be generous—with those they don't know, as well as with those they love. And we hope they will care enough, and be observant enough, to be able to tell when someone else needs a seat more than they do.

What the Nose Knows

James Gorman

Society is losing its odor integrity. Some enterprising souls are actually marketing aerosol cans filled with the aromas of pizza, new cars, anything that might entice people to buy something they would otherwise not. From the inexhaustible engine of commerce have come Aroma Discs, which when warmed in a special container (only $22.50) emit such scents as Passion, Fireplace and After Dinner Mints. And, in what may be the odor crime of the century, a company in Ohio is selling a cherry-scented garden hose.

I may seem like a weird curmudgeon looking for something new to complain about, but it's only the fake smells I don't like, the ones that are meant to fool you. This is a dangerous business because the human nose is emotional and not very bright. Inside the brain, smell seems snuggled right up to the centers for cooking, sex and memory.

I recently discovered a substance whose odor stimulates my memory of childhood like nothing else: Crayola crayons.

I don't expect you to experience the effect of this odor memory just by thinking about crayons, since most people can't recall smells the way they can recall pictures or sounds. But once you get a good whiff of waxy crayon odor, the bells of childhood will ring. Go out and buy a box. Get your nose right down on the crayons and inhale deeply. Pull that crayon smell right up into the old reptile brain. You'll be flooded with a new crayon, untouched-coloring-book feeling— you're young, the world is new, the next thing you know your parents may bring home a puppy.

The smell is part of our culture, in the same class as the Howdy Doody song. Long after my daughters have stopped drawing with crayons, they will have in their brains, as I do now, the subconscious knowledge that if you smell stearic acid—the major component in the smell of Crayola crayons—you're about to have a good time.

Crayons have odor integrity. The Crayola people didn't stick stearic acid into their product to make you buy it. Nobody in his right mind would buy something because it smelled like a fatty acid. If there were a national odor museum, I would give crayons pride of place in it. And I would surround them with other objects emitting the honest aromas that make up American odor culture.

I have a few ideas of what these other objects should be. I got them from William Cain of Yale University and the John B. Pierce Foundation Laboratory in New Haven, Conn. Cain studies what he calls the smell game. He had people sniff 80 everyday things, and then he ranked the substances by how recognizable their odors were. His list is the place for the aroma preservationist to begin.

On it are Juicy Fruit gum and Vicks VapoRub (remember getting it rubbed on your chest?), Ivory soap, Johnson's baby powder and Lysol. Cain also tested Band-Aids, nail-polish remover, shoe polish (which reminds me of church) and bleach.

Crayons are on the list, ranked eighteenth in recognizability. Coffee was first, peanut butter second. Not on the list, but favorites of mine, are rubber cement (which I remember from my newspaper days) and Cutter Insect Repellent.

I know there will be judgment calls. Some people will want to preserve Brut after shave and Herbal Essence shampoo, numbers 35 and 53 on Cain's list, while I will not. Others won't want fresh cow manure in the museum. I think it's a must.

Whatever the choices, it's time to start paying attention to our odor culture. We're responsible for what posterity will smell, and like to smell. If we're not careful, we may end up with a country in which everyone thinks garden hoses are supposed to smell like cherries.

Idiosyncrasies, Anyone?

Bill Bryson

Seeking the Perfect Union Between Custom and Country, I recently discovered a phenomenon that I call the Copenhagen movie house syndrome. I call it that because it was in a Copenhagen movie house that I first thought of it. What I thought was this: Every country in the world does some things far better than every other country and some things far worse, and I began to wonder why that should be. Sometimes a nation's little practices and inventions are so instantly engaging that we associate them with that country alone—double-decker buses in Britain, windmills in Holland, sidewalk cafés in France. But at the same time, there are some things most countries do without difficulty that some can scarcely do at all. Consider the Copenhagen movie house.

When you went into a movie theater in Denmark, at least until recently, you were given a ticket for an assigned seat. On the occasion of my visit, I found that my ticket directed me to sit beside the only other people in the place, a young couple locked in the sort of impassioned embrace associated with dockside reunions at the end of very long wars. I could no more have sat right beside them that I could have asked to join in—it actually would have come to much the same thing—so I took a place a few discreet seats away.

People came into the theater, examined their tickets, and filled the adjacent seats. By the time the movie started, there were about thirty of us sitting together in a tight pack in the middle of a vast and otherwise empty auditorium. A woman laden with shopping bags came in and made her way with difficulty down my row, stopped beside me, and announced in a stern Danish voice, full of glottals and indignation, that I had taken her seat. This caused much play of flashlights by a corps of usherettes and fretful reexamining of tickets by everyone in the vicinity until it became generally realized that I was an American tourist with an evident inability to follow simple seating instructions and was escorted in some shame back to my assigned place.

So we sat all together, thirty or so of us, in crowded discomfort, like refugees in an overloaded lifeboat, rubbing shoulders and sharing small noises, and watched the movie. And I would submit, with all respect to Denmark and her long and noble history as a sovereign state, that that is a pretty nerdy way to run a movie house.

The phenomenon, I hasten to add, is not exclusive to the Danes, even with regard to the movies. The Germans can be equally insensate when it comes to the silver screen. Once, caught in a downpour in Munich, I spied a movie theater across the street showing a Charlie Chaplin silent picture. No language problems there, I thought brightly and dashed in. Barely had I seated myself and wiped the steamy mist from my glasses than the film concluded, and everyone departed.

An usherette came and told me that I must go too. I explained that I had only just arrived and would hang on for the next showing. The usherette indicated severely that this was against the rules. I explained again that I had only just arrived and showed her that the rain was even now dripping from my brow and chin. But this cut *kein* ice with the lady, who conducted me to the back door with the efficiency of a bouncer and left me standing blinking in an alleyway.

The Germans are, of course, famous for such officiousness. I've never been entirely sure whether we notice this streak of Teutonic inflexibility in them because we have been conditioned to look for it or because it genuinely exists. But I do know a couple renting a cottage in the Black Forest who were ordered by their landlady to take down their washing from the clothesline and rehang it in a more orderly and regimented manner before they were allowed to go out for the day.

The great British failing, on the other hand, is a strange uncomfortableness with regard to food, particularly mass catering, a fact that can become evident to the traveler almost from the moment he sets foot in the Country. In his book *Flying Visits*, the Australian critic Clive James describes the food at Heathrow Airport as not fit for a dog to eat. That is perhaps a little unfair—you could certainly feed it to a dog—but it is true that the most charitable thing that can be said of the food there, and at many other public gathering places like train stations and motorway service areas, is that it won't kill you.

More than that, there is among the British a curious inability to grasp the basic idea of many foods—as evidenced by the persistent British habit of eating hamburgers with a knife and fork. In fact, there isn't much to do with dining in Britain that isn't mildly odd to foreign eyes, from the types of food eaten (baked beans on toast) to the manner of their eating (holding the fork upside down and balancing the food precariously on its back). As I write, a commercial is running on British television that shows a man enthusiastically spreading his favorite brand of peanut butter across an ear of sweet corn. I would suggest that this alone is evidence of a kind of national dementia where eating is concerned.

On the credit side, however, the British are consummate queuers—so much so that during riots in Liverpool in 1981 looters formed a line outside the store. I swear it. This is in stark contrast to the French, who have never quite come to terms with the concept of queuing. Wherever you go in Paris, you see orderly lines waiting patiently at bus stops. But as soon as the bus arrives, the line instantly disintegrates into something reminiscent of a fire drill at an insane asylum as everyone scrambles to be the first aboard.

The most bewildering French custom, however, is the practice of putting timers on light switches in hotel corridors and staircases. These are designed, with

—— *Example* ———————————————————————————————————— *79*

uncanny precision, to plunge you into darkness the moment you get near your room, so that you must complete the last stages of the process—feeling your way along the walls, finding the door and doorknob, fumbling with the key—without benefit of vision.

To the casual observer there may seem little point in providing illumination if it's going to poop out at the critical moment, or in forming an orderly line at bus stops if it's just going to lead to anarchy once the bus heaves into view. But that is a crucial feature of the syndrome: The behavior must seem largely inexplicable to any rational outsider, yet be accepted without question by the natives. In its most extreme form, it can even take on a kind of bizarre logic.

Consider the matter of dining out in Norway. I once made the mistake in that country of not thinking about dinner until almost dinnertime. This, I discovered, was several hours too late. Finding myself in Bergen on a Sunday, I ventured out onto the streets at about 5:30 with that agreeable pang of anticipation that comes with having a large appetite in a strange city. I wandered through the empty lanes of the old town and far out into the suburbs, but at every restaurant I came across the windows showed only darkened premises with chairs stacked on the tables.

At one place, I turned forlornly from the window to find an elderly woman watching me. "There's no one there," I croaked in bewilderment. "Yes," she replied in perfect English, "I expect the staff have all gone home to eat. It *is* dinnertime, you know." But of course.

In Spain, the problem comes at the other extreme of the clock. The Spanish wait until all the visitors to the country have put on their pajamas and gone to bed before they eat. For a long time I supposed that this was so they could talk about us, but I am assured by a Spanish friend that it is an ancient practice and there's nothing personal in it. Nonetheless, it is a strange sensation to wander to the hotel desk in the small hours, half expecting to see the night clerk in his bathrobe and everyone else sensibly tucked up in bed, only to find the hotel restaurant packed with laughing people, with children running around and aged grannies plowing into large platters of paella.

Outbreaks of the Copenhagen movie house syndrome can be found in all countries. One of the most prolific, if improbable, sources is the automobile light. In most parts of the world, people work from the assumption that when it is dark you put your car lights on and when it is light you switch them off. This seems pretty basic to most of us. Yet in Sweden there is a law that all drivers must put their lights on all the time, even in brilliant sunshine.

You would think the Swedes would be embarrassed to have saddled themselves with such an ineffably silly law ("It was a bad week; we don't know what came over us"), but evidently not. It is equivalent to making pedestrians wear miners' helmets, yet the Swedes appear to see nothing strange in it.

The British, conversely, use their car lights as sparingly as possible, as if fearful of running up a large quarterly bill for their use. At dusk throughout Britain, you see the strange phenomenon of gray, unilluminated shapes sweeping at you out of the gloom, their drivers peering intently through the windshields, unable to see much of anything. Why, you wonder, don't they put their lights on? It is a mystery that no one can answer. The British, of course, are particularly skilled at doing silly things (viz., requiring their judges to wear little mops on their heads).

And as for us Americans, what are our national shortcomings? Since one of the requirements of the Copenhagen movie house syndrome is that we be blind to our own faults, I am not entirely sure. An informal survey among foreign friends elicited a host of suggested shortcomings, ranging from Tammy Bakker's eyelashes to a misguided affection for plaid pants. But in my view perhaps the most fundamental of all our faults is simply the complete inability to follow simple seating instructions in foreign movie houses.

Were Dinosaurs Dumb?

Stephen Jay Gould

When Muhammad Ali flunked his army intelligence test, he quipped (with a wit that belied his performance on the exam): "I only said I was the greatest; I never said I was the smartest." In our metaphors and fairy tales, size and power are almost always balanced by a want of intelligence. Cunning is the refuge of the little guy. Think of Br'er Rabbit and Br'er Bear; David smiting Goliath with a slingshot; Jack chopping down the beanstalk. Slow wit is the tragic flaw of a giant.

The discovery of dinosaurs in the nineteenth century provided, or so it appeared, a quintessential case for the negative correlation of size and smarts. With their pea brains and giant bodies, dinosaurs became a symbol of lumbering stupidity. Their extinction seemed only to confirm their flawed design.

Dinosaurs were not even granted the usual solace of a giant—great physical prowess. God maintained a discreet silence about the brains of behemoth, but he certainly marveled at its strength: "Lo, now, his strength is in his loins, and his force is in the navel of his belly. He moveth his tail like a cedar. . . . His bones are as strong pieces of brass; his bones are like bars of iron [Job 40:16–18]." Dinosaurs, on the other hand, have usually been reconstructed as slow and clumsy. In the standard illustration, *Brontosaurus* wades in a murky pond because he cannot hold up his own weight on land.

Popularizations for grade school curricula provide a good illustration of prevailing orthodoxy. I still have my third grade copy (1948 edition) of Bertha Morris Parker's *Animals of Yesterday*, stolen, I am forced to suppose, from P.S. 26, Queens (sorry Mrs. McInerney). In it, boy (teleported back to the Jurassic) meets brontosaur:

> *It is huge, and you can tell from the size of its head*
> *that it must be stupid. . . . This giant animal moves*
> *about very slowly as it eats. No wonder it moves*
> *slowly! Its huge feet are very heavy and its great tail*
> *is not easy to pull around. You are not surprised that*

the thunder lizard likes to stay in the water so that
the water will help it hold up its huge body. . . .
Giant dinosaurs were once the lords of the earth.
Why did they disappear? You can probably guess
part of the answer—their bodies were too large for
their brains. If their bodies had been smaller, and
their brains larger, they might have lived on.

Dinosaurs have been making a strong comeback of late, in this age of "I'm OK, you're OK." Most paleontologists are now willing to view them as energetic, active, and capable animals. The *Brontosaurus* that wallowed in its pond a generation ago is now running on land, while pairs of males have been seen twining their necks about each other in elaborate sexual combat for access to females (much like the neck wrestling of giraffes). Modern anatomical reconstructions indicate strength and agility, and many paleontologists now believe that dinosaurs were warm-blooded. . . .

The idea of warm-blooded dinosaurs has captured the public imagination and received a torrent of press coverage. Yet another vindication of dinosaurian capability has received very little attention, although I regard it as equally significant. I refer to the issue of stupidity and its correlation with size. The revisionist interpretation, which I support in this column, does not enshrine dinosaurs as paragons of intellect, but it does maintain that they were not small brained after all. They had the "right-sized" brains for reptiles of their body size.

I don't wish to deny that the flattened, minuscule head of large-bodied *Stegosaurus* houses little brain from our subjective, top-heavy perspective, but I do wish to assert that we should not expect more of the beast. First of all, large animals have relatively smaller brains than related, small animals. The correlation of brain size with body size among kindred animals (all reptiles, all mammals, for example) is remarkably regular. As we move from small to large animals, from mice to elephants or small lizards to Komodo dragons, brain size increases, but not so fast as body size. In other words, bodies grow faster than brains, and large animals have low ratios of brain weight to body weight. In fact, brains grow only about two-thirds as fast as bodies. Since we have no reason to believe that large animals are consistently stupider than their smaller relatives, we must conclude that large animals require relatively less brain to do as well as smaller animals. If we do not recognize this relationship, we are likely to underestimate the mental power of very large animals, dinosaurs in particular.

Second, the relationship between brain and body size is not identical in all groups of vertebrates. All share the same rate of relative decrease in brain size, but small mammals have much larger brains than small reptiles of the same body weight. This discrepancy is maintained at all larger body weights, since brain size increases at the same rate in both groups—two-thirds as fast as body size.

Put these two facts together—all large animals have relatively small brains, and reptiles have much smaller brains than mammals at any common body weight—and what should we expect from a normal, large reptile? The answer, of course, is a brain of very modest size. No living reptile even approaches a middle-sized dinosaur in bulk, so we have no modern standard to serve as a model for dinosaurs.

—— *Example* ————————————————————— *83*

Fortunately, our imperfect fossil record has, for once, not severely disappointed us in providing data about fossil brains. Superbly preserved skulls have been found for many species of dinosaurs, and cranial capacities can be measured. (Since brains do not fill craniums in reptiles, some creative, although not unreasonable, manipulation must be applied to estimate brain size from the hole within a skull.) With these data, we have a clear test for the conventional hypothesis of dinosaurian stupidity. We should agree, at the outset, that a reptilian standard is the only proper one—it is surely irrelevant that dinosaurs had smaller brains than people or whales. We have abundant data on the relationship of brain and body size in modern reptiles. Since we know that brains increase two-thirds as fast as bodies as we move from small to large living species, we can extrapolate this rate to dinosaurian sizes and ask whether dinosaur brains match what we would expect of living reptiles if they grew so large.

Harry Jerison studied the brain sizes of ten dinosaurs and found that they fell right on the extrapolated reptilian curve. Dinosaurs did not have small brains; they maintained just the right-sized brains for reptiles of their dimensions. So much for Ms. Parker's explanation of their demise.

Jerison made no attempt to distinguish among various kinds of dinosaurs; ten species distributed over six major groups scarcely provide a proper basis for comparison. Recently, James A. Hopson of the University of Chicago gathered more data and made a remarkable and satisfying discovery.

Hopson needed a common scale for all dinosaurs. He therefore compared each dinosaur brain with the average reptilian brain we would expect at its body weight. If the dinosaur falls on the standard reptilian curve, its brain receives a value of 1.0 (called an encephalization quotient, or EQ—the ratio of actual brain to expected brain for a standard reptile of the same body weight). Dinosaurs lying above the curve (more brain than expected in a standard reptile of the same body weight) receive values in excess of 1.0, while those below the curve measure less than 1.0.

Hopson found that the major groups of dinosaurs can be ranked by increasing values of average EQ. This ranking corresponds perfectly with inferred speed, agility and behavioral complexity in feeding (or avoiding the prospect of becoming a meal). The giant sauropods, *Brontosaurus* and its allies, have the lowest EQ's—0.20 to 0.35. They must have moved fairly slowly and without great maneuverability. They probably escaped predation by virtue of their bulk alone, much as elephants do today. The armored ankylosaurs and stegosaurs come next with EQ's of 0.52 to 0.56. These animals, with their heavy armor, probably relied largely upon passive defense, but the clubbed tail of ankylosaurs and the spiked tail of stegosaurs imply some active fighting and increased behavioral complexity.

The ceratopsians rank next at about 0.7 to 0.9. Hopson remarks: "The larger ceratopsians, with their great horned heads, relied on active defensive strategies and presumably required somewhat greater agility than the tail-weaponed forms, both in fending off predators and in intraspecific combat bouts. The smaller ceratopsians, lacking true horns, would have relied on sensory acuity and speed to escape from predators." The ornithopods (duckbills and their allies) were the brainiest herbivores, with EQ's from 0.85 to 1.5. They relied upon "acute senses and relatively fast speeds" to elude carnivores. Flight seems to require more acuity and agility than standing defense. Among ceratopsians, small, hornless, and presumably fleeing *Protoceratops* had a higher EQ than great three-horned *Triceratops*.

Carnivores have higher EQ's than herbivores, as in modern vertebrates. Catching a rapidly moving or stoutly fighting prey demands a good deal more upstairs than plucking the right kind of plant. The giant theropods (*Tyrannosaurus* and its allies) vary from 1.0 to nearly 2.0. Atop the heap, quite appropriately at its small size, rests the little coelurosaur *Stenonychosaurus* with an EQ well above 5.0. Its actively moving quarry, small mammals and birds perhaps, probably posed a greater challenge in discovery and capture than *Triceratops* afforded *Tyrannosaurus*.

I do not wish to make a naive claim that brain size equals intelligence or, in this case, behavioral range and agility (I don't know what intelligence means in humans, much less in a group of extinct reptiles). Variation in brain size within a species has precious little to do with brain power (humans do equally well with 900 or 2,500 cubic centimeters of brain). But comparison across species, when the differences are large, seems reasonable. I do not regard it as irrelevant to our achievements that we so greatly exceed koala bears—much as I love them—in EQ. The sensible ordering among dinosaurs also indicates that even so coarse a measure as brain size counts for something.

If behavioral complexity is one consequence of mental power, then we might expect to uncover among dinosaurs some signs of social behavior that demand coordination, cohesiveness, and recognition. Indeed we do, and it cannot be accidental that these signs were overlooked when dinosaurs labored under the burden of a falsely imposed obtuseness. Multiple trackways have been uncovered, with evidence for more than twenty animals traveling together in parallel movement. Did some dinosaurs live in herds? At the Davenport Ranch sauropod trackway, small footprints lie in the center and larger ones at the periphery. Could it be that some dinosaurs traveled much as some advanced herbivorous mammals do today, with large adults at the borders sheltering juveniles in the center?

In addition, the very structures that seemed most bizarre and useless to older paleontologists—the elaborate crests of hadrosaurs, the frills and horns of ceratopsians, and the nine inches of solid bone above the brain of *Pachycephalosaurus*—now appear to gain a coordinated explanation as devices for sexual display and combat. Pachycephalosaurs may have engaged in head-butting contests much as mountain sheep do today. The crests of some hadrosaurs are well designed as resonating chambers; did they engage in bellowing matches? The ceratopsian horn and frill may have acted as sword and shield in the battle for mates. Since such behavior is not only intrinsically complex, but also implies an elaborate social system, we would scarcely expect to find it in a group of animals barely muddling through at a moronic level.

But the best illustration of dinosaurian capability may well be the fact most often cited against them—their demise. Extinction, for most people, carries many of the connotations attributed to sex not so long ago—a rather disreputable business, frequent in occurrence, but not to anyone's credit, and certainly not to be discussed in proper circles. But, like sex, extinction is an ineluctable part of life.

—— *Example* ———————————————————————————— 85

It is the ultimate fate of all species, not the lot of unfortunate and ill-designed creatures. It is no sign of failure.

The remarkable thing about dinosaurs is not that they became extinct, but that they dominated the earth for so long. Dinosaurs held sway for 100 million years while mammals, all the while, lived as small animals in the interstices of their world. After 70 million years on top, we mammals have an excellent track record and good prospects for the future, but we have yet to display the staying power of dinosaurs.

People, on this criterion, are scarcely worth mentioning—5 million years perhaps since *Australopithecus*, a mere 50,000 for our own species, *Homo sapiens*. Try the ultimate test within our system of values: Do you know anyone who would wager a substantial sum, even at favorable odds, on the proposition that *Homo sapiens* will last longer than *Brontosaurus*?

Writing with a Word Processor

William Zinsser

Writing is a deeply personal process, full of mystery and surprise. No two people go about it in exactly the same way. We all have little devices to get us started, or to keep us going, or to remind us of what we think we want to say, and what works for one person may not work for anyone else. The main thing is to get something written—to get the words out of our heads, There is no "right" method. Any method that will do the job is the right method for you.

It helps to remember that writing is hard. Most non-writers don't know this; they think that writing is a natural function, like breathing, that ought to come easy, and they're puzzled when it doesn't. If you find that writing is hard, it's because it is hard. It's one of the hardest things that people do. Among other reasons, it's hard because it requires thinking. You won't write clearly unless you keep forcing yourself to think clearly. There's no escaping the question that has to be constantly asked: What do I want to say next?

So painful is this task that writers, go to remarkable lengths to postpone their daily labor. They sharpen their pencils and change their typewriter ribbon and go out to the store to buy more paper. Now these sacred rituals, as IBM would say, have been obsoleted.

When I began writing this article on my word processor I didn't have any idea what would happen. Would I be able to write anything at all? Would it be any good? I was bringing to the machine what I assumed were wholly different ways of thinking about writing. The units massed in front of me looked cold and sterile. Their steady hum reminded me that they were waiting. They seemed to be waiting for information, not for writing. Maybe what I wrote would also be cold and sterile.

I was particularly worried about the absence of paper. I knew that I would only be able to see as many lines as the screen would hold—twenty lines. How could I review what I had already written? How could I get a sense of continuity and flow? With paper it was always possible to flick through the preceding pages to see where I was coming from—and where I ought to be going. Without paper

—— *Example* ———————————————————————————— 87

I would have no such periodic fix. Would this be a major hardship?

The only way to find out was to find out. I took a last look at my unsharpened pencils and went to work.

My particular hang-up as a writer is that I have to get every paragraph as nearly right as possible before I go on to the next paragraph. I'm somewhat like a bricklayer: I build very slowly, not adding a new row until I feel that the foundation is solid enough to hold up the house. I'm the exact opposite of the writer who dashes off his entire first draft, not caring how sloppy it looks or how badly it's written. His only objective at this early stage is to let his creative motor run the full course at full speed; repairs can always be made later. I envy this writer and would like to have his metabolism. But I'm stuck with the one I've got.

I also care how my writing looks while I'm writing it. The visual arrangement is important to me: the shape of the words, of the sentences, of the paragraphs, of the page. I don't like sentences that are dense with long words, or paragraphs that never end. As I write I want to see the design that my piece will have when the reader sees it in type, and I want that design to have a rhythm and a pace that will invite the reader to keep reading. O.K., so I'm a nut. But I'm not alone; the visual component is important to a large number of people who write.

One hang-up we visual people share is that our copy must be neat. My lifelong writing method, for instance, has gone like this. I put a piece of paper in the typewriter and write the first paragraph. Then I take the paper out and edit what I've written. I mark it up horribly, crossing words out and scribbling new ones in the space between the lines. By this time the paragraph has lost its nature and shape for me as a piece of writing. It's a mishmash of typing and handwriting and arrows and balloons and other directional symbols. So I type a clean copy, incorporating the changes, and then I take that piece of paper out of the typewriter and edit it. It's better, but not much better. I go over it with my pencil again, making more changes, which again make it too messy for me to read critically, so I go back to the typewriter for round three. And round four. Not until I'm reasonably satisfied do I proceed to the next paragraph.

This can get pretty tedious, and I have often thought that there must be a better way. Now there is. The word processor is God's gift, or at least science's gift, to the tinkerers and the refiners and the neatness freaks. For me it was obviously the perfect new toy. I began playing on page 1—editing, cutting and revising—and have been on a rewriting high ever since. The burden of the years has been lifted.

Mostly I've been cutting. I would guess that I've cut at least as many words out of this article as the number that remain. Probably half of those words were eliminated because I saw that they were unnecessary—the sentence worked fine without them. This is where the word processor can improve your writing to an extent that you will hardly believe. Learn to recognize what is clutter and to use the DELETE key to prune it out.

How will you know clutter when you see it? Here's a device I used when I was teaching writing at Yale that my students found helpful; it may be a help here. I would put brackets around every component in a student's paper that I didn't think was doing some kind of work. Often it was only one word—for example, the useless preposition that gets appended to so many verbs (order up, free up), or the adverb whose meaning is already in the verb (blare loudly, clench tightly), or the adjective that tells us what we already know (smooth marble, green grass). The brackets might surround the little qualifiers that dilute a writer's authority (a bit, sort of, in a sense), or the countless phrases in which the writer explains what he is about to explain (it might be pointed out, I'm tempted to say). Often my brackets would surround an entire sentence—the sentence that essentially repeats what the previous sentence has said, or tells the reader something that is implicit, or adds a detail that is irrelevant. Most people's writing is littered with phrases that do no new work whatever. Most first drafts, in fact, can be cut by fifty percent without losing anything organic. (Try it; it's a good exercise.)

By bracketing these extra words, instead of crossing them out, I was saying to the student: "I may be wrong, but I think this can go and the meaning of the sentence won't be affected in any way. But *you* decide: read the sentence without the bracketed material and see if it works." In the first half of the term, the students' papers were festooned with my brackets. Whole paragraphs got bracketed. But gradually the students learned to put mental brackets around their many different kinds of clutter, and by the end of the term I was returning papers to them that had hardly any brackets, or none. It was always a satisfying moment. Today many of those students are professional writers. "I still see your brackets," they tell me. "They're following me through life."

You can develop the same eye. Writing is clear and strong to the extent that it has no superfluous parts. (So is art and music and dance and typography and design.) You will really enjoy writing on a word processor when you see your sentences growing in strength, literally before your eyes, as you get rid of the fat. Be thankful for everything that you can throw away.

I was struck by how many phrases and sentences I wrote in this article that I later found I didn't need. Many of them hammered home a point that didn't need hammering because it had already been made. This kind of overwriting happens in almost everybody's first draft, and it's perfectly natural—the act of putting down our thoughts makes us garrulous. Luckily, the act of editing follows the act of writing, and this is where the word processor will bail you out. It intercedes at the point where the game can be won or lost. With its help I cut hundreds of unnecessary words and didn't replace them.

Hundreds of others were discarded because I later thought of a better word—one that caught more precisely or more vividly what I was trying to express. Here, again, a word processor encourages you to play. The English language is rich in words that convey an exact shade of meaning. Don't get stuck with a word that's merely good if you can find one that takes the reader by surprise with its color or aptness or quirkiness. Root around in your dictionary of synonyms and find words that are fresh. Throw them up on the screen and see how they look.

Also learn to play with whole sentences. If a sentence strikes you as awkward or ponderous, move your cursor to the space after the period and write a new sentence that you think is better. Maybe you can make it shorter. Or clearer. Maybe you can make it livelier by turning it into a question or otherwise altering its rhythm. Change the passive verbs into active verbs. (Passive verbs are the death of clarity and vigor.) Try writing two or three new versions of the awkward sentence and then compare them, or write a fourth version that combines the best elements of all three. Sentences come in an infinite variety of shapes and sizes.

—— *Example* ————————————————————————— 89

Find one that pleases you. If it's clear, and if it pleases you and expresses who you are, trust it to please other people. Then delete all the versions that aren't as good. Your shiny new sentence will jump into position and the rest of the paragraph will rearrange itself as quickly and neatly as if you had never pulled it apart.

Another goal that the word processor will help you to achieve is unity. No matter how carefully you write each sentence as you assemble a piece of writing, the final product is bound to have some ragged edges. Is the tone consistent throughout? And the point of view? And the pronoun? And the tense? How about the transitions? Do they pull the reader along, or is the piece jerky and disjointed? A good piece of writing should be harmonious from beginning to end in the voice of the writer and the flow of its logic. But the harmony usually requires some last-minute patching.

I've been writing a book by the bricklayer method, slowly and carefully. That's all very well as far as it goes—at the end of every chapter the individual bricks may look fine. But what about the wall? The only way to check your piece for unity is to go over it one more time from start to finish, preferably reading it aloud. See if you have executed all the decisions that you made before you started writing.

One such decision is in the area of tone. I decided, for instance, that I didn't want my book to be a technical manual. I'm not a technician; I'm a writer and an editor. The book wouldn't work if I expected the reader to identify with the process of mastering a new technology. He would have to identify with me. The book would be first of all a personal journey and only parenthetically a manual. I knew that this was a hybrid form and that its unities would never be wholly intact. Still, in going over each finished chapter I found places where the balance could be improved—where instructional detail smothered the writer and his narrative, or, conversely, where the writer intruded on the procedures he was trying to explain. With a word processor it was easy to make small repairs—perhaps just a change of pronoun and verb—that made the balance less uneven.

The instructional portions of the book posed a problem of their own—one that I had never faced before. My hope was to try to explain a technical process without the help of any diagrams or drawings. Would this be possible? It would be possible only if I kept remembering one fundamental fact: writing is linear and sequential. This may seem so obvious as to be insulting: everybody knows that writing is linear and sequential. Actually everybody doesn't know. Most people under thirty don't know. They have been reared since early childhood on televisions kaleidoscope of visual images flashed onto their brain—and it doesn't occur to them that sentence B must follow sentence A, and that sentence C must follow sentence B, or all the elegant sentences in the world won't add up to anything but confusion.

I mention this because word processors are going to be widely used by people who need to impart technical information: matters of operating procedure in business and banking, science and technology, medicine and health, education and government and dozens of other specialized fields. The information will only be helpful if readers can grasp it quickly and easily. If it's muddy they will get discouraged or angry, or both, and will stop reading.

You can avoid this dreaded fate for your message, whatever it is, by making sure that every sentence is a logical sequel to the one that preceded it. One way to approach this goal is to keep your sentences short. A major reason why technical prose becomes so tangled is that the writer tries to make one sentence do too many jobs. It's a natural hazard of the first draft. But the solution is simple: see that every sentence contains only one thought. The reader can accommodate only one idea at a time. Help him by giving him only one idea at a time. Let him understand A before you proceed to B.

In writing this article, I was eager to explain the procedures that I had learned, and I would frequently lump several points together in one sentence. Later, editing what I had written, I asked myself if the procedure would be clear to someone who was puzzling through it for the first time—someone who hadn't struggled to figure the procedure out. Often I felt that it wouldn't be clear. I was giving the reader too much. He was being asked to picture himself taking various steps that were single and sequential, and that's how he deserved to get them.

I therefore divided all troublesome long sentences into two short sentences, or even three. It always gave me great pleasure. Not only is it the fastest way for a writer to get out of a quagmire that there seems to be no getting out of, I also like short sentences for their own sake. There's almost no more beautiful sight than a simple declarative sentence. This article is full of simple declarative sentences that have no punctuation and that carry one simple thought. Without a word processor I wouldn't have chopped as many of them down to their proper size, or done it with so little effort. This is one of the main clarifying jobs that your machine can help you to perform, especially if your writing requires you to guide the reader into territory that is new and bewildering.

Not all my experiences, of course, were rosy. The machine had disadvantages as well as blessings. Often, for instance, I missed not being able to see more than twenty lines at a time—to review what I had written earlier. If I wanted to see more lines I had to "scroll" them back into view.

But even this wasn't as painful as I had thought it would be. I found that I could hold in my head the gist of what I had written and didn't need to keep looking at it. Was this need, in fact, still another writer's hang-up that I could shed? To some extent it was. I discovered, as I had at so many other points in this journey, that various crutches I had always assumed I needed were really not necessary. I made a decision to just throw them away and found that I could still function. The only real hardship occurred when a paragraph broke at the bottom of the screen. This meant that the first lines of the paragraph were on one page and the rest were on the next page, and I had to keep flicking the two pages back and forth to read what I was writing. But again, it wasn't fatal. I learned to live with it and soon took it for granted as an occupational hazard.

Bike Wear

Student

In order to get the best performance and most comfort out of serious bicycle riding, proper attire is necessary. A riding jersey is comfortable, and it has pockets sewn into the lower back which let you carry food or light snacks. The jersey can also hold small tools, such as a hex key or a spoke wrench, to make minor repairs to the rear derailleur or adjustments to a wheel that might twist out of true. Riding jerseys are aerodynamic and much more appropriate than a T-shirt or no shirt at all. In addition, it is important to wear riding shorts that are designed with a genuine deerskin chamois to help prevent chafing and irritation which can cause discomfort while riding. Purchasing superior bike wear with major names like Vigorrelli or Duigi can help to insure quality construction, contoured fit and reliable durability. Another important part of attire is cleated shoes made especially for bicycling. The cleats have a narrow notch that slip over the back stage of the pedals. This feature allows the rider to push down on one pedal while simultaneously pulling up on the other pedal. Cleated shoes tremendously affect the smoothness of the pedal stroke and the efficiency of the rider's power. Taking advantage of the specialized riding apparel available, the serious bicycle enthusiast can expect increased performance and comfort.

How to Save Fuel and Money

Student

Rising energy and fuel costs are forcing me to be very careful with my consumption of these expensive commodities. For example, during the winter months my thermostat is turned down as low as I can tolerate which is usually 68 degrees. I turn the thermostat down even lower when I'm not at home. I also wear sweaters and use heavy blankets when I sleep in the effort to not allow the heater to run continuously. My summer months are spent with the doors and windows open to let breezes help cool my home as much as possible. Therefore, the air conditioner is kept idle as much as possible. Moreover, I take shorter showers and do not turn the water temperature up as high as I used to. This helps to conserve on the electricity which is used to warm the water heater. When cooking, I use my microwave oven as much as possible because it is cheaper to run than the electric stove or oven. Also, I am careful to keep nonessential lights turned off, because wasted wattage is one of the main sources of my high electricity bills. Lastly, I have learned to step lighter on the accelerator pedal of my car when driving. I also take shorter trips when traveling in my car. By this practice, I save pocket money for the end of the month which helps to pay my electric bill. Since becoming more conscientious in my efforts to use energy sparingly, I am experiencing lower electric and gasoline expenses and also conserving energy.

How to Be a Successful Basketball Player

Student

When I was in high school, my Uncle Jack convinced me that dedication and hard work are the secret to the success of a basketball player. He first stressed the importance of conditioning. I worked hard getting myself into shape. I got up every morning at five o'clock just to run and stretch out. Every day I pushed myself further and further and soon found myself getting burnt out on the same old routine, but I was dedicated to basketball and continued to work hard. In his second step, he stressed how important it was to handle a basketball every day. I practiced on my dribbling and shooting skills every morning. Initially, I learned how to dribble with my left hand so that I could dribble in any direction with either hand. I would then shoot ten balls from selected spots on the court over and over again until I could hit nine out of ten from each spot. I worked hard at this every morning until basketball season arrived. The third step my uncle continued to stress was how important it was to take the game seriously and put forth my best effort. I did as he instructed, and to this day I'm still the leading scorer of Otis-Bison High School. My dedication and hard work really did pay off.

Ch. 3: Example

Suggestions for writing:

1. Write a paragraph or essay in which you recall some of your favorite or least favorite scents from your past, as James Gorman does in "What the Nose Knows," (p. 75).

2. Write a paragraph or essay giving examples of the most idiosyncratic behavior you have ever witnessed or the worst manners you have ever encountered.

3. Write an example essay or paragraph on one of the following topics or a similar topic:

the contents of a typical attic
miscommunication among friends
obstacles between you and graduation
movie action heroes
a first-time computer user

unfamiliar customs
beliefs you have outgrown
cultural stereotypes
uncomfortable clothing
a personal home page

—— *Example* —————————————————————————————— 95

Example checklist:

1. Did you establish a clear thesis statement or topic sentence?

2. Did you choose an effective example or examples that your reader can identify and relate to?

3. Did you explain and illustrate your example or examples? Did you use plenty of details?

4. Have you followed a logical pattern of organization? Chronological? Least to most important?

5. If writing an essay, have you concluded it effectively?

6. Have you established unity and coherence within your paragraphs?

7. Did you vary your sentence length and type?

8. Did you check for correctness of grammar, punctuation and spelling?

CHAPTER 4

Process Analysis

Explaining Step by Step

Using Process Analysis

Human nature is characterized by the perpetual desire to understand and analyze the process of living well. The bestseller list is always crowded with books on how to know yourself better, how to be assertive, how to become famous, how to avoid a natural disaster, or how to be rich and happy—all explained in three easy lessons. Open almost any popular magazine, and you will find numerous articles on how to lose weight, how elections are run in this country, how to dress for success, how a political rally evolved, how to gain power, or how to hit a successful topspin backhand. People naturally gravitate toward material that tells them how something is done, how something happened, or how something works, especially if they think the information will help them improve their lives in a significant way.

Defining Process Analysis

A *process* is a procedure that follows a series of steps or stages; *analysis* involves taking a subject apart and explaining its components in order to better understand the whole. Process analysis, then, explains an action, a mechanism, or an event from beginning to end. It can concentrate on either a mental or a physical operation: how to solve a chemistry problem, how to tune up your car, how John F. Kennedy was shot, how the telephone system works.

A process analysis can take one of two main forms: (1) It can give directions, thereby explaining how to do something (directive), or (2) it can give information about how something happened (informative). The first type of analysis gives directions for a task the reader might wish to attempt in the future. Examples could include how to make jelly, how to lose weight, how to drive to Los Angeles, how to assemble stereo equipment, how to make money, how to use a microscope, how to knit, how to resuscitate a dying relationship, how to win friends, how to discipline your child, and how to backpack.

The second type of analysis furnishes information about what actually occurred in specific situations. Examples include how Hiroshima was bombed, how certain Hollywood stars live, how the tax system works, how *Batman* was filmed, how Willie Mays earned a place in the Baseball Hall of Fame, how gold was first discovered in California, how computers work, how a kibbutz functions, and how the Gulf War began. These subjects and others like them fulfill a certain fascination we all have with mastering some processes and understanding the intricate details of others. They all provide us with opportunities to raise our own standard of living, either by helping us directly apply certain processes to our own lives or by increasing our understanding of the ways our complex twentieth-century world functions.

The following student paragraph analyzes the process of constructing a garden compost pit. Written primarily for people who might wish to make such a pit, this piece is directive rather than informative. Notice in particular the amount of detail the student calls upon to explain each stage of the process and the clear transitions she uses to guide us through her analysis.

> *No garden is complete without a functioning compost pit. Here's a simple, inexpensive way to make your garbage work for you! To begin with, make a pen out of hog wire or chicken wire, four feet long by eight feet wide by four feet high, splitting it down the middle with another piece of wire so that you end up with a structure that looks like a capital "E" on its side. This is a compost duplex. In the first pen, place a layer of soda ash, just sprinkled on the surface of the dirt. Then, pile an inch or so of leaves, grass clippings, or sawdust on top of the soda ash. You're now ready for the exciting part. Start throwing in all the organic refuse from your kitchen (no meat, bones, or grease, please). After the food is a foot or so deep, throw in a shovelfull of steer manure and cover the entire mess with a thin layer of dirt. Then water it down. Continue this layering process until the pile is about three to three-and-a-half feet high. Allow the pile to sit until it decomposes (from one month in warm climates to six months in colder weather). Next, take your pitchfork and start slinging the contents of pen one into pen two (which will land in reverse order, of course, with the top on the bottom and the bottom on the top). This assures that*

*everything will decompose evenly. Water this down
and begin making a new pile in pen one. That's all
there is to it! You now have a ready supply of fertiliz-
er for your garden.*

How to Write a Process Analysis Essay

Prewriting. As you begin a process analysis assignment, you first need
to become as familiar as you can with the action, mechanism, or event
you are going to describe. If possible, try to go through the process
yourself at least once or twice. Then try to read something about the
process. After all this preparation (and careful consideration of your
audience and purpose), you should be ready to brainstorm, freewrite,
cluster, or use your favorite prewriting technique in response to the
prewriting questions before you start composing your paper.

Writing. The essay should begin with an overview of the process or
event to be analyzed. This initial section should introduce the subject,
divide it into a number of recognizable steps, and describe the result
once the process is complete. Your thesis in a process essay is usually
a purpose statement that clearly and briefly explains your approach to
the procedure you will discuss: "Building model airplanes can be
divided into four basic steps" or "The American courts follow three
stages in prosecuting a criminal case."

Next, the directive or informative essay should proceed through
the various stages of the process in a logical fashion from beginning to
end. The parts of a process usually fall nicely into chronological order,
supported by such transitions as "at first," "in the beginning," "next,"
"then," "after that," and "finally." Some processes, however, are
either simultaneous, forcing the writer to choose a more complex logical order for the essay (such as classification), or cyclical, requiring the
writer to choose a starting point and then explain the cycle stage by
stage. Playing the guitar, for example, involves two separate and simultaneous components that must work together: holding the strings
against the frets with the fingers of one hand and strumming with the
other hand. In analyzing this procedure, you would probably want to
describe both parts of the process and then explain how the hands
work together to produce music. An example of a cyclical process
would be the changing of the seasons. To explain this concept to a
reader, you would need to pick a starting point, such as spring, and
describe the entire cycle stage by stage from that point onward.

In a process paper, you need to be especially sensitive to your
intended audience or they will not be able to follow your explanation.
The amount of information, the number of examples and illustrations,
and the terms to be defined all depend on the prior knowledge and
background of your readers. A writer explaining to a group of ama-
teur cooks how to prepare a soufflé would take an entirely different

approach to the subject than he or she would if the audience were a group of bona fide chefs hoping to land jobs in elegant French restaurants. The professional chefs would need more sophisticated and precise explanations than their recreational counterparts, who would probably find such an approach tedious and complicated because of the extraneous details.

The last section of a process analysis paper should consider the process as a whole. If, for example, the writer is giving directions on how to build a model airplane, the essay might end with a good description or drawing of the plane. The informative essay on our legal system could offer a summary of the stages of judging and sentencing a criminal. And the essay on cooking a soufflé could finish with a photograph of the mouth-watering dish.

Rewriting. In order to revise a process analysis essay, first make sure your main purpose is apparent throughout your paper: Have you written a directive or an informative essay? Is your purpose statement clear? Is your purpose consistent throughout? Next, you need to determine if your paper is aimed at the proper audience: Is your vocabulary, for example, appropriate for that audience? At the beginning of the essay, have you given your readers an overview of the process you are going to discuss? Do you go through the process you are explaining step by step, making sure each phase of the description is comprehensible to your intended audience? Finally, at the end of the essay, do you help your readers see the process as a complete entity?

Student Essay: Process Analysis at Work

The student essay that follows analyzes the process of using a "home permanent" kit. Notice that once the student gives an overview of the process, she discusses each step one at a time, being careful to follow a logical order (in this case, chronological) and to use clear transitions. Then, see how the end of the essay shows the process as a whole.

Follow the Simple Directions

Purpose statement fpr informative process analysis   Although fickle hairstylists in Paris and Hollywood decide what is currently "in," many romanticists disregard fashion and yearn for a mane of delicate tendrils. <u>Sharing this urge but resenting the cost, I opted for a "home perm" kit.</u> Any literate person with normal dexterity could follow illustrated directions, I reasoned, and the eight easy steps would *Overview* energize my limp locks in less than two hours. "Before" and "after" photos of flawless models showed the metamorphosis one might achieve.

First step (chronological order) Confidently, I assembled towels, rollers, hair clips, waving lotion, neutralizer, end papers, and a plastic cap. <u>While shampooing,</u> I chortled about my ingenuity and economy.

Transition   After towel-drying my hair, I applied the gooey, Second
acidic waving lotion thoroughly. Then I wrapped an step
end paper around a parted section and rolled the first Third
curl ("securely but not too tightly"). Despite the reas- step
suring click of the fastened rollers, as I sectioned each
new curl the previous one developed its own volition
and slowly unrolled itself. Resolutely, I reapplied waving lotion and rewound—and rewound—each curl.

Transition Since my hair was already saturated, I regarded the
next direction skeptically: "Apply waving lotion to Fourth
each curl." Faithfully, however, I complied with the step
Transition instructions. Ignoring the fragile state of the fastened
rollers, I then feigned assurance and enclosed my Fifth
entire head in a plastic cap. In forty minutes, chemical step
magic would occur.

Restless with anticipation, I puttered about the
house; while absorbed in small chores, I felt the first
few drops of lotion escape from the plastic tent.
Stuffing wads of cotton around the cap's edges did not
help, and the small drops soon became rivulets that
left red streaks on my neck and face and splattered on
the floor. (Did I overdo the waving lotion?) Ammonia
fumes so permeated each room that I was soon asked
to leave. Retreating to the bathroom, I opened the
window and dreamed of frivolous new hairstyles.

Transition   Finally, the waving time had elapsed; neutralizing Sixth
was next. I removed my plastic cap, carefully heeding step
the caution: "Do not disturb curlers as you rinse waving lotion from hair." With their usual impudence,
however, all the curlers soon bobbed in the sink;
undaunted, I continued. "This next step is critical,"
warned the instructions. Thinking half-hearted curls
were better than no curls at all, I poured the entire bot-
Transition tle of neutralizer on my hair. After a drippy ten-minute
wait, I read the next step: "Carefully remove rollers." Seventh
Transition As this advice was superfluous, I moved anxiously to step
the finale: "Rinse all solution from your hair, and Eighth
enjoy your curls." step

Lifting my head from the sink and expecting
Final visions of Aphrodite, I saw instead Medusa's image in
product the mirror. Limp question-mark spirals fell over my
eyes, and each "curl" ended in an explosion of steel
wool frizz. Reflecting on my ineptitude, I knew why
the direction page was illustrated only with drawings.
After washing a large load of ammonia-scented towels,
I took two aspirin and called my hairdresser. Some Concluding
repair services are cheap at any price. remark

Student Writer's Comments

Any person with normal dexterity probably *could* do it! Even though a process essay is excellent practice for detailing a sequence of ideas or steps, it can sometimes be a bit dull. The satirical approach I chose simultaneously relates the proper procedure while allowing me to poke fun at myself. The obvious hyperbole makes it clear that I was inept and/or failed to follow directions correctly. I'm still not sure I've gotten all the frizz out of my hair!

Some Final Thoughts on Process Analysis

In this chapter, a single process dictates the development and organization of each of the essays. Both directional and informational methods are represented here. Notice in particular the clear purpose statements that set the focus of the essays in each case, as well as the other rhetorical modes (such as narration, comparison/contrast, and definition) that are used to help support the writers' explanations.

A Hairy Experience

Dave Barry

Summer vacation is almost here. Soon it will be time for you parents to pile the kids into the car, show them how to work the ignition key, then watch them roar off down the street, possibly in reverse, as you head back into your house for two weeks of quiet relaxation.

I am pulling your leg, of course. You have to go with them. You also are required, by federal law, to take them to at least one historical or natural site featuring an educational exhibit with a little button that you're supposed to push, except that when you do, nothing happens, because all the little light bulbs which were supposed to light up in an educational manner and tell The Story Of Moss, burned out in 1973. But this does not matter. What matters is that this is a memorable and rewarding and, above all, enjoyable vacation experience that you are providing for your children whether they like it or not,

"DAMMIT YOU KIDS," you might find yourself explaining to them, "IF YOU DON'T TAKE THOSE LEGOS OUT OF YOUR LITTLE BROTHER'S NOSE AND COME LOOK AT THIS EDUCATIONAL EXHIBIT THIS INSTANT, I SWEAR, I WILL NOT TAKE YOU TO THE OYSTER KINGDOM THEME PARK."

This situation demonstrates why you should never set out on a family summer vacation without a complete set of parental threats. You cannot simply assume that when your children have, for example, locked somebody else's child inside the motel ice machine, you'll be able to come up with a good parental threat right there on the spot. You need to prepare your threats in advance and write them on a wallet card for easy reference.

You (sternly): "If you kids don't let that child out of the ice machine this instant, I'm going to (referring to wallet card). . . DONATE MY ORGANS."

First Child: "Huh?"

Second Child: "He's reading from his driver's license again."

You (referring to another wallet card): "OK, here we go: I'm going to TAKE AWAY YOUR GAMEBOY!"

First Child: "We don't have a Game Boy."

Second Child: "Jason threw it into the Water Whiz ride back at Pez Adventure."

You (in a very stern parental voice): "All right then, we'll just have to BUY ANOTHER ONE."

Yes, you need strict discipline on a family vacation. You also should have some kind of theme for your trip, and this year the theme that I am recommending is: Hairballs Across America. Your first stop is Garden City, Kan., home of the Finney County Historical Society Museum, which features, according to news reports sent in by many alert readers, the largest known hairball in captivity, not counting members of Congress. This hairball measures 37 inches in diameter and weighs 55 pounds. That is what we in professional journalism call "a big hairball."

I called up the historical society museum director, Mary Warren, who told me that the hairball was graciously donated by local meat packing plant, which found it inside the stomach of a cow. Cows develop interior hairballs from licking their own coats and swallowing fur, similar to the way cats do, except that cats can get rid of their hairballs by hawking them up onto your face while you sleep. Cows cannot do this, of course; they have no way of getting into your bedroom.

Anyway, the Finney County hairball is larger than the one that recently won a national hairball contest (I am not making any of this up) sponsored by Ripley's Believe It or Not. Mary Warren told me that another local meat-packing plant had recently offered the historical society an even LARGER hairball, but she turned it down. I think this was wise. You put two hairballs of that magnitude in one place, and crowd control becomes a problem.

Anyway, Warren confirmed that the original hairball will be on display this summer, along with other cow-related exhibits that I am sure will have your kids punching each other in the head with delight. After you tear them away, your next stop will be the nearby Midwestern state of Indiana (motto: "It's Also Pretty Flat"), where you will be visiting the city of Alexandria. This is the historic site where, according to a story written by Sarah Mawhorr for The Anderson (Ind.) Herald Bulletin, it took three men to pull a giant hairball out of a manhole last year.

"We thought we had a goat," a city sewer official was quoted as saying.

Needless to say, this hairball was not caused by a cow. Cows do not fare well in the sewer environment, because of the alligators. This hairball was formed by people taking showers, and having their hairs wash down the drain and clump together in a giant mass that would be a wonderful symbol of the Common Bond That Unites All Humanity if it weren't basically a big disgusting wad of sewage-drenched hair.

Tragically—and this is yet another argument for stricter federal guidelines— the giant hairball was left outside, and it disintegrated. But it had already become famous—it got mentioned in USA Today—and a replica hairball (I am still not making this up) appeared in Alexandria's annual Christmas parade. So even though there is, technically, nothing to see, I am recommending that you take your children to Alexandria and let them soak up the historic atmosphere.

"Just think, kids!" you should tell them. "Right here in this town, there was a hairball THE SIZE OF A GOAT! Isn't that amazing? Kids? HEY, YOU KIDS COME BACK HERE!"

You should never have left the keys in the car.

Foundation Waterproofing
Creative Homeowner Press

If regular inside wall waterproofing and crack patching don't solve a leaky foundation wall problem, the very best way to tackle it is to waterproof the exterior of the foundation wall. It is costly to do this, and it is time-consuming. However, it is within a do-it-yourselfer's skills if the job is approached with lots of patience.

Dig a trench around the foundation wide enough for you to fit into the trench and deep enough to reach under the foundation footing. Clean off the foundation wall: use a wide scraper for this such as an ice scraper or a flat tiling spade. Scrub the wall down with water from a garden hose and a stiff broom or brush.

Lay a 3-in. bed of medium-sized gravel in the trench. Then lay a row of field tile on the gravel around the bottom of the foundation.The tile should have a slight pitch.

At one corner of the house, where the tile comes together in the downward pitch, run a length of tile out into the lawn about 10 ft. You will need to dig a trench for this, too. Lay the tile on 3 ins. of gravel.

Coat the foundation walls, from the footing to grade level, with a thick application of asphalt roofing cement. You can apply this with a trowel and brush, Make sure all areas are covered thoroughly.

Embed a vapor barrier of black 4 mil polyethylene film into the asphalt roofing cement. Overlap the joints of the polyfilm about 4 ins., sticking the joints together with asphalt roofing cement.

Let the job dry for a couple of days. Then backfill the earth into the trench. Make sure the fill slopes away from the house at a rate of about 1 in. per foot. Save any leftover dirt. The ground will settle for some time, and you will need this dirt to fill depressions.

On Keeping a Notebook

Joan Didion

"'That woman Estelle,'" the note reads, "'is partly the reason why George Sharp and I are separated today.' *Dirty crepe-de-Chine wrapper, hotel bar, Wilmington RR, 9:45 A.M. August Monday morning.*"

Since the note is in my notebook, it presumably has some meaning to me. I study it for a long while. At first I have only the most general notion of what I was doing on an August Monday morning in the bar of the hotel across from the Pennsylvania Railroad station in Wilmington, Delaware (waiting for a train? missing one? 1960? 1961? why Wilmington?), but I do remember being there. The woman in the dirty crepe-de-Chine wrapper had come down from her room for a beer, and the bartender had heard before the reason why George Sharp and she were separated today. "Sure," he said, and went on mopping the floor. "You told me." At the other end of the bar is a girl. She is talking, pointedly, not to the man beside her but to a cat lying in the triangle of sunlight cast through the open door. She is wearing a plaid silk dress from Peck & Peck, and the hem is coming down.

Here is what it is: the girl has been on the Eastern Shore, and now she is going back to the city, leaving the man beside her, and all she can see ahead are the viscous summer sidewalks and the 3 A.M long-distance calls that will make her lie awake and then sleep drugged through all the steaming mornings left in August (1960? 1961?). Because she must go directly from the train to lunch in New York, she wishes that she had a safety pin for the hem of the plaid silk dress, and she also wishes that she could forget about the hem and the lunch and stay in the cool bar that smells of disinfectant and malt and make friends with the woman in the crepe-de-Chine wrapper. She is afflicted by a little self-pity, and she wants to compare Estelles. That is what that was all about.

Why did I write it down? In order to remember, of course, but exactly what was it I wanted to remember? How much of it actually happened? Did any of it? Why do I keep a notebook at all? It is easy to deceive oneself on all those scores. The impulse to write things down is a peculiarly compulsive one, inexplicable to those who do not share it, useful only accidentally, only secondarily, in the way that any compulsion tries to justify itself. I suppose that it begins or does not begin in the cradle. Although I have felt compelled to write things down since I was five years old, I doubt that my daughter ever will, for she is a singularly blessed and accepting child, delighted with life exactly as life presents itself to her, unafraid to go to sleep and unafraid to wake up. Keepers of private notebooks are a different breed altogether, lonely and resistant rearrangers of things, anxious malcontents, children afflicted apparently at birth with some presentiment of loss.

My first notebook was a Big Five tablet, given to me by my mother with the sensible suggestion that I stop whining and learn to amuse myself by writing down my thoughts. She returned the tablet to me a few years ago; the first entry is an account of a woman who believed herself to be freezing to death in the Arctic night, only to find, when day broke, that she had stumbled onto the Sahara Desert, where she would die of the heat before lunch. I have no idea what turn of a five-year-old's mind could have prompted so insistently "ironic" and exotic a story, but it does reveal a certain predilection for the extreme which has dogged me into adult life; perhaps if I were analytically inclined I would find it a truer story than any I might have told about Donald Johnson's birthday party or the day my cousin Brenda put Kitty Litter in the aquarium.

So the point of my keeping a notebook has never been, nor is it now, to have an accurate factual record of what I have been doing or thinking. That would be a different impulse entirely, an instinct for reality which I sometimes envy but do not possess. At no point have I ever been able successfully to keep a diary; my approach to daily life ranges from the grossly negligent to the merely absent, and on those few occasions when I have tried dutifully to record a day's events, boredom has so overcome me that the results are mysterious at best. What is this business about "shopping, typing piece, dinner with E, depressed"? Shopping for what? Typing what piece? Who is E? Was this "E" depressed, or was I depressed? Who cares?

In fact I have abandoned altogether that kind of pointless entry; instead I tell what some would call lies. "That's simply not true," the members of my family frequently tell me when they come up against my memory of a shared event. "The party was *not* for you, the spider was *not* a black widow, it *wasn't that way at all."* Very likely they are right, for not only have I always had trouble distinguishing between what happened and what merely might have happened, but I remain unconvinced that the distinction, for my purposes, matters. The cracked crab that I recall having for lunch the day my father came home from Detroit in 1945 must certainly be embroidery, worked into the day's pattern to lend verisimilitude; I was ten years old and would not now remember the cracked crab. The day's events did not turn on cracked crab. And yet it is precisely that fictitious crab that makes me see the afternoon all over again, a home movie run all too often, the father bearing gifts, the child weeping, an exercise in family love and guilt. Or that is what it was to me. Similarly, perhaps it never did snow that August in Vermont; perhaps there never were flurries in the night wind, and maybe no one else felt the ground hardening and summer already dead even as we pretended to bask in it, but that was how it felt to me, and it might as well have snowed, could have snowed, did snow.

How it felt to me: that is getting closer to the truth about a notebook. I sometimes delude myself about why I keep a notebook, imagine that some thrifty virtue derives from preserving everything observed. See enough and write it down, I tell myself, and then some morning when the world seems drained of wonder, some day when I am only going through the motions of doing what I am supposed to do, which is write—on that bankrupt morning I will simply open my notebook and there it will all be, a forgotten account with accumulated interest, paid passage back to the world out there: dialogue overheard in hotels and elevators and at the hat-check counter in Pavillon (one middle-aged man shows his hat check to another and says, "That's my old football number"); impressions of Bettina Aptheker and Benjamin Sonnenberg and Teddy ("Mr. Acapulco") Stauffer; careful *aperçus* about tennis bums and failed fashion models and Greek shipping heiresses, one of whom taught me a significant lesson (a lesson I could have learned from F. Scott Fitzgerald, but perhaps we all must meet the very rich for ourselves) by asking, when I arrived to interview her in her orchid-filled sitting room on the second day of a paralyzing New York blizzard, whether it was snowing outside.

I imagine, in other words, that the notebook is about other people. But of course it is not. I have no real business with what one stranger said to another at the hat-check counter in Pavillon; in fact I suspect that the line "That's my old football number" touched not my own imagination at all, but merely some memory of something once read, probably "The Eighty-Yard Run." Nor is my concern with a woman in a dirty crepe-de-Chine wrapper in a Wilmington bar. My stake is always, of course, in the unmentioned girl in the plaid silk dress. Remember what it was to be me: that is always the point.

It is a difficult point to admit. We are brought up in the ethic that others, any others, all others, are by definition more interesting than ourselves; taught to be diffident, just this side of self-effacing. ("You're the least important person in the room and don't forget it," Jessica Mitford's governess would hiss in her ear on the advent of any social occasion; I copied that into my notebook because it is only recently that I have been able to enter a room without hearing some such phrase in my inner ear.) Only the very young and the very old may recount their dreams at breakfast, dwell upon self, interrupt with memories of beach picnics and favorite Liberty lawn dresses and the rainbow trout in a creek near Colorado Springs. The rest of us are expected, rightly, to affect absorption in other people's favorite dresses, other people's trout.

And so we do. But our notebooks give us away, for however dutifully we record what we see around us, the common denominator of all we see is always, transparently, shamelessly, the implacable "I." We are not talking here about the kind of notebook that is patently for public consumption, a structural conceit for binding together a series of graceful *pensées;* we are talking about something private, about bits of the mind's string too short to use, an indiscriminate and erratic assemblage with meaning only for its maker.

And sometimes even the maker has difficulty with the meaning. There does not seem to be, for example, any point in my knowing for the rest of my life that, during 1964, 720 tons of soot fell on every square mile of New York City, yet there it is in my notebook, labeled "FACT." Nor do I really need to remember that Ambrose Bierce liked to spell Leland Stanford's name "£eland $tanford" or that "smart women almost always wear black in Cuba," a fashion hint without much potential for practical application. And does not the relevance of these notes seem marginal at best?

In the basement museum of the Inyo County Courthouse in Independence, California, sign pinned to a mandarin coat: "This MANDARIN COAT was often worn by Mrs. Minnie S. Brooks when giving lectures on her TEAPOT COLLECTION."

Redhead getting out of car in front of Beverly Wilshire Hotel, chinchilla stole, Vuitton bags with tags reading:

MRS LOU FOX

HOTEL SAHARA

VEGAS

Well, perhaps not entirely marginal. As a matter of fact, Mrs. Minnie S. Brooks and her MANDARIN COAT pull me back into my own childhood, for although I never knew Mrs. Brooks and did not visit Inyo County until I was thirty, I grew up in just such a world, in houses cluttered with Indian relics and bits of gold ore and ambergris and the souvenirs my Aunt Mercy Farnsworth brought back from the Orient. It is a long way from that world to Mrs. Lou Fox's world, where we all live now, and is it not just as well to remember that? Might not Mrs. Minnie S. Brooks help me to remember what I am? Might not Mrs. Lou Fox help me to remember what I am not?

But sometimes the point is harder to discern. What exactly did I have in mind when I noted down that it cost the father of someone I know $650 a month to light the place on the Hudson in which he lived before the Crash? What use was I planning to make of this line by Jimmy Hoffa: "I may have my faults, but being wrong ain't one of them"? And although I think it interesting to know where the girls who travel with the Syndicate have their hair done when they find themselves on the West Coast, will I ever make suitable use of it? Might I not be better off just passing it on to John O'Hara? What is a recipe for sauerkraut doing in my notebook? What kind of magpie keeps this notebook? *"He was born the night the Titanic went down.'* That seems a nice enough line, and I even recall who said it, but is it not really a better line in life than it could ever be in fiction?

But of course that is exactly it: not that I should ever use the line, but that I should remember the woman who said it and the afternoon I heard it. We were on her terrace by the sea, and we were finishing the wine left from lunch, trying to get what sun there was, a California winter sun. The woman whose husband was born the night the *Titanic* went down wanted to rent her house, wanted to go back to her children in Paris. I remember wishing that I could afford the house, which cost $1,000 a month. "Someday you will," she said lazily. "Someday it all comes." There in the sun on her terrace it seemed easy to believe in someday, but later I had a low-grade afternoon hangover and ran over a black snake on the way to the supermarket and was flooded with inexplicable fear when I heard the checkout clerk explaining to the man ahead of me why she was finally divorcing her husband. "He left me no choice," she said over and over as she punched the register. "He has a little seven-month-old-baby by her, he left me no choice." I would like to believe that my dread then was for the human condition, but of course it was for me, because I wanted a baby and did not then have one and because I wanted to own the house that cost $1,000 a month to rent and because I had a hangover.

It all comes back. Perhaps it is difficult to see the value in having one's self back in that kind of mood, but I do see it, I think we are well advised to keep on nodding terms with the people we used to be, whether we find them attractive company or not. Otherwise they turn up unannounced and surprise us, come hammering on the mind's door at 4 A.M. of a bad night and demand to know who deserted them, who betrayed them, who is going to make amends. We forget all too soon the things we thought we could never forget. We forget the loves and the betrayals alike, forget what we whispered and what we screamed, forget who we were. I have already lost touch with a couple of people I used to be; one of them, a seventeen-year-old, presents little threat, although it would be of some interest to me to know again what it feels like to sit on a river levee drinking vodka-and-orange-juice and listening to Les Paul and Mary Ford and their echoes sing "How High the Moon" on the car radio. (You see I still have the scenes, but I no longer perceive myself among those present, no longer could even improvise the dialogue.) The other one, a twenty-three-year-old, bothers me more. She was always a good deal of trouble, and I suspect she will reappear when I least want to see her, skirts too long, shy to the point of aggravation, always the injured party, full of recriminations and little hurts and stories I do not want to hear again, at once saddening me and angering me with her vulnerability and ignorance, an apparition all the more insistent for being so long banished.

It is a good idea, then, to keep in touch, and I suppose that keeping in touch is what notebooks are all about. And we are all on our own when it comes to keeping those lines open to ourselves: your notebook will never help me nor mine you, *"So what's new in the whiskey business?"* What could that possibly mean to you? To me it means a blonde in a Pucci bathing suit sitting with a couple of fat men by the pool at the Beverly Hills Hotel. Another man approaches, and they all regard one another in silence for a while. "So what's new in the whiskey business?" one of the fat men finally says by way of welcome, and the blonde stands up, arches one foot and dips it in the pool, looking all the while at the cabaña where Baby Pignatari is talking on the telephone. That is all there is to that, except that several years later I saw the blonde coming out of Saks Fifth Avenue in New York with her California complexion and a voluminous mink coat. In the harsh wind that day she looked old and irrevocably tired to me, and even the skins in the mink coat were not worked the way they were doing them that year, not the way she would have wanted them done, and there is the point of the story. For a while after that I did not like to look in the mirror, and my eyes would skim the newspapers and pick out only the deaths, the cancer victims, the premature coronaries, the suicides, and I stopped riding the Lexington Avenue IRT because I noticed for the first time that all the strangers I had seen for years—the man with the seeing-eye dog, the spinster who read the classified pages every day, the fat girl who always got off with me at Grand Central—looked older than they once had.

It all comes back. Even that recipe for sauerkraut: even that brings it back. I was on Fire Island when I first made that sauerkraut, and it was raining, and we drank a lot of bourbon and ate the sauerkraut and went to bed at ten, and I listened to the rain and the Atlantic and felt safe. I made the sauerkraut again last night and it did not make me feel any safer, but that is, as they say, another story.

How to Say Nothing in Five Hundred Words

Paul Roberts

It's Friday afternoon, and you have almost survived another week of classes. You are just looking forward dreamily to the weekend when the English instructor says: "For Monday you will turn in a five-hundred-word composition on college football."

Well, that puts a good big hole in the weekend. You don't have any strong views on college football one way or the other. You get rather excited during the season and go to all the home games and find it rather more fun than not. On the other hand, the class has been reading Robert Hutchins in the anthology and perhaps Shaw's "Eighty-Yard Run," and from the class discussion you have got the idea that the instructor thinks college football is for the birds. You are no fool. You can figure out what side to take.

After dinner you get out the portable typewriter that you got for high school graduation. You might as well get it over with and enjoy Saturday and Sunday. Five hundred words is about two double-spaced pages with normal margins. You put in a sheet of paper, think up a title, and you're off:

Why College Football Should Be Abolished

College football should be abolished because it's bad for the school and also bad for the players. The players are so busy practicing that they don't have any time for their studies.

This, you feel, is a mighty good start. The only trouble is that it's only thirty-two words. You still have four hundred and sixty-eight to go, and you've pretty well exhausted the subject. It comes to you that you do your best thinking in the morning, so you put away the typewriter and go to the movies. But the next morning you have to do your washing and some math problems, and in the afternoon you go to the game. The English instructor turns up too, and you wonder if you've taken the right side after all. Saturday night you have a date, and Sunday morning you have to go to church. (You can't let English assignments interfere with your religion.) What with one thing and another, it's ten o'clock Sunday night before you get out the typewriter again. You make a pot of coffee and start to fill out your views on college football. Put a little meat on the bones.

Why College Football Should Be Abolished

In my opinion, it seems to me that college football should be abolished. The reason why I think this to be true is because I feel that football is bad for the colleges in nearly every respect. As Robert Hutchins says in his article in our anthology in which he discusses college football, it would be better if the colleges had race horses and had races with one another, because then the horses would not have to attend classes. I firmly agree with Mr. Hutchins on this point, and I am sure that many other students would agree too.

One reason why it seems to me that college football is bad is that it has become too commercial. In the olden times when people played football just for the fun of it, maybe college football was all right, but they do not play football just for the fun of it now as they used to in the old days. Nowadays college football is what you might call a big business. Maybe this is not true at all schools, and I don't think it is especially true here at State, but certainly this is the case at most colleges and universities in America nowadays, as Mr. Hutchins points out in his very interesting article. Actually the coaches and alumni go around to the high schools and offer the high school stars large salaries to come to their colleges and play football for them. There was one case where a high school star was offered a convertible if he would play football for a certain college.

Another reason for abolishing college football is that it is bad for the players. They do not have time to get a college education, because they are so busy playing football. A football player has to practice every afternoon from three to six and then he is so tired that he can't concentrate on his studies. He just feels like dropping off to sleep after dinner, and then the next day he goes to his classes without having studied and maybe he fails the test.

(Good ripe stuff so far, but you're still a hundred and fifty-one words from home. One more push.)

> *Also I think college football is bad for the colleges*
> *and the universities because not very many students*
> *get to participate in it. Out of a college of ten thou-*
> *sand students only seventy-five or a hundred play*
> *football, if that many. Football is what you might call*
> *a spectator sport. That means that most people go to*
> *watch it but do not play it themselves.*

(Four hundred and fifteen. Well, you still have the conclusion, and when you retype it, you can make the margins a little wider.)

> *These are the reasons why I agree with Mr. Hutchins*
> *that college football should be abolished in American*
> *colleges and universities.*

On Monday you turn it in, moderately hopeful, and on Friday it comes back marked "weak in content" and sporting a big "D."

This essay is exaggerated a little, not much. The English instructor will recognize it as reasonably typical of what an assignment on college football will bring in. He knows that nearly half of the class will contrive in five hundred words to say that college football is too commercial and bad for the players. Most of the other half will inform him that college football builds character and prepares one for life and brings prestige to the school. As he reads paper after paper all saying the same thing in almost the same words, all bloodless, five hundred words dripping out of nothing, he wonders how he allowed himself to get trapped into teaching English when he might have had a happy and interesting life as an electrician or a confidence man.

Well, you may ask, what can you do about it? The subject is one on which you have few convictions and little information. Can you be expected to make a dull subject interesting? As a matter of fact, this is precisely what you are expected to do. This is the writer's essential task. All subjects, except sex, are dull until somebody makes them interesting. The writer's job is to find the argument, the approach, the angle, the wording that will take the reader with him. This is seldom easy, and it is particularly hard in subjects that have been much discussed: College Football, Fraternities, Popular Music, Is Chivalry Dead?, and the like. You will feel that there is nothing you can do with such subjects except repeat the old bromides. But there are some things you can do which will make your papers, if not throbbingly alive, at least less insufferably tedious than they might otherwise be.

Avoid the Obvious Content

Say the assignment is college football. Say that you've decided to be against it. Begin by putting down the arguments that come to your mind: it is too commercial, it takes the students' minds off their studies, it is hard on the players, it makes the university a kind of circus instead of an intellectual center, for most schools it is financially ruinous. Can you think of any more arguments, just off hand? All right. Now when you write your paper, *make sure that you don't use any of the material on this list.* If these are the points that leap to your mind, they will leap to everyone else's too, and whether you get a "C" or a "D" may depend on whether the instructor reads your paper early when he is fresh and tolerant or late, when the sentence "In my opinion, college football has become too commercial," inexorably repeated, has brought him to the brink of lunacy.

Be against college football for some reason or reasons of your own. If they are keen and perceptive ones, that's splendid. But even if they are trivial or foolish or indefensible, you are still ahead so long as they are not everybody else's reasons too. Be against it because the colleges don't spend enough money on it to make it worthwhile, because it is bad for the characters of the spectators, because the players are forced to attend classes, because the football stars hog all the beautiful women, because it competes with baseball and is therefore un-American and possibly Communist inspired. There are lots of more or less unused reasons for being against college football.

Sometimes it is a good idea to sum up and dispose of the trite and conventional points before going on to your own. This has the advantage of indicating to the reader that you are going to be neither trite nor conventional. Something like this:

> *We are often told that college football should be abolished because it has become too commercial or because it is bad for the players. These arguments are no doubt very cogent, but they don't really go to the heart of the matter.*

Then you go to the heart of the matter.

Take the Less Usual Side

One rather simple way of getting into your paper is to take the side of the argument that most of the citizens will want to avoid. If the assignment is an essay on dogs, you can, if you choose, explain that dogs are faithful and lovable companions, intelligent, useful as guardians of the house and protectors of children, indispensable in police work—in short, when all is said and done, man's best friends. Or you can suggest that those big brown eyes conceal, more often than not, a vacuity of mind and an inconstancy of purpose; that the dogs you have known most intimately have been mangy, ill-tempered brutes, incapable of instruction; and that only your nobility of mind and fear of arrest prevent you from kicking the flea-ridden animals when you pass them on the street.

Naturally personal convictions will sometimes dictate your approach. If the assigned subject is "Is Methodism Rewarding to the Individual?" and you are a pious Methodist, you have really no choice. But few assigned subjects, if any, will fall in this category. Most of them will lie in broad areas of discussion with much to be said on both sides. They are intellectual exercises, and it is legitimate to argue now one way and now another, as debaters do in similar circumstances. Always take the side that looks to you hardest, least defensible. It will almost always turn out to be easier to write interestingly on that side.

This general advice applies where you have a choice of subjects. If you are to choose among "The Value of Fraternities" and "My Favorite High School

Teacher" and "What I Think About Beetles," by all means plump for the beetles. By the time the instructor gets to your paper, he will be up to his ears in tedious tales about the French teacher at Bloombury High and assertions about how fraternities build character and prepare one for life. Your views on beetles, whatever they are, are bound to be a refreshing change.

Don't worry too much about figuring out what the instructor thinks about the subject so that you can cuddle up with him. Chances are his views are no stronger than yours. If he does have convictions and you oppose him, his problem is to keep from grading you higher than you deserve in order to show he is not biased. This doesn't mean that you should always cantankerously dissent from what the instructor says; that gets tiresome too. And if the subject assigned is "My Pet Peeve," do not begin, "My pet peeve is the English instructor who assigns papers on 'my pet peeve.'" This was still funny during the War of 1812, but it has sort of lost its edge since then. It is in general good manners to avoid personalities.

Slip Out of Abstraction

If you will study the essay on college football [near the beginning of this essay], you will perceive that one reason for its appalling dullness is that it never gets down to particulars. It is just a series of not very glittering generalities: "football is bad for the colleges," "it has become too commercial," "football is a big business," "it is bad for the players," and so on. Such round phrases thudding against the reader's brain are unlikely to convince him, though they may well render him unconscious.

If you want the reader to believe that college football is bad for the players, you have to do more than say so. You have to display the evil. Take your roommate, Alfred Simkins, the second-string center. Picture poor old Alfy coming home from football practice every evening, bruised and aching, agonizingly tired, scarcely able to shovel the mashed potatoes into his mouth. Let us see him staggering up to the room, getting out his econ textbook, peering desperately at it with his good eye, falling asleep and failing the test in the morning. Let us share his unbearable tension as Saturday draws near. Will he fail, be demoted, lose his monthly allowance, be forced to return to the coal mines? And if he succeeds, what will be his reward? Perhaps a slight ripple of applause when the third-string center replaces him, a moment of elation in the locker room if the team wins, of despair if it loses. What will he look back on when he graduates from college? Toil and torn ligaments. And what will be his future? He is not good enough for pro football, and he is too obscure and weak in econ to succeed in stocks and bonds. College football is tearing the heart from Alfy Simkins and, when it finishes with him, will callously toss aside the shattered hulk.

This is no doubt a weak enough argument for the abolition of college football, but it is a sight better than saying, in three or four variations, that college football (in your opinion) is bad for the players.

Look at the work of any professional writer and notice how constantly he is moving from the generality, the abstract statement, to the concrete example, the facts and figures, the illustration. If he is writing on juvenile delinquency, he does not just tell you that juveniles are (it seems to him) delinquent and that (in his opinion) something should be done about it. He shows you juveniles being delinquent, tearing up movie theatres in Buffalo, stabbing high school principals in Dallas, smoking marijuana in Palo Alto. And more than likely he is moving toward some specific remedy, not just a general wringing of the hands.

It is no doubt possible to be *too* concrete, too illustrative or anecdotal, but few inexperienced writers err this way. For most the soundest advice is to be seeking always for the picture, to be always turning general remarks into seeable examples. Don't say, "Sororities teach girls the social graces." Say, "Sorority life teaches a girl how to carry on a conversation while pouring tea, without sloshing the tea into the saucer." Don't say, "I like certain kinds of popular music very much." Say, "Whenever I hear Gerber Sprinklittle play 'Mississippi Man' on the trombone, my socks creep up my ankles."

Get Rid of Obvious Padding

The student toiling away at his weekly English theme is too often tormented by a figure: five hundred words. How, he asks himself, is he to achieve this staggering total? Obviously by never using one word when he can somehow work in ten.

He is therefore seldom content with a plain statement like "Fast driving is dangerous." This has only four words in it. He takes thought, and the sentence becomes:

In my opinion, fast driving is dangerous.

Better, but he can do better still:

In my opinion, fast driving would seem to be rather dangerous.

If he is really adept, it may come out:

*In my humble opinion, though I do not claim to be an
expert on this complicated subject, fast driving, in most
circumstances, would seem to be rather dangerous in
many respects, or at least so it would seem to me.*

Thus four words have been turned into forty, and not an iota of content has been added.

Now this is a way to go about reaching five hundred words, and if you are content with a "D" grade, it is as good a way as any. But if you aim higher, you must work differently. Instead of stuffing your sentences with straw, you must try steadily to get rid of the padding, to make your sentences lean and tough. If you are really working at it, your first draft will greatly exceed the required total, and then you will work it down, thus:

*It is thought in some quarters that fraternities do not contribute
as much as might be expected to campus life.*

Some people think that fraternities contribute little to campus life.

*The average doctor who practices in small towns or in the coutry
must toil night and day to heal the sick.*

Most country doctors work long hours.

*When I was a little girl, I suffered from shyness and embarrament
in the presence of others.*

I was a shy little girl.

It is absolutely necessary for the person employed as a marine fireman to give the matter of steam pressure his undivided atttion at all times.

The fireman has to keep his eye on the steam gauge.

You may ask how you can arrive at five hundred words at this rate. Simple. You dig up more real content. Instead of taking a couple of obvious points off the surface of the topic and then circling warily around them for six paragraphs, you work in and explore, figure out the details. You illustrate. You say that fast driving is dangerous, and then you prove it. How long does it take to stop a car at forty and at eighty? How far can you see at night? What happens when a tire blows? What happens in a head-on collision at fifty miles an hour? Pretty soon your paper will be full of broken glass and blood and headless torsos, and reaching five hundred words will not really be a problem.

Call a Fool a Fool

Some of the padding in freshman themes is to be blamed not on anxiety about the word minimum but on excessive timidity. The student writes, "In my opinion, the principal of my high school acted in ways that I believe every unbiased person would have to call foolish." This isn't exactly what he means. What he means is, "My high school principal was a fool." If he was a fool, call him a fool. Hedging the thing about with "in-my-opinion's" and "it-seems-to-me's" and "as-I-see-it's" and "at-least-from-my-point-of-view's" gains you nothing. Delete these phrases whenever they creep into your paper.

The student's tendency to hedge stems from a modesty that in other circumstances would be commendable. He is, he realizes, young and inexperienced, and he half suspects that he is dopey and fuzzy-minded beyond the average. Probably only too true. But it doesn't help to announce your incompetence six times in every paragraph. Decide what you want to say and say it as vigorously as possible, without apology and in plain words.

Linguistic diffidence can take various forms. One is what we call *euphemism*. This is the tendency to call a spade "a certain garden implement" or women's underwear "unmentionables." It is stronger in some eras than others and in some people than others but it always operates more or less in subjects that are touchy or taboo: death, sex, madness, and so on. Thus we shrink from saying "He died last night" but say instead "passed away," "left us," "joined his Maker," "went to his reward." Or we try to take off the tension with a lighter cliché: "kicked the bucket," "cashed in his chips," "handed in his dinner pail." We have found all sorts of ways to avoid saying *mad*: "mentally ill," "touched," "not quite right upstairs," "feeble-minded," "innocent," "simple," "off his trolley," "not in his right mind." Even such a now plain word as *insane* began as a euphemism with the meaning "not healthy."

Modern science, particularly psychology, contributes many polysyllables in which we can wrap our thoughts and blunt their force. To many writers there is no such thing as a bad schoolboy. Schoolboys are maladjusted or unoriented or misunderstood or in the need of guidance or lacking in continued success toward satisfactory integration of the personality as a social unit, but they are never bad. Psychology no doubt makes us better men and women, more sympathetic and tolerant, but it doesn't make writing any easier. Had Shakespeare been confronted with psychology, "To be or not to be" might have come out, "To continue as a social unit or not to do so. That is the personality problem. Whether 'tis a better sign of integration at the conscious level to display a psychic tolerance toward the maladjustments and repressions induced by one's lack of orientation in one's environment or—" But Hamlet would never have finished the soliloquy.

Writing in the modern world, you cannot altogether avoid modern jargon. Nor, in an effort to get away from euphemism, should you salt your paper with four-letter words. But you can do much if you will mount guard against those roundabout phrases, those echoing polysyllables that tend to slip into your writing to rob it of its crispness and force.

Beware of Pat Expressions

Other things being equal, avoid phrases like "other things being equal." Those sentences that come to you whole, or in two or three doughy lumps, are sure to be bad sentences. They are no creation of yours but pieces of common thought floating in the community soup.

Pat expressions are hard, often impossible, to avoid, because they come too easily to be noticed and seem too necessary to be dispensed with. No writer avoids them altogether, but good writers avoid them more often than poor writers.

By "pat expressions" we mean such tags as "to all practical intents and purposes," "the pure and simple truth," "from where I sit," "the time of his life," "to the ends of the earth," "in the twinkling of an eye," "as sure as you're born," "over my dead body," "under cover of darkness," "took the easy way out," "when all is said and done," "told him time and time again," "parted the best of friends," "stand up and be counted," "gave him the best years of her life," "worked her fingers to the bone." Like other clichés, these expressions were once forceful. Now we should use them only when we can't possibly think of anything else.

Some pat expressions stand like a wall between the writer and thought. Such a one is "the American way of life." Many student writers feel that when they have said that something accords with the American way of life or does not they have exhausted the subject. Actually, they have stopped at the highest level of abstraction. The American way of life is the complicated set of bonds between a hundred and eighty million ways. All of us know this when we think about it, but the tag phrase too often keeps us from thinking about it.

So with many another phrase dear to the politician: "this great land of ours," "the man in the street," "our national heritage." These may prove our patriotism or give a clue to our political beliefs, but otherwise they add nothing to the paper except words.

Colorful Words

The writer builds with words, and no builder uses a raw material more slippery and elusive and treacherous. A writer's work is a constant struggle to get the right word in the right place, to find that particular word that will convey his meaning exactly, that will persuade the reader or soothe him or startle or amuse him. He never succeeds altogether—sometimes he feels that he scarcely succeeds at all—but such successes as he has are what make the thing worth doing.

There is no book of rules for this game. One progresses through everlasting experiment on the basis of ever-widening experience. There are few useful generalizations that one can make about words as words, but there are perhaps a few.

Some words are what we call "colorful." By this we mean that they are calculated to produce a picture or induce an emotion. They are dressy instead of plain, specific instead of general, loud instead of soft. Thus, in place of "Her heart beat," we may write, "Her heart *pounded, throbbed, fluttered, danced.*" Instead of "He sat in his chair," we may say, "He *lounged, sprawled, coiled.*" Instead of "It was hot," we may say, "It was *blistering, sultry, muggy, suffocating, steamy, wilting.*"

However, it should not be supposed that the fancy word is always better. Often it is as well to write "Her heart beat" or "It was hot" if that is all it did or all it was. Ages differ in how they like their prose. The nineteenth century liked it rich and smoky. The twentieth has usually preferred it lean and cool. The twentieth century writer, like all writers, is forever seeking the exact word, but he is wary of sounding feverish. He tends to pitch it low, to understate it, to throw it away. He knows that if he gets too colorful, the audience is likely to giggle.

See how this strikes you: "As the rich, golden glow of the sunset died away along the eternal western hills, Angela's limpid blue eyes looked softly and trustingly into Montague's flashing brown ones, and her heart pounded like a drum in time with the joyous song surging in her soul." Some people like that sort of thing, but most modern readers would say, "Good grief," and turn on the television.

Colored Words

Some words we would call not so much colorful as colored—that is, loaded with associations, good or bad. All words—except perhaps structure words—have associations of some sort. We have said that the meaning of a word is the sum of the contexts in which it occurs. When we hear a word, we hear with it an echo of all the situations in which we have heard it before.

In some words, these echoes are obvious and discussible. The word *mother,* for example, has for most people, agreeable associations. When you hear *mother* you probably think of home, safety, love, food, and various other pleasant things. If one writes, "She was like a mother to me," he gets an effect which he would not get in "She was like an aunt to me." The advertiser makes use of the associations of *mother* by working it in when he talks about his product. The politician works it in when he talks about himself.

So also with such words as *home, liberty, fireside, contentment, patriot, tenderness, sacrifice, childlike, manly, bluff, limpid.* All of these words are loaded with associations that would be rather hard to indicate in a straight-forward definition. There is more than a literal difference between "They sat around the fireside" and "They sat around the stove." They might have been equally warm and happy around the stove, but *fireside* suggests leisure, grace, quiet tradition, congenial company, and *stove* does not.

Conversely, some words have bad associations. *Mother* suggests pleasant things, but *mother-in-law* does not. Many mothers-in-law are heroically, lovable and some mothers drink gin all day and beat their children insensible, but these facts of life are beside the point. The point is that *mother* sounds good and *mother-in-law* does not.

Or consider the word *intellectual*. This would seem to be a complimentary term, but in point of fact it is not, for it has picked up associations of impracticality and ineffectuality and general dopiness. So also such words as *liberal, reactionary, Communist, socialist, capitalist, radical, schoolteacher, truck driver, undertaker, operator, salesman, huckster, speculator*. These convey meaning on the literal level, but beyond that—sometimes, in some places—they convey contempt on the part of the speaker.

The question of whether to use loaded words or not depends on what is being written. The scientist, the scholar, try to avoid them; for the poet, the advertising writer, the public speaker, they are standard equipment. But every writer should take care that they do not substitute for thought. If you write, "Anyone who thinks that is nothing but a Socialist (or Communist or capitalist)," you have said nothing except that you don't like people who think that, and such remarks are effective only with the most naive readers. It is always a bad mistake to think your readers more naive than they really are.

Colorless Words

But probably most student writers come to grief not with words that are colorful or those that are colored but with those that have no color at all. A pet example is nice, a word we would find it hard to dispense with in casual conversation but which is no longer capable of adding much to a description. Colorless words are those of such general meaning that in a particular sentence they mean nothing. Slang adjectives like *cool* ("That's real cool") tend to explode all over the language. They are applied to everything, lose their original force, and quickly die.

Beware also of nouns of very general meaning, like *circumstances, cases, instances, aspects, factors, relationships, attitudes, eventualities*, etc. In most circumstances you will find that those cases of writing which contain too many instances of words like these will in this and other aspects have factors leading to unsatisfactory relationships with the reader resulting in unfavorable attitudes on his part and perhaps other eventualities, like a grade of "D." Notice also what "etc." means. It means "I'd like to make this list longer, but I can't think of any more examples."

How to Write with Style

Kurt Vonnegut

Newspaper reporters and technical writers are trained to reveal almost nothing about themselves in their writings. This makes them freaks in the world of writers, since almost all of the other ink-stained wretches in that world reveal a lot about themselves to readers. We call these revelations, accidental and intentional, elements of literary style.

These revelations are fascinating to us as readers. They tell is what sort of person it is with whom we are spending time. Does the writer sound ignorant or informed, crazy or sane, stupid or bright, crooked or honest, humorless or playful—? And on and on.

When you yourself put words on paper, remember that the most damning revelation you can make about yourself is that you do not know what is interesting and what is not. Don't you yourself like or dislike writers mainly for what they choose to show you or make you think about? Did you ever admire an empty-headed writer for his or her mastery of the language? No.

So your own winning literary style must begin with interesting ideas in your head. Find a subject you care about and which you in your heart feel others should care about. It is this genuine caring, and not your games with language, which will be the most compelling and seductive element in your style.

I am not urging you to write a novel, by the way—although I would not be sorry if you wrote one, provided you genuinely cared about something. A petition to the mayor about a pothole in front of your house or a love letter to the girl next door will do.

Do not ramble, though.

As for your use of language: Remember that two great masters of our language, William Shakespeare and James Joyce, wrote sentences which were almost childlike when their subjects were most profound. "To be or not to be?" asks Shakespeare's Hamlet. The longest word is three letters long. Joyce, when he was frisky, could put together a sentence as intricate and glittering as a necklace for Cleopatra, but my favorite sentence in his short story "Eveline" is this one: "She was tired." At that point in the story, no other words could break the heart of a reader as those words do.

Simplicity of language is not only reputable, but perhaps even sacred. The Bible opens with a sentence well within the writing skills of a lively fourteen-year-old: "In the beginning God created the heavens and the earth."

It may be that you, too, are capable of making necklaces for Cleopatra, so to speak. But your eloquence should be the servant of the ideas in your head. Your rule might be this: If a sentence, no matter how excellent, does not illuminate my subject in some new and useful way, scratch it out. Here is the same rule paraphrased to apply to storytelling, to fiction: Never include a sentence which does not either remark on character or advance the action.

The writing style which is most natural for you is bound to echo speech you heard when a child. English was the novelist Joseph Conrad's third language, and much that seems piquant in his use of English was no doubt colored by his first language, which was Polish. And lucky indeed is the writer who has grown up in Ireland, for the English spoken there is so amusing and musical. I myself grew up in Indianapolis, Indiana, where common speech sounds like a band saw cutting galvanized tin, and employs a vocabulary as unornamental as a monkey wrench.

In some of the more remote hollows of Appalachia, children still grow up hearing songs and locutions of Elizabethan times. Yes, and many Americans grow up hearing a language other than English, or an English dialect a majority of Americans cannot understand.

All these varieties of speech are beautiful, just as the varieties of butterflies are beautiful. No matter what your first language, you should treasure it all your life. If it happens not to be standard English, and if it shows itself when you write standard English, the result is usually delightful, like a very pretty girl with one eye that is green and one that is blue.

I myself find that I trust my own writing most, and others seem to trust it most, too, when I sound most like a person from Indianapolis, which is what I am. What alternatives do I have? The one most vehemently recommended by teachers has no doubt been pressed on you, as well: that I write like cultivated Englishmen of a century or more ago.

I used to be exasperated by such teachers, but am no more. I understand now that all those antique essays and stories with which I was to compare my own work were not magnificent for their datedness or foreignness, but for saying precisely what their authors meant them to say. My teachers wished me to write accurately, always selecting the most effective words, and relating the words to one another unambiguously, rigidly, like parts of a machine. The teachers did not want to turn me into an Englishman after all. They hoped that I would become understandable—and therefore understood.

And there went my dream of doing with words what Pablo Picasso did with paint or what any number of jazz idols did with music. If I broke all the rules of punctuation, had words mean whatever I wanted them to mean, and strung them together higgledy-piggledy, I would simply not be understood. So you, too, had better avoid Picasso-style or jazz-style writing, if you have something worth saying and wish to be understood.

If it were only teachers who insisted that modern writers stay close to literary styles of the past, we might reasonably ignore them. But readers insist on the very same thing. They want our pages to look very much like pages they have seen before.

Why? It is because they themselves have a tough job to do, and they need all the help they can get from us. They have to identify thousands of little marks on paper, and make sense of them immediately. They have to *read*, an art so difficult that most people do not really master it even after having studied it all through grade school and high school—for twelve long years.

So this discussion, like all discussions of literary styles, must finally acknowledge that our stylistic options as writers are neither numerous nor glamorous, since our readers are bound to be such imperfect artists. Our audience requires us to be sympathetic and patient teachers, ever willing to simplify and clarify—whereas we would rather soar high above the crowd, singing like nightingales.

That is the bad news. The good news is that we Americans are governed under a unique Constitution, which allows us to write whatever we please without fear of punishment. So the most meaningful aspect of our styles, which is what we choose to write about, is unlimited.

Also: we are members of an egalitarian society, so there is no reason for us to write, in case we are not classically educated aristocrats, as though we were classically educated aristocrats.

For a discussion of literary style in a narrower sense, in a more technical sense, I commend to your attention *The Elements of Style* by William Strunk, Jr., and E. B. White (Macmillan, 1979). It contains such rules as this: "A participial phrase at the beginning of a sentence must refer to the grammatical subject," and so on. E. B. White is, of course, one of the most admirable literary stylists this country has so far produced.

You should realize, too, that no one would care how well or badly Mr. White expressed himself, if he did not have perfectly enchanting things to say.

Let's Get Vertical!

Beth Wald

Here I am, 400 feet up on the steep west face of Devil's Tower, a tiny figure in a sea of petrified rock. I can't find enough footholds and handholds to keep climbing. My climbing partner anxiously looks up at me from his narrow ledge. I can see the silver sparkle of the climbing devices I've jammed into the crack every eight feet or so.

I study the last device I've placed, a half-inch aluminum wedge 12 feet below me. If I slip, it'll catch me, but only after a 24-foot fall, a real "screamer." It's too difficult to go back; I have to find a way up before my fingers get too tired. I must act quickly.

Finding a tiny opening in the crack, I jam two fingertips in, crimp them, pull hard, and kick my right foot onto a sloping knob, hoping it won't skid off. At the same time, I slap my right hand up to what looks like a good hold. To my horror, it's round and slippery.

My fingers start to slide. Panic rivets me for a second, but then a surge of adrenalin snaps me back into action. I scramble my feet higher, lunge with my left hand, and catch a wider crack. I manage to get a better grip just as my right hand pops off its slick hold. My feet find edges, and I regain my balance, whipping a chock (wedge) off my harness, I slip it into the crack and clip my rope through a carabiner (oblong metal snaplink). After catching my breath, I start moving again, and the rest of the climb flows upward like a vertical dance.

The Challenges and Rewards

I've tried many sports, but I haven't found any to match the excitement of rock climbing. It's a unique world, with its own language, communities, controversies, heroes, villains, and devoted followers. I've lived in vans, tepees, tents, and caves; worked three jobs to save money for expenses; driven 24 hours to spend a weekend at a good rock; and lived on beans and rice for months at a time—all of this to be able to climb. What is it about scrambling up rocks that inspires such a passion? The answer is, no other sport offers so many challenges and so many rewards.

The physical challenges are obvious. You need flexibility, balance, and strength. But climbing is also a psychological game of defeating your fear, and it demands creative thinking. It's a bit like improvising a gymnastic routine 200 feet in the air while playing a game of chess.

Climbers visit some of the most spectacular places on earth and see them from a unique perspective—the top! Because the sport is so intense, friendships between climbers tend to be strong and enduring.

Anyone Can Climb

Kids playing in trees or on monkey bars know that climbing is a natural activity, but older people often have to relearn to trust their instincts. This isn't too hard, though. The ability to maintain self-control in difficult situations is the most important trait for a beginning climber to have. Panic is almost automatic when you run out of handholds 100 feet off the ground. The typical reaction is to freeze solid until you fall off. But with a little discipline, rational thinking, and/or distraction tactics such as babbling to yourself, humming, or even screaming, fear can change to elation as you climb out of a tough spot.

Contrary to popular belief, you don't have to be superhumanly strong to climb. Self-confidence, agility, a good sense of balance, and determination will get you farther up the rock than bulging biceps. Once you've learned the basics, climbing itself will gradually make you stronger, though many dedicated climbers speed up the process by training at home or in the gym.

Nonclimbers often ask, "How do the ropes get up there?" It's quite simple; the climbers bring them up as they climb. Most rock climbers today are "free climbers." In free climbing, the rope is used only for safety in case of a fall, *not* to help pull you up. (Climbing without a rope, called "free soloing," is a *very* dangerous activity practiced only by extremely experienced—and crazy—climbers.)

First, two climbers tie into opposite ends of a 150-foot-long nylon rope. Then one of them, the belayer, anchors himself or herself to a rock or tree. The other, the leader, starts to climb, occasionally stopping to jam a variety of aluminum wedges or other special gadgets, generically referred to as protection, into cracks in the rock. To each of these, he or she attaches a snaplink, called a carabiner, and clips the rope through. As the leader climbs, the belayer feeds out the rope, and it runs through the carabiners. If the leader falls, the belayer holds the rope, and the highest piece of protection catches the leader. The belayer uses special techniques and equipment to make it easy to stop falls.

When the leader reaches the end of a section of rock—called the pitch—and sets an anchor, he or she becomes the belayer. This person pulls up the slack of the rope as the other partner climbs and removes the protection. Once together again, they can either continue in the same manner or switch leaders. These worldwide techniques work on rock formations, cliffs, peaks, even buildings.

Rocks, Rocks Everywhere

Some of the best climbing cliffs in the country are in the Shawangunk Mountains, only two hours from New York City. Seneca Rocks in West Virginia draws climbers from Washington, D.C., and Pittsburgh, Pennsylvania. Chattanooga, Tennessee, has a fine cliff within the city limits. Most states in the U.S. and provinces in Canada offer at least one or two good climbing opportunities.

Even if there are no large cliffs or rock formations nearby, you can climb smaller rocks to practice techniques and get stronger. This is called bouldering. Many climbers who live in cities and towns have created climbing areas out of old stone walls and buildings. Ask someone at your local outdoor shop where you can go to start climbing.

Get a Helping Hand

There's no substitute for an expert teacher when it comes to learning basic techniques and safety procedures. One of the best (and least expensive) ways to learn climbing is to convince a veteran climber in your area to teach you. You can usually meet these types at the local crag or climbing shop.

As another option, many universities and colleges, some high schools, and some YMCAs have climbing clubs. Their main purpose is to introduce people to climbing and to teach the basics. Other clubs, such as the Appalachian Mountain Club in the eastern U.S. and the Mountaineers on the West Coast, also provide instruction. Ask at your outdoor shop for the names of clubs in your area.

If you live in a place completely lacking rocks and climbers, you can attend one of the fine climbing schools at the major climbing area closest to you. Magazines like *Climbing*, *Rock & Ice*, and *Outside* publish lists of these schools. Once you learn the basics, you're ready to get vertical.

In rock climbing, you can both lose yourself and find yourself. Life and all its troubles are reduced to figuring out the puzzle of the next section of cliff or forgotten in the challenge and delight of moving through vertical space. And learning how to control anxiety, how to piece together a difficult sequence of moves, and how to communicate with a partner are all skills that prove incredibly useful back on the ground!

Collecting Stamps
Student

The beginning stamp collector, before he does anything else, should read. Every public library has a good collection of philatelic books and periodicals that will acquaint the new collector with all the ins and outs of this fascinating but complex hobby. After acquiring a good general background of information, the new collector should decide on a specialty, for general stamp collections tend to become unmanageable. At the same time, it is wise to decide whether the collection is to include only mint (unused) stamps, used stamps, or both. Then, the beginning collector should explore the various sources of supply, such as dealers, the philatelic divisions of post offices, friends and acquaintances. Once the new collector begins to acquire stamps, he must develop a system for arranging and storing his collection. At every step of the way, the new collector should make it his business to become acquainted with experienced collectors and learn from them. Getting off to a good start in stamp collecting is getting off to the beginning of many years of pleasurable reward.

Ch. 4: Process Analysis

Suggestions for writing:

1. Write a detailed process analysis of a task you have performed as part of a job or hobby, a task that you think probably no one else in your class has ever done. Try thinking of either your favorite task or the most unpleasant one you've encountered.

2. In paragraph or essay form, write a set of instructions on how to make a bad impression on your girlfriend or boyfriend's parents.

3. Write a set of instructions on how to get an A, or an F, on a specific test or assignment.

4. Write a process analysis paragraph or essay on one of the following topics or a similar topic:

    planting a garden   writing an essay
    performing a search on the Internet   changing a flat tire
    hiring or firing an employee   staying awake in class
    designing a Web page   taking effective notes
    overcoming insomnia   buying a new suit

Process checklist:

1. Did you begin with an overview of the process to be analyzed?

2. Did you introduce the subject and then break it down into a number of recognizable steps?

3. Did you use a topic sentence (for a paragraph) or a thesis sentence (for an essay) that clearly and briefly explains your approach to the procedure that you will discuss?

4. Did you proceed through the various stages of the process logically?

5. Did you follow a chronological order and do you use chronological transitions (first, next, then, finally, etc.)?

6. Did you provide a sufficient amount of explanation and detailed description for your reader to clearly understand each step?

7. Did you vary your vocabulary and sentences?

8. Did you check grammar, punctuation, and spelling?

CHAPTER 5

Division / Classification

Finding Categories

Using Division/Classification

Both division and classification play important roles in our everyday lives: Bureau drawers separate one type of clothing from another; kitchen cabinets organize food, dishes, and utensils into proper groups; grocery stores shelve similar items together so shoppers can easily locate what they want to buy; school notebooks with tabs help students divide up their academic lives; newspapers classify local and national events in order to organize a great deal of daily information for the general public; and our own personal classification systems assist us in separating what we like from what we don't so that we can have access to our favorite foods, our favorite cars, our favorite entertainment, our favorite people. The two processes of division and classification are so natural to us, in fact, that we sometimes aren't even aware we are using them.

Defining Division/Classification

Division and classification are actually mirror images of each other. Division is the basic feature of process analysis, which we studied in the last chapter: It moves from a general concept to subdivisions of that concept or from a single category to multiple subcategories. Classification works in the opposite direction, moving from specifics to a group with common traits or from multiple subgroups to a single, larger, and more inclusive category. These techniques work together in many ways: A college, for example, is *divided* into departments (single to multiple), whereas courses are *classified* by department (multiple to single); the medical field is divided into specialties, whereas each doctor is *classified* by a single specialty; a cookbook is *divided* into chapters, whereas recipes are *classified* according to type; and athletics is *divided* into specific sports, whereas athletes are *classified* by the sport in which they participate. Division is the separation of an idea or item into its basic parts, such as a home into rooms, a course into assignments, or a job into various duties or responsibilities; classification is the organization of items with similar features into a group or groups, such as ordering furniture to decorate a dining room, dropping all carbohydrates from your diet, or preferring to date only tall, sun-tanned swimmers.

Classification is an organizational system for presenting a large amount of material to a reader or listener. This process helps us make sense of the complex world we live in by letting us work with smaller, more understandable units of that world. Classification must be governed by some clear, logical purpose (such as focusing on all lower-division course requirements), which will then dictate the system of categories to be used. The plan of organization that results should be as flexible as possible, and it should illustrate the specific relationship of items in a group to each other and of the groups themselves to one another.

As you already know, many different ways of classifying the same elements are possible. If you consider the examples at the outset of this chapter, you will realize that bureau drawers vary from house to house and even from person to person; that no one's kitchen is set up exactly the same way as someone else's; and that grocery stores have similar but not identical systems of food classification. (Think, for instance, of the many different schemes for organizing dairy products, meats, foreign foods, etc.) In addition, your friends probably use a method different from yours to organize their school notebooks; different newspapers vary their presentation of the news; and two professors will probably teach the same course material in divergent ways. We all have distinct and uniquely logical methods of classifying elements in our own lives.

The following student paragraph about friends illustrates both division and classification. As you read it, notice how the student writer moves back and forth smoothly from general to specific and from multiple to single.

> *The word "friend" can refer to many different types*
> *of relationships. Close friends are "friends" at their*
> *very best: people for whom we feel respect, esteem,*
> *and, quite possibly, even love. We regard these people*
> *and their well-being with kindness, interest, and good*
> *will; we trust them and will go out of our way to*
> *help them. Needless to say, we could all use at least*
> *one close friend. Next come "casual friends," people*
> *with whom we share a particular interest or activity.*
> *The investment of a great amount of time and energy*
> *in developing this type of friendship is usually not*

required, though casual friends often become close friends with the passage of time. The last division of "friend" is most general and is composed of all those individuals whose acquaintance we have made and who feel no hostility toward us. When one is counting friends, this group should certainly be included, since such friendships often develop into "casual" or "close" relationships. Knowing people in all three groups is necessary, however, because all types of friends undoubtedly help us live healthier, happier lives.

How to Write a Division/Classification Essay

Preparing to Write. You should approach a division/classification essay in the same way you have begun all your other writing assignments—with some kind of prewriting activity that will help you generate ideas. Before you even consider selection and arrangement of details, you need to explore your subject, choose a topic, and decide on a specific purpose and audience.

Writing. As you begin to write, certain guidelines will help you structure your ideas for a division/classification essay: (1) First declare an overall purpose for your classification; (2) then divide the item or concept you are dealing with into categories; (3) arrange these categories into a logical sequence; (4) define each category, explaining the difference between one category and another and demonstrating that difference through examples; and (5) explain the significance of your classification system (Why is it worth reading? What will your audience learn from it?). All discussion in such an essay should reinforce the purpose stated at the beginning of the theme. Other rhetorical modes—such as narration, example, and comparison/contrast—will naturally be used to supplement your classification. To make your classification as workable as possible, take special care that your categories do not overlap and that all topics fail into their proper places. If, for example, you were classifying all the jobs performed by students in your writing class, the categories of (1) indoor work and (2) outdoor work would probably be inadequate. Most delivery jobs, for example, fall into both categories. At a pizza parlor, a florist, or a gift shop, a delivery person's time would be split between indoor and outdoor work. So you would need to design a different classification system to avoid this problem. The categories of (1) indoor work, (2) outdoor work, and (3) a combination of indoor and outdoor work would be much more useful for this task. The last suggestion in particular will help make your classification essays more readable and more accurate.

Rewriting. As you rewrite your division/classification essay, consider carefully the probable reactions of your readers to the form and content of your paper: Does your thesis communicate your purpose clearly? Have you divided your topic into separate and understandable categories? Are your categories original and unique? Are these categories arranged logically? Are the distinctions between your categories as clear as possible? Will your audience appreciate the significance of your particular classification system?

Student Essay: Division/Classification at Work

The following student essay divides skiers into interesting categories based on their physical abilities. As you read it, notice how the student writer weaves the significance of his study into his opening statement of purpose. Also, pay particular attention to his logical method of organization and clear explanation of categories as he moves with ease from multiple to single and back to multiple again throughout the essay.

People on the Slopes

<u>When I first learned to ski</u>, I was amazed by the ^{Subject} shapes who whizzed by me and slipped down trails marked only by a black diamond signifying "most difficult," while others careened awkwardly down the "bunny slopes." ^{Thesis} <u>These skiers, I discovered, could be divided into</u> ^{statement} <u>distinct categories</u>—for my own entertainment and for the purpose of finding appropriate skiing partners.

^{First} First are the <u>poetic skiers</u>. They glide down the ^{category} mountainside silently with what seems like no effort at ^{Support-} all. They float from side to side on the intermediate ^{ing details} slopes, their knees bent perfectly above parallel skis, while their sharp skills allow them to bypass slower skiers with safely executed turns at remarkable speeds.

^{Second} The <u>crazy skiers</u> also get down the mountain ^{category} quickly, but with a lot more noise attending their descent. At every hill, they yell a loud "Yahoo!" and ^{Support-} slam their skis into the snow. These go-for-broke ath- ^{ing details} letes always whiz by faster than everyone else, and ^{(with} ^{humor)} they especially seem to love the crowded runs where they can slide over the backs of other people's skis. I often find crazy skiers in mangled messes at the bottoms of steep hills, where they are yelling loudly, but not the famous "Yahoo!"

After being overwhelmed by the crazy skiers, I am ^{Third} always glad to find other skiers like myself: <u>the aver-</u> ^{category} <u>age ones.</u> We are polite on the slopes, concentrate on improving our technique with every run, and ski the beginner slopes only at the beginning of the day to warm up. We go over the moguls (small hills) much more cautiously than the crazy or poetic skiers, but still seek adventure with a slight jump or two each day.

We remain a silent majority on the mountain.

Below us in talent, but much more evident on the mountainside, are what I call the <u>eternal beginners</u>. These skiers stick to the same beginner slope almost every run of the day during their vacation. Should they venture onto an intermediate slope, they quickly assume the snowplow position (a pigeon-toed stance) and never leave it. Eternal beginners weave from one side of the run to the other and hardly ever fall, because they proceed so slowly; however, they do yell quite a bit at the crazies who like to run over the backs of their skis.

<u>Having always enjoyed people-watching, I have fun each time I am on the slopes observing the myriad of skiers around me. I use these observations to pick out possible ski partners for myself and others.</u> Since my mother is an eternal beginner, she has more fun skiing with someone who shares her interests than with my dad, who is a poetic skier with solitude on his mind. After taking care of Mom, I am free to find a partner I'll enjoy. My sister, the crazy skier of the family, just heads for the rowdiest group she can find! <u>As the years go by and my talents grow, I am trusting my perceptions of skier types to help me find the right partner for life on and off the slopes. No doubt watching my fellow skiers will always remain an enjoyable plastime.</u>

Margin notes: Supporting details (comparitive); Fourth category; Supporting details; Significance of classification system; Concluding remarks

Student Writer's Comments

To begin this paper—the topic of which occurred to me as I flew over snow-capped mountains on a trip—I brainstormed. I jotted down the general groups I believed existed on the slopes, then noted characteristics as they came to me. The ideas flowed quite freely, and I enjoyed picturing the people I was describing. The difficult part came when I had to organize the groups. The order of presentation in my last draft is totally different from my initial draft. The greatest part of this paper was realizing that I had used these mental groupings before in pairing my family and friends with other skiers; I had just never organized or verbalized the categories. Writing this paper helped me do that and was a lot of fun.

Some Final Thoughts on Division/Classification

The following essays collected in this chapter use division and/or classification as their primary organizing principle. Most of these essays show both techniques at work, but a few demonstrate how division works by itself.

The Big Five Fears of Our Time

Stephanie Brush

In a recent survey, 1,000 Americans were asked to name the fear that torments them the most. They're listed here in no particular order-of-fearsomeness, but most everyone has a personal favorite on this list.

1. Fear of Gradual Hysteria

Gradual hysteria is what happens when you feel your life is completely out of control.

Many of us attempt to exert control by redecorating our homes, for example. We move a picture and find that there is a rectangular spot on the wall where the picture used to be. Then we move the TV stand and find that there are four identical indentations in the rug. Then we move the TV stand back and find that there are now eight identical indentations in the rug. Then someone starts drilling into the pavement outside the window, and the phone rings exactly once, and stops, and we run to answer it, and hear only a metallic click and start to scream, very quietly. We feel that God is talking to us. "Just try it," He is saying, "Just try and make something out of your life."

Gradual hysteria happens in this way to just about everybody. It is usually triggered by loud noises, helplessness, and cumulative stress, and yes, it has the power to destroy everything in its path. But you'd rather have that happening to you than to someone else, wouldn't you?

2. Fear of People Who Have Had Too Much Assertiveness Training

There was a movement back in the seventies in which thousands of ineffectual nebbishes decided that they were not standing firm where it counted in life, and they went out and shelled out $300 at adult-education classes around the country, so that they could Learn to Say No! To Get Their Needs Met! To Not Take a Lot of BS From the Guy at the Auto Body Shop!

They walk among us now, and the threat they pose is inestimable.

Have they become, in fact, "assertive" people? Let's be serious. Assertiveness comes from being *born* knowing you're going to get the goods in life, whatever they may be. You don't have to take *courses* in this stuff, okay? And the reason an assertiveness-trained nebbish is a dangerous commodity is that he suspects he is still a nebbish but he's not sure whether it shows or not. It *shows*, all right?

He starts to breathe heavily at the cleaners' because he's just found a spot on his jacket that wasn't there before, and now he is trying to remember his "lines" for the big confrontation to come.

Sometimes, Assertiveness-Trained Nebbishes get the heady feeling of "being honest" and "owning their feelings"—and they do embarrassing things like embrace you and say, "I hate your rug, but the honesty of this moment feels beautiful."

Whatever we do, it is essential for us to impress on our friends that we liked them better when they were obsequious, waffling little toadies. At least then we knew what we were dealing with. At least life had some kind of structure.

There is some work being done to "de-program" these people, sort of like former members of cults. But it is too soon to tell whether this technique is going to have any effect.

3. Insomnia: Fear of Consciousness

"Consciousness" is a state of awareness of all the realities of life. If we had to live in a state of total awareness all the time, if we had to dwell on realities like crime and war and what happens to the members of "Menudo" after they turn fifteen, then we should all surely become mad and highly depressed.

So sleep was invented to spare us from total consciousness. But the more we can't sleep, the more conscious—and therefore *anxious*—we become. The same scientists who have clocked things like REM cycles and muscle-activity cycles have also clocked pre-sleep anxiety cycles.

• Cycle I usually involves WORK ANXIETY. Did I remember to turn off my office light? Does my boss like me? Would my boss recognize me if he saw me in a small crowd?

• Cycle II involves CURRENT-EVENTS ANXIETY. IS there plutonium in my drinking water? Will the world be safe for my children? With street crime in the state it's in, would it be all right if I asked my dog to walk himself at night?

• Cycle III occurs when the mind drifts off to a netherworld of halfformed dreads and sinister potentialities. What if my family got sick and died? What if they were tied to a stake in the Amazon rain forest and eaten by termites? What if I were on a quiz show and had to know the Gross National Product of Burma?

Some of these fears, unfortunately, have more than a little merit (although for what it's worth, the GNP of Burma is 657,000 Bwenzii a year, and there are no termites in the Amazon rain forest. Then again, there's nothing to stop them from being flown in.)

It is estimated that over 45 percent of the population suffers from insomnia on any given night; which means that on any given night YOU ARE ALONE WITH 150 MILLION OTHER AMERICANS. So when you think about it, it would make sense if you were given these people's phone numbers, so you'd at least have someone to talk to. (And yet, paradoxically, if you called them, they would scream into the receiver, "What are you, *crazy*? It's *three o'clock in the morning*!" And they would call the police.)

4. Fear of Amnesia

There are really three varieties of amnesia we need to talk about here: "Random" amnesia strikes about 5 million Americans a year, including an undisclosed number of dental patients who "forget" to floss between meals, and a number of hotel guests who "forget" to return the towels, stationery, and light fixtures to the rooms where they found them. Also every year, twelve or thirteen natives of Florence, Oregon, fall victim to *group* amnesia and awaken and imagine themselves to be natives of Florence, Italy. They immediately start painting frescoes all over the sides of municipal buildings, and each year the frescoes have to be sandblasted off, at the expense of thousands to the taxpayers, since no one in Oregon is known to have any artistic talent.

By far the most virulent form of amnesia is SOAPSTAR amnesia, which occurs relentlessly in daytime television. Hardly a day goes by when someone on one of the major networks is not suffering from a complete memory loss—"*What do you mean 'Nicki Matuszak?' I've never heard of a 'Nicki Matuszak' in my life! I'm a beekeeper! Stay away from me!*"

These poor doomed sufferers are destined to wander around strange towns in brunette wigs and unattractive clothing, marry people they have never met before, and ignore the pleas of their husbands and wives on television ("Nicki! It's me, Stefano! I never meant to shoot you in the brain! Please come home!").

Naturally, if we watch a lot of daytime TV, we are afraid that this fate could befall us (although we secretly wonder how TV amnesiacs can use their American Express cards for months at a time, pay the finance charge, and still not have a clue to their identity).

5. Fear of Major Brain-Loss

Many people are afraid of appearing helpless, foolish, and "brainless." For example, of being in serious car crashes and becoming "vegetables." (Although if you get incinerated in a *plane* crash, you get to become a "mineral," which is probably much, much worse.)

A far greater threat than this, however, is that of having a song you really hate running through your head that you just can't get rid of. It certainly happens more frequently. NO ONE EVER HAS A SONG THEY *LIKE* RUNNING THROUGH THEIR HEAD. Large numbers of college graduates still hear "Yummy, Yummy, Yummy," by the Ohio Express, and some people have gone nearly insane with a continual rendition of "Hey! You! Get Offa My Cloud!" as performed by the Ray Conniff Singers.

Add to the dangers of brain-loss the persistent lure of religious cults, lurking tantalizingly with "all the answers" around every corner. Beyond even the Hare Krishnas and the Unification Church lies the "Pepsi Generation," a dangerous cult headed by singer LIONEL RICHIE. Instead of working regular hours and contributing to the Gross National Product, the Pepsi Generation spends hours taking dancing lessons and having their teeth professionally polished. They venerate organized volleyball and drive dune buggies to all their major appointments. Fortunately, they are closely watched and monitored by a number of federal agencies.

The Plot Against People

Russell Baker

WASHINGTON, JUNE 17—Inanimate objects are classified scientifically into three major categories—those that don't work, those that break down and those that get lost.

The goal of all inanimate objects is to resist man and ultimately to defeat him, and the three major classifications are based on the method each object uses to achieve its purpose. As a general rule, any object capable of breaking down at the moment when it is most needed will do so. The automobile is typical of the category.

With the cunning typical of its breed, the automobile never breaks down while entering a filling station with a large staff of idle mechanics. It waits until it reaches a downtown intersection in the middle of the rush hour, or until it is fully loaded with family and luggage on the Ohio turnpike.

Thus it creates maximum misery, inconvenience, frustration and irritability among its human cargo, thereby reducing its owner's life span.

Washing machines, garbage disposals, lawn mowers, light bulbs, automatic laundry dryers, water pipes, furnaces, electrical fuses, television tubes, hose nozzles, tape recorders, slide projectors—all are in league with the automobile to take their turn at breaking down whenever life threatens to flow smoothly for their human enemies.

Many inanimate objects, of course, find it extremely difficult to break down. Pliers, for example, and gloves and keys are almost totally incapable of breaking down. Therefore, they have had to evolve a different technique for resisting man.

They get lost. Science has still not solved the mystery of how they do it, and no man has ever caught one of them in the act of getting lost. The most plausible theory is that they have developed a secret method of locomotion which they are able to conceal the instant a human eye falls upon them.

It is not uncommon for a pair of pliers to climb all the way from the cellar to the attic in its single-minded determination to raise its owner's blood pressure. Keys have been known to burrow three feet under mattresses. Women's purses, despite their great weight, frequently travel through six or seven rooms to find hiding space under a couch.

Scientists have been struck by the fact that things that break down virtually never get lost, while things that get lost hardly ever break down.

A furnace, for example, will invariably break down at the depth of the first winter cold wave, but it will never get lost. A woman's purse, which after all does have some inherent capacity for breaking down, hardly ever does; it almost invariably chooses to get lost.

Some persons believe this constitutes evidence that inanimate objects are not entirely hostile to man, and that a negotiated peace is possible. After all, they point out, a furnace could infuriate a man even more thoroughly by getting lost than by breaking down, just as a glove could upset him far more by breaking down than by getting lost.

Not everyone agrees, however, that this indicates a conciliatory attitude among inanimate objects. Many say it merely proves that furnaces, gloves and pliers are incredibly stupid.

The third class of objects—those that don't work—is the most curious of all. These include such objects as barometers, car clocks, cigarette lighters, flashlights and toy-train locomotives. It is inaccurate, of course, to say that they never work. They work once, usually for the first few hours after being brought home, and then quit. Thereafter, they never work again.

In fact, it is widely assumed that they are built for the purpose of not working. Some people have reached advanced ages without ever seeing some of these objects—barometers, for example—in working order.

Science is utterly baffled by the entire category. There are many theories about it. The most interesting holds that the things that don't work have attained the highest state possible for an inanimate object, the state to which things that break down and things that get lost can still only aspire.

They have truly defeated man by conditioning him never to expect anything of them, and in return they have given man the only peace he receives from inanimate society. He does not expect his barometer to work, his electric locomotive to run, his cigarette lighter to light or his flashlight to illuminate, and when they don't it does not raise his blood pressure.

He cannot attain that peace with furnaces and keys, and cars and women's purses as long as he demands that they work for their keep.

Why I Want a Wife

Judy Brady

I belong to that classification of people known as wives. I am A Wife. And, not altogether incidentally, I am a mother.

Not too long ago a male friend of mine appeared on the scene fresh from a recent divorce. He had one child, who is, of course, with his ex-wife. He is looking for another wife. As I thought about him while I was ironing one evening, it suddenly occurred to me that I, too, would like to have a wife. Why do I want a wife?

I would like to go back to school so that I can become economically independent, support myself, and, if need be, support those dependent upon me. I want a wife who will work and send me to school. And while I am going to school I want a wife to take care of my children. I want a wife to keep track of the children's doctor and dentist appointments. And to keep track of mine, too. I want a wife to make sure my children eat properly and are kept clean. I want a wife who will wash the children's clothes and keep them mended. I want a wife who is a good nurturant attendant to my children, who arranges for their schooling, makes sure that they have an adequate social life with their peers, takes them to the park, the zoo, etc. I want a wife who takes care of the children when they are sick, a wife who arranges to be around when the children need special care, because, of course, I cannot miss classes at school. My wife must arrange to lose time at work and not lose the job. It may mean a small cut in my wife's income from time to time, but I guess I can tolerate that. Needless to say, my wife will arrange and pay for the care of the children while my wife is working.

I want a wife who will take care of *my* physical needs. I want a wife who will keep my house clean. A wife who will pick up after my children, a wife who will pick up after me. I want a wife who will keep my clothes clean, ironed, mended, replaced when need be, and who will see to it that my personal things are kept in their proper place so that I can find what I need the minute I need it. I want a wife who cooks the meals, a wife who is a *good* cook. I want a wife who will plan the menus, do the necessary grocery shopping, prepare the meals, serve them pleasantly, and then do the cleaning up while I do my studying. I want a wife who will care for me when I am sick and sympathize with my pain and loss of time from school. I want a wife to go along when our family takes a vacation so that someone can continue to care for me and my children when I need a rest and change of scene.

I want a wife who will not bother me with rambling complaints about a wife's duties. But I want a wife who will listen to me when I feel the need to explain a rather difficult point I have come across in my course of studies. And I want a wife who will type my papers for me when I have written them.

I want a wife who will take care of the details of my social life. When my wife and I are invited out by my friends, I want a wife who will take care of the baby-sitting arrangements. When I meet people at school that I like and want to entertain, I want a wife who will have the house clean, will prepare a special meal, serve it to me and my friends, and not interrupt when I talk about things that interest me and my friends. I want a wife who will have arranged that the children are fed and ready for bed before my guests arrive so that the children do not bother us. I want a wife who takes care of the needs of my guests so that they feel comfortable, who makes sure that they have an ashtray, that they are passed the hors d'oeuvres, that they are offered a second helping of the food, that their wine glasses are replenished when necessary, that their coffee is served to them as they like it. And I want a wife who knows that sometimes I need a night out by myself.

I want a wife who is sensitive to my sexual needs, a wife who makes love passionately and eagerly when I feel like it, a wife who makes sure that I am satisfied. And, of course, I want a wife who will not demand sexual attention when I am not in the mood for it. I want a wife who assumes the complete responsibility for birth control, because I do not want more children. I want a wife who will remain sexually faithful to me so that I do not have to clutter up my intellectual life with jealousies. And I want a wife who understands that *my* sexual needs may entail more than strict adherence to monogamy. I must, after all, be able to relate to people as fully as possible.

If, by chance, I find another person more suitable as a wife than the wife I already have, I want the liberty to replace my present wife with another one. Naturally, I will expect a fresh, new life; my wife will take the children and be solely responsible for them so that I am left free.

When I am through with school and have a job, I want my wife to quit working and remain at home so that my wife can more fully and completely take care of a wife's duties.

My God, who *wouldn't* want a wife?

It's Only a Paper World

Kathleen Fury

Many experts claimed that the computer age heralded the advent of the paperless office. Clearly, this is not to be. If anything, offices are overwhelmed by even more paper, much of it now with sprocket holes.

Humankind is adapting, fortunately. According to the dictates of our varied individual natures, we have developed ways of coping with our changing ecosystem.

The beaver uses paper to build. It may not be exactly clear to observers just what she's building, but deep in her genetic code she knows.

On one side of the typical beaver's desk leans a foot-high stack of papers. Close by is a vertical file stuffed with bulging folders, some waving in the air, unable to touch bottom. In between, the beaver constructs a clever "dam" to prevent the entire structure from falling over: Her two-tier In/Out box supports the pile and allows movement of papers from one place to another.

Incredibly, to nonbeaver observers, the beaver has an uncanny ability to locate a two-month-old report buried within the pile. With deft precision, she can move her hand four millimeters down the pile and extract what she's looking for, confident that the dam will hold.

In this way, the beaver has evolved a protective mechanism that makes her invaluable within the organization, for nobody else, including her secretary, can find anything on her desk. When the beaver goes away on vacation, her department simply ceases work until she returns. She is thus assured that the cliché "nobody's indispensable" doesn't apply to her.

The squirrel's desk, by contrast, is barren. Throughout the year, in all kinds of weather, the squirrel energetically stores away what her brain tells her she may need someday. In her many file cabinets, drawers and bookcases she neatly stores memos, letters, printouts and receipts she believes will nourish her in the months and years to come.

Unlike her coworker, the beaver, the squirrel does not always know exactly where she has hidden a particular item. She knows she has it but is not skilled at remembering the exact location.

Like the maple tree, which produces enough seeds to reforest a continent, the squirrel illustrates nature's method of "overkill." By saving and storing everything, she increases her chance of retrieving something.

Of necessity, squirrels have developed the ability to move through a wide territorial range. When a squirrel moves up to another job, as she tends to do rather often due to lack of space, management must hire a special team of search-and-destroy experts to go through her files.

Nature's scavengers, her "clean-up crew," crows are regarded with wary admiration by squirrels and beavers, who recognize their contribution to keeping the corporate ecosystem tidy.

Crows are responsible for such paper-management advice as "Act on it—or throw it away." They are deeply drawn to paper shredders, trash compactors and outsized waste receptacles and will buy them if they happen to work in purchasing.

Crows belie the common epithet "bird-brained," for it has taken centuries of evolution to create a mind disciplined enough to know with certainty that it is OK to throw the CEO's Statement of Corporate Policy in the wastebasket after a glance.

Other species, who must adapt to the corporate food chain, quickly learn not to address any crow with a sentence that begins, "Do you have a copy of. . . ?"

The clever bees are among the wonders of the corporate world. A bee neither hoards nor destroys paper; she redistributes it, moving from office to office as if between flowers.

Her methods are various and unpredictable, but there is no madness in them. Sometimes she arrives in an office with paper in hand and, distracting a colleague with conversation, simply leaves the paper inconspicuously on his desk. Sometimes she moves paper through seemingly legitimate channels, sending it through interoffice mail with ingenious notes like "Please look into this when you get a chance." More often, she employs the clever notation invented by bees, "FYI."

Whatever her method, she ensures that paper floats outward and does not return to her. Students of human behavior have come to call this cross-pollination "delegation." Though to the bee it is simply a genetic imperative.

While others of the species hoard, distribute and destroy paper, the possum follows the evolutionary dictates of all marsupials and carries it with her.

Instead of a pouch, the office possum has a briefcase—in some cases, several. It is large and soft sided to accommodate her needs. Some possums, as an auxiliary system, carry handbags, large enough to hold legal-size files. When a possum needs to retrieve paper, she goes not to a file cabinet or an In box but to her bags. She protects her paper by carrying it with her at all times—to her home, to the health club, to lunch.

Though she has no natural predators, the possum's habits create special risks. She must spend considerable time at the lost-and-found department of theaters and restaurants and knows by heart the telephone number of the taxi commissioner. One of her arms is longer than the other.

But in nature, all things serve a purpose. And if the office burned down, the lowly possum would be the sole possessor of the paper that is the raison d'être of all the other animals.

Predictable Crises of Adulthood

Gail Sheehy

We are not unlike a particularly hardy crustacean. The lobster grows by developing and shedding a series of hard, protective shells. Each time it expands from within, the confining shell must be sloughed off. It is left exposed and vulnerable until, in time, a new covering grows to replace the old.

With each passage from one stage of human growth to the next we, too, must shed a protective structure. We are left exposed and vulnerable—but also yeasty and embryonic again, capable of stretching in ways we hadn't known before. These sheddings may take several years or more. Coming out of each passage, though, we enter a longer and more stable period in which we can expect relative tranquillity and a sense of equilibrium regained.

As we shall see, each person engages the steps of development in his or her own characteristic *step-style*. Some people never complete the whole sequence. And none of us "solves" with one step—by jumping out of the parental home into a job or marriage, for example—the problems in separating from the caregivers of childhood. Nor do we "achieve" autonomy once and for all by converting our dreams into concrete goals, even when we attain those goals. The central issues or tasks of one period are never fully completed, tied up, and cast aside. But when they lose their primacy and the current life structure has served its purpose, we are ready to move on to the next period.

Can one catch up? What might look to others like listlessness, contrariness, a maddening refusal to face up to an obvious task may be a person's own unique detour that will bring him out later on the other side. Developmental gains won can later be lost—and rewon. It's plausible, though it can't be proven, that the mastery of one set of tasks fortifies us for the next period and the next set of challenges. But its important not to think too mechanistically. Machines work by units. The bureaucracy (supposedly) works step by step. Human beings, thank God, have an individual inner dynamic that can never be precisely coded.

Although I have indicated the ages when Americans are likely to go through each stage, and the differences between men and women where they are striking, do not take the ages too seriously. The stages are the thing, and most particularly the sequence.

Here is the briefest outline of the developmental ladder.

Pulling Up Roots

Before 18, the motto is loud and clear: "I have to get away from my parents." But the words are seldom connected to action. Generally still safely part of our families, even if away at school, we feel our autonomy to be subject to erosion from moment to moment.

After 18, we begin Pulling Up Roots in earnest. College, military service, and short-term travels are all customary vehicles our society provides for the first round trips between family and a base of ones own. In the attempt to separate our view of the world from our family's view; despite vigorous protestations to the contrary—"I know exactly what I want!"—we cast about for any beliefs we can call our own. And in the process of testing those beliefs we are often drawn to fads, preferably those most mysterious and inaccessible to our parents.

Whatever tentative memberships we try out in the world, the fear haunts us that we are really kids who cannot take care of ourselves. We cover that fear with acts of defiance and mimicked confidence. For allies to replace our parents, we turn to our contemporaries. They become conspirators. So long as their perspective meshes with our own, they are able to substitute for the sanctuary of the family. But that doesn't last very long. And the instant they diverge from the shaky ideals of "our group," they are seen as betrayers. Rebounds to the family are common between the ages of 18 and 22.

The tasks of this passage are to locate ourselves in a peer group role, a sex role, an anticipated occupation, an ideology or world view. As a result, we gather the impetus to leave home physically and the identity to *begin* leaving home emotionally.

Even as one part of us seeks to be an individual, another part longs to restore the safety and comfort of merging with another. Thus one of the most popular myths of this passage is: We can piggyback our development by attaching to a Stronger One. But people who marry during this time often prolong financial and emotional ties to the family and relatives that impede them from becoming self-sufficient.

A stormy passage through the Pulling Up Roots years will probably facilitate the normal progression of the adult life cycle. If one doesn't have an identity crisis at this point, it will erupt during a later transition, when the penalties may be harder to bear.

The Trying Twenties

The Trying Twenties confront us with the question of how to take hold in the adult world. Our focus shifts from the interior turmoils of late adolescence—"Who am I?" "What is truth?"—and we become almost totally preoccupied with working out the externals. "How do I put my aspirations into effect?" "What is the best way to start?" "Where do I go?" "Who can help me?" "How did *you* do it?"

In this period, which is longer and more stable compared with the passage that leads to it, the tasks are as enormous as they are exhilarating: To shape a Dream, that vision of ourselves which will generate energy, aliveness, and hope. To prepare for a lifework, to find a mentor if possible. And to form the capacity for intimacy, without losing in the process whatever consistency of self we have thus far mustered. The first test structure must be erected around the life we choose to try.

Doing what we "should" is the most pervasive theme of the twenties. The "shoulds" are largely defined by family models, the press of the culture, or the prejudices of our peers. If the prevailing cultural instructions are that one should get married and settle down behind one's own door, a nuclear family is born. If instead the peers insist that one should do one's own thing, the 25-year-old is likely to harness himself onto a Harley-Davidson and burn up Route 66 in the commitment to have no commitments.

One of the terrifying aspects of the twenties is the inner conviction that the choices we make are irrevocable. It is largely a false fear. Change is quite possible, and some alteration of our original choices is probably inevitable.

Two impulses, as always, are at work. One is to build a firm, safe structure for the future by making strong commitments, to "be set." Yet people who slip into a ready-made form without much self-examination are likely to find themselves *locked in*.

The other urge is to explore and experiment, keeping any structure tentative and therefore easily reversible. Taken to the extreme, these are people who skip from one trial job and one limited personal encounter to another, spending their twenties in the *transient* state.

Although the choices of our twenties are not irrevocable, they do set in motion a Life Pattern. Some of us follow the locked-in pattern, others the transient pattern, the wunderkind pattern, the caregiver pattern, and there are a number of others. Such patterns strongly influence the particular questions raised for each person during each passage. . . .

Buoyed by powerful illusions and belief in the power of the will, we commonly insist in our twenties that what we have chosen to do is the one true course in life. Our backs go up at the merest hint that we are like our parents, that two decades of parental training might be reflected in our current actions and attitudes.

"Not me," is the motto, "I'm different."

Catch-30

Impatient with devoting ourselves to the "shoulds," a new vitality springs from within as we approach 30. Men and women alike speak of feeling too narrow and restricted. They blame all sorts of things, but what the restrictions boil down to are the outgrowth of career and personal choices of the twenties. They may have been choices perfectly suited to that stage. But now the fit feels different. Some inner aspect that was left out is striving to be taken into account. Important new choices must be made, and commitments altered or deepened. The work involves great change, turmoil, and often crisis—a simultaneous feeling of rock bottom and the urge to bust out.

One common response is the tearing up of the life we spent most of our twenties putting together. It may mean striking out on a secondary road toward a new vision or converting a dream of "running for president" into a more realistic goal. The single person feels a push to find a partner. The woman who was previously content at home with children chafes to venture into the world. The childless couple reconsiders children. And almost everyone who is married, especially those married for seven years, feels a discontent.

If the discontent doesn't lead to a divorce, it will, or should, call for a serious review of the marriage and of each partner's aspirations in their Catch-30 condition. The gist of that condition was expressed by a 29-year-old associate with a Wall Street law firm:

"I'm considering leaving the firm. I've been there four years now; I'm getting good feedback, but I have no clients of my own. I feel weak. If I wait much longer, it will be too late, too close to that fateful time of decision on whether or not to become a partner. I'm success-oriented. But the concept of being 55 years old and stuck in a monotonous job drives me wild. It drives me crazy now, just a little bit. I'd say that 85 percent of the time I thoroughly enjoy my work. But when I get a screwball case, I come away from court saying, 'What am I doing here?' It's a *visceral* reaction that I'm wasting my time. I'm trying to find some way to make a social contribution or a slot in city government. I keep saying, 'There's something more.'"

Besides the push to broaden himself professionally, there is a wish to expand his personal life. He wants two or three more children. "The concept of a home has become very meaningful to me, a place to get away from troubles and relax. I love my son in a way I could not have anticipated. I never could live alone."

Consumed with the work of making his own critical life-steering decisions, he demonstrates the essential shift at this age: an absolute requirement to be more self-concerned. The self has new value now that his competency has been proved.

His wife is struggling with her own age-30 priorities. She wants to go to law school, but he wants more children. If she is going to stay home, she wants him to make more time for the family instead of taking on even wider professional commitments. His view of the bind, of what he would most like from his wife, is this:

"I'd like not to be bothered. It sounds cruel, but I'd like not to have to worry about what she's going to do next week. Which is why I've told her several times that I think she should do something. Go back to school and get a degree in social work or geography or whatever. Hopefully that would fulfill her, and then I wouldn't have to worry about her line of problems. I want her to be decisive about herself."

The trouble with his advice to his wife is that it comes out of concern with *his* convenience, rather than with *her* development. She quickly picks up on this lack of goodwill: He is trying to dispose of her. At the same time, he refuses her the same latitude to be "selfish" in making an independent decision to broaden her own horizons. Both perceive a lack of mutuality. And that is what Catch-30 is all about for the couple.

Rooting and Extending

Life becomes less provisional, more rational and orderly in the early thirties. We begin to settle down in the full sense. Most of us begin putting down roots and sending out new shoots. People buy houses and become very earnest about climbing career ladders. Men in particular concern themselves with "making it." Satisfaction with marriage generally goes downhill in the thirties (for those who have remained together) compared with the highly valued, vision-supporting marriage of the twenties. This coincides with the couple's reduced social life outside the family and the in-turned focus on raising their children.

The Deadline Decade

In the middle of the thirties we come upon a crossroads. We have reached the halfway mark. Yet even as we are reaching our prime, we begin to see there is a place where it finishes. Time starts to squeeze.

The loss of youth, the faltering of physical powers we have always taken for granted, the fading purpose of stereotyped roles by which we have thus far identified ourselves, the spiritual dilemma of having no absolute answers—any or all of these shocks can give this passage the character of crisis. Such thoughts usher in a decade between 35 and 45 that can be called the Deadline Decade. It is a time of both danger and opportunity. All of us have the chance to rework the narrow identity by which we defined ourselves in the first half of life. And those of us who make the most of the opportunity will have a full-out authenticity crisis.

To come through this authenticity crisis, we must reexamine our purposes and reevaluate how to spend our resources from now on. "Why am I doing all this? What do I really believe in?" No matter what we have been doing, there will be parts of ourselves that have been suppressed and now need to find expression. "Bad" feelings will demand acknowledgment along with the good.

It is frightening to step off onto the treacherous footbridge leading to the second half of life. We can't take everything with us on this journey through uncertainty. Along the way, we discover that we are alone. We no longer have to ask permission because we are the providers of our own safety. We must learn to give ourselves permission. We stumble upon feminine or masculine aspects of our natures that up to this time have usually been masked. There is grieving to be done because an old self is dying. By taking in our suppressed and even our unwanted parts, we prepare at the gut level for the reintegration of an identity that is ours and ours alone—not some artificial form put together to please the culture or our mates. It is a dark passage at the beginning. But by disassembling ourselves, we can glimpse the light and gather our parts into a renewal.

Women sense this inner crossroads earlier than men do. The time pinch often prompts a woman to stop and take an all-points survey at age 35. Whatever options she has already played out, she feels a "my last chance" urgency to review those options she has set aside and those that aging and biology will close off in the *now foreseeable* future. For all her qualms and confusion about where to start looking for a new future, she usually enjoys an exhilaration of release. Assertiveness begins rising. There are so many firsts ahead.

Men, too, feel the time push in the mid-thirties. Most men respond by pressing down harder on the career acceleration. It's "my last chance" to pull away from the pack. It is no longer enough to be the loyal junior executive, the promising young novelist, the lawyer who does a little *pro bono* work on the side. He wants now to become part of top management, to be recognized as an established writer, or an active politician with his own legislative program. With some chagrin, he discovers that he has been too anxious to please and too vulnerable to criticism. He wants to put together his own ship.

During this period of intense concentration on external advancement, it is common for men to be unaware of the more difficult, gut issues that are propelling them forward. The survey that was neglected at 35 becomes a crucible at 40. Whatever rung of achievement he has reached, the man of 40 usually feels stale, restless, burdened, and unappreciated. He worries about his health. He wonders, "Is this all there is?" He may make a series of departures from well established lifelong base lines, including marriage. More and more men are seeking second careers in midlife. Some become self-destructive. And many men in their forties experience a major shift of emphasis away from pouring all their energies into their own advancement. A more tender, feeling side comes into play. They become interested in developing an ethical self.

Renewal or Resignation

Somewhere in the mid-forties, equilibrium is regained. A new stability is achieved, which may be more or less satisfying.

If one has refused to budge through the midlife transition, the sense of staleness will calcify into resignation. One by one, the safety and supports will be withdrawn from the person who is standing still. Parents will become children; children will become strangers; a mate will grow away or go away; the career will become just a job—and each of these events will be felt as an abandonment. The crisis will probably emerge again around 50. And although its wallop will be greater, the jolt may be just what is needed to prod the resigned middle-ager toward seeking revitalization.

On the Other Hand . . .

If we have confronted ourselves in the middle passage and found a renewal of purpose around which we are eager to build a more authentic life structure, these may well be the best years. Personal happiness takes a sharp turn upward for partners who can now accept the fact: "I cannot expect *anyone* to fully understand me." Parents can be forgiven for the burdens of our childhood. Children can be let go without leaving us in collapsed silence. At 50, there is a new warmth and mellowing. Friends become more important than ever, but so does privacy. Since it is so often proclaimed by people past midlife, the motto of this stage might be "No more bullshit."

DeVry Students and Financial Aid

Student

We routinely accept that DeVry students are *serious about success*. They vary in their diligence; however, student financial aid demands their attention. Most of the institute's patrons regularly receive some form of fiducairy assistance that allows them to finance their education. Their management of the associated responsibility categorizes them as financial aid angels, financial aid users, and financial aid nightmares.

A select few of the student body are angels in the eyes of the Financial Aid Office. Scholarship winners and independently wealthy students whose files are thin and free of excess paperwork require little effort by advisors. Advisors look fondly even upon students who require loans and grants when the students actually read directions and complete their paperwork flawlessly every time.

The vast majority of DeVry students are financial aid users. Financial aid is important to their educational careers but occupies only a minuscule portion of their thoughts. Users are the students who bring their partially completed paperwork into the Financial Aid Office and say, "I have a few questions." Although an advisor may occasionally need to call the student or add a name to the Call List, the user responds to the requests made of him and his problems are quickly resolved. Even students whose files are complex, such as those who attended previous colleges, defaulted on but paid back a prior student loan, or left school for a term are users because their financial aid processing generally follows a well-defined path that is quickly traversed. Delays or mistakes with financial aid administration occasionally frustrate them, but they recognize these obstacles as part of life, and move on without any genuine contempt for the financial aid office.

Angels and users are the majority at DeVry, and the administration designs the processes of financial aid primarily for them. But there are a few students who add dark flair to financial assistance.

The nightmare is the student whose file is considered to be possessed by financial aid demons. Their contact logs overflow from the many times they have entered the financial aid office with complex problems they have created for themselves—seemingly on purpose, for these problems are not the natural results of daily events. Their six-inch-thick files bulge out of the file cabinets as evidence of the times they have abandoned their classes only to enroll again. They ignore the letters, calls, and signs that demand their attention to financial aid, then enter the Financial Aid Office and ask, "Why don't I have any money this term?" They take advantage of DeVry's lenient deadline policies, then return their required documents months late while still expecting immediate action. They apply for federal assistance, and when an advisor requests their absent tax information, they don puzzled looks and declare, "I didn't know I had to file taxes last year." They request that thousands of dollars be loaned to them and sign their promissory notes, only to exclaim in surprise months later, "I have to pay that money back?" Some even come to our school from foreign lands; they practice their limited grasp of our language as the painful sounds of the last crash of the INS, IRS, and Department of Education still echo through their advisors' memories. Financial aid workers throw the nightmares' names about as insults and expletives as their stories become the urban legends of financial aid.

Every day, hordes of students parade through the financial aid office. As financial aid angels, financial aid users, and financial aid nightmares, they add variety and challenge to the otherwise redundant and tedious work of managing student financial assistance.

Spare Time at DeVry
Student

Break time is really when students exercise their options, rather than simply a time to relax from a typical day's demands. Really anywhere, but particularly at DeVry, students or employees have a number of choices for break, and what they do says a lot about themselves. Generally, one finds people either sleeping, relaxing/sleeping, studying, playing, or feeding their addictions.

It's not a very big group of people, but the "nodders and dozers" are unique, so I've got to include them. Occasionally, we see them strewn about the floor like so much debris, or on a makeshift cot, or even slumped over in one of our Hezbollah-designed chairs. Oddly, these are not the most agreeable of people, but that may be because they only talk after you trip over them. Maybe they've been deprived of sleep recently, or perhaps they would just as soon sleep as to do anything productive or enjoyable—that's not for me to say, but I know as long as I don't bother them, they won't bother me.

The polar opposites of the sleepers are, horror of horrors, the studiers. These academic warriors not only use their time, but they use it judiciously. What possesses them to spend what little time they can enjoy or at least waste, doing work is beyond my capacity to understand. Whenever I walk by one of these heathens, I am almost overcome by the need to spread the gospel of good news: "Gather ye rosebuds while ye may," man, join the fold.

Thus far, what we have dealt with are the anti-social types, but I know of at least two other groups (not necessarily only two others) which could really stand examination. Now, these two related groups don't actually mix much, mostly because of the nature of their addiction, so we can deal with them separately. I'm talking about the addicts and the free-recreators—two groups that probably form the majority of DeVry students.

The arcade is packed at break time almost every day with people who are, whether quickly or slowly, surely relieved of their pocket money. Really, it costs enough, don't you think, to come to DeVry without being hypnotized and pickpocketed daily by school sanctioned no-armed bandits? I'm trying to cut back myself, but this school doesn't make it easy; and come to think of it, why should it?

Smokers have nothing on the gamers, even though they don't overtly stand there pumping quarters into a mindless machine of evil—they just spend it elsewhere. The tobacco industry is some kind of racket, I've got to tell you, because not only do they addict you endlessly to this thing, they make sure it kills you s-l-o-w-l-y, so as to milk you for everything they can, no doubt. (Who invented these things anyway, Satan?) But as long as they're smoking, smokers are *very* easy to get along with, even if they make an ashtray of whatever is handy, like your WHOLE FREAKING PORCH.

I guess what I've proved is that we can be defined by our free time, and our free time is defined by our problems, so we can be defined in part by our problems—a flawless syllogism. Furthermore, we all have problems, so at least we must all have free time. I can only hope this has been educational, and in closing, please get help!

Ch. 5: Division / Classification

Suggestions for writing:

1. Write a paper in which you classify the types of people you work with at your job, like Kathleen Fury does in "It's Only a Paper World,"(p.144), and then label them as different animals (or cars or holidays or vegetables or whatever you prefer).

2. What unique perspective do you have on your fellow students? How do you see them like no one else does? Write a paper in which you classify some or all of your classmates according to this personal outlook.

3. Write a classification paragraph or essay using one of the following topics or a similar topic:

   customers or patrons you've dealt with   professional sports coaches
   different professors you've had   types of shoppers
   managers and supervisors   types of college courses
   reasons for attending school   types of web pages

Division / Classification checklist:

1. Did you use a topic sentence (paragraph) or thesis sentence (essay)?

2. Did you break your subject up into at least three categories?

3. Do any of your categories overlap? If so, how can you remedy this?

4. Did you categorize like things?

5. Did you arrange these categories in a logical sequence?

6. Did you define and explain each category so that it is distinct from the other categories?

7. Did you also use description, example, or narration to develop your categories?

8. Did you explain the significance of your classification system?

9. Did you vary your vocabulary and sentences?

10. Did you check for correctness of grammar, punctuation, and spelling?

CHAPTER 6

Comparison / Contrast

Discovering Similarities and Differences

Using Comparison/Contrast

The ability to make comparisons is such a natural and necessary part of our everyday lives that we often do so without conscious effort. When we were children, we compared our toys with those of our friends, we contrasted our height and physical development to other children's, and we constantly evaluated our relative happiness in comparison with that evidenced by our parents and childhood companions. As we grew older, we habitually compared our dates, teachers, parents, friends, cars, and physical attributes. In college, we learn about anthropology by writing essays on the similarities and differences between two African tribes, about political science by contrasting the Republican and Democratic platforms, about business by comparing annual production rates, and about literature by comparing Shakespeare with Marlowe or Browning with Tennyson. Comparing and contrasting various elements in our lives helps us make decisions, such as which course to take or which house to buy, and it justifies preferences that we already hold, such as liking one city more than another or loving one person more than the next. In these ways and in many others, the skillful use of comparison and contrast is clearly essential to our social and professional lives.

Defining Comparison/Contrast

Both comparison and contrast are ways of understanding one subject by putting it next to another. Comparing involves discovering likenesses or similarities, whereas contrasting is based on finding differences. Like division and classification, both comparison and contrast are generally considered part of the same process, because we usually have no reason for comparing unless some contrast is also involved. Each technique implies the existence of the other. For this reason, the word "compare" is often used to mean both techniques.

Comparison and contrast are most profitably applied to two items that have something in common, such as cats and dogs or cars and motorcycles. A discussion of cats and motorcycles, for example, would probably not be very rewarding or stimulating, because they do not have much in common. If more than two items are compared in an essay, they are still most profitably discussed in pairs: for instance, motorcycles and cars, cars and bicycles, or bicycles and motorcycles.

An analogy is an extended, sustained comparison. Often used to explain unfamiliar, abstract, or complicated thoughts, this rhetorical technique can add energy and vividness to a wide variety of college-level writing. The process of analogy differs slightly from comparison/contrast in three important ways: Comparison/contrast begins with subjects from the same class and then places equal weight on both of them. In addition, it addresses both the similarities and the differences of these subjects. Analogy, conversely, seldom explores subjects from the same class and focuses principally on one familiar subject in an attempt to explain another, more complex one. Furthermore, it deals only with similarities, not with contrasts. A comparison/contrast essay, for example, might study two veterans' ways of coping with the trauma of the Gulf War by pointing out the differences between their methods as well as the similarities. An analogy essay might use the familiar notion of a fireworks display to reveal the chilling horror of the lonely hours after dark during this war: "Nights in the Persian Gulf were similar to a loud, unending fireworks display. We had no idea when the next blast was coming, how loud it would be, or how close. We cringed in terror after dark, hoping the next surprise would not be our own death." In this example, rather than simply hearing about an event, we participate in it through this highly refined form of comparison.

The following student paragraph compares and contrasts married and single life. As you read it, notice how the author compares similar social states and, in the process, justifies her current lifestyle.

> *Recently I saw a bumper sticker that read, "It used to be wine, women, and song, and now it's beer, the old lady, and TV." Much truth may be found in this comparison of single and married lifestyles. When my husband and I used to date, for example, we'd go out for dinner and drinks and then maybe see a play or concert. Our discussions were intelligent, often ranging over global politics, science, literature, and other lofty topics. He would open doors for me, buy me flowers, and make sure I was comfortable and happy. Now, three years later, after marriage and a child, the baby bottle has replaced the wine bottle, the smell of diapers wipes out the scent of roses, and our nights*

*on the town are infrequent, cherished events. But
that's okay. A little bit of the excitement and mystery
may be gone, but these intangible qualities have given
way to a sturdy, dependable trust in each other and a
quiet confidence about our future together.*

How to Write a Comparison/Contrast Essay

Preparing to Write. As you consider various topics for a comparison/contrast essay, use the prewriting techniques to generate more ideas on these topics. As you focus your attention on a particular topic, keep the following suggestions in mind:

1. Always compare/contrast items in the same category (e.g., compare two professors, but not a professor and a swimming pool).
2. Have a specific purpose or reason for writing your essay.
3. Discuss the same qualities for each subject (if you evaluate teaching techniques for one professor, do so for the other professor as well).
4. Use as many pertinent details as possible to expand your comparison/contrast and accomplish your stated purpose.
5. Deal with all aspects of the comparison that are relevant to the purpose.
6. Balance the treatment of the different subjects of your comparison (i.e., don't spend more time on one than on another).
7. Determine your audience's background and knowledge so you will know how much of your comparison should be explained in detail and how much can be skimmed over.

Next, in preparation for a comparison/contrast project, you might list all the elements of both subjects that you want to compare. This list can then help give your essay structure as well as substance. At this stage in the writing process, the task may seem similar to pure description, but a discussion of two subjects in relation to one another rapidly changes the assignment from description to comparison.

Writing. The introduction of a comparison/contrast essay should (1) clearly identify your subjects, (2) explain the basis of your comparison/contrast, and (3) state your purpose and the overall limits of your particular study. Identifying your subject is, of course, a necessary and important task in any essay. Similarly, justifying the elements you will be comparing and contrasting creates reader interest and gives your audience some specifics to look for in the essay. Finally, your statement of purpose or thesis (for example, to prove that one professor is superior to another) should include the boundaries of your discussion. You cannot cover all the reasons for your preference in one short essay, so you must limit your consideration to three or four basic categories (perhaps teaching techniques, clarity of assignments given, classroom attitude, and grading standards). The introduction is the place to make all these limits known.

The body of your paper can be organized in one of four ways: (1) a point-by-point or alternating comparison, (2) a subject-by-subject or divided comparison, (3) a combination of these two methods, or (4) a division between the similarities and differences.

The point-by-point comparison evaluates both subjects in terms of each category. If the issue, for example, is which of two cars to buy, you might discuss both models' gasoline mileage first, then their horsepower, next their ease in handling, and finally their standard equipment. Following the second method of organization, subject by subject, you would discuss the gasoline mileage, horsepower, ease in handling, and standard equipment of car A first, then follow the same format for car B. The third option would allow you to introduce, say, the interior design of each car point by point (or car by car) and then explain the mechanical features of the automobiles (MPG, horsepower, gear ratio, and braking system) subject by subject. To use the last method of organization, you might discuss the similarities between the two models first and the differences second (or vice versa). If the cars you are comparing have similar MPG ratings but completely different horsepower, steering systems, and optional equipment, you could discuss the gasoline mileage first and then emphasize the differences by mentioning them later in the essay. If, instead, you are trying to emphasize the fact that the MPG of these models remains consistent despite their differences, then reverse the order of your essay.

Methods of Organization

Point by Point	Subject by Subject
MPG, car A MPG, car B horsepower, car A horsepower, car B handling, car A handling, car B	MPG, car A horsepower, car A handling, car A equipment, car A MPG, car B horsepower, car B handling, car B equipment, car B

Combination	Similarities/Differences
Interior, car A Interior, car B ——— MPG, car A horsepower, car A MPG, car B horsepower, car B	similarities: MPG, car A & B differences: MPG, car A & B horsepower, car A & B handling, car A & B equipment, car A & B

When confronted with the task of choosing a method of organization for a comparison/contrast essay, you need to find the pattern that best suits your purpose. If you want single items to stand out in a discussion, for instance, the best choice will be the point-by-point system; it is especially appropriate for long essays but has a tendency to turn into an exercise in listing if you don't pay careful attention to your transitions. If, however, the subjects themselves (rather than the itemized points) are the most interesting feature of your essay, you should use the subject-by-subject comparison; this system is particularly good for short essays in which the readers can retain what was said about one subject while they read about a second subject. Through this second system of organization, both subjects become unified wholes, which is generally a positive feature of an essay unless the theme becomes awkwardly divided into two separate parts. You must also remember, if you choose this second method of organization, that the second (or last) subject is in the most emphatic position, because that is what your readers will have seen most recently. The final two options for organizing a comparison/contrast essay give you some built-in flexibility so you can create emphasis and attempt to manipulate reader opinion simply by the structure of your essay.

Using logical transitions in your comparison/contrast essays will establish clear relationships between the items in your comparisons and will also move your readers smoothly from one topic to the next. If you wish to indicate comparisons, use such words as "like," "as," "also," "in like manner," "similarly," and "in addition"; to signal contrasts, try "but," "in contrast to," "unlike," "whereas," and "on the one hand/on the other hand."

The conclusion of a comparison/contrast essay summarizes the main points and states the deductions drawn from those points. As you choose your method of organization, remember not to get locked into a formulaic approach to your subjects, which will adversely affect the readability of your essay. To avoid making your reader feel like a spectator at a verbal ping-pong match, be straightforward, honest, and patient as you discover and recount the details of your comparison.

Rewriting. When you review the draft of your comparison/contrast essay, you need once again to make sure that you communicate your purpose as effectively as possible to your intended audience. Three guidelines previously mentioned should help you accomplish this goal: Do you identify your subjects clearly? Do you explain the basis of your comparison/contrast? Does your thesis clearly state the purpose and overall limits of your particular study?

You will also need to pay close attention to the development of your essay: Are you attempting to compare/contrast items from the same general category? Do you discuss the same qualities for each subject? Do you use as many pertinent details as possible to expand your essay? Do you deal with all aspects of the topic that are relevant to your purpose? Do you balance the treatment of the different subjects of your essay? Did you organize your topic as effectively as possible?

Student Essay: Comparison/Contrast at Work

The following student essay compares the advantages and disadvantages of macaroni and cheese versus tacos in the life of a harried college freshman. As you read it, notice how the writer states his intention in the first paragraph and then expands his discussion with appropriate details to produce a balanced essay. Also, try to determine what effect he creates by using two methods of organization: first subject by subject, then point by point.

Dormitory Chef

Back-ground   To this day, I will not eat either macaroni and cheese or tacos. No, it's not because of any allergy; it's because during my freshman year at college, I prepared one or the other of these scrumptious dishes more times than I care to remember. <u>However, my choice of which</u> Thesis <u>culinary delight to cook on any given night was not as</u> statement <u>simple a decision as one might imagine.</u>

Paragraph on Subject A: Macaroni and cheese   Macaroni and cheese has numerous advantages Point 1 for the dormitory chef. <u>First of all, it is inexpensive</u>. (Price) No matter how poor one may be, there's probably enough change under the couch cushion to buy a box at the market. All that starch for only 89¢. What a Point 2 bargain! <u>Second, it can be prepared in just one pan</u>. (Preparation) This is especially important given the meager resources Point 3 of the average dorm kitchen. <u>Third, and perhaps most</u> (Odor) <u>important, macaroni and cheese is odorless</u>. By odorless, I mean that no one else can smell it. It is a well-known fact that dorm residents hate to cook and that they love nothing better than to wander dejectedly around the kitchen with big, sad eyes after someone else has been cooking. But with macaroni and cheese, no enticing aromas are going to find their way into the nose of any would-be mooch.

Paragraph on Subject B: Tacos   Tacos, <u>on the other hand</u>, are a different matter Transition altogether. For the dorm cook, <u>the most significant dif-</u> Point 1 <u>ference is obviously the price</u>. To enjoy tacos for din- (Price) ner, the adventurous dorm gourmet must purchase no fewer than five ingredients from the market: corn tortillas, beef, lettuce, tomatoes, and cheese. Needless to say, this is a major expenditure. <u>Second, the chef must</u> Point 2 <u>adroitly shuffle these ingredients back and forth</u> (Preparation) <u>among his very limited supply of pans and bowls. And</u> tion) <u>finally, tacos smell great</u>. That wouldn't be a problem Point 3 if the tacos didn't also smell great to about twenty of (Odor) the cook's newest—if not closest—friends, who appear with those same pathetic, starving eyes mentioned earlier. When this happens, the cook will be lucky to get more than two of his own creations.

Transition   Tacos, then, wouldn't stand much of a chance if   Subject B
they didn't outdo macaroni and cheese in one area—   Subject A
Paragraph taste. Taste is almost—but not quite—an optional
on Point requirement in the opinion of a frugal dormitory hash-
4: Taste slinger. Taste is just important enough so that tacos are occasionally prepared, despite their disadvantages.

Transition   But tacos have other advantages besides their   Subject B
taste. With their enticing, colorful ingredients, they
Paragraph even look good. The only thing that can be said about
on Point the color of macaroni and cheese is that it's a color not   Subject A
5: Color found in nature.

Transition   On the other hand, macaroni and cheese is quick.   Subject A
It can be prepared in about ten minutes, while tacos
Paragraph take more than twice as long. And there are occa-
on Point sions—such as final exam week—when time is a scarce   Subject B
6: Time and precious resource.

Transition   As you can see, quite a bit of thinking went into
my choice of food in my younger years. These two
dishes essentially got me through my freshman year
and indirectly taught me how to make important deci-
sions (like what to eat). But I still feel a certain revul-   Concluding
sion when I hear their names today.   statement

Student Writer's Comments

I compare and contrast so many times during ordinary thoughts that I took this rhetorical technique for granted; I overlooked it. Just be sure that there are enough parallel points in the subjects you want to compare, and then apply the same logic you use every day. The most difficult part of writing this essay was finding two appropriate topics to compare. Ideally, they should be united by a similarity. For example, macaroni and cheese and tacos are two very different kinds of food. Proving this fact is easy and doesn't provide for an interesting essay. But their similar property of being popular dorm foods unites the two despite their differences. This similarity supplies the basic structure for the entire essay. It is the common theme against which I compared these two different topics.

Some Final Thoughts on Comparison/Contrast

The essays in this section demonstrate various methods of organiza-
tion as well as a number of distinct stylistic approaches to writing a comparison/contrast essay. As you read these selections, pay particular attention to the clear, well-focused introductions; the different logical methods of organization; and the smooth transitions between sentences and paragraphs.

Neat People vs. Sloppy People

Susan Britt

I've finally figured out the difference between neat people and sloppy people. The distinction is, as always, moral. Neat people are lazier and meaner than sloppy people.

Sloppy people, you see, are not really sloppy. Their sloppiness is merely the unfortunate consequence of their extreme moral rectitude. Sloppy people carry in their mind's eye a heavenly vision, a precise plan, that is so stupendous, so perfect, it can't be achieved in this world or the next.

Sloppy people live in Never-Never-Land. Someday is their metier. Someday they are planning to alphabetize all their books and set up home catalogues. Someday they will go through their wardrobes and mark certain items for tentative mending and certain items for passing on to relatives of similar shape and size. Someday sloppy people will make family scrapbooks into which they will put newspaper clippings, postcards, locks of hair, and the dried corsage from their senior prom. Someday they will file everything on the surface of their desks, including the cash receipts from coffee purchases at the snack shop. Someday they will sit down and read all the back issues of *The New Yorker*.

For all these noble reasons and more, sloppy people never get neat. They aim too high and wide. They save everything, planning someday to file, order, and straighten out the world. But while these ambitious plans take clearer and clearer shape in their heads, the books spill from the shelves onto the floor, the clothes pile up in the hamper and closet, the family mementos accumulate in every drawer, the surface of the desk is buried under mounds of paper, and the unread magazines threaten to reach the ceiling.

Sloppy people can't bear to part with anything. They give loving attention to every detail. When sloppy people say they're going to tackle the surface of the desk, they really mean it. Not a paper will go unturned; not a rubber band will go unboxed. Four hours or two weeks into the excavation, the desk looks exactly the same, primarily because the sloppy person is meticulously creating new piles of papers with new headings and scrupulously stopping to read all the old book catalogues before he throws them away. A neat person would just bulldoze the desk.

Neat people are bums and clods at heart. They have cavalier attitudes toward possessions, including family heirlooms. Everything is just another dust-catcher to them. If anything collects dust, it's got to go and that's that. Neat people will toy with the idea of throwing the children out of the house just to cut down the clutter.

Neat people don't care about process. They like results. What they want to do is get the whole thing over with so they can sit down and watch the rasslin' on TV. Neat people operate on two unvarying principles: Never handle any item twice, and throw everything away.

The only thing messy in a neat person's house is the trash can. The minute something comes to a neat person's hand, he will look at it, try to decide if it has immediate use and, finding none, throw it in the trash.

Neat people are especially vicious with mail. They never go through their mail unless they are standing directly over a trash can. If the trash can is beside the mailbox, even better. All ads, catalogues, pleas for charitable contributions, church bulletins, and money-saving coupons go straight into the trash can without being opened. All letters from home, postcards from Europe, bills and paychecks are opened, immediately responded to, then dropped in the trash can. Neat people keep their receipts only for tax purposes. That's it. No sentimental salvaging of birthday cards or the last letter a dying relative ever wrote. Into the trash it goes.

Neat people place neatness above everything, even economics. They are incredibly wasteful. Neat people throw away several toys every time they walk through the den. I knew a neat person once who threw away a perfectly good dish drainer because it had mold on it. The drainer was too much trouble to wash. And neat people sell their furniture when they move. They will sell a La-Z-Boy recliner while you are reclining in it.

Neat people are no good to borrow from. Neat people buy everything in expensive little single portions. They get their flour and sugar in two-pound bags. They wouldn't consider clipping a coupon, saving a leftover, reusing plastic nondairy whipped cream containers, or rinsing off tin foil and draping it over the unmoldy dish drainer. You can never borrow a neat person's newspaper to see what's playing at the movies. Neat people have the paper all wadded up and in the trash by 7:05 A.M.

Neat people cut a clean swath through the organic as well as the inorganic world. People, animals, and things are all one to them. They are so insensitive. After they've finished with the pantry, the medicine cabinet, and the attic, they will throw out the red geranium (too many leaves), sell the dog (too many fleas), and send the children off to boarding school (too many scuff marks on the hardwood floors).

Nursing Practices—England and America

Mary Madden

I left my native Ireland after I had completed a high school education. I studied to become a nurse and midwife in England, and I eventually came to the United States of America. Because I have worked five years in hospitals in England and the U.S.A., my friends frequently ask about differences, as I see them, in the practice of nursing on both sides of the Atlantic.

Until I realized how different the licensing laws of Great Britain are from those in the United States, I was surprised at the number of restrictions placed on a nurse's actions in this country. A nurse licensed in Britain may practice anywhere in the British Isles and in some countries abroad; in the United States, the nurse must apply in every state in which she hopes to work.

In Britain, a nurse is a deeply respected, devoted woman, entrusted with a vast amount of responsibility. The patients place unquestioned confidence in her judgment and advice. The doctor relies on her report of her observations, and he seldom interferes in what is considered a nursing duty.

The nurse decides when the patient is allowed out of bed or what type of bath he may have. I do not recall ever seeing an order on a physician's chart such as "OOR in 24 hours" or "may take a shower." The nurse judges when a wound is healed and when sutures may be removed. She is always consulted about the patient's requirements and his progress. And because of the structure of most hopitals in England, the nurse is in view of the patient constantly. Whenever he needs attention, the nurse is there in the ward, and she may observe him, too, unobtrusively.

Furthermore, the nurse is a member of the health team who sees the patient most frequently. To the patient she is the most familiar person in the strange hospital world.

In the United States, the patient is likely to be under the care of the same doctor in and out of the hospital, so the doctor is the person the patient knows best and the one in whom he confides most easily. But though the patient's treatment and care are discussed with the nursing staff, a nurse is not allowed much freedom to advise a patient. Also, I have seen doctors visit patients without a word of communication to the nurse. Personally I think it difficult to be ignored when a patient's care is concerned and I think it prevents full utilization of the nurse's knowledge and skills.

I myself found nursing practice easier, in a way, under the so-called "socialized medicine" of Great Britain than the more individual type of medical care found in the United States. It involved much less writing and left me at the patient's bedside, where I am happiest. There was no need to write several charges and requests for the needs of the patient. Stocks of drugs and other medicines were kept on each ward, so that when medication was ordered, it was at hand. All charges were met by "National Health"— including all supplies and equipment used on the ward. The nurse tends a person who is free from much anxiety and hence more easily cared for while he is an inpatient.

On the other hand, I found that my introduction to an American hospital was a happy experience. As a new nurse, I was guided by an orientation program given by another nurse and quickly found my place on the patient care team. I had never experienced such an orientation in England.

Policy, drug reference, and procedure books at the nurses' station provide a ready reference where a nurse may check facts when she is in doubt, and she can instruct a new nurse on the staff without confusion. The active U.S. nurse, while working, can keep informed about new trends, discoveries, and inventions in a rapidly changing world of medicine.

Here in the United States the nurse is regarded as an individual person and her personal life outside the hospital is given consideration. She develops interests in arts, sport or a creative hobby; she is encouraged to further her education. Time and means are available to her to expand her horizons and to enrich her personality. Many nurses combine marriage and a career very ably in this country, but not in England or Ireland. All this tends to involve her more with people other than the sick. She is an interesting, informed, and happy person and at the bedside she can show understanding and perception.

In Britain, like most nurses, I lived in a nurses' home on the hospital grounds and was thus isolated in a special hospital community. Theoretically I worked eight hours each day that I was on duty. But these hours were so arranged that one went to work twice in one day. One might work four hours in the morning, have a few hours free, and then go back to the ward for the evening. This schedule demands most of one's waking hours, and so mingling in the larger community outside the hospital was quite limited. The nurse was expected to find full satisfaction in her vocation, and thoughts of increases in salary were considered unworthy. Now, such attitudes are beginning to change and the winds of unrest are blowing through nursing in England, ruffling many a well-placed cap.

Grant and Lee: A Study in Contrasts

Bruce Catton

When Ulysses S. Grant and Robert E. Lee met in the parlor of a modest house at Appomattox Court House, Virginia, on April 9, 1865, to work out the terms for the surrender of Lee's Army of Northern Virginia, a great chapter in American life came to a close, and a great new chapter began.

These men were bringing the Civil War to its virtual finish. To be sure, other armies had yet to surrender, and for a few days the fugitive Confederate government would struggle desperately and vainly, trying to find some way to go on living now that its chief support was gone. But in effect it was all over when Grant and Lee signed the papers. And the little room where they wrote out the terms was the scene of one of the poignant, dramatic contrasts in American history.

They were two strong men, these oddly different generals, and they represented the strengths of two conflicting currents that, through them, had come into final collision.

Back of Robert E. Lee was the notion that the old aristocratic concept might somehow survive and be dominant in American life.

Lee was tidewater Virginia, and in his background were family, culture, and tradition . . . the age of chivalry transplanted to a New World which was making its own legends and its own myths. He embodied a way of life that had come down through the age of knighthood and the English country squire. America was a land that was beginning all over again, dedicated to nothing much more complicated than the rather hazy belief that all men had equal rights and should have an equal chance in the world. In such a land Lee stood for the feeling that it was somehow of advantage to human society to have a pronounced inequality in the social structure. There should be a leisure class, backed by ownership of land; in turn, society itself should be keyed to the land as the chief source of wealth and influence. It would bring forth (according to this ideal) a class of men with a strong sense of obligation to the community; men who lived not to gain advantage for themselves, but to meet the solemn obligations which had been laid on them by the very fact that they were privileged. From them the country would get its leadership; to them it could look for the higher values—of thought, of conduct, of personal deportment—to give it strength and virtue.

Lee embodied the noblest elements of this aristocratic ideal. Through him, the landed nobility justified itself. For four years, the Southern states had fought a desperate war to uphold the ideals for which Lee stood. In the end, it almost seemed as if the Confederacy fought for Lee; as if he himself was the Confederacy . . . the best thing that the way of life for which the Confederacy stood could ever have to offer. He had passed into legend before Appomattox. Thousands of tired, underfed, poorly clothed Confederate soldiers, long since past the simple enthusiasm of the early days of the struggle, somehow considered Lee the symbol of everything for which they had been willing to die. But they could not quite put this feeling into words. If the Lost Cause, sanctified by so much heroism and so many deaths, had a living justification, its justification was General Lee.

Grant, the son of a tanner on the Western frontier, was everything Lee was not. He had come up the hard way and embodied nothing in particular except the eternal toughness and sinewy fiber of the men who grew up beyond the mountains. He was one of a body of men who owed reverence and obeisance to no one, who were self-reliant to a fault, who cared hardly anything for the past but who had a sharp eye for the future.

These frontier men were the precise opposites of the tidewater aristocrats. Back of them, in the great surge that had taken people over the Alleghenies and into the opening Western country, there was a deep, implicit dissatisfaction with a past that had settled into grooves. They stood for democracy, not from any reasoned conclusion about the proper ordering of human society, but simply because they had grown up in the middle of democracy and knew how it worked. Their society might have privileges, but they would be privileges each man had won for himself. Forms and patterns meant nothing. No man was born to anything, except perhaps to a chance to show how far he could rise. Life was competition.

Yet along with this feeling had come a deep sense of belonging to a national community. The Westerner who developed a farm, opened a shop, or set up in business as a trader, could hope to prosper only as his won community prospered—and his community ran from the Atlantic to the Pacific and from Canada down to Mexico. If the land was settled, with towns and highways and accessible markets, he could better himself. He saw his fate in terms of the nation's own destiny. As its horizons expanded, so did his. He had, in other words, an acute dollars-and-cents stake in the continued growth and development of his country.

And that, perhaps, is where the contrast between Grant and Lee becomes most striking. The Virginia aristocrat, inevitably, saw himself in relation to his own region. He lived in a static society which could endure almost anything except change. Instinctively, his first loyalty would go to the locality in which that society existed. He would fight to the limit of endurance to defend it, because in defending it he was defending everything that gave his own life its deepest meaning.

The Westerner, on the other hand, would fight with an equal tenacity for the broader concept of society. He fought so because everything he lived by was tied to growth, expansion, and a constantly widening horizon. What he lived by would survive or fall with the nation itself. He could not possibly stand by unmoved in the face of an attempt to destroy the Union. He would combat it with everything he had, because he could only see it as an effort to cut the ground out from under his feet.

So Grant and Lee were in complete contrast, representing two diametrically opposed elements in American life. Grant was the modern man emerging; beyond him, ready to come on the stage, was the great age of steel and machinery, of crowded cities and a restless burgeoning vitality. Lee might have ridden down from the old age of chivalry, lance in hand, silken banner fluttering over his head. Each man was the perfect champion of his cause, drawing both his strengths and his weaknesses from the people he led.

Yet it was not all contrast, after all. Different as they were—in background, in personality, in underlying aspiration—these two great soldiers had much in common. Under everything else, they were marvelous fighters. Furthermore, their fighting qualities were really very much alike.

Each man had, to begin with, the great virtue of utter tenacity and fidelity. Grant fought his way down the Mississippi Valley in spite of acute personal discouragement and profound military handicaps. Lee hung on in the trenches at Petersburg after hope itself had died. In each man there was an indomitable quality . . . the born fighter's refusal to give up as long as he can still remain on his feet and lift his two fists.

Daring and resourcefulness they had, too; the ability to think faster and move faster than the enemy. These were the qualities which gave Lee the dazzling campaigns of Second Manassas and Chancellorsville and won Vicksburg for Grant.

Lastly, and perhaps greatest of all, there was the ability, at the end, to turn quickly from war to peace once the fighting was over. Out of the way these two men behaved at Appomattox came the possibility of a peace of reconciliation. It was a possibility not wholly realized, in the years to come, but which did, in the end, help the two sections to become one nation again . . . after a war whose bitterness might have seemed to make such a reunion wholly impossible. No part of either man's life became him more than the part he played in this brief meeting in the McLean house at Appomattox. Their behavior there put all succeeding generations of Americans in their debt. Two great Americans, Grant and Lee—very different, yet under everything very much alike. Their encounter at Appomattox was one of the great moments of American history.

Second Thoughts on the Information Highway

Cliff Stoll

Surely you've heard the predictions of our future digital age: "Multimedia will revolutionize the classroom," "Interactive electronic information will make books obsolete," "Businesses will flock to the computer networks for instant, low cost information. Visionaries see a future of telecommuting office workers, interactive libraries, and multimedia classrooms. They speak of electronic town meetings and virtual communities. Commerce and business will shift from offices and malls to networks and modems. Electronic mail will replace slow and inefficient snail mail. And thanks to the freedom of electronic networks, government will become profoundly democratic and efficient.

Such claims are utterly bogus. These glowing predictions of a digital nirvana make me wonder if some lemming-like madness has cursed our technologists. Do our computer pundits lack all common sense? I'm astonished at the wide gulf between their utopian dreams and the dreary reality that pours into my modem.

The truth is that no online database will replace your daily newspaper, no CD-ROM can take the place of a competent teacher, and no computer network will change the way government works. Work has never been easy; learning isn't painless, and bureaucracies have never been quick to change. The computer ain't gonna do it for you.

Consider today's online world. The Usenet, a worldwide bulletin board, allows anyone to post messages across the globe. Your word gets out, leapfrogging editors and publishers. Every voice can be heard cheaply and instantly. The result is that every voice is heard. The resultant cacophony more closely resembles Citizen Band Radio, complete with handles, harassment, and anonymous threats. When most everyone shouts, few listen.

How about electronic publishing? Try reading a book on your monitor. At best, it's an unpleasant chore: the myopic glow of a clunky computer replaces the friendly pages of a book. And you can't tote that laptop to the beach or leave it in your car—it'll get stolen. Yet Nicholas Negroponte, director of the MIT Media Center, predicts that we'll soon buy books straight over the Internet. Uh, sure.

What the Internet hucksters won't tell you is that the World Wide Web is an ocean of unedited data, without any pretense of completeness. Lacking editors, reporters, reviewers, or critics, the Internet has become a wasteland of unreviewed, unedited, unfiltered data. You don't know what to ignore and what's worth reading.

Logged onto the World Wide Web, I hunt for the date of the battle of Trafalgar. Hundreds of files show up, including Napoleon.txt, Trafalg.zip, and J41N32.gif. It takes fifteen minutes to unravel them—one's a biography written by an 8th grader, the second is a computer game that doesn't work, and the third is an image of a London monument. None answer my question, and my search is periodically interrupted by messages like, "Too many connections, try again later." This searching is a great way to waste time but hardly an efficient research tool.

Won't the Internet be useful in governing? Internet addicts clamor for government reports to be uploaded to the networks. But when Andy Speno ran for County Executive in Westchester County, NY, he put every press release and position paper onto a bulletin board. In that affluent county, with plenty of computer companies, how many voters logged in? Fewer than thirty did. This is hardly a good omen for the electronic democracy.

The strongest hype comes from those who are forcing computers into schools. We're told that multimedia and interactive video systems will make learning easy and schoolwork fun. Students will happily learn from animated characters while being taught by expertly tailored software. Teachers won't be as essential when we have computer-aided education.

Bah. These expensive toys are difficult to use in classrooms, require extensive teacher preparation, and waste what few dollars trickle into schools. Sure, kids love to play video games—but think of your own experience: Can you recall even one educational filmstrip of decades past? I'll bet you remember the two or three great teachers who made a difference in your life.

Cyberbusiness? We're promised instant catalog shopping—just point and click for great deals. We'll order airline tickets over the network, make restaurant reservations, and negotiate sales contracts. Stores will become obsolete. So how come my local mall does more business in an afternoon than the entire Internet handles in a month? Even if there were a trustworthy way to send money over the network—which there isn't—the networks are missing a most essential ingredient of capitalism: salespeople. Without the personal attention and human interactions of good salesfolk, the Internet can't blossom into an electronic shopping mail.

What's missing from this electronic wonderland? Human contact. Discount the fawning technoburble about virtual communities—computers and networks isolate us from each other. A network chat line is a limp substitute for meeting friends over coffee. No interactive multimedia display comes close to the excitement of a live concert. And who'd prefer cybersex to the real thing?

Is it likely that you can enjoy a rich online world and a plentiful personal life? Nope. Every hour that you spend linked through your modem is sixty minutes that you're not visiting with your friends or shagging fly balls with the kid down the block. While the Internet beckons brightly, seductively flashing an icon of knowledge-as-power, this non-place lures us to surrender our time on Earth. A poor substitute it is, this virtual reality where frustration is legion and where—in the holy names of Education and Progress—important aspects of human interactions are relentlessly devalued.

Get a Life?

Nicholas Negroponte

Any significant social phenomenon creates a backlash. The Net is no exception. It is odd, however, that the loudest complaints are shouts of "Get a life!"—suggesting that online living will dehumanize us, insulate us, and create a world of people who won't smell flowers, watch sunsets, or engage in face-to-face experiences. Out of this backlash comes a warning to parents that their children will "cocoon" and metamorphose into social invalids.

Experience tells us the opposite. So far, evidence gathered by those using the Net as a teaching tool indicates that kids who go online gain social skills rather than lose them. Since the distance between Athens, Georgia, and Athens, Greece, is just a mouse click away, children attain a new kind of worldliness. Young people on the Net today will intevitably experience some of the sophistication of Europe. In earlier days, only children from élite families could afford to interact with European culture during their summer vacations abroad.

I know that visiting Web pages in Italy or interacting with Italians via e-mail isn't the same as ducking the pigeons or listening to music in Piazza San Marco—but it sure beats never going there at all. Take all the books in the world, and they won't offer the real-time global experience a kid can get on the Net: here a child becomes the driver of the intellectual vehicle, not the passenger.

Mitch Resnick of the MIT Media Lab recently told me of an autistic boy who has great difficulty interacting with people, often giving inappropriate visual cues (like strange facial expressions) and so forth. But this child has thrived on the Net. When he types, he gains control and becomes articulate. He's an active participant in chat rooms and newsgroups. He has developed strong online friendships, which have given him greater confidence in face-to-face situations.

It's an extreme case, but isn't it odd how parents grieve if their child spends six hours a day on the Net but delight if those same hours are spent reading books? With the exception of sleep, doing anything six hours a day, every day, is not good for a child.

Adults on the Net enjoy even greater opportunity, as more people discover they can work from almost anywhere. Granted, if you make pizzas you need to be close to the dough; if you're a surgeon you must be close to your patients (at least for the next two decades). But if your trade involves bits (not atoms), you probably don't need to be anywhere specific—at least most of the time. In fact, it might be beneficial all around if you were in the Caribbean or Mediterranean—then your company wouldn't have to tie up capital in expensive downtown real estate.

Certain early users of the Net (bless them!) are now whining about its vulgarization, warning people of its hazards as if it were a cigarette. If only these whiners were more honest, they'd admit that it was they who didn't have much of a life and found solace on the Net, they who woke up one day with midlife crises and discovered there was more to living than what was waiting in their e-mail boxes. So, what took you guys so long? Of course there's more to life than e-mail, but don't project your empty existence onto others and suggest "being digital" is a form of virtual leprosy for which total abstinence is the only immunization.

My own lifestyle is totally enhanced by being online. I've been a compulsive e-mail user for more than 25 years; more often than not, it's allowed me to spend more time in scenic places with interesting people. Which would you prefer: two weeks' vacation totally offline or four to six weeks online? This doesn't work for all professions, but it is a growing trend among so-called "knowledge workers."

Once, only the likes of Rupert Murdoch or Aga Khan could cut deals from their satellite-laden luxury yachts off the coast of Sardinia. Now all sorts of people from Tahoe to Telluride can work from the back seat of a Winnebago if they wish.

I don't know the statistics, but I'm willing to guess that the executives of corporate America spend 70 to 80 percent of their time in meetings. I *do* know that most of those meetings, often a canonical one hour long, are 70 to 80 percent posturing and leveling (bringing the others up to speed on a common subject). The posturing is gratuitous, and the leveling is better done elsewhere—online, for example. This alone would enhance US productivity far more than any trade agreement.

I am constantly astonished by just how offline corporate America is. Wouldn't you expect executives at computer and communications companies to be active online? Even household names of the high-tech industry are *offline* human beings, sometimes more so than execs in extremely low-tech fields. I guess this is a corollary to the shoemaker's children having no shoes.

Being online not only makes the inevitable face-to-face meetings so much easier—it allows you to look outward. Generally, large companies are so inwardly directed that staff memorandums about growing bureaucracy get more attention than the dwindling competitive advantage of being big in the first place. David, who has a life, needn't use a slingshot. Goliath, *who doesn't*, is too busy reading office memos.

In the mid-1700s, mechanical looms and other machines forced cottage industries out of business. Many people lost the opportunity to be their own bosses and to enjoy the profits of hard work. I'm sure I would have been a Luddite under those conditions.

But the current sweep of digital living is doing exactly the opposite. Parents of young children find exciting self-employment from home. The "virtual corporation" is an opportunity for tiny companies (with employees spread across the world) to work together in a global market and set up base wherever they choose. If you don't like centralist thinking, big companies, or job automation, what better place to go than the Net? Work for yourself and get a life.

Kansas vs. Hawaii

Student

Imagine you are lying in bed. It is a warm and humid night. You feel a faint breeze and hear a distant rhythmic roar. Where could you be? You could be in a beach front home with the seaward house vents open, listening to the distant pulsating of the Pacific Ocean on the shore. Or, you could be in a suburban home in the middle of the heartland with the ceiling fans on, listening to the distant roar of a nearby busy road in late spring. From personal experience, it is amazing how similar these two sensations are. Even though Kansas and Hawaii do share some similar attributes, when it comes to comparing their overall sceneries, cultures, and weather patterns, their vast differences become apparent.

For instance, Kansas and Hawaii's sceneries contrast in quality and physical attributes. Kansas stands out with its vast flat lands, many lakes, and seasonally varied vegetation. In particular, the flat lands and rolling hills of Kansas allow you to drive long scenic distances and view beautiful multi-colored sunsets. You can travel in all directions for hundreds and thousands of miles viewing the countryside before even reaching an ocean. In addition, the flat lands provide an excellent stage in displaying the gorgeous Kansas sunsets. Specifically, prairie sunsets are more dramatic than ocean sunsets because of the increase of dust particles in the air that intensify the brilliant colors of the sun's final rays. Another feature Kansas has is its many fresh water lakes that are available for recreational purposes. Furthermore, Kansas distinctively stands out with the ability to naturally support the growth of grass and deciduous trees due to having a season where they can die and regenerate. The growth of grass is widespread and naturally common along most roadways. Also, deciduous leaf trees are abundant in Kansas which provides a dynamic array of beautiful colors to enjoy in the Fall season.

Meanwhile, Hawaii's scenery is distinctively different from Kansas with its island attributes, volcanic mountains, and tropical vegetation. Since Hawaii is made up of several small islands, the road systems are limited and the chances of coming across a beach or ocean cliff shore is inevitable. In Hawaii, it is hard to become lost on the roads because typically there is only one main artery that circles the island along with a few internal public roadways. Due to the island attributes, there are no shortages of beautiful beaches and majestic ocean cliffs to view. The beaches provide a relaxing setting for observing the hypnotizing waves on the sand or the crashing breakers against the reefs. The many remnants of volcanoes are another unique and contrasting aspect of the Hawaiian islands. Hawaii is spotted with gorgeous volcanic ridges, craters and mountains that have in turn created additional scenic wonders, such as, natural waterfalls. Also, Hawaii consists of large exotic tropical forests that are wondrous to experience. The lush, thick vegetation, that includes palm trees and unbelievably beautiful and aromatic flowers, is abundant because of Hawaii's climate. This same climate, however, hampers Hawaii from growing grass on any large scale since there is no distinct change of season for it to repopulate.

Along with the scenic differences, Kansas and Hawaii culturally differ in their ethnic demographics, traditional activities, and native foods. First, the ethnic demographics of Kansas do not vary dramatically due to its geographical location. Approximately 90% of the population in Kansas are White. Since Kansas is in the middle of the United States, it is not prone to large settlement of differing nationalities. In addition, some of the activities that typify the culture of Kansas can be seen in the large number of rodeos and barbecues Kansas entertains. The rodeo events carry a historic heritage of the Old West which Kansas appears to take pride in identifying with, as evident in one particular event, the American Royal. Furthermore, the barbecue events are a way of life for Kansans. In the summertime, it is rare to go one week without hearing of a formal barbecuing contest or a friendly barbecue gathering. Another way in which Kansas differs is in the types of food that it can abundantly produce. In Kansas, there are a large number of ranches and farms that raise beef and grow various kinds of grains and vegetables.

In contrast, Hawaii's cultural aspects differ from Kansas. Demographically, Hawaii's population is over 60% Asian. This large Asian population is mainly due to Hawaii's location in the western part of the Pacific Ocean. Besides the ethnic structure, Hawaii's culture differs in the activities that are typified by their tribal dance performances and beach activities. A large portion of the native population appears to take pride in sharing the Hawaiian culture through the various island tribe dances. In the two weeks I stayed in Hawaii, I did not come across a day that I was not eagerly given instructions or had not viewed a demonstration of the various Pacific tribe dances. In addition, Hawaii is renowned for its treacherous surfs on the North Shore. According to a prior Hawaiian roommate of mine, spending time at the beach, both in and out of the water, is a way of life for many native Hawaiians. Moreover, Hawaii's culture differs in the types of native foods that can be abundantly produced and harvested. In Hawaii, the main native foods come from either plantations, which harvest all types of tropical fruits; or the ocean, where fishermen are able to catch large quantities of seafood.

Furthermore, Kansas and Hawaii's weather differ in their climatic features, such as temperatures, precipitations, and severest storm types. In Kansas, for example, you will experience a seasonal change in temperature. In one day, it is not uncommon for the temperature to change up to thirty degrees. These fluctuations, both daily and seasonally, open up the need for Kansans to keep a varied wardrobe to meet the possible hundred degree heats of summer to the sub-zero cold of winter. Similarly, the types of precipitation and their duration appear more extreme in Kansas. In Kansas you can have rain, sleet, hail, and snow. Also, the storms that produce these various degrees of precipitations are typically more intense and last longer. In fact, there are times when I remember having not seen the sun and sky for weeks on end. Typically, the worst storms Kansans have to face are tornadoes. Tornadoes and their destructive funnel clouds are a factor that is typical of flat expanses of land mixed with high winds and violent storm conditions. Tornadoes are erratic and do not provide much advance notice to those in its path. Because of the characteristics of tornadoes, most homes in Kansas have basements that serve the dual purpose as shelters from these potentially deadly storms.

On the other hand, if you reside in Hawaii, you will experience moderate temperatures. The temperature fluctuates little throughout the year unless you travel between the leeward and windward side of the islands; even then, you may only experience about a five to ten degree change in temperature. Typically, the temperature on the islands averages around seventy to eighty degrees. Since the temperature does not vary widely, there is less of a need for Hawaiians to maintain a large seasonal wardrobe. Besides the temperature differences between the two states, the patterns of precipitation are not as extreme for Hawaii but do occur more often. On most given days, if you venture outside and you do not like the weather, there is hope. I have learned first hand that rain does not particularly mean a wasted day. Most of the time, you only have to wait about ten to fifteen minutes for a storm to move on and the sun to come out again. Or else, you can often drive from a cloudy windward coast to find sun at a leeward beach. The precipitation variances come into play because of the mixture of volcanic mountains and wind currents from the Pacific Ocean that often create sporadic rain showers.

In Hawaii, the severest storms you have to guard against are hurricanes. Even though these storms can approach the islands at a very fast pace, typically hurricanes provide the residents with some advance warning. Basements are not practical to guard against severe storms in Hawaii. In actuality, high ground is to a Hawaiian in a hurricane as a basement is to a Kansan in a tornado.

On the whole, I have grown to appreciate both Kansas and Hawaii for the unique qualities and the exciting contrasts they have provided in my life experiences. If I had to choose between living in either Kansas or Hawaii, I would have to choose Kansas because I have grown to love the natural beauty, culture and dramatic weather it has to offer.

A Comparison Between Business and the Life of the Non-Traditional Student

Student

I returned to college from a business career as a training manager in California, for a variety of reasons. During my year's time at DeVry, I've noticed many similarities and dissimilarities between business life and existence, a la DeVry. However, it is in the realms of responsibilities, management of time, and how others view me, that the differences and similarities seem most clear.

Perhaps the most crucial difference in responsibility between business and the student life is to whom you ultimately answer. All moralistic yearnings and sky high wishes aside, in business, the person who comes around every two weeks with that envelope filled with pictures of Presidents is your ultimate responsibility. He/she does rule your life, and by their nature and management style can dictate everything from the tone of your workday to the pace of your advancement, if any. In comparison, many students have only themselves to own up to. However, my situation is more akin to business. The millstones of pressure, lack of time and financial burdens are also around my wife's neck. Though not ultimately responsible to her, I am to us as a family. In this respect my situation is not all that dissimilar to the business arena.

The management of one's time may be the area that contains the most similarities between business and student life. This applies even more so to DeVry which is designed, it seems, to simulate business conditions. Business is fast paced and so is DeVry. I worked as a computer trainer and manager of a Customer Service district. Serving over 3,000 on-line customers in meetings, trainings, answering their questions and traveling all required diligent planning of my day-to-day schedule. I see no difference in my present life as a student. To try to get the massive amount of reading, projects, etc. done takes the same coordinating. In business you must set aside time for customers. Playing their games, courting them, buttering them up takes lots of time. It's the political side of business. Here my life as a student has no equivalent. However, one area where the two comparisons almost merge is the projects required. Though they're not the same type, the volume stayed the same. In business I had training manuals to write, or computer works to prepare for my bosses' meetings. They all took careful management of time and the management of my projects here is no different. The major disparity between the two in time allocation is the weekends. In my business, you could mostly count the weekends as your own. I have had very few of them since hoisting the student's banner. At least 75 percent of these dubiously named weekends are spent studying, preparing projects, etc. Though responsibilities and management of time strike a balance between differences and similarities, it is not so with the way I believe I'm seen by my peers.

Where I worked in California I was the baby. This even held true in my job before I started school. Everyone, including my co-workers, the secretaries, etc. was older. Now my associates weren't exactly museum pieces, but usually five years more advanced, at the least. To lightly understate the matter, this is not the case at DeVry. With two or three exceptions, I'm the oldest member of my class. This difference was and is a great jolt to me. I don't see myself as ready to be measured for the pine box, but some of my peers probably firmly believe I personally knew Abraham Lincoln, or at latest Franklin Roosevelt. In my first term, a student, obviously direct from wherever high school, seriously asked me if I wouldn't be too old to work after graduating. I never experienced this attitude in business. Usually if you can contribute to the bottom line you're accepted. I've known many business people who have followed this same course of returning to school for a second career. My experience from California says it's not frowned upon, but accepted. The line between this attitude and the student's view is different yet subtle. They accept it, but I sense because they are too young to have had a first career, they see returning, older students as ones who couldn't cut it in their first.

I don't have a preference between these two lifestyles. Business and the real world can honestly be the most exciting, boring and mundane existence imaginable, all in the same day. But, the life of learning, and experimentation of a student possesses the same blood pulsing and snore inducing qualities. The numbers of non-traditional students (that is what they call us now) will grow for social, economic and demographic reasons. Life and business in this country move and change with the pace of a Cheetah chasing prey. Learning and studying will likely be a constant for all American professionals from now on. Since I am equally adept at both lifestyles, I might have a jump on the competition.

Ch. 6: Comparison / Contrast

Suggestions for writing:

1. Complete the following sentence: "There are two types of people in this world: the_____ and the_____." Now write an essay or paragraph in which, through description and illustration, you compare and contrast these two types of people. Try substituting the word "teachers" or "parents" or "students" for the word "people."

2. Compare Kansas City to the town or city you moved here from. What are the three or four areas of greatest difference? Write an essay or paragraph in which you describe and illustrate these major differences.

3. Write a paragraph or an essay in which you compare and contrast one of the following topics or a similar topic:

    two schools you have attended   college vs. the military
    marriage vs. single life   two web sites
    two countries you have lived in   two movies with the same star
    city drivers vs. rural drivers   a good boss vs. a bad boss
    married with children vs. without   IBM vs. Apple

Comparison/contrast checklist:

1. Did you begin with a topic sentence (paragraph) or thesis statement (essay)?

2. Have you used specific criteria for contrast and comparison?

3. Have you organized your work point to point or topic to topic?

4. Have you arranged the major points within your text logically?

5. Did you use effective transitions within and between paragraphs?

6. Have you devoted about 50 percent of your paper to each of your two topics?

7. Have you given your reader a clear understanding of the similarities and differences that you are illustrating?

8. Did you vary your sentences and vocabulary?

9. Did you check for correctness of grammar, punctuation, and spelling?

CHAPTER 7

Cause / Effect

Tracing Reasons and Results

Using Cause/Effect

Wanting to know why things happen is one of our earliest, most basic instincts: Why can't I go out, Mommy? Why are you laughing? Why won't the dog stop barking? Why can't I swim faster than my big brother? These questions, and many more like them, reflect the innately inquisitive nature that dwells within each of us. Closely related to this desire to understand why is our corresponding interest in what will happen in the future as a result of some particular action: What will I feel like tomorrow if I stay up late tonight? How will I perform in the track meet Saturday if I practice all week? What will be the result if I mix together these two potent chemicals? What will happen if I turn in my next English assignment two days early?

A daily awareness of this intimate relationship between causes and effects allows us to begin to understand the complex and interrelated series of events that make up our lives and the lives of others. For example, trying to understand the various causes of the conflict in the Persian Gulf can teach us about international relations; knowing our biological reactions to certain foods will help us make decisions about what to eat; understanding the interrelated reasons for the outbreak of World War II offers us insight into historical trends and human nature; knowing the effects of sunshine on various parts of our bodies can help us make decisions about how much ultraviolet exposure we can tolerate and what suntan lotion to use; and understanding the causes of America's most recent recession will help us respond appropriately to the next economic crisis we encounter. More than anything else, tracing causes and effects teaches us how to think clearly and react intelligently to our multifaceted environment.

In college you will often be asked to use this natural interest in causes and effects to analyze particular situations and discern general principles. For example, you might be asked some of the following questions on essay exams in different courses:

> *Anthropology: Why did the Mayan culture disintegrate?*
> *Psychology: Why do humans respond to fear in different ways?*
> *Biology: How do lab rats react to caffeine?*
> *History: What were the positive effects of the Spanish-American War?*
> *Business: Why did so many computer manufacturing companies go bankrupt in the early 1980s?*

Your ability to answer such questions will depend in large part on your skill at writing a cause/effect essay.

Defining Cause/Effect

Cause/effect analysis requires the ability to look for connections between different elements and to analyze the reasons for those connections. As the name implies, this rhetorical mode has two separate components: cause and effect. A particular essay might concentrate on cause (Why do you live in a dorm?), on effect (What are the resulting advantages and disadvantages of living in a dorm?), or on some combination of the two. In working with causes, we are searching for any circumstances from the past that might have caused a single event; in looking for effects, we seek occurrences that took place after a particular event and resulted from that event. Like process analysis, cause/effect makes use of our intellectual ability to analyze. Process analysis addresses how something happens, whereas causal analysis discusses why it happened and what the result was. A process analysis paper, for example, might explain how to advertise more effectively to increase sales, whereas a cause/effect study would discover that three specific reasons contributed to the increase in sales: effective advertising, personal service, and selective discounts. The study of causes and effects, therefore, provides many different and helpful ways for humans to clarify their views of the world.

Looking for causes and effects requires an advanced form of thinking. It is more complex than most rhetorical strategies we have studied, because it can exist on a number of different and progressively more difficult levels. The most accurate and effective causal analysis accrues from digging for the real or ultimate causes or effects, as opposed to those that are merely superficial or immediate. Actress Angela Lansbury would have been out of work on an episode of the television show "Murder, She Wrote," for example, if her character had stopped her investigation at the immediate cause of death (slipping in the bath tub) rather than searching diligently for the real reason (an overdose of cocaine administered by an angry companion, thereby causing the slip in the tub). Similarly, voters would be easy to manipulate if they considered only the immediate effects of a tax increase (a slightly higher tax bill) rather than the ultimate benefits that would result (the many years of improved education our children would receive because of the specialized programs created by such an increase). Only the discovery of the actual reasons behind an event or an idea will lead to a logical and accurate analysis of causes and effects.

Faulty reasoning assigns causes to a sequence of actions without adequate justification. One such logical fallacy is called post hoc, ergo propter hoc ("after this, therefore because of this"): The fact that someone lost a job after walking under a ladder does not mean that the two events are causally related; by the same token, if we get up every morning at 5:30 a.m., just before the sun rises, we cannot therefore conclude that the sun rises because we get up (no matter how self-centered we are). Faulty reasoning can also occur when we oversimplify a particular situation. Most events are connected to a multitude of causes and effects. Sometimes one effect can have many causes: A student might fail a history exam because she's been working two part-time jobs, she was sick, she didn't study hard enough, and she found the instructor very boring. One cause can also have many effects. If a house burns down, the people who lived in it will be out of a home. If we look at such a tragic scene more closely, however, we might also note that the fire traumatized a child who lived there, helped the family learn what good friends they had, encouraged the family to double their future fire insurance, and provided the happy stimulus they needed to make a long-dreamed-of move to another city. One event has thus resulted in many interrelated effects. The act of building an argument on insecure foundations or oversimplifying the causes or effects connected with an event will seriously hinder the construction of a rational essay. No matter what the nature of the cause/effect analysis, it must always be based on clear observation, accurate facts, and rigorous logic.

In the following paragraph, a student writer analyzes some of the causes and effects connected with the controversial issue of euthanasia. Notice how he makes connections and then analyzes those connections as he consistently explores the immediate and ultimate effects of being able to stretch life beyond its normal limits through new medical technology.

> *Along with the many recent startling advancements in medical technology have come a number of complex moral, ethical, and spiritual questions which beg to be answered. We now have the ability to prolong the life of the human body for a very long time. But what rights do patients and their families have to curtail cruel and unusual medical treatment that stretches life beyond its normal limits? This dilemma has produced a ripple effect in society. Is the extension of*

life an unquestionable goal in itself, regardless of the quality of that life? Modern scientific technology has forced doctors to reevaluate the exact meaning and purpose of their profession. For example, many medical schools and undergraduate university programs now routinely offer classes on medical ethics—an esoteric and infrequently taught subject only a few years ago. Doctors and scholars alike are realizing that medical personnel alone cannot be expected to determine the exact parameters of life. In like manner, the judicial process must now evaluate the legal complexities of mercy killings and the rights of patients to die with dignity and without unnecessary medical intervention. The insurance business, too, wrestles with the catastrophic effects new technology has had on the costs of today's hospital care. In short, medical progress entails more than microscopes, chemicals, and high-tech instruments. If we are to develop as a thoughtful, just, and merciful society, we must consider not only the physical well-being of our nation's patients, but their emotional, spiritual, and financial status as well.

How to Write a Cause/Effect Essay

Preparing to Write. Beginning a cause/effect essay requires—as does any other essay—exploring and limiting your subject, specifying a purpose, and identifying an audience. For cause/effect essays, determining a purpose is even more important than usual, because your readers can get hopelessly lost without a clear focus for your analysis.

Writing. For all its conceptual complexity, a cause/effect essay can be organized quite simply. The introduction generally presents the subject(s) and states the purpose of the analysis in a clear thesis. The body of the paper then explores all relevant causes and/or effects, typically progressing either from least to most influential or from most to least influential. Finally, the concluding section summarizes the various cause-and-effect relationships established in the body of the paper and clearly states the conclusions that can be drawn from those relationships.

The following additional guidelines should assist you in producing an effective cause/effect essay in all academic disciplines:

1. Narrow and focus your material as much as possible.
2. Consider all possibilities before assigning real or ultimate causes or effects.
3. Show connections between ideas by using transitions and key words—such as "because," "reasons," "results," "effects," and "consequences"—to guide your readers smoothly through your essay.
4. Support all inferences with concrete evidence.

5. Be as objective as possible in your analysis so you don't distort logic with personal biases.
6. Understand your audience's opinions and convictions, so that you know what to emphasize in your essay.
7. Qualify your assertions to avoid overstatement and oversimplification.

These suggestions apply to both cause/effect essay assignments and exam questions.

Rewriting. As you revise your cause/effect essay, ask yourself the following important questions: Is your thesis stated clearly at the outset of your paper? Do you accomplish your purpose as effectively as possible for your particular audience? Do you use logical reasoning throughout the essay? Do you carefully explore all relevant causes and/or effects, searching for the real (as opposed to the immediate) reasons in each case? Do you state clearly the conclusions that can be drawn from the various cause/effect relationships discussed in your paper?

Student Essay: Cause/Effect at Work

In the following essay, the student writer analyzes the effects of contemporary TV soap operas on young people: Notice how she states her subject and purpose at the beginning of the essay and then presents a combination of facts and opinions in her exploration of the topic. Notice also that, in her analysis, the writer is careful to draw clear connections between her perceptions of the issue and various objective details in an attempt to trace the effects of this medium in our society today. At the end of her essay, look at her summary of the logical relationships she establishes in the body of the essay and her statements about the conclusions she draws from these relationships.

Distortions of Reality

Background   Television's contributions to society, positive and negative, have been debated continually since this piece of technology invaded the average American household in the 1950s. Television has brought an unlimited influx of new information, ideas, and cultures into our homes. However, based on my observations of my thirteen-year-old cousin, Katie, and her friends, I think we need to take a closer look at the effects of soap operas on adolescents today. <u>The distortions of reality portrayed on these programs are</u> Thesis statement <u>frightenly misleading and, in my opinion, can be very confusing to young people.</u>

Transition   <u>During the late 1980s, the lifestyle of the typical soap opera "family" has been radically transformed from comfortable pretentiousness to blatant and unre-</u> First distortion of reality <u>alistic decadence. The characters neither live nor dress like the majority of their viewers, who are generally</u>

middle-class Americans. These television families live in large, majestic homes that are flawlessly decorated. The **Concrete examples** actors are often adorned in beautiful designer clothing, fur coats, and expensive jewelry, but this opulent lifestyle is sustained by people with no visible means of income. Very few of the characters seem to "work" for a living. When they do, upward mobility—without the benefit of the proper education or suitable training— and a well-planned marriage come quickly.

Transition From this constant barrage of conspicuous con- **First effect** sumption, my cousin and her friends seem to have a distorted view of everyday economic realities. I see Katie and her group becoming obsessed with the appearance of their clothes and possessions. I frequently hear them berate their parents' jobs and modest **Concrete examples** homes. With noticeable arrogance, these young adolescents seem to view their parents' lives as "failures" when compared to the effortless, luxurious lifestyles portrayed in the soaps.

Transition One of the alluring features of this genre is its masterful use of deception. Conflicts between characters in soap operas are based on secrecy and misinformation. **Concrete examples** Failure to tell the truth and to perform honorable deeds further complicates the entangled lives and love affairs of the participants. But when the truth finally **Second** comes out and all mistakes and misdeeds become pub- **distortion** lic, the culprits and offenders hardly ever suffer for **of reality** their actions. In fact, they appear to leave the scene of the crime guilt-free.

Transition Regrettably, Katie and her friends consistently express an alarming indifference in response to this lack of moral integrity. In their daily viewing, they **Concrete examples** shrug off underhanded scenes of scheming and conniving, and they marvel at how the characters manipulate each other into positions of powerlessness or grapple in distasteful love scenes. I can only conclude that contin- **Second** ued exposure to this amoral behavior is eroding the **effect** fundamental values of truth and fidelity in these kids.

Transitions Also in the soaps, the powers-that-be conveniently **Third** disregard any sense of responsibility for wrongdoing. **distortion** Characters serve jail terms quickly and in relative **of reality** comfort. Drug or alcohol abuse does not mar anyone's **Concrete examples** physical appearance or behavior, and poverty is virtually nonexistent. Usually, the wrongdoer's position, wealth, and prestige are quickly restored—with little pain and suffering.

Adolescents are clearly learning that people can _{Third} act without regard for the harmful effects of their _{effect} actions on themselves and others when they see this type of behavior go unpunished. Again, I notice the result of this delusion in my cousin. Recently, when a businessman in our community was convicted of _{Concrete} embezzling large sums of money from his clients, Katie _{examples} was outraged because he was sentenced to five years in prison, unlike her daytime T.V. "heartthrob" who was given a suspended sentence for a similar crime. With righteous indignation, Katie claimed the victims, many of whom had lost their entire savings, should have realized that any business investment involves risk and the threat of loss. Logic and common sense evaded Katie's reasoning as she insisted on comparing television justice with real-life scruples.

The writers and producers of soap operas argue that the shows are designed to entertain viewers and are not meant to be reflections of reality. Theoretically, this may be true, but I can actually see how these soap operas are affecting my cousin and her crowd. Although my personal observations are limited, I cannot believe they are unique or unusual. Too many young people _{Ultimate} think that they can amass wealth and material posses- _{effect} sions without an education, hard work, or careful financial planning; that material goods are the sole measure of a person's success in life; and that honesty and integrity are not necessarily admirable qualities.

_{Proposed} Soap operas should demonstrate a realistic lifestyle _{solution} and a responsible sense of behavior. The many hours adolescents spend in front of the television can obviously influence their views of the world. As a society, we cannot afford the consequences resulting from the distortions of reality portrayed every day in these shows.

Student Writer's Comments

Writing this essay was not as easy as I had anticipated in my prewriting phase. Although I was interested in and familiar with my topic, the challenge was in selecting specific examples to support my thesis statement and then in narrowing my focus to a few main points. Although all writing requires support and focus, a cause/effect essay demands special attention to the relationship between specific examples and their ultimate causes and/or effects.

Some Final Thoughts on Cause/Effect

The essays in this chapter deal with both causes and effects in a variety of ways. As you read each essay, try to discover its primary purpose and the ultimate causes and/or effects of the issue under discussion. Note also the clear causal relationships each author sets forth on solid foundations supported by logical reasoning. Although the subjects of these essays vary dramatically, each essay exhibits the basic elements of effective causal analysis.

Children and Violence in America
Dudley Erskine Devlin

Violence seems to be everywhere in America, but increasingly both the victims and the perpetrators are likely to be children and teenagers. According to a recent Department of Education study, 81 percent of the victims of violent crimes are now preteens and teenagers. Teenagers also lead adults in the number of serious crimes committed. As if to prove this point, recently a stray bullet from gang violence in Denver struck a 10-month-old child who was visiting the zoo. In another incident, a 13-year-old boy accidently shot his friend, and then in despair shot and killed himself. Even this morning's newspaper carries the story of a 15-year-old boy who accidently shot his 9-year-old sister while showing her how to load and unload his father's .22 semi-automatic handgun. The gun went off, and the bullet shattered her spine. The 9-year-old girl is now paralyzed. When people read these shocking and unbelievable stories, they begin to wonder about the causes of the problem. Why are children so frequently the victims or the perpetrators of violence? (1)

The debate in America today is about the causes of violence involving children. But what exactly is the basic, underlying cause? Conventional explanations take an either/or approach: Either the cause lies in TV programs which promote violence or the cause is a society riddled with family instability, drugs, and poverty. It's a classic chicken-or-the-egg question: Does TV and movie violence promote social violence, or is social violence merely reflected in violent movies and television programs? (2)

I believe that we should not be fooled by this either/or logic. There is, after all, a third possible answer. Instead of the primary cause being TV violence or the decline in family values, I believe that the news media themselves are the underlying cause of our crisis. The truth is that the liberal media—particularly newspapers and network TV news—have cleverly staged this crisis of violence by hyping a few statistics and isolated cases of violence. To prove this claim, I need to review the conventional arguments. (3)

First, let's analyze the belief that violence on TV and in the movies is causing increased violence among children and teenagers. The self-appointed liberal reformers usually trot out a bunch of statistics and examples like the following:

• By the age of 18, the average American child will have seen 200,000 violent acts on television, including 40,000 murders. By the time an American child has left elementary school, he or she has witnessed 8,000 murders on TV.

• Today, television programs and films strive for high body counts, not high morals. *Terminator 2* seems like one long machine-gunning. In *RoboCop*, 32 people are killed. *Die Hard 2* may have the unofficial record with 264 people killed.

• In 1950, approximately 15 percent of America's homes had television; by 1990, 93 percent of America's homes had television. In that 40-year period, the murder rate per 100,000 people jumped from 5.3 to 10.2. That's almost a 100 percent increase in murders.

Using examples like these, the TV and media critics like Tipper Gore argue that children confuse images on TV with the real world, that they become desensitized to repeated acts of violence, and that they say that "it's fun" to do violence to others. Researchers like University of Illinois psychologists Leonard Eron and Rowell Huesmann argue that violence on TV does cause violent behavior: "Television violence affects youngsters of all ages, of both genders, at all socioeconomic levels. It cannot be denied or explained away." (4)

On the other side of this either/or argument are those who believe that social violence causes violent behavior in children and teenagers. Those who make this argument point to drug use, poverty, and the decline in family values. Their best evidence is that violence already exists in our children's public schools. They like to cite figures released by the National Education Association (NEA) that show that violence is an everyday part of every child's education. Every school day, the NEA claims, at least 100,000 students bring guns to school; 40 are hurt or killed by firearms; 6,250 teachers are threatened with bodily injury; and 260 teachers are physically assaulted. Everywhere, schools are installing metal detectors and police are stationed in the hallways. (5)

Obviously, each of these arguments represents a half-truth. Possibly there is some TV and movie violence that adds to the culture of violence in America. And yes, we can believe that there are a few, isolated pockets of violence in society and schools. But the real truth is that the newspaper media and the network news have actually invented this epidemic of violence in order to promote their product and frighten the public. Every day, reporters search for a few examples of violence to teens and children, plaster them on the front page, and blow the whole thing out of proportion. (6)

To be sure, there are violent TV shows and movies that a few people watch, but there are also family shows like *Home Improvement* and *Home Alone* that don't get the publicity of *RoboCop* or *Terminator 2*. There are, of course, one or two cities in America, like Los Angeles and Washington, D.C., where there is occasional violence on the streets and in children's schools. But the liberal establishment press has done its thing again, trying to scare the daylights out of the public in order to sell newspapers and raise their Neilsen ratings. (7)

So when you pick up your paper in the morning or turn on the TV news and see another story about teenage violence, take it with a big lump of salt and don't believe everything you read. As they say, one swallow doesn't make a summer, and one infant shot in the Denver Zoo does not mean that we have this huge crisis of violence. In terms of "telling it like it is," you'll find more truth if you turn to the comics and check out "Peanuts." When Lucy hits Charlie Brown, at least you know it's make-believe. (8)

The Agony Must End

Paul Zimmerman

They are the assassins waiting behind the door in a dark room. They are pro football's unpredictable—yet only too predictable—curse. Injuries. As the fractures, concussions and bruises that play havoc with America's No. 1 sport struck down 183 NFL starters in the first half of the season, medical reports like these became commonplace:

Two defensive backs, Anthony Young of Indianapolis and Tim Lewis of Green Bay, damaged nerves in their necks while making fairly routine tackles. They will never make any more. To do so would be to risk paralysis.

On Oct. 26 the San Francisco 49ers fielded only 37 healthy players out of a possible 45 for their game with Green Bay.

Dallas running back Tony Dorsett, after nine relatively injury-free years, missed three of his first eight games this season and hobbled through three more on an ailing knee.

Two Kansas City Chiefs, linebacker Ken McAlister and wide receiver Anthony Hancock, underwent surgery after their knees buckled on artificial turf without having been hit. (1)

"Injuries," says Philip Rosenthal, the assistant director of New York's Nicholas Institute of Sports Medicine and Athletic Trauma, "are inherent to football. It's the nature of the beast."(2)

O.K., but where does it stop? When do we make the breakthrough and start reducing injuries? The average playing career, 4.6 years in 1983, is now 3.6 years. Speed has increased through natural selection and lighter equipment. Size has shown a natural gain, too, but it also has an unnatural side because of the anabolic steroids that are such a major part of the weight-training programs favored by a number of players. (3)

Artificial turf abounds, and it's still as hated by the players as it was 21 years ago when the Houston Astrodome opened. Where's the end of it? Today's 240-pounder is a pumped-up 280, thanks to the steroids. In five years maybe he'll be 300, moving even faster, inflicting greater damage. Can medical science keep up with that? Or will the incidence of injury be even higher? It's time that the NFL takes a long look at the problem and steps in, before football becomes Rollerball. (4)

Questionable and conflicting data from the league, the Players Association and the trainers make it hard to determine exact percentages on injuries and whether they're up a great deal, up only slightly or staying more or less level. One thing that's certain is that they're not declining, and this in itself is frightening. Modern equipment is supposedly safer, and rule changes meant to protect players from injuries have been adopted. Then why, in a world in which modern medicine has discovered how to transplant organs, are pro football players still getting hurt at the same rate as they were in the old days? (5)

The medical breakthroughs in football have been curative, not preventive. For example, arthroscopic surgery can mend a wounded knee and have a player who once would have been out for the season back on the field in three weeks. Arthroscopy can diagnose a minute fracture that used to be called water on the knee. Medical science and the equipment people are in a race against the changing physics of pro football, and they're not winning. They can't gain any ground on the steroid labs, which are turning out bigger, artificially built-up athletes, who move at higher speeds on faster tracks, thanks to synthetic turf. The result is higher-speed collisions by larger people, a ferocity of hitting never before seen in football or any other sport. (6)

Injuries are publicized most heavily when quarterbacks are hurt. The quarterback thrashing is a constant. NFL figures show that after eight weeks of the ' '84 season there had been 41 different starting quarterbacks, 12 getting the call because of injury. Last year the midseason numbers were 40 and 11; this year they are 44 and 14. (7)

So the damage goes on, week after week, year after year. What should be done? Steroids are a good place to start. Everybody hates them, everybody knows the long-range damage they can cause, and lots of players in the NFL use them— and don't admit it. (8)

"That's about right," Los Angeles Raider defensive end Howie Long says. "At least 50 percent of the big guys. The offensive line—75 percent. Defensive line 40 percent, plus 35 percent of the linebackers. I don't know about the speed positions, but I've heard they're used there, too." (9)

The dangers are threefold: No. 1, the long-range risks—cancers, urinary tract problems and other perils. No. 2, turning pro football games into a game for artificially created giants, able to inflict great damage by their sheer mass. Danger No. 3 is that the artificial bulk causes more insidious injuries—muscle pulls and tendon strains that won't go away. (10)

"Eighty percent of the time when a big guy tears a muscle, steroids are probably the reason why," Long says. "You put 50 pounds of muscle on a player, and he goes from a baggage carrier in the jungle to Tarzan, and he says, 'Wow, this is great!' But something has to give. You're putting too much muscle fiber on a body not designed for it." (11)

Trainers around the league are slowly starting to realize he might be right. "I look with suspicion on some of those injuries when you can't determine how they happened," Saints trainer Dean Kleinschmidt says. "Steroids do strange things to your body. When a guy is pumped up on steroids, there's always a weak link, maybe an Achilles, maybe a patellar tendon." (12)

Solution: Attack anabolic steroids at the league level. A tough project. There hasn't been much concern about the question until recently. Steroids are not illegal unless they are obtained without a prescription. Testing is expensive. Each test costs about $100. O.K., it's worth it. Two spot checks for each player, every year, will cost a club about $10,000. (13)

Any effective antisteroid effort must become part of the new Players Association contract. The program will certainly have more bite and greater impact if the NFLPA enters into a joint endorsement with the league. (14)

The Players Association has another duty to perform, if it wishes to do something about the injury problem. It has to take a serious position on artificial turf. Both the NFL-sponsored Stanford Research Institute International's 1974 study and the NCAA's 1982 study showed that the incidence of injury on synthetic turf was significantly higher than on grass. Since then, the NFL has offered no research to the contrary. Two weeks ago in Giants Stadium, the Jets lost two Pro Bowlers, noseguard Joe Klecko for a game and linebacker Lance Mehl for the season, because of noncontact injuries attributable to the artificial turf. (15)

New, softer carpets, with better cushions, are more comfortable to fall on, but according to some people they also increase traction so that the cleats catch, causing knee injuries. "When the nap of the turf is new there's just too much traction," Cincinnati trainer Paul Sparling says. "Archie Griffin tried to cut once on new turf and his foot stuck so firmly that he tore up his abdominal muscles in addition to his leg. He was out for the year." (16)

The players' general hatred of artificial turf is well documented. Very few of them like fake grass, but in the last two contract sessions, while elimination of synthetics was a blanket demand, it quickly became a throwaway issue in former executive director Ed Garvey's negotiating strategy when the heavy matters came up—like money. Note to current association director Gene Upshaw: Worker safety is a top priority for a responsible union. It's not a throwaway. (17)

San Francisco coach Bill Walsh's idea of a joint player-management committee to examine the carpets every year and replace them when necessary or at least to eliminate the more unsafe aspects, is a good one. If a particular field proves to be unsafe no matter what is done, then bring back the grass in that particular stadium—assuming it's outdoors (sad to say, grass won't grow properly in the domes). Make that a keynote demand at the contract talks. (18)

Cheap shots cause injuries, too. It's a fact of life in football—always was, always will be. The problem is that the people responsible for the cheap shots are now so much better equipped to deliver the crippling blow—again, the size and speed factors. The NFL takes a curious approach to cheap shots—protect the quarterback, protect the head. The cosmetic approach. Granted, quarterbacks must be protected from late hits, out-of-bounds hits and general mayhem. (19)

Consistency in officiating is the key. But why protect only the quarterback? How about the running back who gets teed up by two tacklers and finished off by a third one as Bengal fullback Bill Johnson was against the Steelers (he missed one game with a neck injury). That's the play that really needs the quick whistle. (20)

The NFL's interpretation of anatomy is strange. Head skots are severely penalized, but the crippling blindsider to the knee is O.K., especially when linemen do it to each other. It's time to take intent into account. Deliberate attempts to maim must be punished, even in cases in which a blow to the head is not involved. (21)

Solution: Pass a rule that says no cut-blocking unless you're face-up with a man. Clipping is illegal everywhere else on the field. It should be on the line, too. (22)

But how about the illegal, career-ending type of injury? New Orleans safety Antonio Gibson put the Giants' Lionel Manuel out six weeks ago with a vicious knee shot in the end zone after a pass had sailed out of reach. No flag. No nothing. The intent? Well, you don't go to break up a pass at knee level, and there's nothing to be gained by a low tackle in the end zone. Instead of worrying about hands-to-the-face calls, this is the type of thing the NFL should go after. (23)

Solution: Biblical justice. An eye-for-an-eye penalty. If a player puts someone out for a week with a blatantly illegal blow, suspend him for a week. If the other guy is out for a month, suspend the culprit for a month, a year for a year, a career for a career. Think about it. If you want to eliminate the really bad cheap shots, then hand out really tough punishment. (24):

Drastic problems need bold solutions. I have this to say:

• To Gene Upshaw—get your union members a safe surface to play on. The owners won't do it; it's up to you. The membership deserves it.

• To [NFL Commissioner] Pete Rozelle—begin steroid testing right now. Get rid of the freak show in the NFL.

• To Art McNally—make sure your refs are working on the same page. Get them to recognize intent to maim and punish it accordingly.

• To the Competition Committee—no more clipping. Don't build up the passing stats at the sake of people's knees.

• To the owners—spend some dough to preserve careers. Too many are being cut short. Just ask all those guys with casts on their knees and arms. (25)

My Wood

E. M. Forster

A few years ago I wrote a book which dealt in part with the difficulties of the English in India. Feeling that they would have had no difficulties in India themselves, the Americans read the book freely. The more they read it the better it made them feel, and a cheque to the author was the result. I bought a wood with the cheque. It is not a large wood—it contains scarcely any trees, and it is intersected, blast it, by a public footpath. Still, it is the first property that I have owned, so it is right that other people should participate in my shame, and should ask themselves, in accents that will vary in horror, this very important question. What is the effect of property upon the character? Don't let's touch economics; the effect of private ownership upon the community as a whole is another question—a more important question, perhaps, but another one. Let's keep to psychology. If you own things, what's their effect on you? What's the effect on me of my wood?

In the first place, it makes me feel heavy. Property does have this effect. Property produces men of weight, and it was a man of weight who failed to get into the Kingdom of Heaven. He was not wicked, that unfortunate millionaire in the parable, he was only stout; he stuck out in front, not to mention behind, and as he wedged himself this way and that in the crystalline entrance and bruised his well-fed flanks, he saw beneath him a comparatively slim camel passing though the eye of a needle and being woven into the robe of God. The Gospels all through couple stoutness and slowness. They point out what is perfectly obvious, yet seldom realized: that if you have a lot of things you cannot move about a lot, that furniture requires dusting, dusters require servants, servants require insurance stamps, and the whole tangle of them makes you think twice before you accept an invitation to dinner or go for a bathe in the Jordan. Sometimes the Gospels proceed further and say with Tolstoy that property is sinful; they approach the difficult ground of asceticism here, where I cannot follow them. But as to the immediate effects of property on people, they just show straightforward logic. It produces men of weight. Men of weight cannot, by definition, move like the lightning from the East unto the West, and the ascent of a fourteen-stone bishop into a pulpit is thus the exact antithesis of the coming of the Son of Man. My wood makes me feel heavy.

In the second place, it makes me feel it ought to be larger.

The other day I heard a twig snap in it. I was annoyed at first, for I thought that someone was blackberrying, and depreciating the value of the undergrowth. On coming nearer, I saw it was not a man who had trodden on the twig and snapped it, but a bird, and I felt pleased. My bird. The bird was not equally pleased. Ignoring the relation between us, it took fright as soon as it saw the shape of my face, and flew straight over the boundary hedge into a field, the property of Mrs. Henessy, where it sat down with a loud squawk. It had become Mrs. Henessy's bird. Something seemed grossly amiss here, something that would not have occurred had the wood been larger. I could not afford to buy Mrs. Henessy out, I dared not murder her, and limitations of this sort beset me on every side. Ahab did not want that vineyard—he only needed it to round off his property, preparatory to plotting a new curve—and all the land around my wood has become necessary to me in order to round off the wood. A boundary protects. But—poor little thing—the boundary ought in its turn to be protected. Noises on the edge of it. Children throw stones. A little more, and then a little more, until we reach the sea. Happy Canute! Happier Alexander! And after all, why should even the world be the limit of possession? A rocket containing a Union Jack, will, it is hoped, be shortly fired at the moon. Mars. Sirius. Beyond which . . . But these immensities ended by saddening me. I could not suppose that my wood was the destined nucleus of universal dominion—it is so very small and contains no mineral wealth beyond the blackberries. Nor was I comforted when Mrs. Henessy's bird took alarm for the second time and flew clean away from us all, under the belief that it belonged to itself.

In the third place, property makes its owner feel that he ought to do something to it. Yet he isn't sure what. A restlessness comes over him, a vague sense that he has a personality to express—the same sense which, without any vagueness, leads the artist to an act of creation. Sometimes I think I will cut down such trees as remain in the wood, at other times I want to fill up the gaps between them with new trees. But impulses are pretentious and empty. They are not honest movements towards money-making or beauty. They spring from a foolish desire to express myself and from an inability to enjoy what I have got. Creation, property, enjoyment form a sinister trinity in the human mind. Creation and enjoyment are both very, very good, yet they are often unattainable without a material basis, and at such moments property pushes itself in as a substitute, saying, "Accept me instead—I'm good enough for all three." It is not enough. It is, as Shakespeare said of lust, "the expense of spirit in a waste of shame"; it is "Before, a joy proposed; behind, a dream." Yet we don't know how to shun it. It is forced on us by our economic system as the alternative to starvation. It is forced on us by an internal defect in the soul, by the feeling that in property may lie the germs of self-development and of exquisite or heroic deeds. Our life on earth is, and ought to be, material and carnal. But we have not learned to manage our materialism and carnality properly; they are still entangled with the desire for ownership, where (in the words of Dante) "Possession is one with loss."

And this brings us to our fourth and final point: the blackberries.

Blackberries are not plentiful in the meagre grove, but they are easily seen from the public footpath which traverses it, and all too easily gathered. Foxgloves, too—people will pull up the foxgloves, and ladies of an educational tendency even grub for toadstools to show them on the Monday in class. Other ladies, less educated, roll down the bracken in the arms of their gentlemen friends. There is paper, there are tins. Pray, does my wood belong to me or doesn't it? And, if it does, should I not own it best by allowing no one else to walk there? There is a wood near Lyme Regis, also cursed by a public footpath, where the owner has not hesitated on this point. He has built high stone walls on each side of the path, and has spanned it by bridges, so that the public circulate like termites while he gorges on the blackberries unseen. He really does own his wood, this able chap. Dives in Hell did pretty well, but the gulf dividing him from Lazarus could be traversed by vision, and nothing traverses it here. And perhaps I shall come to this in time. I shall wall in and fence out until I really taste the sweets of property. Enormously stout, endlessly avaricious, pseudocreative, intensely selfish, I shall weave upon my forehead the quadruple crown of possession until those nasty Bolshies come and take it off again and thrust me aside into the outer darkness.

Why We Crave Horror Movies

Stephen King

I think that we're all mentally ill; those of us outside the asylums only hide it a little better—and maybe not all that much better, after all. We've all known people who talk to themselves, people who sometimes squinch their faces into horrible grimaces when they believe no one is watching, people who have some hysterical fear—of snakes, the dark, the tight place, the long drop . . . and, of course, those final worms and grubs that are waiting so patiently underground.

When we pay our four or five bucks and seat ourselves at tenth-row center in a theater showing a horror movie, we are daring the nightmare.

Why? Some of the reasons are simple and obvious. To show that we can, that we are not afraid, that we can ride this roller coaster. Which is not to say that a really good horror movie may not surprise a scream out of us at some point, the way we may scream when the roller coaster twists through a complete 360 or plows through a lake at the bottom of the drop. And horror movies, like roller coasters, have always been the special province of the young; by the time one turns 40 or 50, one's appetite for double twists or 360-degree loops may be considerably depleted.

We also go to reestablish our feelings of essential normality; the horror movie is innately conservative, even reactionary. Freda Jackson as the horrible melting woman in *Die, Monster, Die!* confirms for us that no matter how far we may be removed from the beauty of a Robert Redford or a Diana Ross, we are still lightyears from true ugliness.

And we go to have fun.

Ah, but this is where the ground starts to slope away, isn't it? Because this is a very peculiar sort of fun, indeed. The fun comes from seeing others menaced—sometimes killed. One critic has suggested that if pro football has become the voyeur's version of combat, then the horror film has become the modern version of the public lynching.

It is true that the mythic, "fairy-tale" horror film intends to take away the shades of gray. . . . It urges us to put away our more civilized and adult penchant for analysis and to become children again, seeing things in pure blacks and whites. It may be that horror movies provide psychic relief on this level because this invitation to lapse into simplicity, irrationality, and even outright madness is extended so rarely. We are told we may allow our emotions a free rein . . . or no rein at all.

If we are all insane, then sanity becomes a matter of degree. If your insanity leads you to carve up women, like Jack the Ripper or the Cleveland Torso Murderer, we clap you away in the funny farm (but neither of those two amateur-night surgeons was ever caught, heh-heh-heh); if, on the other hand, your insanity leads you only to talk to yourself when you're under stress or to pick your nose on your morning bus, then you are left alone to go about your business . . . though it is doubtful that you will ever be invited to the best parties.

The potential lyncher is in almost all of us (excluding saints, past and present; but then, most saints have been crazy in their own ways), and every now and then, he has to be let loose to scream and roll around in the grass. Our emotions and our fears form their own body, and we recognize that it demands its own exercise to maintain proper muscle tone. Certain of these emotional muscles are accepted—even exalted—in civilized society; they are, of course, the emotions that tend to maintain the status quo of civilization itself. Love, friendship, loyalty, kindness—these are all the emotions that we applaud, emotions that have been immortalized in the couplets of Hallmark cards and in the verses (I don't dare call it poetry) of Leonard Nimoy.

When we exhibit these emotions, society showers us with positive reinforcement; we learn this even before we get out of diapers. When, as children, we hug our rotten little puke of a sister and give her a kiss, all the aunts and uncles smile and twit and cry, "Isn't he the sweetest little thing?" Such coveted treats as chocolate-covered graham crackers often follow. But if we deliberately slam the rotten little puke of a sister's fingers in the door, sanctions follow—angry remonstrance from parents, aunts and uncles; instead of a chocolate-covered graham cracker, a spanking.

But anticivilization emotions don't go away, and they demand periodic exercise. We have such "sick" jokes as, "What's the difference between a truckload of bowling balls and a truckload of dead babies?" (You can't unload a truckload of bowling balls with a pitchfork . . . a joke, by the way, that I heard originally from a ten-year-old.) Such a joke may surprise a laugh or a grin out of us even as we recoil, a possibility that confirms the thesis: If we share a brotherhood of man, then we also share an insanity of man. None of which is intended as a defense of either the sick joke or insanity but merely as an explanation of why the best horror films, like the best fairy tales, manage to be reactionary, anarchistic, and revolutionary all at the same time.

The mythic horror movie, like the sick joke, has a dirty job to do. It deliberately appeals to all that is worst in us. It is morbidity unchained, our most base instincts let free, our nastiest fantasies realized . . . , and it all happens, fittingly enough, in the dark. For those reasons, good liberals often shy away from horror films. For myself, I like to see the most aggressive of them—*Dawn of the Dead*, for instance—as lifting a trap door in the civilized forebrain and throwing a basket of raw meat to the hungry alligators swimming around in that subterranean river beneath.

Why bother? Because it keeps them from getting out, man. It keeps them down there and me up here. It was Lennon and McCartney who said that all you need is love, and I would agree with that.

As long as you keep the gators fed.

Fear of Dearth

Carl Tucker

I hate jogging. Every dawn, as I thud around New York City's Central Park reservoir, I am reminded of how much I hate it. It's so tedious. Some claim jogging is thought conducive: others insist the scenery relieves the monotony. For me, the pace is wrong for contemplation of either ideas or vistas. While jogging, all I can think about is jogging—or nothing. One advantage of jogging around a reservoir is that there's no dry shortcut home.

From the listless looks of some fellow trotters, I gather I am not alone in my unenthusiasm: Bill-paying, it seems, would be about as diverting. Nonetheless, we continue to jog; more, we continue to *choose* to jog. From a practically infinite array of opportunities, we select one that we don't enjoy and can't wait to have done with. Why?

For any trend, there are as many reasons as there are participants. This person runs to lower his blood pressure. That person runs to escape the telephone or a cranky spouse or a filthy household. Another person runs to avoid doing anything else, to dodge a decision about how to lead his life or a realization that his life is leading nowhere. Each of us has his carrot and stick. In my case, the stick is my slackening physical condition, which keeps me from beating opponents at tennis whom I overwhelmed two years ago. My carrot is to win.

Beyond these disparate reasons, however, lies a deeper cause. It is no accident that now, in the last third of the twentieth century, personal fitness and health have suddenly become a popular obsession. True, modern man likes to feel good, but that hardly distinguishes him from his predecessors.

With zany myopia, economists like to claim that the deeper cause of everything is economic. Delightfully, there seems no marketplace explanation for jogging. True, jogging is cheap, but then not jogging is cheaper. And the scant and skimpy equipment which jogging demands must make it a marketer's least favored form of recreation.

Some scout-masterish philosophers argue that the appeal of jogging and other body-maintenance programs is the discipline they afford. We live in a world in which individuals have fewer and fewer obligations. The work week has shrunk.

Weekend worship is less compulsory. Technology gives us more free time. Satisfactorily filling free time requires imagination and effort. Freedom is a wide and risky river; it can drown the person who does not know how to swim across it. The more obligations one takes on, the more time one occupies, the less threat freedom poses. Jogging can become an instant obligation. For a portion of his day, the jogger is not his own man; he is obedient to a regimen he has accepted.

Theologists may take the argument one step further. It is our modern irreligion, our lack of confidence in any hereafter, that makes us anxious to stretch our mortal stay as long as possible. We run, as the saying goes, for our lives, hounded by the suspicion that these are the only lives we are likely to enjoy.

All of these theorists seem to me more or less right. As the growth of cults and charismatic religions and the resurgence of enthusiasm for the military draft suggest, we do crave commitment. And who can doubt, watching so many middle-aged and older persons torturing themselves in the name of fitness, that we are unreconciled to death, more so perhaps than any generation in modern memory?

But I have a hunch there's a further explanation of our obsession with exercise. I suspect that what motivates us even more than a fear of death is a fear of dearth. Our era is the first to anticipate the eventual depletion of all natural resources. We see wilderness shrinking; rivers losing their capacity to sustain life; the air, even the stratosphere, being loaded with potentially deadly junk. We see the irreplaceable being squandered, and in the depths of our consciousness we are fearful that we are creating an uninhabitable world. We feel more or less helpless and yet, at the same time, desirous to protect what resources we can. We recycle soda bottles and restore old buildings and protect our nearest natural resource— our physical health—in the almost superstitious hope that such small gestures will help save an earth that we are blighting. Jogging becomes a sort of penance for our sins of gluttony, greed, and waste. Like a hair shirt or a bed of nails, the more one hates it, the more virtuous it makes one feel.

That is why *we* jog. Why *I* jog is to win at tennis.

My Decision to Attend DeVry

Student

With only a weeks forethought, I found myself sitting in the office of a DeVry recruitment counselor discussing what DeVry may have to offer for me. Prior to that week, I would have never thought that I would have ever stepped foot back into a formal educational environment. I entered the interview with high skepticism, but I slowly came to the realization that this was where I belonged. All of my excuses of why formal education was no longer applicable to me lost their validity. "Student" was now going to become my identity for the next two years. As a result of my decision to attend DeVry, my personal, financial, and educational life has changed dramatically.

For instance, my resolve to return to school personally altered my independence, my self-esteem, and my family relationships. Basically, I had to let go of the self-sufficient independence I had embraced over the last nine years. In order for me to attend school, it became necessary for me to move back in with my parents. Then, my employer of the last three years was unable to retain me on a part-time basis, so I lost my job. Also, due to my accelerated class schedule and studies, I had to modify my social activities. Even with losing some of my independence, the decision to attend DeVry personally provided me with a deeper sense of self-esteem. I was now imagining a future with a wealth of possibilities. I, also, grew more confident after realizing I would acquire new skills. Furthermore, I felt a sense of pride in coming to terms with my half-completed education, receiving satisfaction at the prospect of possessing a usable degree in the near future. Surprisingly, my decision to attend DeVry even enhanced my relationship with my family. Moving back in with my parents provided me the opportunity to interact with my family on a daily basis. Besides conversing with my parents more, I was also sharing many of my meals and helping them with their 40-acre horse farm.

In addition to the personal changes I have experienced from my decision to attend DeVry, financially I have increased my debt liabilities, eliminated the last of my long term investments, and provided a future potential for increased income. Attending DeVry exposed me to a whole new world of incurring long term debts to support both personal and educational obligations. Financial creativity and loans have become a necessity in order to support my various personal expenses. Little experiences of joy have occurred every once in a while, such as when I realized for the first time in my life that I would actually receive a tax refund for this next year. Unfortunately, tax refunds alone will not support both my personal and educational expenses incurred while at DeVry. Once I made the decision to attend, I was quickly introduced to the confusing world of student loans and the ever growing debt that follows. As a result of my decision to become a student, I had to sacrifice my present day financial security. Regular employment was no longer feasible with the twenty credit hour terms I carried. Also, the mounting expenses caused me to sell the last of my long term investments. On the other hand, the projected financial rewards of increasing my skills and marketability by attending DeVry compensates for any present day sacrifices. The skills and knowledge I will acquire at DeVry will give me an edge on having more of a choice on my future employment and salary level. In addition, receiving my education from DeVry will increase my ability to secure employment sooner because of DeVry's reputation and its placement program.

Moreover, the decision to attend DeVry reminded me of the value of gaining an education, opened up to me new knowledge and skills, and provided me the ability to visualize the application of this education. I discovered how much I missed the awe of learning, the moment when a completely foreign idea formulates into a comprehensible concept. In addition, I received a reawakened desire to seek out knowledge and not to be satisfied with only the status quo. Also, DeVry has enhanced my knowledge base through the various courses they offer with the Telecommunication Management Bachelors of Science degree. The telecommunication courses have made me aware of a whole new developing segment of technology and the need to manage it. The business and finance classes have provided me with a better understanding of the economy around me. Similarly, each of the remaining courses has provided me with a refining education that will add to my value in the workplace. Finally, my decision to attend DeVry played a key factor in enabling me to visualize completing my education and applying the acquired knowledge to future employment. Only when I firmly decided to attend DeVry was I hit with the momentousness of my decision. For the first time in all of my educational experiences, I could actually visualize completing school and receiving a college degree. DeVry successfully converted me to the pursuit of a higher level of education. Through the various courses I have already taken, I have now become a stronger advocate of education. Experience may be very important to an employer but education is the foundation upon which I can firmly build that experience.

On the whole, my decision to attend and complete my education at DeVry has resulted in many changes in my life, both present and future. Just as a caterpillar needs to develop a cocoon to someday become a beautiful butterfly, it appears I, too, have felt the effects of the need to develop and change to reach my potential.

This Is Not a Tall Person's World

Student

I feel that our world is made for tall people and not short people like me. No one ever makes a comment about being too tall, it is always the short people like me that comments are made to. I do not make it through the day without a comment being made about my height. I can do just as many things as tall people can do. Being short hinders playing some sports, creates problems with everyday activities, and causes many remarks to be made.

Being short makes some sports hard to do. The teams for basketball have tall people on them. I never got to be one of the starting five, because my coach felt I was not tall enough to play basketball. I could shoot and score just as well as the starters, but because of my height, I could not start. I had to wait until one of the starters made a mistake before I could get a chance to play. I do not see many short people playing football. When football is mentioned tall guys come to mind. The short guys would get knocked down easier than the tall guys would. Volleyball is another sport that I have had trouble with because of my height. I can serve, bump, and set the ball fine, but the spiking part of the game is a different story. The net is too tall for me to get above it to have a good spike or block. My coach wanted someone that could spike and block, so I had to work extra hard to convince her to let me start. My other good abilities outweighed the weakness of spiking and blocking.

Being short creates some problems with my everyday activities. If I want something out of the top cabinet in our kitchen, I have to get a chair or climb up on the cabinet to reach it. This takes extra time for me that a person with ordinary height would never encounter. Some of the mirrors on the restroom walls are too high that I can not see myself without having to jump. When I go to the store, I can not reach some things off the top shelf. I can not take a chair with me of climb up on the shelf like I do at home. I have to ask a clerk from the store to get it of me. Some seats in place are made too tall, when I sit in them my feet dangle. My feet do not reach the floor like a person's with normal height would. Some of the peepholes on motel rooms and apartment doors are up too high for me to see out of. By the time I get a chair to see outside, the person waiting is wondering if anyone is going to answer the door. When I am driving my car, I have to have the seat up close to see over the dashboard. When there are crowds of people around, I can never see what is actually going on because I can not see over the people in front of me. I always have to move up front if I want to see what is happening. When I am with my friends, I am usually the only one who has to show some type of identification to verify my age. When I walk with my dad, I feel like I am in a walking marathon trying to keep up with him. He is six feet tall, and one of his strides make up two of mine. These are just some of the problems that I encounter thanks to my height.

I have been called a variety of names. At my last job it was not 'Hello Jennifer,' but 'Hello Munchkin.' Shorty is probably the most ordinary name used. Tidbit and short-stuff are some other names that I hear. People will ask me if I get the children's discount, even though they know my age. Some of my friend's will make the remark that I should look at the children's menu or ask me if I need a highchair to eat in a restaurant. When people tell me to grow up, they think that this might disturb me, but I have heard this remark too many times to let it bother me. Just because I am short does not mean that I am still a child.

I can do just about anything that people with ordinary height can do. I may have a few more problems, but it is not my fault that I did not grow a few more inches.

Ch. 7: Cause / Effect

———————————

Suggestions for writing:

1. What is the most or one of the most important decisions you've ever had to make? Write an essay or paragraph on the effect this decision has had on your later life.

2. What was the most important advice anyone ever gave you? Did you follow it? Write an essay or paragraph on how following or not following this advice has affected your life.

3. What was the major cause of your coming to school here? What were some of the less important but still significant causes? Write an essay or paragraph discussing the three or four causes of your decision to attend college here.

4. Write an essay or paragraph on one of the following topics or a similar topic:

how a grandparent influenced your life

how living abroad affected you

why you went through a certain phase

what staying up late does to you

why you enlisted in the military

why you live where you live

why you got married

why you bought a computer

Cause / Effect checklist:

1. Did you include a thesis statement (essay) or topic sentence (paragraph)?

2. Have you dealt with all of the important causes or effects that pertain to your topic? If not, have you explained to your reader why you're leaving some out?

3. Have you arranged the causes or effects that you're explaining logically and effectively? What organizational pattern have you used?

4. Have you fully explained, described, and illustrated the causes or effects so that they are understandable?

5. Did you use effective transitions within and between paragraphs?

6. Did you vary your sentence patterns and vocabulary?

7. Did you check for correctness of grammar, punctuation, and spelling?

CHAPTER 8

Definition

Limiting the Frame of Reference

Using Definition

Definitions help us function smoothly in a complex world. All effective communication, in fact, is continuously dependent on our unique human ability to understand and employ accurate definitions of a wide range of words, phrases, and abstract ideas. If we did not work from a set of shared definitions, we would not be able to carry on coherent conversations, write comprehensible letters, or respond to even the simplest radio and television programs. Definitions help us understand basic concrete terms (such as automobiles, laser beams, and the gross national product), discuss various events in our lives (such as snow skiing, legal proceedings, and a Cinco de Mayo celebration), and grasp difficult abstract ideas (such as the concepts of democracy, ambition, and resentment). The ability to comprehend definitions and use them effectively helps us keep our oral and written level of communication accurate and accessible to a wide variety of people.

Defining Definition

Definition is the process of explaining a word, object, or idea in such a way that the reader (or listener) knows as precisely as possible what we mean. A good definition sets up intellectual boundaries by focusing on the special qualities of a word or phrase that set it apart from other similar words or phrases. Clear definitions always give the writer and reader a mutual starting point on the sometimes bumpy road to successful communication.

Definitions vary from short, dictionary-length summaries to longer, "extended" accounts that determine the form of an entire essay. Words or ideas that require expanded definitions are usually abstract, complex, or unavoidably controversial; they generally bear many related meanings or many shades of meaning. Definitions can be *objective* (technically precise and generally dry) or *subjective* (colored with personal opinion), and they can be used to instruct, entertain, or accomplish a combination of these two fundamental rhetorical goals.

In the following excerpt, a student defines "childhood" by putting it into perspective with other important stages of life. Though mostly entertaining, the paragraph is also instructive as the student objectively captures the essence of this phase of human development.

> *Childhood is a stage of growth somewhere between infancy and adolescence. Just as each developmental period in our lives brings new changes and concerns, childhood serves as the threshold to puberty—the time we learn to discriminate between good and bad, right and wrong, love and lust. Childhood is neither a time of irresponsible infancy nor responsible adulthood. Rather, it is marked by duties that we don't really want, challenges that excite us, feelings that puzzle and frighten us, and limitless opportunities that help us explore the world around us. Childhood is a time when we solidify our personalities in spite of pressures to be someone else.*

How to Write a Definition Essay

Preparing to Write. As with other essays, you should begin the task of writing a definition essay by prewriting and then by exploring your subject and generating other ideas. Be sure you know what you are going to define and how you will approach your definition. You should then focus on a specific audience and purpose as you approach the writing assignment.

Writing. The next step toward developing a definition essay is usually to describe the general category to which the word belongs and then to contrast the word with all other words in that group. To define "exposition," for example, you might say that it is a type of writing. Then, to differentiate it from other types of writing, you could go on to say that its main purpose is to "expose" or present information, as opposed to rhetorical modes such as description or narration, which have different purposes. In addition, you might want to cite some expository methods—such as example, process analysis, division/classification, or comparison/contrast.

Yet another way to begin a definition essay is to provide a term's etymology. Tracing a word's origin often illuminates its current meaning and usage as well. "Exposition," for example, comes from the Latin *exponere*, meaning "to put forth, set forth, display, declare, or publish" (*ex* = out; *ponere* = to put or place). This information can generally be found in any good dictionary or in a good encyclopedia.

Another approach to defining a term is to explain what it does not mean. "Exposition" is not description or narration; nor is it poetry of any kind. By limiting the readers' frame of reference in these various ways, you are helping to establish a working definition for the term under consideration.

Finally rhetorical methods that we have already studied, such as description, narration, example, process analysis, division/classification, and comparison/contrast, are particularly useful to writers in expanding their definitions. To clarify the term "exposition," you might describe the details of an expository theme, narrate a story about the wide use of the term in today's classroom, or give examples of assignments that would produce good expository writing. In other situations, you could analyze various writing assignments and discuss the process of producing an expository essay, classify exposition apart from creative writing and then divide it into categories similar to the headings of this book, or compare and contrast it with creative writing. Writers also use definition quite often to support other rhetorical modes.

Rewriting. Reviewing and revising a definition essay is a relatively straightforward task: Have you chosen an effective beginning for your paper? Have you used appropriate rhetorical strategies for developing your ideas? Will your explanation be clear to your intended audience? Do you achieve your overall purpose as effectively as possible?

Student Essay: Definition at Work

In the following essay, a student defines "the perfect yuppie." Notice how the writer puts this term in a category, then explains the limits of that category and the uniqueness of this term within the category. To further inform her audience about the features of "yuppiedom," the student calls upon the word's etymology, its dictionary definition, an itemization of the term's basic characteristics, a number of examples that explain those characteristics, and, finally, a general discussion of cause/effect.

The Perfect Yuppie

Many people already know that the letters "Y.U.P" stand for "young urban professional." "Young" in this content is understood to mean thirtyish; "urban" often means suburban; and "professional" means most definitely college-educated. Double the "P" and add an "I" and an "E" at the end, and you get yuppie—that 1980s bourgeois, the marketers' darling, and the sixties' inheritance. But let's not generalize. Not every 30-year-old suburban college graduate qualifies as a yuppie. Nor is every yuppie in his or her thirties. True yuppiness involves much more than the words that make up the acronym. Being the little sister

[Margin annotations: Etymology/dictionary definition; Subject; Limitations set; General category of word being defined; Why the dictionary definition is inadequate]

Writer
establishes
credibility of a couple of yups, I am in an especially good position to define the perfect yuppie. I watched two develop.

The essence of yuppiness is generally <u>new money</u>. General character-istic In the yuppie's defense, I will admit that most yuppies have worked hard for their money and social status. Moreover, the baby boom of which they are a part has caused a glut of manpower in their age bracket, forcing them to be competitive if they want all the nice things retailers have designed for them. But with new General character-istic money comes <u>an interesting combination of wealth, naiveté, and pretentiousness</u>.

Specific example For example, most yuppies worthy of the title have long ago <u>traded in their fringed suede jackets for fancy fur coats</u>. Although they were animal rights activists in the sixties, they will not notice the irony of this change. In fact, they may be shameless enough to <u>parade in their fur coats—fashion-show style—for</u> Specific example <u>friends and family</u>. Because of their "innocence," yuppies generally will not see the vulgarity of their actions.

Because they are often quite wealthy, yuppies <u>tend</u> General character-istic <u>to have a lot of "things."</u> They are simply overwhelmed with the responsibility of spending all that money. For example, <u>one yup I know has 14 pairs of sunglasses and 7 watches</u>. She, her husband, and their Specific example three children own at least <u>twenty collections of every-thing from comic books to Civil War memorabilia.</u> Specific example Most yuppies have so much money that I often wonder why the word "yuppie" does not have a $ in it somewhere.

Perhaps in an effort to rid themselves of this financial burden, <u>all good yuppies go to Europe</u> as soon as possible. Not Germany or France or Portugal, mind you, but Europe. They do not know what they are doing there, and thus generally spend much more money than they need to—but, after all, no yuppie ever claimed to be frugal. Most important, they <u>bring</u> General character-istic <u>home slides of Europe and show them</u> to everyone they know. A really good yuppie will forget and show you his or her slides more than once. Incidentally, when everyone has seen the slides of Europe twice, the yuppie's next stop is Australia.

General character-istic A favorite pastime of yuppies is having <u>wine-tast-ing parties</u> for their yuppie friends. At these parties, Specific example they must <u>make a great to-do about tasting the wine</u>, cupping their faces over the glass with their palms (as if they were having a facial), and even sniffing the cork, for goodness sake. I once knew a yuppie who <u>did</u>

Specific example
not understand that a bottle of wine could not be rejected simply because he found he "did not like that kind." Another enjoyed making a show of having his wife choose and taste the wine occasionally, which they both thought was adorable.

Specific example

What it is not
Some yuppie wanna-be's drive red or black BMW's; but don't let them fool you. A genuine, hard-core yuppie will usually own a gold or silver Volvo station wagon. In this yuppie-mobile, the yuppie wife will chauffeur her young yupettes to and from their modeling classes, track meets, ballet, the manicurist, and boy scouts, for the young yuppie is generally as competitive and socially active as his or her parents. On the same topic, one particularly annoying trait of yuppie parents is bragging about their yupettes. You will know yuppies by the fact that they have the smartest, most talented children in the world. They will show you their kids' report cards, making sure you notice any improvements from last quarter.

General characteristic

Specific example

General characteristic

Specific example

Perhaps I have been harsh in my portrayal of the perfect yuppie, and, certainly, I will be accused by some of stereotyping. But consider this: I never classify people as yuppies who do not so classify themselves. The ultimate criterion for being yuppies is that they will always proudly label themselves as such.

General characteristic and concluding statement

Student Writer's Comments

For me, the most difficult part about writing a definition essay was choosing a topic. I knew it had to be a word or phrase with different shades of meaning; but it also had to be either something I know more about than the average person or something I have an unusual perspective on. I figured "yuppie" was a good word, not only because it has different meanings for different people, but also because it is an acronym, and acronyms tend to be greater than the sum of their parts. I started by looking the word up in the dictionary and using the etymology for my opening sentence. After explaining why the dictionary definition was inadequate, I gave some general characteristics of yuppies, working with humorous examples from my personal experience. I suppose you could say I also used a little argument and persuasion, because I was trying to make a point about how some yuppies have lost the 1960s values they once had.

Some Final Thoughts on Definition

The following selections feature extended definitions whose main purpose is to explain a specific term or idea to their readers. Each essay in its own way helps the audience identify with various parts of its definitions, and each successfully communicates the unique qualities of the term or idea in question. Notice what approaches to definition each writer takes and how these approaches limit the readers' frame of reference in the process of effective communication.

Barrier Signals

Desmond Morris

People feel safer behind some kind of physical barrier. If a social situation is in any way threatening, then there is an immediate urge to set up such a barricade. For a tiny child faced with a stranger, the problem is usually solved by hiding behind its mother's body and peeping out at the intruder to see what he or she will do next. If the mother's body is not available, then a chair or some other piece of solid furniture will do. If the stranger insists on coming closer, then the peeping face must be hidden too. If the insensitive intruder continues to approach despite these obvious signals of fear, then there is nothing for it but to scream or flee.

This pattern is gradually reduced as the child matures. In teenage girls it may still be detected in the giggling cover-up of the face, with hands or papers, when acutely or jokingly embarrassed. But by the time we are adult, the childhood hiding which dwindled to adolescent shyness, is expected to disappear altogether, as we bravely stride out to meet our guests, hosts, companions, relatives, colleagues, customers, clients, or friends. Each social occasion involves us, once again, in encounters similar to the ones which made us hide as scared infants and, as then, each encounter is slightly threatening. In other words, the fears are still there, but their expression is blocked. Our adult roles demand control and suppression of any primitive urge to withdraw and hide ourselves away. The more formal the occasion and the more dominant or unfamiliar our social companions, the more worrying the moment of encounter becomes. Watching people under these conditions, it is possible to observe the many small ways in which they continue to 'hide behind their mother's skirts.' The actions are still there, but they are transformed into less obvious movements and postures. It is these that are the Barrier Signals of adult life.

The most popular form of Barrier Signal is the Body-cross. In this, the hands or arms are brought into contact with one another in front of the body, forming a temporary 'bar' across the trunk, rather like a bumper or fender on the front of a motor-car. This is not done as a physical act of fending off the other person, as when raising a forearm horizontally across the front of the body to push through a struggling crowd. It is done, usually at quite a distance, as a nervous guest approaches a dominant host. The action is performed unconsciously and, if tackled on the subject immediately afterwards, the guest will not be able to remember having made the gesture. It is always camouflaged in some way, because if it were performed as a primitive fending-off or covering-up action, it would obviously be too transparent. The disguise it wears varies from person to person. Here are some examples:

The special guest on a gala occasion is alighting from his official limousine. Before he can meet and shake hands with the reception committee, he has to walk alone across the open space in front of the main entrance to the building where the function is being held. A large crowd has come to watch his arrival and the press cameras are flashing. Even for the most experienced of celebrities this is a slightly nervous moment, and the mild fear that is felt expresses itself just as he is halfway across the 'greeting-space'. As he walks forward, his right hand reaches across his body and makes a last-minute adjustment to his left cuff-link. It pauses there momentarily as he takes a few more steps, and then, at last, he is close enough to reach out his hand for the first of the many handshakes.

On a similar occasion, the special guest is a female. At just the point where her male counterpart would have fiddled with his cuff, she reaches across her body with her right hand and slightly shifts the position of her handbag, which is hanging from her left forearm.

There are other variations on this theme. A male may finger a button or the strap of a wristwatch instead of his cuff. A female may smooth out an imaginary crease in a sleeve, or re-position a scarf or coat held over her left arm. But in all cases there is one essential feature: at the peak moment of nervousness there is a Body-cross, in which one arm makes contact with the other across the front of the body, constructing a fleeting barrier between the guest and the reception committee.

Sometimes the barrier is incomplete. One arm swings across but does not actually make contact with the other. Instead it deals with some trivial clothing-adjustment task on the opposite side of the body. With even heavier camouflage, the hand comes up and across, but goes no further than the far side of the head or face, with a mild stroking or touching action.

Less disguised forms of the Body-cross are seen with less experienced individuals. The man entering the restaurant, as he walks across an open space, rubs his hands together, as if washing them. Or he advances with them clasped firmly in front of him.

Such are the Barrier Signals of the greeting situation, where one person is advancing on another. Interestingly, field observations reveal that it is most unlikely that both the greeter *and* the greeted will perform such actions. Regardless of status, it is nearly always the new arrival who makes the body-cross movement, because it is he who is invading the home territory of the greeters. They are on their own ground or, even if they are not, they were there first and have at least temporary territorial 'rights' over the place. This gives them an indisputable dominance at the moment of the greeting. Only if they are extremely subordinate to the new arrival, and perhaps in serious trouble with him, will there be a likelihood of them taking the 'body-cross role'. And if they do, this will mean that the new arrival on the scene will omit it as he enters.

These observations tell us something about the secret language of Barrier Signals, and indicate that, although the sending and receiving of the signals are both unconsciously done, the message gets across, nonetheless. The message says: 'I am nervous but I will not retreat'; and this makes it into an act of subordination which automatically makes the other person feel slightly more dominant and more comfortable.

The situation is different after greetings are over and people are standing about talking to one another. Now, if one man edges too close to another, perhaps to hear better in all the noise of chattering voices, the boxed-in companion may feel the same sort of threatening sensation that the arriving celebrity felt as he walked towards the reception committee. What is needed now, however, is something more long-lasting than a mere cuff-fumble. It is simply not possible to go fiddling with a button for as long as this companion is going to thrust himself forward. So a more composed posture is needed. The favorite Body-cross employed in this situation is the arm-fold, in which the left and right arms intertwine themselves across the front of the chest. This posture, a perfect, frontal Barrier Signal, can be held for a very long time without appearing strange. Unconsciously it transmits a 'come-no-farther' message and is used a great deal at crowded gatherings. It has also been used by poster artists as a deliberate 'They-shall-not pass!' gesture, and is rather formally employed by bodyguards when standing outside a protected doorway.

The same device of arm-folding can be used in a sitting relationship where the companion is approaching too close, and it can be amplified by a crossing of the legs *away* from the companion. Another variant is to press the tightly clasped hands down on to the crotch and squeeze them there between the legs, as if protecting the genitals. The message of this particular form of barrier is clear enough, even though neither side becomes consciously aware of it. But perhaps the major Barrier Signal for the seated person is that ubiquitous device, the desk. Many a businessman would feel naked without one and hides behind it gratefully every day, wearing it like a vast, wooden chastity-belt. Sitting beyond it he feels fully protected from the visitor exposed on the far side. It is the supreme barrier, both physical and psychological, giving him an immediate and lasting comfort while he remains in its solid embrace.

Baseball's Hot Dogs

Jim Kaplan

Here's Rickey Henderson at the plate. Taking forever to situate himself in the batter's box, the New York Yankees outfielder crouches low and extends a shy left foot, like a man inching into a cold swimming pool. A pitch arrives on the inside corner. Henderson twists away and then looks shocked when the umpire calls it a strike. Finally, Rickey sees a pitch he likes and rides it out of the park.

Now the real fun begins. Playing shamelessly to the crowd and camera, Henderson chucks his bat high over his head, ambles to first by way of the Yankee dugout, lowers his head and proceeds around the bases in an endless, mock-serious trot. The fans love it. The opponents do not.

Henderson is baseball's foremost "hot dog"—and his repertoire is so varied and controversial that his employers have actually put pressure on him to modify his style. This spring, the Yankees proposed banning Henderson's famous "snatch," a one-handed catch in which he snaps his glove down like a teacher scrawling a semicircle on a blackboard and finishes with it pressed to his heart.

"They said, 'Rickey, the only snatch you can make is the last out of the World Series,'" explained Henderson, adding that he thought he could still get away with it on occasion. "I want to show I can do more than catch. I want to show I can *catch*. To me, the snatch isn't hot-dogging; it's style. People say I'm a hot dog. What *is* a hot dog?"

Good question. "A hot dog is someone whose actions put down someone on another team," says Doug DeCinces, the former major-league third baseman now playing for Tokyo's Yakult Swallows.

"Hot-dogging is unnecessarily calling attention to yourself," adds Roy Smalley, the well traveled former American League infielder.

But there's another point of view: that hot-dogging is flair and zest, the very ingredients that make baseball so entertaining on the air or in person. Hot dogs contribute to baseball science, strategy and style. Some hot dogs show off; others motivate themselves; still others intimidate the opposition; most are entertaining.

Henderson may qualify on every count. "I never try to put anyone down," he says. "I take my time getting into the box because I'm thinking of the pitches I'm going to get." But he knows only too well the effect his apparent stalling has. Even as imperturbable a pitching pro as the now retired Tom Seaver got so flustered that he had to turn his back on the mound until Henderson had set himself to hit.

"Rickey has always played with flair," says Milwaukee manager Tom Trebelhorn, who handled Henderson in the minors. "When he played for me, he drove the other side crazy. Now he drives *me* crazy."

National League managers echo those sentiments about the San Francisco Giants' Jeffrey "Hac-Man" Leonard, who showcased his trademark "flap down" homerun trot (one arm pinned to his side) four times during the 1987 League Championship Series.

"[One flap down] is entertaining, a guy having fun," the unflappable Leonard has told reporters. "Anything that provides energy gets me up. Like Muhammad Ali, we'll bring out the best in our opponents, and that'll make us better."

Oh, there are many kinds of baseball hot dogs—kosher and otherwise. Cleveland's Mel Hall used to round the bases with a batting glove in each back pocket arranged to flap "bye-bye." He has since contained his act. But there's no containing Dennis "Oil Can" Boyd, the Boston Red Sox pitcher who celebrates good fortune by variously high-fiving and lowfiving teammates, waving to the crowd, doing clenched-fist "out" calls and Michael Jackson struts, and snapping his fingers as he walks off the mound.

Oil Can (the nickname is Mississippi slang for beer can) grew up playing with older men who had starred in the Negro leagues. "I had a leadoff hitter who drag-bunted with the bat behind his back," says Boyd. "My fielders would turn [the double play] by throwing the ball between their legs. A first baseman named Bud Moore said to throw to him in the dirt so he could pick it and look good. When I punched [struck] a guy out, I'd say, 'Get outta here—next guy up.' To hot-dog was the way to play."

TV may be the biggest boon to hot-dogging since the invention of mustard. Midway through the 1982 World Series, St. Louis pitcher Joaquin Andujar was struck on the leg by a line drive and carried off in apparent agony. NBC sportscaster Bob Costas raced down to the dugout expecting to report on a broken leg. The Cardinals made faces and winked at him. "Television time," they were saying. Sure enough, Andujar returned to pitch and win the final game.

"These days there are fewer characters but more character-acting," says Costas. "You can almost choreograph your own moment, and the camera will do the rest."

Hot dog!

The Bureaucrat

Citicorp N. A.

Bureaucracy is a state of mind. True, every bureaucrat needs an organization, a milieu—to choose another useful word from the French—but it is the bureaucrat who makes the milieu, not the other way around.

Most of us associate bureaucracy and all its attendant evils with large organizations, especially governments, and we are not surprised to see it getting worse. As the earth's population grows and computers multiply along with the people, burgeoning bureaucracy appears a natural consequence. What Thomas Carlyle, a hundred years ago, could dismiss contemptuously as "the Continental nuisance called 'Bureaucracy'" is now to become the fate of all humanity because there are so many of us.

Before resigning ourselves to the inevitable, however, we might pause to consider that one of the most pervasive bureaucracies the world has ever known was oppressing the population of the Nile Valley 5,000 years ago, when there were fewer people in the entire world than now live in North America. Add to this the thought that the same number of people can be organized into *(a)* an army, *(b)* a crowd or *(c)* a mob, and it is clear that something more must be involved than time and numbers.

What distinguishes each of the aforementioned groups is not how many people it contains, nor where they happen to congregate, but their purpose for being there. And so it is with the bureaucrat.

The true bureaucrat is any individual who has lost sight of the underlying purpose of the job at hand, whether in government, industry—or a bank. The purpose of a library, for example, is to facilitate the reading of books. Yet to a certain type of librarian, perfection consists of a well-stocked library with a place for every book—and every book in its place. The reader who insists on taking books home, leaving empty spaces on shelves, is this librarian's natural enemy.

It is a cast of mind invulnerable even to the vicissitudes of war. We see it in James Jones's novel *From Here to Eternity* where American soldiers under surprise attack by Japanese planes at the outbreak of World War II rush to the arsenal for weapons, only to find the door barred by a comrade-in-arms loudly proclaiming that he cannot pass out live ammunition without a written request signed by a commissioned officer.

One of these custodians forgot the purpose of a library, the other the purpose of an army. Both illustrate how, in institutionalized endeavors, means have a way of displacing the ends they are originally designed to serve. In fact, it is one of the bureaucrat's distinguishing features that, for him or for her, the means become the ends.

The struggle to prevent this subtle subversion is—or should be—a continual challenge to every policy maker in any organization, public or private. Bureaucrats love any policy and can be counted on to enforce it faithfully, as in, "I'm sorry, but that's the policy here." Unfortunately, they don't understand what a policy is.

A policy is a standard solution to a constantly recurring problem, not an inviolable law. As a weapon in the hands of literal-minded people, however, a "firm policy'" can be as deadly as a repeating rifle. When matters finally become intolerable, the harassed administrator will usually "change the policy." Of course, this never helps because the problem was not the policy in the first place, but the manner of its application.

Every college student seeking entry into a course for which he lacks the exact prerequisite, every shopper trying to return a gift without receipt of purchase, every bank customer seeking to correct an error in an account is in danger of discovering that the rules imagined by Joseph Heller are in service wherever rote is more revered than reason.

The application of binary logic to human affairs through electronic computers has done nothing to retard the spread of *Catch 22* into the wider world. And thus the thought occurs that modern bureaucracy does, after all, present some problems new to history. Nothing lends itself so readily to "a standard solution to a constantly recurring problem" as a computer.

In the best of all possible worlds we might look forward to the day when computers handle all standard solutions, freeing human brains to concentrate on the singular and the exceptional. In the real world, it does not always work out that way—as anyone knows who has ever become trapped in a two-way correspondence with a computer and appealed in vain for human intervention.

A favorite student protest sign of the sixties read, "I am a Human Being. Do not fold, spindle or mutilate." What they objected to is real, only the fault is not in our computers, but in ourselves. It lies in our human propensity to let means become ends, and all too often to resemble Santayana's description of a fanatic; one who, having forgotten his purpose, redoubles his efforts.

We can denounce the bureaucrats and condemn their works, but they will not go away. They have been with us since the dawn of history, and if they seem to be getting worse, it is because we are getting worse. For, in the words of the comic strip *Pogo*: "We has met the enemy, and they is us."

Bureaucracy is a state of mind, and the best way to fight it—whether you work for government, industry, a private foundation or a bank—is not to be a bureaucrat. Or at least try not to.

The Sweet Smell of Success Isn't All That Sweet

Laurence Shames

John Milton was a failure. In writing "Paradise Lost," his stated aim was to "jus-tify the ways of God to men." Inevitably, he fell short of accomplishing that and only wrote a monumental poem. Beethoven, whose music was conceived to tran-scend Fate, was a failure, as was Socrates, whose ambition was to make people happy by making them reasonable and just. The inescapable conclusion seems to be that the surest, noblest way to fail is to set one's own standards titanically high.

The flip-side of that proposition also seems true, and it provides the safe but dreary logic by which most of us live: The surest way to succeed is to keep one's strivings low—at least to direct them along already charted paths. Don't set your-self the probably thankless task of making the legal system better; just shoot at becoming a partner in the firm. Don't agonize over questions about where your talents and proclivities might most fulfillingly lead you; just do a heads-up job of determining where the educational or business opportunities seem most secure.

After all, if "success" itself—rather than the substance of the achievements that make for success—is the criterion by which we measure ourselves and from which we derive our self-esteem, why make things more difficult by reaching for the stars?

What is this contemporary version of success really all about?

According to certain beer commercials, it consists in moving up to a premi-um brand that costs a dime or so more per bottle. Credit-card companies would have you believe success inheres in owning their particular piece of plastic.

If these examples sound petty, they are. But take those petty privileges, weave them into a fabric that passes for a value system and what you've got is a nation-al mood that has vast motivating power that can shape at least the near future of the entire country.

Under the flag of success, modern-style, liberal arts colleges are withering while business schools are burgeoning—and yet even business schools are having an increasingly hard time finding faculty members, because teaching isn't considered "successful" enough. Amid a broad consensus that there is a glut of lawyers and an epidemic of strangling litigation, record numbers of young people continue to flock to law school because, for the individual practitioner, a law degree is still considered a safe ticket.

The most sobering thought of all is that today's M.B.A.s and lawyers are tomorrow's M.B.A.s and lawyers: Having invested so much time and money in their training, only a tiny percentage of them will ever opt out of their early chosen fields. Decisions made in accordance with today's hothouse notions of ambition are locking people into careers that will define and also limit their activities and yearnings for virtually the rest of their lives.

Many by external standards, will be "successes." They will own homes, eat in better restaurants, dress well and, in some instances, perform socially useful work. Yet there is a deadening and dangerous flaw in their philosophy: It has little room, little sympathy and less respect for the noble failure, for the person who ventures past the limits, who aims gloriously high and falls unashamedly short.

That sort of ambition doesn't have much place in a world where success is proved by worldly reward rather than by accomplishment itself. That sort of ambition is increasingly thought of as the domain of irredeemable eccentrics, of people who haven't quite caught on—and there is great social pressure not to be one of them.

The result is that fewer people are drawn to the cutting edge of noncommercial scientific research. Fewer are taking on the sublime, unwinnable challenges of the arts. Fewer are asking questions that matter—the ones that can't be answered. Fewer are putting themselves on the line, making as much of their minds and talents as they might.

The irony is that today's success-chasers seem obsessed with the idea of *not settling*. They take advanced degrees in business because they won't settle for just a so-so job. They compete for slots at law firms and investment houses because they won't settle for any but the fastest track. They seem to regard it as axiomatic that "success" and "settling" are opposites.

Yet in doggedly pursuing the rather brittle species of success now in fashion, they are restricting themselves to a chokingly narrow swath of turf along the entire range of human possibilities. Does it ever occur to them that, frequently, success is what people settle for when they can't think of something noble enough to be worth failing at?

Television Addiction

Marie Winn

Cookies or Heroin?

The word "addiction" is often used loosely and wryly in conversation. People will refer to themselves as "mystery book addicts" or "cookie addicts." E. B. White wrote of his annual surge of interest in gardening: "We are hooked and are making an attempt to kick the habit." Yet nobody really believes that reading mysteries or ordering seeds by catalogue is serious enough to be compared with addictions to heroin or alcohol. The word "addiction" is here used jokingly to denote a tendency to overindulge in some pleasurable activity.

People often refer to being "hooked on TV." Does this, too, fall into the light-hearted category of cookie eating and other pleasures that people pursue with unusual intensity, or is there a kind of television viewing that falls into the more serious category of destructive addiction?

When we think about addiction to drugs or alcohol we frequently focus on negative aspects, ignoring the pleasures that accompany drinking or drug-taking. And yet the essence of any serious addiction is a pursuit of pleasure, a search for a "high" that normal life does not supply. It is only the inability to function without the addictive substance that is dismaying, the dependence of the organism upon a certain experience and an increasing inability to function normally without it. Thus people will take two or three drinks at the end of the day not merely for the pleasure drinking provides, but also because they "don't feel normal" without them.

Real addicts do not merely pursue a pleasurable experience one time in order to function normally. They need to *repeat* it again and again. Something about that particular experience makes life without it less than complete. Other potentially pleasurable experiences are no longer possible, for under the spell of the addictive experience, their lives are peculiarly distorted. The addict craves an experience and yet is never really satisfied. The organism may be temporarily sated, but soon it begins to crave again.

Finally, a serious addiction is distinguished from a harmless pursuit of pleasure by its distinctly destructive elements. Heroin addicts, for instance, lead a damaged life: their increasing need for heroin in increasing doses prevents them from working, from maintaining relationships, from developing in human ways. Similarly alcoholics' lives are narrowed and dehumanized by their dependence on alcohol.

Let us consider television viewing in the light of the conditions that define serious addictions.

Not unlike drugs or alcohol, the television experience allows the participant to blot out the real world and enter into a pleasurable and passive mental state. The worries and anxieties of reality are as effectively deferred by becoming absorbed in a television program as by going on a trip induced by drugs or alcohol. And just as alcoholics are only vaguely aware of their addiction, feeling that they control their drinking more than they really do ("I can cut it out any time I want—I just like to have three or four drinks before dinner"), people similarly overestimate their control over television watching. Even as they put off other activities to spend hour after hour watching television, they feel they could easily resume living in a different, less passive style. But somehow or other, while the television set is present in their homes, the click doesn't sound. With television pleasures available, those other experiences seem less attractive, more difficult somehow.

A heavy viewer (a college English instructor) observes:

"I find television almost irresistible. When the set is on, I cannot ignore it. I can't turn it off. I feel sapped, will-less, enervated. As I reach out to turn off the set, the strength goes out of my arms. So I sit there for hours and hours."

Self-confessed television addicts often feel they "ought" to do other things—but the fact that they don't read and don't plant their garden or sew or crochet or play games or have conversations means that those activities are no longer as desirable as television viewing. In a way the lives of heavy viewers are as imbalanced by their television "habit" as a drug addict's or an alcoholic's. They are living in a holding pattern, as it were, passing up the activities that lead to growth or development or a sense of accomplishment. This is one reason people talk about their television viewing so ruefully, so apologetically. They are aware that it is an unproductive experience, that almost any other endeavor is more worthwhile by any human measure.

Finally it is the adverse effect of television viewing on the lives of so many people that defines it as a serious addiction. The television habit distorts the sense of time. It renders other experiences vague and curiously unreal while taking on a greater reality for itself. It weakens relationships by reducing and sometimes eliminating normal opportunities for talking, for communicating.

And yet television does not satisfy, else why would the viewer continue to watch hour after hour, day after day? "The measure of health," writes Lawrence Kubie, "is flexibility . . . and especially the freedom to cease when sated." But heavy television viewers can never be sated with their television experience—these do not provide the true nourishment that satiation requires—and thus they find that they cannot stop watching.

A former heavy watcher (filmmaker) describes such a syndrome:

"I remember when we first got the set I'd watch for hours and hours, whenever I could, and I remember that feeling of tiredness and anxiety that always followed those orgies, a sense of time terribly wasted. It was like eating cotton candy; television promised so much richness, I couldn't wait for it, and, then it just evaporated into air. I remember feeling terribly drained after watching for a long time."

Similarly a nursery school teacher remembers her own childhood television experience:

"I remember bingeing on television when I was a child and having that vapid feeling after watching hours of TV. I'd look forward to watching whenever I could, but it just didn't give back a real feeling of pleasure. It was like no orgasm, no catharsis, very frustrating. Television just wasn't giving me the promised satisfaction, and yet I kept on watching. It filled some sort of need, or had to do with an inability to get something started."

The testimonies of ex-television addicts often have the evangelistic overtones of stories heard at Alcoholics Anonymous meetings.

A handbag repair shop owner says:

"I'd get on the subway home from work with the newspaper and immediately turn to the TV page to plan out my evening's watching. I'd come home, wash, change my clothes, and tell my wife to start the machine so it would be warmed up. (We had an old-fashioned set that took a few seconds before an image appeared.) And then we'd watch TV for the rest of the evening. We'd eat our dinner in the living room while watching, and we'd only talk every once in a while, during the ads, if at all. I'd watch anything, good, bad, or indifferent.

"All the while we were watching I'd feel terribly angry at myself for wasting all that time watching junk. I could never go to sleep until at least the eleven o'clock news, and then sometimes I'd still stay up for the late-night talk show. I had a feeling that I *had* to watch the news programs, that I *had* to know what was happening, even though most of the time nothing much was happening and I could easily find out what was by reading the paper the next morning. Usually my wife would fall asleep on the couch while I was watching. I'd get angry at her for doing that. Actually, I was angry at myself. I had a collection of three years of back issues of different magazines that I planned to read sometime, but I never got around to reading them. I never got around to sorting or labeling my collection of slides I had made when traveling. I only had time for television. We'd take the telephone off the hook while watching so we wouldn't be interrupted! We like classical music, but we never listened to any, never!

"Then one day the set broke. I said to my wife, 'Let's not fix it. Let's just see what happens.' Well, that was the smartest thing we ever did. We haven't had a TV in the house since then.

"Now I look back and I can hardly believe we could have lived like that. I feel that my mind was completely mummified for all those years. I was glued to that machine and couldn't get loose, somehow. It really frightens me to think of it. Yes, I'm frightened of TV now. I don't think I could control it if we had a set in the house again. I think it would take over no matter what I did.

A further sign of addiction is that "an exclusive craving for something is accompanied by a loss of discrimination towards the object which satisfies the craving. . . . The alcoholic is not interested in the taste of liquor that is available; likewise the compulsive eater is not particular about what he eats when there is food around" write the authors of a book about the nature of addiction. And just so, for many viewers the process of *watching* television is far more important than the actual contents of the programs being watched. The knowledge that the act of watching is more important than *what* is being watched lies behind the practice of "road blocking," invented by television advertisers and adopted by political candidates who purchase the same half-hour on all three channels in order to force-feed their message to the public. As one prominent candidate put it, "People will watch television no matter what is on, and if you allow them no other choice they will watch your show."

The comparison between television addiction and drug addictions is often made by addicts themselves. A lawyer says:

"I watch TV the way an alcoholic drinks. If I come home and sit in front of the TV, I'll watch any program at all, even if there's nothing on that especially appeals to me. Then the next thing I know it's eleven o'clock and I'm watching the Johnny Carson show, and I'll realize I've spent the whole evening watching TV. What's more, I can't stand Johnny Carson! But I'll still sit there watching him. I'm addicted to TV, when it's there, and I'm not happy about the addiction. I'll sit there getting madder and madder at myself for watching, but still I'll sit there. I can't turn it off."

Nor is the television addict always blind to the dysfunctional aspects of his addiction. A housewife says:

"Sometimes a friend will come over while I'm watching TV. I'll say, 'Wait a second. Just let me finish watching this,' and then I'll feel bad about that, letting the machine take precedence over people. And I'll do that for the stupidest programs, just because I have to watch, somehow."

In spite of the potentially destructive nature of television addiction, it is rarely taken seriously in American society. Critics mockingly refer to television as a "cultural barbiturate" and joke about "mainlining the tube." Indeed, a spectacle called a "Media Burn," which took place in San Francisco in 1975 and which involved the piling of 44 old television sets on top of each other in the parking lot of the old Cow Palace, soaking them with kerosene, and applying a torch, perfectly illustrates the feeling of good fun that surrounds the issue of television addiction. According to the programs distributed before the event, everybody was supposed to experience "a cathartic explosion" and "be free at last from the addiction to television."

The issue of television addiction takes on a more serious air when the addicts are our own children. A mother reports:

"My ten-year-old is as hooked on TV as an alcoholic is hooked on drink. He tries to strike desperate bargains: 'If you let me watch just ten more minutes, I won't watch at all tomorrow,' he says. It's pathetic. It scares me."

Another mother tells about her six-year-old son:

"We were in Israel last summer where the TV stations sign off for the night at about ten. Well, my son would turn on the set and watch the Arabic stations that were still on, even though he couldn't understand a word, just because he had to watch *something*."

Other signs of serious addiction come out in parents' descriptions of their children's viewing behavior:

"We used to have very bad reception before we got on Cable TV. I'd come into the room and see my eight-year-old watching this terrible, blurry picture and I'd say, 'Heavens, how can you see? Let me try to fix it,' and he'd get frantic and scream, 'Don't touch it!' It really worried me, that he wanted to watch so badly that he was even willing to watch a completely blurred image."

Another mother tells of her eight-year-old son's behavior when deprived of television:

"There was a time when both TV sets were out for about two weeks, and Jerry reached a point where I felt that if he didn't watch something, he was really going to start climbing the walls. He was fidgety and nervous. He'd crawl all over the furniture. He just didn't know what to do with himself, and it seemed to get worse every day. I said to my husband, 'He's having withdrawal symptoms,' and I really think that's what it was. Finally I asked one of my friends if he could go and watch the Saturday cartoons at their house."

The Right Stuff

Tom Wolfe

A young man might go into military flight training believing that he was entering some sort of technical school in which he was simply going to acquire a certain set of skills. Instead, he found himself all at once enclosed in a fraternity. And in this fraternity, even though it was military, men were not rated by their outward rank as ensigns, lieutenants, commanders, or whatever. No, herein the world was divided into those who had it and those who did not. This quality, this *it*, was never named, however, nor was it talked about in any way.

As to just what this ineffable quality was . . . well, it obviously involved bravery. But it was not bravery in the simple sense of being willing to risk your life. The idea seemed to be that any fool could do that, if that was all that was required, just as any fool could throw away his life in the process. No, the idea here (in the all-enclosing fraternity) seemed to be that a man should have the ability to go up in a hurtling piece of machinery and put his hide on the line and then have the moxie, the reflexes, the experience, the coolness, to pull it back in the last yawning moment—and then to go up again *the next day*, and the next day, and every next day, even if the series should prove infinite—and, ultimately, in its best expression, do so in a cause that means something to thousands, to a people, nation, to humanity, to God. Nor was there *a test* to show whether or not a pilot had this righteous quality. There was, instead, a seemingly infinite series of tests. A career in flying was like climbing one of those ancient Babylonian pyramids made up of a dizzy progression of steps and ledges, a ziggurat, a pyramid extraordinarily high and steep; and the idea was to prove at every foot of the way up that pyramid that you were one of the elected and anointed ones who had *the right stuff* and could move higher and higher and even—ultimately, God willing, one day—that you might be able to join that special few at the very top, that elite who had the capacity to bring tears to men's eyes, the very Brotherhood of the Right Stuff itself.

None of this was to be mentioned, and yet it was acted out in a way that a young man could not fail to understand. When a new flight (i.e., a class) of trainees arrived at Pensacola, they were brought into an auditorium for a little lecture. An officer would tell them: "Take a look at the man on either side of you." Quite a few actually swiveled their heads this way and that, in the interest of appearing diligent. Then the officer would say: "One of the three of you is not going to make it!"—meaning, not get his wings. That was the opening theme, the *motif* of primary training. We already know that one-third of you do not have the right stuff—it only remains to find out who.

Furthermore, that was the way it turned out. At every level in one's progress up that staggeringly high pyramid, the world was once more divided into those men who had the right stuff to continue the climb and those who had to be *left behind* in the most obvious way. Some were eliminated in the course of the opening classroom work, as either not smart enough or not hard-working enough, and were left behind. Then came the basic flight instruction, in single-engine, propeller-driven trainers, and a few more—even though the military tried to make this stage easy—were washed out and left behind. Then came more demanding levels, one after the other, formation flying, instrument flying, jet training, all-weather flying, gunnery, and at each level more were washed out and left behind. By this point easily a third of the original candidates had been, indeed, eliminated . . . from the ranks of those who might prove to have the right stuff.

In the Navy, in addition to the stages that Air Force trainees went through, the neophyte always had waiting for him, out in the ocean, a certain grim gray slab; namely, the deck of an aircraft carrier; and with it perhaps the most difficult routine in military flying, carrier landings. He was shown films about it, he heard lectures about it, and he knew that carrier landings were hazardous. He first practiced touching down on the shape of a flight deck painted on an airfield. He was instructed to touch down and gun right off. This was safe enough—the shape didn't move, at least—but it could do terrible things to, let us say, the gyroscope of the soul. *That shape!—it's so damned small!* And more candidates were washed out and left behind. Then came the day, without warning, when those who remained were sent out over the ocean for the first of many days of reckoning with the slab. The first day was always a clear day with little wind and a calm sea. The carrier was so steady that it seemed, from up there in the air, to be resting on pilings, and the candidate usually made his first carrier landing successfully, with relief and even *élan*. Many young candidates looked like terrific aviators up to that very point—and it was not until they were actually standing on the carrier deck that they first began to wonder if they had the proper stuff, after all. In the training film the flight deck was a grand piece of gray geometry, perilous, to be sure, but an amazing abstract shape as one looks down upon it on the screen. And yet once the newcomer's two feet were on it . . . *Geometry*—my God, man, this is a . . . skillet! It *heaved*, it moved up and down underneath his feet. It pitched up, it pitched down, it rolled to port (this great beast *rolled!*), and it rolled to starboard, as the ship moved into the wind and, therefore, into the waves, and the wind kept sweeping across, sixty feet up in the air out in the open sea, and there were no railings whatsoever. This was a *skillet!*—a flying pan!—a short-order grill!—not gray but black smeared with skid marks from one end to the other and glistening with pools of hydraulic fluid and the occasional jet-fuel slick, all of it still hot, sticky, greasy, runny, virulent from God knows what traumas—still ablaze!—consumed in detonations, explosions, flames, combustion, roars, shrieks, whines, blasts, horrible shudders, fracturing impacts, as little men in screaming red and yellow and purple and green shirts with black Mickey Mouse helmets over their ears skittered about on the surface as if for their very lives (you've said it now!), hooking fighter planes onto the catapult shuttles so that they can explode their afterburners and be slung off the deck in a red-mad fury with a *kaboom!* that pounds through the entire deck—a procedure that seems absolutely controlled, orderly, sublime, however, compared to what he is about to watch as aircraft return to the ship for what is known in the engineering stoicisms of the military as "recovery and arrest." To say that an F-4 was coming back onto this heaving barbecue from out of the sky at a speed of 135 knots . . . that might have been the truth in the training lecture, but it did not begin to get across the idea of what the newcomer saw from the deck itself, because it created the notion that perhaps the plane was gliding in. On the deck one knew differently! As the aircraft came closer and the carrier heaved on into the waves and the plane's speed did not diminish and the deck did not grow steady—indeed, it pitched up and down five or ten feet per greasy heave—one experienced a neural alarm that no lecture could have prepared him for: This is not an *airplane* coming toward me, it is a brick with some poor sonofabitch riding it (*someone much like myself!*), and it is not *gliding*, it is *falling*, a thirty-thousand-pound brick, headed not for a stripe on the deck but for *me*—and with a horrible *smash!* it hits the skillet, and with a blur of momentum as big as a freight train's it hurtles toward the far end of the deck—another blinding storm!—another roar as the pilot pushes the throttle up to full military power and another smear of rubber screams out over the skillet—and this is nominal!—quite okay!—for a wire stretched across the deck has grabbed the hook on the end of the plane as it hit the deck tail down, and the smash was the rest of the fifteen-ton brute slamming onto the deck, as it tripped up, so that it is now straining against the wire at full throttle, in case it hadn't held and the plane had "boltered" off the end of the deck and had to struggle up into the air again. And already the Mickey Mouse helmets are running toward the fiery monster. . . .

And the candidate, looking on, begins to *feel* that great heaving sun-blazing deathboard of a deck wallowing in his own vestibule system—and suddenly he finds himself backed up against his own limits. He ends up going to the flight surgeon with so-called conversion symptoms. Overnight he develops blurred vision or numbness in his hands and feet or sinusitis so severe that he cannot tolerate changes in altitude. On one level the symptom is real. He really cannot see too well or use his fingers or stand the pain. But somewhere in his subconscious he knows it is a plea and a beg-off; he shows not the slightest concern (the flight surgeon notes) that the condition might be permanent and affect him in whatever life awaits him outside the arena of the right stuff.

Those who remained, those who qualified for carrier duty—and even more so those who later on qualified for *night* carrier duty—began to feel a bit like Gideon's warriors. *So many have been left behind!* The young warriors were now treated to a deathly sweet and quite unmentionable sight. They could gaze at length upon the crushed and wilted pariahs who had washed out. They could inspect those who did not have that righteous stuff.

The military did not have very merciful instincts. Rather than packing up these poor souls and sending them home, the Navy, like the Air Force and the Marines, would try to make use of them in some other role, such as flight controller. So the washout has to keep taking classes with the rest of his group, even though he can no longer touch an airplane. He sits there in the classes staring at sheets of paper with cataracts of sheer human mortification over his eyes while the rest steal looks at him . . . this man reduced to an ant, this untouchable, this poor sonofabitch. And in what test had he been found wanting? Why, it seemed to be nothing less than *manhood* itself. Naturally, this was never mentioned, either. Yet there it was. *Manliness, manhood, manly courage* . . . there was something ancient, primordial, irresistible about the challenge of this stuff, no matter what a sophisticated and rational age one might think he lived in.

What Is a Lamer?

Student

What is a lamer? A lamer is a person who thinks that the online world belongs to him or her. The lamer doesn't take well to threats, and genuinely has less knowledge than the average user, although the lamer will often seem full of knowledge and godlike to other users. A lamer is a person who is a frequent member of the online community, especially chat rooms, who thinks he or she knows everything, when really knowing less than the average user.

First, a lamer is very ignorant. The lamer throws around phrases that he or she has picked up in chat rooms though not having a clue as how to use these phrases, for example, something outrageous like "My mainframe is my sound-card." First of all, a mainframe doesn't have a soundcard. Second, the average Joe Blow doesn't have a mainframe. Finally, if a mainframe did have a soundcard, it would be an accessory, not part of the system. The irony of it all is that the words "soundcard" and "mainframe" are not common words, and your average online user may think the lamer is pretty smart because he or she knows words that the average user doesn't.

Second, a lamer is obnoxiously egotistical. The lamer has an ego the size of the universe, so big it can't be defined. A lamer will not only go around blabbing fallacies around the online forum, but also says them in such a way as to make him or her look cool, for instance, typing the word "elite" as "31337" to look so cool. The substituting of letters for numbers is called "elite speak." Talking in "elite speak" really just takes a lot more time and makes the message of the lamer less substantial than it already is. The lamer also will brag about what warez (pirated software) he or she has. In truth, all the lamer does to get the software he or she wants is tell an unknowing person that he or she has certain software and then rip them off by taking their software and not trading, as agreed. But the biggest problem concerning a lamer's ego is not knowing when to stop. The lamer will keep rambling on and on, bragging about things that he or she doesn't have a clue about, and—boom— the lamer is kicked out of the channel or chat room that he or she is typing in and not allowed back. The members of the channel then rejoice and talk about how lame the lamer was.

Third, a lamer is sadly unskillful; in fact, the lamer has very few computer skills at all. The lamer, unfortunately, does have the skills to get online, but the learning process seems to stop there. The lamer will brag on and on about how much skill he or she has, but knows nothing about what he or she is talking about. The lamer simply has picked up something along the way and types it. The lamer has no idea what it means, just that it sounds smart. The lamer also will say that he or she has hacked web sites, etc., but what the lamer really has done is modified his or her own web site and act like it was hacked. Hacking your own web site is probably one of the lamest things a person can do.

Fourth, a lamer is undoubtedly lazy and does not want to learn anything. If you ever run into a lamer, he or she will ask you for information instead of taking the initiative to find it on his or her own. Lamers will also ask you questions revealing their own stupidity and then try to prove that they aren't lamers by putting out a little, tiny bit of effort to show you up. Then they will simply accuse you of being wrong and go on like nothing happened.

A lamer, most of all, is insecure, having one of the biggest insecurity problems any one person can. If the lamer is made fun of or called a "lamer," the lamer will resort to saying "shut up" and using some non-intelligent, substance-lacking, slang expletives. He or she will continue saying how elite and better than you he or she is. The lamer, after being made fun of long enough, probably goes home and cries to his or her mommy because of this insecurity problem.

Overall, a lamer is just that —"lame." Being a lamer should be illegal on the planet Earth, but the Internet, with free speech and free reign, means that the lamer has just as much a right to be online as you or I. This having been said, you have the ethical right to put the lamer in his or her place because, again, the Internet grants you free speech and free reign.

Failure

Student

What is my definition of failure? *I believe failure is when you set goals for yourself and do nothing to achieve them.* It is like you say you are going to do something and never do it because something comes up. There is always an excuse for not pushing yourself to do what you need to do to be successful. Other people believe that not reaching a goal that you have set for yourself is failure. I don't believe that is true. If they really try to reach a goal but just can't accomplish the task, they are still a success because they at least tried to see what would happen and how close they could get to their goal. Just setting goals and honestly trying to reach them is the key to not becoming a failure.

Success

Student

Success is defined in many different ways by many different people. To me success is achieving something that I strived for a long time. In my life I have only one instance of success. I started training for that moment when I was eleven. It took six months of training and practicing every year. Six years later, I was ready to give up and quit, but I decided to keep trying and not give up until I succeeded. My freshman year in college I made the varsity football team, and I thought that maybe finally this was my chance. We were three and zero, and we were playing a team that had not won all year. They had us down 23 to zero with only five minutes left in the game, and we ended up coming back for the win. We won all of our games that year and became national champions of our division. This was my lifelong dream, and it had finally came true. This was something that I had worked my whole life to try and be a part of, and this is why I feel that I have succeeded in my life.

Ch. 8: Definition

Suggestions for writing:

1. Write an essay or paragraph defining what you think failure and success are, without resorting to merely stating that "success is attaining the goals that you set for yourself."

2. Write an essay or paragraph defining what you think the "right stuff' is for being a successful student.

3. Write a definition essay or paragraph using one of the following topics or a similar topic:

an act of true courage	a loyal friend
happiness/unhappiness	unconditional love
faith	the perfect gift
the most difficult exam	a learning experience
a boring job	anger
an easy-to-use search engine	the best computer

Definition checklist:

1. Did you begin by describing the general category to which your term (the topic of your essay or paragraph) belongs?

2. Did you distinguish your term from other related terms in this category?

3. Did you define your term's etymology?

4. Did you define your term by saying what it is not?

5. If writing an essay, does each body paragraph relate to the thesis? Did you develop the body paragraphs using example, description, illustration, etc.?

6. Do you speak to your audience's needs?

7. Do you vary your vocabulary? The type and length of your sentences?

8. If writing an essay, did you conclude it logically and effectively?

9. Did you check for correctness of grammar, punctuation and spelling?

CHAPTER 9

Argument and Persuasion

Inciting People to Thought or Action

Using Argument and Persuasion

Almost everything we do or say is an attempt to persuade. Whether we dress up to impress a potential employer or argue openly with a friend about an upcoming election, we are trying to convince various people to see the world our way. Some aspects of life are particularly dependent upon persuasion. Think, for example, of all the television, magazine, and billboard ads we see urging us to buy certain products or of the many impassioned appeals we read and hear on such controversial issues as school prayer, abortion, gun control, and nuclear energy. Religious leaders devote their professional lives to convincing people to live a certain way and believe in certain religious truths, whereas scientists and mathematicians use rigorous logic and natural law to convince us of various hypotheses. Politicians make their living persuading voters to elect them and then support them throughout their terms of office. In fact, anyone who wants something from another person or agency, ranging from federal money for a research project to a new bicycle for Christmas, must use some form of persuasion to get what he or she desires. The success or failure of this type of communication is easily determined: If the people being addressed change their actions or attitudes in favor of the writer or speaker, the attempt at persuasion has been successful.

Defining Argument and Persuasion

The terms argument and persuasion are often used interchangeably, but one is actually a subdivision of the other. Persuasion names a purpose for writing. To persuade your readers is to convince them to think, act, or feel a certain way. Much of the writing you have been doing in this book has persuasion as one of its goals: A description of an African tribe has a "dominant impression" you want your readers to accept; in an essay comparing various ways of celebrating Thanksgiving, you are trying to convince your readers to believe that these similarities and differences actually exist, and in writing an essay exam on the causes of the Vietnam War, you are trying to convince your instructor that your reasoning is clear and your conclusions sound. In a sense, some degree of persuasion propels all writing.

More specifically, however, the process of persuasion involves appealing to one or more of the following: to reason, to emotion, or to a sense of ethics. An *argument* is an appeal predominantly to your readers' reason and intellect. You are working in the realm of argument when you deal with complex issues that are debatable; opposing views (either explicit or implicit) are a basic requirement of argumentation. But argument and persuasion are taught together because good writers are constantly blending these three appeals and adjusting them to the purpose and audience of a particular writing task. Although reason and logic are the focus of this chapter, you need to learn to use all three methods of persuasion as skillfully as possible to write effective essays.

An appeal to reason relies upon logic and intellect and is usually most effective when you are expecting your readers to disagree with you in any way. This type of appeal can help you change your readers' opinions or influence their future actions through the sheer strength of logical validity. If you wanted to argue, for example, that pregnant women should refrain from smoking cigarettes, you could cite abundant statistical evidence that babies born to mothers who smoke have lower birth weights, more respiratory problems, and a higher incidence of sudden infant death syndrome than the children of nonsmoking mothers. Because smoking clearly endangers the health of the unborn child, reason dictates that mothers who wish to give birth to the healthiest possible babies should avoid smoking during pregnancy.

Emotional appeals, however, attempt to arouse your readers' feelings, instincts, senses, and biases. Used most profitably when your readers already agree with you, this type of essay generally validates, reinforces, and/or incites in an effort to get your readers to share your feelings or ideas. In an attempt to urge our lawmakers to impose stricter jail sentences for alcohol abuse, you might describe a recent tragic accident involving a local twelve-year-old girl who was killed by a drunk driver as she rode her bicycle to school one morning. By focusing on such poignant visual details as the condition of her mangled bike, the bright blood stains on her white dress, and the anguish on the faces of parents and friends, you could build a powerfully persuasive essay that would be much more effective than a dull recitation of impersonal facts and nationwide statistics.

An appeal to ethics, the third technique writers often use to encourage readers to agree with them, involves cultivating a sincere, honest tone that will establish your reputation as a reliable, qualified, experienced, well-informed, and knowledgeable person whose opinions on the topic under discussion are believable because they are ethically sound. Such an approach is often used in conjunction with logical or emotional appeals to foster a verbal environment that will result in minimal resistance from its readers. Ed McMahon, Johnny Carson's congenial announcer on the "Tonight Show" for many years and the host of "Star Search," is an absolute master at creating this ethical, trustworthy persona as he coaxes his television viewers to purchase everything from dog food to beer. In fact, the old gag question "Would you buy a used car from this man?" is our instinctive response to all forms of attempted persuasion, whether the salesperson is trying to sell us Puppy Chow or gun control, hair spray or school prayer. The more believable we are as human beings, the better chance we will have of convincing our audience.

The following student paragraph is directed primarily toward the audience's logical faculties. Notice how the writer states her assertion and then gives reasons to convince her readers to change their ways. The student writer also brings both emotion and ethics into the argument by choosing her words and examples with great precision.

> *Have you ever watched a pair of chunky thighs, a jiggling posterior, and an extra-large sweatshirt straining to cover a beer belly and thought, "Thank God I don't look like that! I'm in pretty good shape. . . for someone my age." Well, before you become too smug and self-righteous, consider what kind of shape you're really in. Just because you don't look like Shamu the Whale doesn't mean you're in good condition. What's missing, you ask? Exercise. You can diet all day, wear the latest slim-cut designer jeans, and still be in worse shape than someone twice your age if you don't get a strong physical workout at least three times a week. Exercise is not only good for you, but it can also be fun—especially if you find a sport that makes you happy while you sweat. Your activity need not be expensive: Jogging, walking, basketball, tennis, and handball are not costly, unless you're seduced by the glossy sheen of the latest sporting fashions and accessories. Most of all, however, regular exercise is important for your health. You can just as easily drop dead from a sudden heart attack in the middle of a restaurant when you're slim and trim as when you're a slob. Your heart and lungs need regular workouts to stay healthy. So do yourself a favor and add some form of exercise to your schedule. You'll feel better and live longer, and your looks will improve, too!*

How to Write Persuasive Essays

Preparing to Write. The first stage of writing an essay of this sort involves, as usual, exploring and then limiting your topic. As you prepare to write your persuasive paper, first try to generate as many ideas as possible—regardless of whether they appeal to logic, emotion, or ethics. Then, choose a topic. Next, focus on a purpose and specific audience before you begin to write.

Writing. Most persuasive essays should begin with an assertion or proposition stating what you believe about a certain issue. This thesis should generally be phrased as a debatable statement, such as, "If individual states reinstituted the death penalty, Americans would notice an immediate drop in violent crimes." At this point in your essay, you should also justify the significance of the issue you will be discussing: "Such a decline in the crime rate would affect all our lives and make this country a safer place in which to live."

The essay should then support your thesis in a variety of ways. This support might take the form of facts, figures, examples, opinions by recognized authorities, case histories, narratives/anecdotes, comparisons, contrasts, or cause/effect studies. This evidence is most effectively organized from least to most important when you are confronted with a hostile audience (so that you can lead your readers through the reasoning step by step) and from most to least important when you are facing a supportive audience (so that you can build on their loyalty and enthusiasm as you advance your thesis). In fact, you will be able to engineer your best support if you know your audience's opinions, feelings, and background before you write your essay so that your intended "target" is as clear as possible, the body of your essay will undoubtedly consist of a combination of logical, emotional, and ethical appeals—all leading to some final summation or recommendation.

The concluding paragraph of a persuasive essay should restate your main assertion (in slightly different terms than your original statement) and offer some constructive recommendations about the problem you have been discussing (if you haven't already done so). This section of your paper should clearly bring your argument to a close in one final attempt to move your audience to accept or act upon the viewpoint you present. Let's look more closely now at each of the three types of appeals used in such essays: logical, emotional, and ethical.

To construct a logical argument, you have two principal patterns available to you: inductive reasoning or deductive reasoning. The first encourages an audience to make what is called an "inductive leap" from several particular examples to a single, useful generalization. In the case of the death penalty, you might cite a number of examples, figures, facts, and case studies illustrating the effectiveness of capital punishment in various states, thereby leading up to your firm belief that the death penalty should be reinstituted. Used most often by detectives, scientists, and lawyers, the process of inductive reasoning addresses the audience's ability to think logically by moving them systematically from an assortment of selected evidence to a rational and ordered conclusion.

In contrast, deductive reasoning moves its audience from a broad, general statement to particular examples supporting that statement. In writing such an essay, you would present your thesis statement about capital punishment first and then offer clear, orderly evidence to support that belief. Although the mental process we go through in creating a deductive argument is quite sophisticated, it is based upon a three-step form of reasoning called the "syllogism," which most logicians believe is the foundation of logical thinking. The traditional syllogism has

> a major premise: *All humans fear death.*
> a minor premise: *Criminals are humans.*
> and a conclusion: *Therefore, criminals fear death.*

As you might suspect, this type of reasoning is only as accurate as its original premises, so you need to be careful with the truth of the premises as well as with the logical validity of your argument.

In constructing a logical argument, you should take great care to avoid the two types of fallacies in reasoning found most frequently in lower-division college papers: giving too few examples to support an assertion, or citing examples that do not represent the assertion fairly. If you build your argument on true statements and abundant, accurate evidence, your essay will be effective.

Persuading through emotion necessitates controlling your readers' instinctive reactions to what you are saying. You can accomplish this goal in two different ways: (1) by choosing your words with even greater care than usual and (2) by using figurative language whenever appropriate. In the first case, you must be especially conscious of using words that have the same general denotative (or dictionary) meaning but bear decidedly favorable or unfavorable connotative (or implicit) meanings: For example, notice the difference between "slender" and "scrawny," "patriotic" and "chauvinistic," or "compliment" and "flattery." Your careful attention to the choice of such words can help readers form visual images with certain positive or negative associations that subtly encourage them to follow your argument and adopt your opinions. Second, the effective use of figurative language—especially similes and metaphors—makes your writing more vivid, thus triggering your readers' senses and encouraging them to accept your views. Both of these techniques will help you manipulate your readers into the position of agreeing with your ideas.

Ethical appeals, which establish you as a reliable, well-informed person, are accomplished through (1) the tone of your essay and (2) the number and type of examples you cite. Tone is created through deliberate word choice: Careful attention to the mood implied in the words you use can convince your readers that you are serious, friendly, authoritative, jovial, or methodical—depending on your intended purpose. In like manner, the examples you supply to support your assertions can encourage readers to see you as experienced, insightful, relaxed, or intense. In both of these cases, winning favor for yourself will usually also gain approval for your opinions.

Rewriting. To rework your persuasive essays, you should play the role of your readers and impartially evaluate the different appeals you have used to accomplish your purpose: Is your thesis statement clear? Is the main thrust of your essay argumentative (an appeal to reason)? Which of your supporting details appeal to emotion? To ethics? Will the balance of these appeals effectively accomplish your purpose with your intended audience? You should also look closely at the way your appeals work together in your essay: When you use logic, is that section of your paper arranged through either inductive or deductive reasoning? Is that the most effective order to achieve your purpose? In appealing to the emotions, have you chosen your words with proper attention to their denotative and connotative effects? Have you used figurative language whenever appropriate? And in your ethical appeals, have you created the right tone for your essay? Is it suitable for your purpose and your audience? Have you chosen examples carefully to support your thesis statement?

Student Essay: Argument and Persuasion at Work

The following student essay uses all three appeals to make its point about the power of language in shaping our view of the world. First, the writer sets forth her character references (ethical appeal) in the first paragraph, after which she presents her thesis and its significance in paragraph 2. The support for her thesis is a combination of logical and emotional appeals, heavy on the logical, as the writer moves her paragraphs from general to particular in an effort to convince her readers to adopt her point of view and adjust their language use accordingly.

The Language of Equal Rights

Ethical appeal — Up front, I admit it. I'm a woman's libber, a card-carrying feminist since junior high school. I want to see an Equal Rights Amendment to the U.S. Constitution, equal pay for equal—and comparable—work, and I go dutch on dates. Furthermore, I am quite prickly on the subject of language. I'm one of those women who bristles at terms like "lady doctor" — Emotional appeal — (you know they don't mean a gynecologist), "female policeman" (a paradox), and "mankind" instead of humanity (are they really talking about me?)

Many people ask "How important are mere words, anyway? You know what they really mean." A question like this ignores the symbolic and psychological importance of language. What words "mean" can go beyond what a speaker or writer consciously intends,

Assertion or thesis statement

Signifi-
cance of
assertion reflecting personal and cultural biases that run so deep that most of the time we aren't even aware they exist. "Mere words" are incredibly important—they are our framework for seeing and understanding the world.

Logical
appeal "Man," we are told, means woman as well as man, just as "mankind" supposedly stands for all of humanity. In the introduction of a sociology textbook I read recently, the author was anxious to demonstrate his awareness of the controversy over sexist language and to assure his female readers that, despite his use of Examples
organized
deductively noninclusive terms, he was not forgetting the existence or importance of women in society. He was making a conscious decision to continue to use "man" and "mankind" instead of "people," "humanity," etc., because of ease of expression and esthetic reasons. "Man" simply sounds better, he explained. I flipped through the table of contents and found "Man and Society," "Man and Nature," "Man and Technology," and near the end, "Man and Woman." At what point Emotional
appeal did "Man" quit meaning people and start meaning men again? The writer was obviously unaware of the answer to this question, because it is one he would never think to ask. Having consciously addressed the issue only to dismiss it, he reverted to form.

Logical
appeal The very ambiguity of "man" as the generic word for our species ought to be enough to combat any arguments that we keep it because we all "know what it means" or because it is both traditional and sounds better. And does it really sound all that better, or are we just more used to it, more comfortable? Our own national history proves that we can be comfortable Examples
organized
deductively with a host of words and attitudes that strike us as unjust and ugly today. A lot of White folks probably thought that Negroes were getting pretty stuffy and picky when they began to insist on being called Blacks. After all, weren't there more important things to worry about, like civil rights? Emotional
appeal But Black activists recognize the emotional and symbolic significance of having a name that was parallel to the name the dominant race used for itself—a name equal in dignity, lacking that vaguely alien, anthropological sound. After all, Whites were called Caucasians only in police reports, textbooks, and autopsies. "Negro" may have sounded better to people in the bad old days of blatant racial bigotry, but we've adjusted to the word "Black," and more and more people of each race are adjusting to the wider implications and demands of practical, as well as verbal, equality.

In a world where "man" and "human" are offered
as synonymous terms, I don't think it is a coincidence

Logical that women are still vastly underrepresented in posi-
appeal tions of money, power, and respect. Children grow up
learning a language that makes maleness the norm for
anything that isn't explicitly designated as female, giving little girls a very limited corner of the universe to
picture themselves in. Indeed, the language that non-
feminists today claim to be inclusive was never intend- Examples
ed to cover women in the first place. "One man, one organized
vote" and "All men are created equal" meant just that. deduc-
Women had to fight for decades to be included even as tively
an afterthought; it took constitutional amendments to
convince the government and the courts that women
are human, too.

The message is clear. We have to start speaking

Conclu- about people, not men, if we are going to start think-
sion/ ing in terms of both women and men. A "female man"
restate- will never be the equal of her brother.
ment

Student Writer's Comments

The hardest task for me on this essay was trying to come up with a
topic! The second hardest task was trying to be effective without getting preachy, strident, or wordy. I wanted to persuade an audience that
would no doubt include the bored, the hostile, and the indifferent, and
I was worried about losing their attention. Although my main
approach to the topic is argumentative, I strategically introduce emotional and ethical appeals in the essay. I appeal to ethics to establish
my credibility, and I appeal to emotion to vary my pace and help my
argument gain a little momentum. After many revisions, I think the
balance of appeals finally works.

Some Final Thoughts on Argument and Persuasion

As you can tell from the selections that follow, the three different types
of persuasive appeals usually complement each other in practice. Most
good persuasive essays use a combination of these methods to achieve
their purposes. Good persuasive essays also rely upon various rhetorical modes we have already studied—such as example, process analysis, division/classification, comparison/contrast, definition, and
cause/effect—to advance their arguments. In the following essays, you
will see a combination of appeals at work and a number of different
rhetorical modes furthering the arguments.

Get a Knife, Get a Dog, but Get Rid of Guns

Molly Ivins

Guns. Everywhere guns.

Let me start this discussion by pointing out that I am not antigun. I'm pro-knife. Consider the merits of the knife.

In the first place, you have to catch up with someone in order to stab him. A general substitution of knives for guns would promote physical fitness. We'd turn into a whole nation of great runners. Plus, knives don't ricochet. And people are seldom killed while cleaning their knives.

As a civil libertarian, I of course support the Second Amendment. And I believe it means exactly what it says:

A well-regulated militia being necessary to the security of a free state, the right of the people to keep and bear arms shall not be infringed. Fourteen-year-old boys are not part of a well-regulated militia. Members of wacky religious cults are not part of a well-regulated militia. Permitting unregulated citizens to have guns is destroying the security of this free state.

I am intrigued by the arguments of those who claim to follow the judicial doctrine of original intent. How do they know it was the dearest wish of Thomas Jefferson's heart that teenage drug dealers should cruise the cities of this nation perforating their fellow citizens with assault rifles? Channeling?

There is more hooey spread about the Second Amendment. It says quite clearly that guns are for those who form part of a well-regulated militia, that is, the armed forces, including the National Guard. The reasons for keeping them away from everyone else get clearer by the day.

The comparison most often used is that of the automobile, another lethal object that is regularly used to wreak great carnage. Obviously, this society is full of people who haven't enough common sense to use an automobile properly. But we haven't outlawed cars yet.

We do, however, license them and their owners, restrict their use to presumably sane and sober adults, and keep track of who sells them to whom. At a minimum, we should do the same with guns.

In truth, there is no rational argument for guns in this society. This is no longer a frontier nation in which people hunt their own food. It is a crowded, overwhelmingly urban country in which letting people have access to guns is a continuing disaster. Those who want guns—whether for target shooting, hunting, or potting rattlesnakes (get a hoe)—should be subject to the same restrictions placed on gun owners in England, a nation in which liberty has survived nicely without an armed populace.

The argument that "guns don't kill people" is patent nonsense. Anyone who has ever worked in a cop shop knows how many family arguments end in murder because there was a gun in the house. Did the gun kill someone? No. But if there had been no gun, no one would have died. At least not without a good foot race first. Guns do kill. Unlike cars, that is all they do.

Michael Crichton makes an interesting argument about technology in his thriller *Jurassic Park*. He points out that power without discipline is making this society into a wreckage. By the time someone who studies the martial arts becomes a master—literally able to kill with bare hands—that person has also undergone years of training and discipline. But any fool can pick up a gun and kill with it.

"A well-regulated militia" surely implies both long training and long discipline. That is the least, the very least, that should be required of those who are permitted to have guns, because a gun is literally the power to kill. For years I used to enjoy taunting my gun-nut friends about their psychosexual hang-ups—always in a spirit of good cheer, you understand. But letting the noisy minority in the NRA force us to allow this carnage to continue is just plain insane.

I do think gun nuts have a power hang-up. I don't know what is missing in their psyches that they need to feel they have the power to kill. But no sane society would allow this to continue.

Ban the damn things. Ban them all.

You want protection? Get a dog.

Putting in a Good Word for Guilt

Ellen Goodman

Feeling guilty is nothing to feel guilty about. Yes, guilt can be the excess baggage that keeps us paralyzed unless we dump it. But it can also be the engine that fuels us. Yes, it can be a self-punishing activity, but it can also be the conscience that keeps us civilized.

Not too long ago I wrote a story about that amusing couple, Guilt and the Working Mother. I'll tell you more about that later. Through the mail someone sent me a gift coffee mug carrying the message "I gave up guilt for Lent."

My first reaction was to giggle. But then it occurred to me that this particular Lent has been too lengthy. For the past decade or more, the pop psychologists who use book jackets rather than couches all were busy telling us that I am okay, you are okay and whatever we do is okay.

In most of their books, guilt was given a bad name—or rather, an assortment of bad names. It was a (1) Puritan (2) Jewish (3) Catholic hangover from our (1) parents (2) culture (3) religion. To be truly liberated was to be free of guilt about being rich, powerful, number one, bad to your mother, thoughtless, late, a smoker or about cheating on your spouse.

There was a popular notion, in fact, that self-love began by slaying one's guilt. People all around us spent a great portion of the last decade trying to tune out guilt instead of decoding its message and learning what it was trying to tell us.

With that sort of success, guilt was ripe for revival. Somewhere along the I'm-okay-you're-okay way, many of us realized that, in fact, I am not always okay and neither are you. Furthermore, we did not want to join the legions who conquered their guilt en route to new depths of narcissistic rottenness.

At the deepest, most devastating level, guilt is the criminal in us that longs to be caught. It is the horrible, pit-of-the-stomach sense of having done wrong. It is, as Lady Macbeth obsessively knew, the spot that no one else may see . . . and we can't see around.

To be without guilt is to be without a conscience. Guilt-free people don't feel bad when they cause pain to others, and so they go on guilt-freely causing more pain. The last thing we need more of is less conscience.

Freud once said, "As regards conscience, God has done an uneven and careless piece of work, for a large majority of men have brought along with them only a modest amount of it, or scarcely enough to be worth mentioning."

Now, I am not suggesting that we all sign up for a new guilt trip. But there has to be some line between the accusation that we all should feel guilty for, say, poverty or racism and the assertion that the oppressed have "chosen" their lot in life.

There has to be something between Puritanism and hedonism. There has to be something between the parents who guilt-trip their children across every stage of life and those who offer no guidance, no—gulp—moral or ethical point of view.

At quite regular intervals, for example, my daughter looks up at me in the midst of a discussion (she would call it a lecture) and says: "You're making me feel guilty." For a long time this made me, in turn, feel guilty. But now I realize that I am doing precisely what I am supposed to be doing: instilling in her a sense of right and wrong so that she will feel uncomfortable if she behaves in hurtful ways.

This is, of course, a very tricky business. Guilt is ultimately the way we judge ourselves. It is the part of us that says, "I deserve to be punished." But we all know people who feel guilty just for being alive. We know people who are paralyzed by irrational guilt. And we certainly don't want to be among them, or to shepherd our children into their flock.

But it seems to me that the trick isn't to become flaccidly nonjudgmental, but to figure out whether we are being fair judges of ourselves. Karl Menninger once wrote that one aim of psychiatric treatment isn't to get rid of guilt but "to get people's guilt feelings attached to the 'right' things."

In his book *Feelings*, Willard Gaylin quotes a Reverend Tillotson's definition of guilt as "nothing else but trouble arising in our mind from our consciousness of having done contrary to what we are verily persuaded [sic] was our Duty."

We may, however, have wildly different senses of duty. I had lunch with two friends a month ago when they both started talking about feeling guilty for neglecting their mothers. One, it turned out, worried that she didn't call "home" every day; the other hadn't even chatted with her mother since Christmas.

We are also particularly vulnerable to feelings of duty in a time of change. Today an older and ingrained sense of what we should do may conflict with a new one. In the gaps that open between what we once were taught and what we now believe grows a rich crop of guilt.

Mothers now often tell me that they feel guilty if they are working and guilty if they aren't. One set of older expectations, to be a perfect milk-and-cookies supermom, conflicts with another, to be an independent woman or an economic helpmate.

But duty has its uses. It sets us down at the typewriter, hustles us to the job on a morning when everything has gone wrong, pushes us toward the crying baby at 3 A.M.

If guilt is a struggle between our acceptance of should and should nots, it is a powerful and intensely human one. Gaylin writes, "Guilt represents the noblest and most painful of struggles. It is between us and ourselves." It is better to struggle with ourselves than give up on ourselves.

This worst emotion, in a sense, helps bring out the best in us. The desire to avoid feeling guilty makes us avoid the worst sort of behavior. The early guilt of a child who has hurt a younger sister or brother, even when no one else knows, is a message. The adult who has inflicted pain on an innocent, who has cheated, lied, stolen, to get ahead of another—each of us has a list—wakes up in the middle of the night and remembers it.

In that sense guilt is the great civilizer, the internal commandment that helps us choose to be kind to each other rather than to join in a stampede of me-firsts. "If guilt is coming back," said Harvard Professor David Riesman, who wrote *The Lonely Crowd*, "one reason is that a tremendous surge of young people overpowered the adults in the sixties. You might say the barbarians took Rome. Now there are more adults around who are trying to restore some stability."

Guilt is the adult in each of us, the parent, the one who upholds the standards. It is the internal guide against which we argue in vain that "everybody else is doing it."

We even wrestle with ethical dilemmas and conflicts of conscience so that we an live with ourselves more comfortably. I know two people who were faced with a crisis about their infidelities. One woman resolved the triangle she was in by ending her marriage. The other ended her affair. In both cases, it was the pain that had motivated them to change.

It is not easy to attach our guilt to the right things. It is never easy to separate right from wrong, rational guilt from neurotic guilt. We may resolve one by changing our view of it and another by changing our behavior.

In my own life as a working mother, I have done both half a dozen times. When my daughter was small and I was working, I worried that I was not following the pattern of the good mother, my mother. Only through time and perspective and reality did I change that view; I realized that my daughter clearly did not feel neglected and I clearly was not uncaring. Good child care, love, luck and support helped me to resolve my early guilt feelings.

Then again, last winter I found myself out of town more than I was comfortable with. This time I changed my schedule instead of my mind.

For all of us, in the dozens of daily decisions we make, guilt is one of the many proper motivations. I am not saying our lives are ruled by guilt. Hardly. But guilt is inherent in the underlying question: "If I do that, can I live with myself?"

People who don't ask themselves that question, people who never get no for an answer, may seem lucky. They can, we think, be self-centered without self-punishment, hedonistic without qualms. They can worry about me-first and forget about the others.

It is easy to be jealous of those who go through life without a moment of wrenching guilt. But envying the guiltless is like envying a house pet. Striving to follow their lead it like accepting a catatonic as your role model. They are not the free but the antisocial. In a world in which guilt is one of the few emotions experienced only by human beings, they are, even, inhuman.

Guilt is one of the most human of dilemmas. It is the claim of others on the self, the recognition both of our flaws and of our desire to be the people we want to be.

I Have a Dream

Martin Luther King, Jr.

I am happy to join with you today in what will go down in history as the greatest demonstration for freedom in the history of our nation.

Five score years ago, a great American, in whose symbolic shadow we stand today, signed the Emancipation Proclamation. This momentous decree came as a great beacon light of hope to millions of Negro slaves who had been seared in the flames of withering injustice. It came as a joyous daybreak to end the long night of their captivity.

But one hundred years later, the Negro still is not free; one hundred years later, the life of the Negro is still sadly crippled by the manacles of segregation and the chains of discrimination; one hundred years later, the Negro lives on a lonely island of poverty in the midst of a vast ocean of material prosperity; one hundred years later, the Negro is still languishing in the corners of American society and finds himself in exile in his own land.

So we've come here today to dramatize a shameful condition. In a sense we've come to our nation's capital to cash a check. When the architects of our republic wrote the magnificent words of the Constitution and the Declaration of Independence, they were signing a promissory note to which every American was to fall heir. This note was the promise that all men, yes, black men as well as white men, would be guaranteed the unalienable rights of life, liberty, and the pursuit of happiness.

It is obvious today that America has defaulted on this promissory note in so far as her citizens of color are concerned. Instead of honoring this sacred obligation, America has given the Negro people a bad check; a check which has come back marked "insufficient funds." But we refuse to believe that the bank of justice is bankrupt. We refuse to believe that there are insufficient funds in the great vaults of opportunity of this nation. And so we've come to cash this check, a check that will give us upon demand the riches of freedom and the security of justice.

We have also come to this hallowed spot to remind America of the fierce urgency of now. This is no time to engage in the luxury of cooling off or to take the tranquilizing drug of gradualism. Now is the time to make real the promises of democracy; now is the time to rise from the dark and desolate valley of segregation to the sunlit path of racial justice; now is the time to lift our nation from the quicksand's of racial injustice to the solid rock of brotherhood; now is the time to make justice a reality for all of God's children. It would be fatal for the nation to overlook the urgency of the moment. This sweltering summer of the Negro's legitimate discontent will not pass until there is an invigorating autumn of freedom and equality.

Nineteen sixty-three is not an end, but a beginning. And those who hope that the Negro needed to blow off steam and will now be content will have a rude awakening if the nation returns to business as usual. There will be neither rest nor tranquility in America until the Negro is granted his citizenship rights. The whirlwinds of revolt will continue to shake the foundations of our nation until the bright day of justice emerges.

But there is something that I must say to my people, who stand on the worn threshold which leads into the palace of justice. In the process of gaining our rightful place, we must not be guilty of wrongful deeds. Let us not seek to satisfy our thirst for freedom by drinking from the cup of bitterness and hatred. We must forever conduct our struggle on the high plain of dignity and discipline. We must not allow our creative protests to degenerate into physical violence. Again and again we must rise to the majestic heights of meeting physical force with soul force. The marvelous new militancy, which has engulfed the Negro community, must not lead us to a distrust of all white people. For many of our white brothers, as evidenced by their presence here today, have come to realize that their destiny is tied up with our destiny. And they have come to realize that their freedom is inextricably bound to our freedom. We cannot walk alone. And as we walk, we most make the pledge that we shall always march ahead. We cannot turn back.

There are those who are asking the devotees of Civil Rights. "When will you be satisfied?" We can never be satisfied as long as the Negro is the victim of the unspeakable horrors of police brutality: we can never be satisfied as long as our bodies, heavy with the fatigue of travel, cannot gain lodging in the motels of the highways and the hotels of the cities; we cannot be satisfied as long as the Negro's basic mobility is from a smaller ghetto to a larger one; we can never be satisfied as long as our children are stripped of their selfhood and robbed of their dignity by signs stating "For White Only"; we cannot be satisfied as long as the Negro in Mississippi cannot vote and a Negro in New York believes he has nothing for which to vote. No! No, we are not satisfied, and we will not be satisfied until justice rolls down like waters and righteousness like a mighty stream.

I am not unmindful that some of you have come here out of great trials and tribulations. Some of you have come fresh from narrow jail cells. Some of you have come from areas where your quest for freedom left you battered by the storms of persecution and staggered by the winds of police brutality. You have been the veterans of creative suffering. Continue to work with the faith that unearned suffering is redemptive. Go back to Mississippi. Go back to Alabama. Go back to South Carolina. Go back to Georgia. Go back to Louisiana. Go back to the slums and ghettos of our Northern cities, knowing that somehow this situation can and will be changed. Let us not wallow in the valley of despair.

I say to you today, my friends, that even though we face the difficulties of today and tomorrow, I still have a dream. It is a dream deeply rooted in the American dream. I have a dream that one day this nation will rise up and live out the true meaning of its creed, "We hold these truths to be self-evident, that all men are created equal." I have a dream that one day on the red hills of Georgia, sons of former slaves and the sons of former slave owners will be able to sit down together at the table of brotherhood. I have a dream that one day even the state of Mississippi, a state sweltering with the heat of injustice, sweltering with the heat of oppression, will be transformed into an oasis of freedom and justice. I have a dream that my four little children will one day live in a nation where they will not be judged by the color of their skin, but by the content of their character.

I HAVE A DREAM TODAY!

I have a dream that one day down in Alabama—with its vicious racists, with its Governor having his lips dripping with the words of interposition and nullification—one day right there in Alabama, little black boys and black girls will be able to join hands with little white boys and white girls as sisters and brothers.

I HAVE A DREAM TODAY!

I have a dream that one day every valley shall be exalted, every hill and mountain shall be made low. The rough places will be plain and the crooked places will be made straight, "and the glory of the Lord shall be revealed, and all flesh shall see it together."

This is our hope. This is the faith that I go back to the South with. With this faith we will be able to hew out of the mountain of despair, a stone of hope. With this faith we will be able to transform the jangling discords of our nation into a beautiful symphony of brotherhood. With this faith we will be able to work together, to pray together, to struggle together, to go to jail together, to stand up for freedom together, knowing that we will be free one day. And this will be the day. This will be the day when all of God's children will be able to sing with new meaning, "My country 'tis of thee, sweet land of liberty, of thee I sing. Land where my fathers died, land of the pilgrim's pride, from every mountain side, let freedom ring." And if America is to be a great nation, this must become true.

So let freedom ring from the prodigious hilltops of New Hampshire; let freedom ring from the mighty mountains of New York; let freedom ring from the heightening Alleghenies of Pennsylvania; let freedom ring from the snow-capped Rockies of Colorado; let freedom ring from the curvaceous slopes of California. But not only that. Let freedom ring from Stone Mountain of Georgia; let freedom ring from Lookout Mountain of Tennessee: let freedom ring from every hill and mole hill of Mississippi. "From every mountainside, let freedom ring."

And when this happens, and when we allow freedom to ring, when we let it ring from every village and every hamlet, from every state and every city, we will be able to speed up that day when all of God's children, black men and white men, Jews and Gentiles, Protestants and Catholics, will be able to join hands and sing in the words of the old Negro spiritual: "Free at last. Free at last. Thank God Almighty, we are free at last."

Gettysburg Address

Abraham Lincoln

Speech at the Dedication of the National Cemetery of Gettysburg

November 19, 1863

Four score and seven years ago our fathers brought forth on this continent a new nation, conceived in liberty and dedicated to the proposition that all men are created equal. Now we are engaged in a great civil war, testing whether that nation or any nation so conceived and so dedicated can long endure. We are met on a great battlefield of that war. We have come to dedicate a portion of that field as a final resting-place for those who here gave their lives that that nation might live. It is altogether fitting and proper that we should do this. But in a larger sense, we cannot dedicate, we cannot consecrate, we cannot hallow this ground. The brave men, living and dead who struggled here have consecrated it far above our poor power to add or detract. The world will little note nor long remember what we say here, but it can never forget what they did here. It is for us the living rather to be dedicated here to the unfinished work which they who fought here have thus far so nobly advanced. It is rather for us to be here dedicated to the great task remaining before us, that from these honored dead we take increased devotion to that cause for which they gave the last full measure of devotion; that we here highly resolve that these dead shall not have died in vain, that this nation under God shall have a new birth of freedom, and that government of the people, by the people, for the people shall not perish from the earth.

Drug Testing Violates Workers' Rights

The New Republic

The President's Commission on Organized Crime spent 32 months and nearly five million dollars preparing its report on drug abuse and trafficking. There's something for everyone in the panel's 1,000-page study, but here's the gist of its recommendation: since law-enforcement techniques have failed to curtail the supply of illegal narcotics, we should try to diminish the demand. In pursuit of that goal, the commission argues, the president should direct all federal agencies to implement "suitable drug testing programs." State and local governments and the private sector should follow suit, and federal contracts should be denied to firms that don't test for drugs. In other words, practically everyone should have his or her urine tested. Laboratory owners and manufacturers of small plastic cups should be delighted with the scheme.

Several members of the panel have dissented publicly, saying that the controversial suggestion was added without their knowledge. U.S. Court of Appeals Judge Irving R. Kaufman, who chairs the commission, and supports the idea, has refused to answer their objections. But the report has been greeted with signs of approbation as well. Attorney General Edwin Meese III caused some confusion in the press when he stopped short of endorsing the plan (saying it might be too expensive), yet argued that drug testing doesn't violate anyone's constitutional rights. Representative Clay Shaw of Florida embraced the idea unreservedly. He volunteered himself and his staff for urine tests as soon as they can be arranged.

Too Close for Comfort

In fact, we are already much closer to universal urine testing than most people realize. One-quarter of all Fortune 500 companies, including IBM and General Motors, now administer urinalysis tests to applicants or current employees. Another 20 percent are planning to institute programs. . . . According to a *USA Today* survey cited in the Kaufman Commission report, two-thirds of those firms won't hire anyone who fails a test. Of those testing current employees, 25 percent fire those who fail, while 64 percent require treatment, strongly recommend it, or take disciplinary action. Since a urine sample is usually taken as part of a medical examination, applicants and employees often don't know that they are being checked for drug use.

The tests are probably justified for air traffic controllers and Drug Enforcement Administration agents who now undergo them regularly. There's even a case to be made for testing professional athletes, part of whose job is to serve as role models to children. But need the same standards be applied to the entire work force? The *Los Angeles Times*, the *Chicago Tribune*, and the *New York Times*, for example, screen all new employees for drug use. Although the *New York Times* doesn't tell applicants that their urine will be tested for narcotics, a spokesman says the company's policy is to not hire anyone whose medical examination indicates use of illegal drugs, including marijuana. Once you are hired, there are no further tests.

And urinalysis is only one of the more intrusive new ways to search people for drugs. Many bus drivers and amusement park ride operators are required to produce saliva samples, which are tested for the presence of marijuana. . . . It is now possible to test hair samples for drugs. Some companies have searched lockers and cars, frisked workers on their way into the factory, and set up hidden video cameras. G.M. hired undercover agents to pose as assembly-line workers in order to catch drug dealers. Capital Cities/ABC and the *Kansas City Times* and *Star* called off the drug-sniffing dogs after reporters ridiculed their plans for canine searches in the newsroom.

There is already a body of case law on the Fourth Amendment questions raised by the various drug tests. If a warrant is required to search someone's home, you need a probable cause to impound some of his urine. The Kaufman report notes that the Supreme Court ruled in favor of the Federal Railroad Administration's right to employ a range of tests for drugs and alcohol. But the commission ignores the fact that the railroad regulations delineate the need for "reasonable suspicion" that employees are under the influence on the job—not that they've used drugs away from work in previous weeks.

Invasion of Privacy

Beyond the constitutional questions, most would agree that asking people to produce a urine specimen if they want to apply for a job, or to keep the one they've got, is an unwarranted invasion of their privacy. To assure an honest sample, a supervisor must witness its production. The Coast Guard has someone follow each of its 38,000 employees into the bathroom. "We don't want them to bring in baby's urine," one Coast Guard officer told the *Washington Post*.

Why are these officers and supervisors, who administer the tests, always assumed to be clean? Programs for widespread testing almost always reflect class bias. Regulations are usually written for equipment operators or assembly-line workers without reference to supervisors or management. Isn't it just as important that they be drug-free? If we test train conductors, shouldn't we also analyze the urine of the railroad bosses? As the Kaufman Commission report indicates, heroin has been climbing up the socioeconomic ladder as cocaine has been descending. Yet lawyers, stock brokers, and senators are rarely included in drug-testing programs, perhaps because they are better able to fight the imposition of such indignities.

Besides running roughshod over personal privacy, the tests are impractical and imprecise. Urinalysis can't tell you whether someone is high on the job—only whether she has traces of narcotics in her system. Cocaine, heroin, and PCP—the drugs employers claim to be most worried about—vanish from the bloodstream in less than 48 hours. If the tests are scheduled, as most are, an employee can avoid detection by staying clean for a couple of days.

But THC, the active chemical in marijuana, remains in the blood months after it is ingested. That's why the vast majority of those who fail drug tests register positive for pot. What do we do with them? Nearly 40 million citizens smoke marijuana at least once a year. Half that number use the drug regularly. Should all of them be fired? If passing a drug test ought to be a condition of all kinds of employment, should a large segment of the population be unemployable? Eleven states have eliminated criminal penalties for possession of marijuana, and Alaskans can grow it legally in their backyards. Rather than weeding 20 million weed-smokers from the work force, employers ought to discipline, treat, or fire those who perform poorly at work, whether or not they use drugs. Axing workers who test positive but demonstrate no other problems doesn't make sense.

Unconstitutional

Even if drug tests were free and 100 percent accurate, they would still be unconstitutional. There is going to be a lot of legal rhubarb over this, and I don't know what a Rehnquist-led Supreme Court is finally going to decide. But I take the same attitude toward the Constitution as Reformation Protestants took toward the Bible: Anyone can read it and witness the truth thereof. Amendment Four is perfectly straightforward:

The right of the people to be secure in their persons, houses, papers and effects against unreasonable searches and seizures shall not be violated, and no warrants shall issue but upon probable cause, supported by an oath or affirmation and particularly describing the place to be searched and the persons or things to be seized.

It's hard to see how scatter-shot drug testing could be legal under the Fourth Amendment, no matter how particularly the Government describes the way you take a leak. (P.J. O'Rourke, Playboy, February 1987.)

Like those who advocate widespread use of polygraph tests, the Kaufman panel puts boundless faith in far-from-perfect scientific techniques. Although the tests have been widely used for only a few years, they've ruined lives and fingered thousands of innocent people. The Pentagon, which administers six million urinalysis tests a year, provides plenty of examples. Urinalysis tests said time and again that a Navy doctor named Dale Mitchell was using morphine. When he failed a polygraph test, he began sending out job applications. Then someone at the Navy lab figured out that Mitchell was testing positive for poppy seed bagels. In 1982 and 1983 a group of 9,100 employees the Army said were using illegal drugs weren't so lucky. They had already gotten their dishonorable discharges when the Pentagon tried to track them down to apologize for convicting them on faulty evidence including mixed-up samples.

Most drug-testing laboratories acknowledge a margin of error of two or three percent. Even by that conservative estimate, four million innocents would lose their jobs if we tested the entire work force. But the conclusions of a secret study of the labs by the National Centers for Disease Control are far less optimistic. According to an article in the *Journal of the American Medical Association,* the worst laboratories indicated false positive results as much as 66 percent of the time. Only one lab was credited with acceptable performance in testing for cocaine. The CDC study didn't include any marijuana samples, which pose similar, if not more severe, lab problems. Herbal tea and prescription drugs can trigger false positive results, as can being in a room with people smoking marijuana. Those terminated unfairly may waste years and fortunes proving their innocence, if they are able to do so at all.

Little Plastic Cups

Despite the abundant hype, the use of legal and illegal drugs has decreased markedly over the past several years. Fewer people are taking heroin, PCP, marijuana, alcohol, and tobacco than they were ten years ago. LSD and Quaaludes have all but vanished. Cocaine use has increased slightly, but may well decline when its dangers become better known—which is what happened with heroin and PCP.

The failure of our policy of interdiction has combined with the hysteria to send the law-enforcement establishment on a search for sweeping solutions. [Attorney General Edwin] Meese suggested stepping up efforts to prosecute consumers of illegal drugs. What sort of indiscriminate check will catch the corporate imagination next? Strip searches for weapons? Polygraphs for potential office thieves? Blood tests for AIDS? All hold forth a similar promise of purity in the workplace, which is why they appeal so strongly to those who run businesses and governments. But such forms of social control, which force people to prove their innocence of crimes they haven't even been charged with, are abhorrent. What starts with little plastic cups ends in the urinalysis state.

Affirmative Action: It's Not Progress

Thomas Sowell

A whole industry exists to explain away the "failures" of blacks and other low-income groups. Seldom has so much time and talent been so completely wasted. These groups have not failed. There are painful problems in minority communities, but that does not mean that these communities have not progressed. Many theories and preconceptions have been disappointed, but that is something else.

The history of blacks as a free people in the United States is little more than a century old. To find people as badly off, in so many ways, as black Americans were at the time of emancipation, you would have to go to some of the poorest of the Third World nations. Few people in such conditions have kept pace with the advancement of blacks in the past century.

It has been called an "educational explosion" that the people of India have gone from 5 percent literacy to 36 percent literacy in 80 years. Among black Americans, 80 years after emancipation, the literacy rate had risen to almost 90 percent. A distinguished economic historian has called this "an accomplishment seldom witnessed in human history."

Yet it might as well never have happened, for all the effect it has had on the thinking of those who are busy explaining failure, denouncing society and promoting their own brand of instant salvation. Others wring their hands in despair, wondering how they can *possibly* bring advancement to blacks—a people who have been advancing in virtually every decade of their history, even against determined opposition.

Those who start from the arbitrary assumption that all groups should be at "the national average" in income, education and other social indicators, have set standards that guarantee massive failures. If blacks and whites in the United States were the same, they would be the only two groups on this planet who are the same.

Group differences cannot even be discussed, as long as we are paralyzed by the phobia that every difference means innate inferiority. Yet virtually no one does things in the same way, or with the same effect, as anyone else—whether comparing individuals or groups. Nor does the same individual or group have the same performance over time. It was little more than half a century ago that American Jews scored below the national average on mental tests. They were also over represented in basketball before the 1950s.

Jews are only one of a number of groups whose I.Q. scores have risen over time as their other circumstances changed. The same has been true of Italians and Poles in the United States. Whole nations, such as Japan and New Zealand, have had significant increases in I.Q. scores over the past generation. That means that these scores are not set in concrete. It does not mean that they are "irrelevant."

More than a decade ago, a well-known black intellectual urged me *not* to do research on I.Q. differences among groups. This lack of confidence speaks volumes about the mindset of those who are publicly defenders and "explainers" of blacks. The research in fact showed that neither the level nor the pattern of black I.Q. scores was unique. Other groups, here and abroad, have had similar I.Q. levels in similar circumstances. But the mindset that closes its eyes to uncomfortable facts has made it legally or politically impossible to study the progress of black I.Q. scores in many parts of the United States.

Recently released data on the Scholastic Aptitude Test show blacks to be the fastest-rising group—though rising from the lowest scores. Recent data on black IQs in California by Professor Arthur Jensen show these I.Q. scores now to be in the 90s, compared to a national average of 100 and an historic black I.Q. average of 85. It is truly ironic that one must turn to the research of Arthur Jensen—who favors genetic theories of intelligence—for a glimpse of black progress, because "defenders" of blacks are afraid to let the facts be looked at.

Multiple Causes of Progress

Innumerable factors go into the economic, social, medical and other characteristics of a people. It would be an incredible coincidence if all these factors worked out to produce the same results for all groups, in all institutions and activities. Yet a whole social vision in our time proceeds as if that was what would happen, in the absence of institutional bias. No doubt institutional bias and public policy have had an effect—but how big an effect is a question, not a foregone conclusion.

Virtually everyone is aware that the number of blacks in high-level occupations increased strikingly in the decade following passage of the Civil Rights Act of 1964. But virtually no one seems to be aware that the rise of blacks in such occupations was even more striking in the decade before passage of the Civil Rights Act of 1964.

This was part of historic, ongoing progress, created by one of the great social transformations of a people. This historic transformation is too easily overlooked by the American habit of thinking of progress in terms of rags-to-riches. But a black secretary or mechanic represents a long social journey in a short span of time, as history is measured. Blacks did not come to America as secretaries and mechanics.

Even those who talk incessantly of "change" often overlook this kind of internal change. To them, "change" is what the anointed bring to the stagnant multitudes.

National political developments within the past generation have had great impact in dismantling politically created barriers, epitomized by the Jim Crow system in the South. Civil rights are enormously important in and of themselves. If they have not also created the economic or educational results expected, that is a failure of prevailing assumptions—not a failure of civil rights.

Government policy has historically been largely ineffective in holding back or advancing a people. The prosperity of Jews, Chinese and Japanese in many countries around the world is a mockery of innumerable political efforts to hold them back. Even the pervasive Jim Crow laws, supplemented by vigilante terrorism, were only able to slow the advance of blacks in the United States. By the same token, far-reaching preferential advantages have yet to advance any group from poverty to parity. This is true even where such policies go back much further than "affirmative action" in the United States—for the Malays in Malaysia or any of a number of groups in India, the Assamese for example.

If we do not understand what has produced economic progress in the past, we are not likely to understand how to enhance the prospects of more economic advancement in the future. Skills, education and work habits may be corny, but they have worked. And they have worked for all sorts of groups in all sorts of countries, down through history. When something has been around long enough to be considered corny, there may be something to it.

Among the many specific ways by which groups around the world have advanced from poverty to prosperity, politics seems conspicuous by its absence. The most dramatic examples of destitute immigrants evolving into an affluent middle class are the Jews, the Chinese and the Japanese—not only in the United States, but throughout the Western Hemisphere and on other continents.

All three groups have been notably slow to develop political clout in the many countries in which they have settled, and the Japanese have it virtually nowhere. Only after substantial economic advancement did Jews begin to acquire political strength in the United States. Immigrants from Germany, Italy and India have likewise lacked political clout during their economic rise in the many countries in which they have settled and prospered.

Those groups that have acquired political power and attempted to use it to advance themselves economically have not come close to duplicating the success of non-political minorities. The Malays in Malaysia and numerous locally dominant ethnic groups in various parts of India have voted themselves preferential employment, university admissions and numerous other benefits. Their progress has been marginal, and largely confined to those already more fortunate.

The progress of blacks and other disadvantaged groups in the United States does not mean that things are rosy. In some respects, there have been serious and even dangerous retrogressions in the past generation. Teenage pregnancy, soaring crime rates and massive unemployment among ghetto youths are among the worst of these retrogressions. Leaders and movements that eagerly seize credit for progress never question for a moment whether they may have contributed to the retrogressions. Nor do the media force them to face such questions.

Is it possible to din into the heads of a whole generation that their problems are all other people's fault, that the world owes them an enormous debt, that everything they have yet to achieve is an injustice; that violence is excusable when the world is flawed—and yet expect it all to have no effect on attitudes? Is the arduous process of acquiring skills and discipline supposed to be endured for years by people who are told, by word and deed, that skills are not the real issue?

The Dangers of Racial Ideology

The ideological vision of race is more than an economic handicap. In the longer run, it is a serious danger.

The whole climate of creeds and taboos, villains and rescuers, crusades and symbols, is more suitable to melodrama than to serious social policy. This kind of melodrama has left many multiethnic societies literally bleeding in the streets. Lebanon is only one of the more publicized examples. Inter group violence in India has taken hundreds of lives among the Sikhs in the Punjab alone. Last year it took thousands of lives in the state of Assam, at the opposite end of India. Similar—and worse—intergroup violence has occurred in various nations of Africa. And we need only say the words "Northern Ireland" to conjure up an image of intergroup violence erupting again and again.

Tragic as the history of intergroup conflict and violence has been in the United States, it does not begin to compare with what has happened in many other nations. If a mob of Americans attacked another group of Americans from a different race or ethnicity, and killed even one-tenth as many people as the hundreds of Tamils killed by Sinhalese last year in Sri Lanka, it would shake this republic to its foundation and reverberate around the world for years. Every nation in the United Nations would lecture us, including Sri Lanka.

We have not escaped this fate by nobility but by circumstances. Americans are not made of different flesh and blood than other people. If we go down the road to polarization, we will find the same things at the end of it.

If it were necessary to take such risks in order to ensure advancement of the disadvantaged, then a case could be made for doing it. But most of the things that polarize Americans—busing and quotas, for example—have no such track record of advancing the disadvantaged.

Supporters of such policies have ringing rhetoric, but they avoid hard evidence like the plague. Well they might. Masses of data show that groups that perform differently in separate schools also perform differently when in the same schools. This is not peculiar to blacks and whites, or even to the United States. You can find the same evidence from Hong Kong to the Virgin Islands. History shows huge test-score and dropout differences among American immigrant groups that lived cheek by jowl, and whose children sat side by side in the same schools.

Where the other ingredients of a good education have been present, blacks have advanced in all-black schools or in racially mixed schools. This still continues to be the case.

The track record of the other great polarizer—"affirmative action"—is even poorer. The truly disadvantaged—those with little education or job experience, or from broken families—have fallen even further behind during the era of affirmative action. As in other countries, the benefits of preferential programs go disproportionately to those already more fortunate. It may help a black professor get an endowed chair, but it is counterproductive for the black teenager trying to get a job. There are economic reasons why this is so, as well as much hard evidence that it is.

Again, this is not unique to the United States. A number of studies of preferential programs for untouchables in India have concluded that little or no benefit actually accrues to these poverty-stricken people. Yet it is precisely the poor untouchable who suffers from the backlash against the great privileges he is thought to be enjoying. Violence against untouchables doubled in less than a decade during the 1970s, amid rising denunciations of preferential policies in their behalf. What is the answer?

Nowadays, you are not supposed to say that the emperor has no clothes, unless you are prepared to design a whole wardrobe for him. Yet there has never been a shortage of blueprints for salvation. What there has been a shortage of is a factual approach to what does and does not work.

Standards work—whether in schools or the job market. Yet there is a whole set of rhetoric that dismisses standards as mere excuses for racism. The success of black institutions or particular black groups (such as West Indians) are dismissed out of hand by another set of rhetoric. How they did it doesn't matter. It is treated as almost an embarrassment that they did.

No one seems to care what there is about certain economic sectors, such as sports and entertainment, that has made them more accessible to all sorts of disadvantaged groups trying to rise. They are certainly not sectors where government policy or preferential treatment have played any great role. On the contrary, some of the most dog-eat-dog competition in the economy takes place there—almost a textbook example of *laissez-faire*. This evidence may not be conclusive, but at least it is evidence, rather than rhetoric.

There is no such thing as "the" answer. But we need to start asking different questions. We need to start asking "Does it work?" instead of, "How does that sound?" We need to start asking what our own purpose is. Is it to advance the disadvantaged or to ease guilt, buy off "trouble" or preserve an image? It would be a remarkable coincidence if the things that accomplish these other purposes were also best for the disadvantaged.

Above all, we need to stop thinking of the disadvantaged as guinea pigs, or thinking that we can move them around like pieces on a chess board. Nor do we need to confuse the interests of hoodlums and hustlers with the interests of the ghetto. Wrongdoers in the ghetto are almost adopted as mascots by some civil libertarians, even when that means sacrificing the safety of the old or the education of the young.

Once the disadvantaged are seen as human beings with minds and hearts of their own, the issue becomes one of how to allow them more choices—letting parents select their children's schools, for example—instead of unleashing "experts" on them. Letting teenagers get job experience is more important than letting humanitarians feel noble by pricing them out of the market with minimum wage laws. (Black teenage unemployment today is several times larger than it was in 1950, when the minimum wage began escalating and the coverage spreading.) Examples are virtually endless—once the focus is on the advancement of the disadvantaged rather than on promoting other people's image, visions and—God help us—"expertise."

Affirmative Action: The Price of Preference

Shelby Steele

In a few short years, when my two children will be applying to college, the affirmative action policies by which most universities offer black students some form of preferential treatment will present me with a dilemma. I am a middle-class black, a college professor, far from wealthy, but also well-removed from the kind of deprivation that would qualify my children for the label "disadvantaged." Both of them have endured racial insensitivity from whites. They have been called names, have suffered slights, and have experienced firsthand the peculiar malevolence that racism brings out in people. Yet, they have never experienced racial discrimination, have never been stopped by their race on any path they have chosen to follow. Still, their society now tells them that if they will only designate themselves as black on their college applications, they will likely do better in the college lottery than if they conceal this fact. I think there is something of a Faustian bargain in this.

Of course, many blacks and a considerable number of whites would say that I was sanctimoniously making affirmative action into a test of character. They would say that this small preference is the meagerest recompense for centuries of unrelieved oppression. And to these arguments other very obvious facts must be added. In America, many marginally competent or flatly incompetent whites are hired every day—some because their white skin suits the conscious or unconscious racial preference of their employer. The white children of alumni are often grandfathered into elite universities in what can only be seen as a residual benefit of historic white privilege. Worse, white incompetence is always an individual matter, while for blacks it is often confirmation of ugly stereotypes. The Peter Principle was not conceived with only blacks in mind. Given that unfairness cuts both ways, doesn't it only balance the scales of history that my children now receive a slight preference over whites? Doesn't this repay, in a small way, the systematic denial under which their grandfather lived out his days?

So, in theory, affirmative action certainly has all the moral symmetry that fairness requires—the injustice of historical and even contemporary white advantage is offset with black advantage; preference replaces prejudice, inclusion answers exclusion. It is reformist and corrective, even repentant and redemptive. And I would never sneer at these good intentions. Born in the late forties in Chicago, I started my education (a charitable term in this case) in a segregated school and suffered all the indignities that come to blacks in a segregated society. My father, born in the South, only made it to the third grade before the white man's fields took permanent priority over his formal education. And though he educated himself into an advanced reader with an almost professorial authority, he could only drive a truck for a living and never earned more than ninety dollars a week in his entire life. So yes, it is crucial to my sense of citizenship, to my ability to identify with the spirit and the interests of America, to know that this country, however imperfectly, recognizes its past sins and wishes to correct them.

Yet good intentions, because of the opportunity for innocence they offer us, are very seductive and can blind us to the effects they generate when implemented. In our society, affirmative action is, among other things, a testament to white goodwill and to black power, and in the midst of these heavy investments, its effects can be hard to see. But after twenty years of implementation, I think affirmative action has shown itself to be more bad than good and that blacks—whom I will focus on in this essay—now stand to lose more from it than they gain.

In talking with affirmative action administrators and with blacks and whites in general, it is clear that supporters of affirmative action focus on its good intentions while detractors emphasize its negative effects. Proponents talk about "diversity" and "pluralism"; opponents speak of "reverse discrimination": the unfairness of quotas and set-asides. It was virtually impossible to find people outside either camp. The closest I came was a white male manager at a large computer company who said, "I think it amounts to reverse discrimination, but I'll put up with a little of that for a little more diversity." I'll live with a little of the effect to gain a little of the intention, he seemed to be saying. But this only makes him a halfhearted supporter of affirmative action. I think many people who don't really like affirmative action support it to one degree or another anyway.

I believe they do this because of what happened to white and black Americans in the crucible of the sixties when whites were confronted with their racial guilt and blacks tasted their first real power. In this stormy time white absolution and black power coalesced into virtual mandates for society. Affirmative action became a meeting ground for these mandates in the law, and in the late sixties and early seventies it underwent a remarkable escalation of its mission from simple antidiscrimination enforcement to social engineering by means of quotas, goals, timetables, set-asides, and other forms of preferential treatment.

Legally, this was achieved through a series of executive orders and EEOC [Equal Employment Opportunity Commission] guidelines that allowed racial imbalances in the workplace to stand as proof of racial discrimination. Once it could be assumed that discrimination explained racial imbalances, it became easy to justify group remedies to presumed discrimination, rather than the normal case-by-case redress for proven discrimination. Preferential treatment through quotas, goals, and so on is designed to correct imbalances based on the assumption that they always indicate discrimination. This expansion of what constitutes discrimination allowed affirmative action to escalate into the business of social engineering in the name of anti-discrimination, to push society toward statistically proportionate racial representation, without any obligation of proving actual discrimination.

What accounted for this shift, I believe, was the white mandate to achieve a new racial innocence and the black mandate to gain power. Even though blacks had made great advances during the sixties without quotas, these mandates, which came to a head in the very late sixties, could no longer be satisfied by anything less than racial preferences. I don't think these mandates in themselves were wrong, since whites clearly needed to do better by blacks and blacks needed more real power in society. But, as they came together in affirmative action, their effect was to distort our understanding of racial discrimination in a way that allowed us to offer the remediation of preference on the basis of mere color rather than actual injury. By making black the color of preference, these mandates have reburdened society with the very marriage of color and preference (in reverse) that we set out to eradicate. The old sin is reaffirmed in a new guise.

But the essential problem with this form of affirmative action is the way it leaps over the hard business of developing a formerly oppressed people to the point where they can achieve proportionate representation on their own (given equal opportunity) and goes straight for the proportionate representation. This may satisfy some whites of their innocence and some blacks of their power, but it does very little to truly uplift blacks.

A white female affirmative action officer at an Ivy League university told me what many supporters of affirmative action now say: "We're after diversity. We ideally want a student body where racial and ethnic groups are represented according to their proportion in society." When affirmative action escalated into social engineering, diversity became a golden word. It grants whites an egalitarian fairness (innocence) and blacks an entitlement to proportionate representation (power). *Diversity* is a term that applies democratic principles to races and cultures rather than to citizens, despite the fact that there is nothing to indicate that real diversity is the same thing as proportionate representation. Too often the result of this on campuses (for example) has been a democracy of colors rather than of people, an artificial diversity that gives the appearance of an educational parity between black and white students that has not yet been achieved in reality. Here again, racial preferences allow society to leapfrog over the difficult problem of developing blacks to parity with whites and into a cosmetic diversity that covers the blemish of disparity—a full six years after admission, only about 26 percent of black students graduate from college.

Racial representation is not the same thing as racial development, yet affirmative action fosters a confusion of these very different needs. Representation can be manufactured; development is always hard-earned. However, it is the music of innocence and power that we hear in affirmative action that causes us to cling to it and to its distracting emphasis on representation. The fact is that after twenty years of racial preferences, the gap between white and black median income is greater than it was in the seventies. None of this is to say that blacks don't need policies that ensure our right to equal opportunity, but what we need more is the development that will let us take advantage of society's efforts to include us.

I think that one of the most troubling effects of racial preferences for blacks is a kind of demoralization, or put another way, an enlargement of self-doubt. Under affirmative action the quality that earns us preferential treatment is an implied inferiority. However this inferiority is explained—and it is easily enough explained by the myriad deprivations that grew out of our oppression—it is still inferiority. There are explanations, and then there is the fact. And the fact must be borne by the individual as a condition apart from the explanation, apart even from the fact that others like himself also bear this condition. In integrated situations where blacks must compete with whites who may be better prepared, these explanations may quickly wear thin and expose the individual to racial as well as personal self-doubt.

All of this is compounded by the cultural myth of black inferiority that blacks have always lived with. What this means in practical terms is that when blacks deliver themselves into integrated situations, they encounter a nasty little reflex in whites, a mindless, atavistic reflex that responds to the color black with alarm. Attributions may follow this alarm if the white cares to indulge them, and if they do, they will most likely be negative—one such attribution is intellectual ineptness. I think this reflex and the attributions that may follow it embarrass most whites today; therefore, it is usually quickly repressed. Nevertheless, on an equally atavistic level, the black will be aware of the reflex his color triggers and will feel a stab of horror at seeing himself reflected in this way. He, too, will do a quick repression, but a lifetime of such stabbings is what constitutes his inner realm of racial doubt.

The effects of this may be a subject for another essay. The point here is that the implication of inferiority that racial preferences engender in both the white and black mind expands rather than contracts this doubt. Even when the black sees no implication of inferiority in racial preferences, he knows that whites do, so that—consciously or unconsciously—the result is virtually the same. The effect of preferential treatment—the lowering of normal standards to increase black representation—puts blacks at war with an expanded realm of debilitating doubt, so that the doubt itself becomes an unrecognized preoccupation that undermines their ability to perform, especially in integrated situations. On largely white campuses, blacks are five times more likely to drop out than whites. Preferential treatment, no matter how it is justified in the light of day, subjects blacks to a midnight of self-doubt and so often transforms their advantage into a revolving door.

Another liability of affirmative action comes from the fact that it indirectly encourages blacks to exploit their own past victimization as a source of power and privilege. Victimization, like implied inferiority, is what justifies preference, so that to receive the benefits of preferential treatment one must, to some extent, become invested in the view of one's self as a victim. In this way, affirmative action nurtures a victim-focused identify in blacks. The obvious irony here is that we become inadvertently invested in the very condition we are trying to overcome. Racial preferences send us the message that there is more power in our past suffering than our present achievements—none of which could bring us a *preference* over others.

When power itself grows out of suffering, then blacks are encouraged to expand the boundaries of what qualifies as racial oppression, a situation that can lead us to paint our victimization in vivid colors, even as we receive the benefits of preference. The same corporations and institutions that give us preference are also seen as our oppressors. At Stanford University minority students—some of whom enjoy as much as $15,000 a year in financial aid—recently took over the president's office demanding, among other things, more financial aid. The power to be found in victimization, like any power, is intoxicating and can lend itself to the creation of a new class of super-victims who can feel the pea of victimization under twenty mattresses. Preferential treatment rewards us for being underdogs rather than for moving beyond that status—a misplacement of incentives that, along with its deepening of our doubt, is more a yoke than a spur.

But, I think, one of the worst prices that blacks pay for preference has to do with an illusion. I saw this illusion at work recently in the mother of a middle-class black student who was going off to his first semester of college. "They owe us this, so don't think for a minute that you don't belong there." This is the logic by which many blacks, and some whites, justify affirmative action—it is something "owed" a form of reparation. But this logic overlooks a much harder and less digestible reality, that it is impossible to repay blacks living today for the historic suffering of the race. If all blacks were given a million dollars tomorrow morning it would not amount to a dime on the dollar of three centuries of oppression, nor would it obviate the residues of that oppression that we still carry today. The concept of historic reparation grows out of man's need to impose a degree of justice on the world that simply does not exist. Suffering can be endured and overcome; it cannot be repaid. Blacks cannot be repaid for the injustice done to the race, but we can be corrupted by society's guilty gestures of repayment.

Affirmative action is such a gesture. It tells us that racial preferences can do for us what we cannot do for ourselves. The corruption here is in the hidden incentive not to do what we believe preferences will do. This is an incentive to be reliant on others just as we are struggling for self-reliance. And it keeps alive the illusion that we can find some deliverance in repayment. The hardest thing for any sufferer to accept is that his suffering excuses him from very little and never has enough currency to restore him. To think otherwise is to prolong the suffering.

Several blacks I spoke with said they were still in favor of affirmative action because of the "subtle" discrimination blacks were subject to once on the job. One photojournalist said, "They have ways of ignoring you." A black female television producer said, "You can't file a lawsuit when your boss doesn't invite you to the insider meetings without ruining your career. So we still need affirmative action." Others mentioned the infamous "glass ceiling" through which blacks can see the top positions of authority but never reach them. But I don't think racial preferences are a protection against this subtle discrimination; I think they contribute to it.

In any workplace, racial preferences will always create two-tiered populations composed of preferred and unpreferreds. This division makes automatic a perception of enhanced competence for the unpreferreds and of questionable competence for the preferreds—the former earned his way, even though others were given preference, while the latter made it by color as much as by competence. Racial preferences implicitly mark whites with an exaggerated superiority just as they mark blacks with an exaggerated inferiority. They not only reinforce America's oldest racial myth but, for blacks, they have the effect of stigmatizing the already stigmatized.

I think that much of the "subtle" discrimination that blacks talk about is often (not always) discrimination against the stigma of questionable competence that affirmative action delivers to blacks. In this sense, preferences scapegoat the very people they seek to help. And it may be that at a certain level employers impose a glass ceiling, but this may not be against the race so much as against the race's reputation for having advanced by color as much as by competence. Affirmative action makes a glass ceiling virtually necessary as a protection against the corruption's of preferential treatment. This ceiling is the point at which corporations shift the emphasis from color to competency and stop playing the affirmative action game. Here preference backfires for blacks and becomes a taint that holds them back. Of course, one could argue that this taint, which is, after all, in the minds of whites, becomes nothing more than an excuse to discriminate against blacks. And certainly the result is the same in either case—blacks don't get past the glass ceiling. But this argument does not get around the fact that racial preferences now taint this color with a new theme of suspicion that makes it even more vulnerable to the impulse in others to discriminate. In this crucial yet gray area of perceived competence, preferences make whites look better than they are and blacks worse, while doing nothing whatever to stop the very real discrimination that blacks may encounter. I don't wish to justify the glass ceiling here, but only to suggest the very subtle ways that affirmative action revives rather than extinguishes the old rationalizations for racial discrimination.

In education, a revolving door; in employment, a glass ceiling.

I believe affirmative action is problematic in our society because it tries to function like a social program. Rather than ask it to ensure equal opportunity we have demanded that it create parity between the races. But preferential treatment does not teach skills, or educate, or instill motivation. It only passes out entitlement by color, a situation that in my profession has created an unrealistically high demand for black professors. The social engineer's assumption is that this high demand will inspire more blacks to earn Ph.D.'s and join the profession. In fact, the number of blacks earning Ph.D.'s has declined in recent years. A Ph.D. must be developed from preschool on. He requires family and community support. He must acquire an entire system of values that enables him to work hard while delaying gratification. There are social programs, I believe, that can (and should) help blacks *develop* in all these areas, but entitlement by color is not a social program; it is a dubious reward for being black.

It now seems clear that the Supreme Court, in a series of recent decisions, is moving away from racial preferences. It has disallowed preferences except in instances of "identified discrimination," eroded the precedent that statistical racial imbalances are *prima facie* evidence of discrimination, and in effect granted white males the right to challenge consent decrees that use preference to achieve racial balances in the workplace. One civil rights leader said, "Night has fallen on civil rights." But I am not so sure. The effect of these decisions is to protect the constitutional rights of everyone rather than take rights away from blacks. What they do take away from blacks is the special entitlement to more rights than others that preferences always grant. Night has fallen on racial preferences, not on the fundamental rights of black Americans. The reason for this shift, I believe, is that the white mandate for absolution from past racial sins has weakened considerably during the eighties. Whites are now less willing to endure unfairness to themselves in order to grant special entitlements to blacks, even when these entitlements are justified in the name of past suffering. Yet the black mandate for more power in society has remained unchanged. And I think part of the anxiety that many blacks feel over these decisions has to do with the loss of black power they may signal. We had won a certain specialness and now we are losing it.

But the power we've lost by these decisions is really only the power that grows out of our victimization—the power to claim special entitlements under the law because of past oppression. This is not a very substantial or reliable power, and it is important that we know this so we can focus more exclusively on the kind of development that will bring enduring power. There is talk now that Congress will pass new legislation to compensate for these new limits on affirmative action. If this happens, I hope that their focus will be on development and antidiscrimination rather than entitlement, on achieving racial parity rather than jerry-building racial diversity.

I would also like to see affirmative action go back to its original purpose of enforcing equal opportunity—a purpose that in itself disallows racial preferences. We cannot be sure that the discriminatory impulse in America has yet been shamed into extinction, and I believe affirmative action can make its greatest contribution by providing a rigorous vigilance in this area. It can guard constitutional rather than racial rights and help institutions evolve standards of merit and selection that are appropriate to the institution's needs yet as free of racial bias as possible (again, with the understanding that racial imbalances are not always an indication of racial bias). One of the most important things affirmative action can do is to define exactly what racial discrimination is and how it might manifest itself within a specific institution. The impulse to discriminate *is* subtle and cannot be ferreted out unless its many guises are made clear to people. Along with this there should be monitoring of institutions and heavy sanctions brought to bear when actual discrimination is found. This is the sort of affirmative action that America owes to blacks and to itself. It goes after the evil of discrimination itself, while preferences only sidestep the evil and grant entitlement to its *presumed* victims.

But if not preferences, then what? I think we need social policies that are committed to two goals: the educational and economic development of disadvantaged people, regardless of race, and the eradication from our society—through close monitoring and severe sanctions—of racial, ethnic, or gender discrimination. Preferences will not deliver us to either of these goals, since they tend to benefit those who are not disadvantaged—middle-class white women and middle-class blacks—and attack one form of discrimination with another. Preferences are inexpensive and carry the glamour of good intentions—change the numbers and the good deed is done. To be against them is to be unkind. But I think the unkindest cut is to bestow on children like my own an undeserved advantage while neglecting the development of those disadvantaged children on the East Side of my city who will likely never be in a position to benefit from a preference.

Give my children fairness; give disadvantaged children a better shot at development—better elementary and secondary schools, job training, safer neighborhoods, better financial assistance for college, and so on. Fewer blacks go to college today than ten years ago; more black males of college age are in prison or under the control of the criminal justice system than in college. This despite racial preferences.

The mandates of black power and white absolution out of which preferences emerged were not wrong in themselves. What was wrong was that both races focused more on the goals of these mandates than on the means to the goals. Blacks can have no real power without taking responsibility for their own educational and economic development. Whites can have no racial innocence without earning it by eradicating discrimination and helping the disadvantaged to develop. Because we ignored the means, the goals have not been reached, and the real work remains to be done.

The Psychology of the Future
Alvin Toffler

All education springs from some image of the future. If the image of the future held by a society is grossly inaccurate, its education system will betray its youth.

Imagine an Indian tribe which for centuries has sailed its dugouts on the river at its doorstep. During all this time the economy and culture of the tribe have depended upon fishing, preparing and cooking the products of the river, growing food in soil fertilized by the river, building boats and appropriate tools. So long as the rate of technological change in such a community stays slow, so long as no wars, invasions, epidemics or other natural disasters upset the even rhythm of life, it is simple for the tribe to formulate a workable image of its own future, since tomorrow merely repeats yesterday.

It is from this image that education flows. Schools may not even exist in the tribe; yet there is a curriculum's cluster of skills, values and rituals to be learned. Boys are taught to scrape bark and hollow out trees, just as their ancestors did before them. The teacher in such a system knows what he is doing, secure in the knowledge that tradition—the past—will work in the future.

What happens to such a tribe, however, when it pursues its traditional methods unaware that five hundred miles upstream men are constructing a gigantic dam that will dry up their branch of the river? Suddenly the tribe's image of the future, the set of assumptions on which its members base their present behavior, becomes dangerously misleading. Tomorrow will not replicate today. The tribal investment in preparing its children to live in a riverine culture becomes a pointless and potentially tragic waste. A false image of the future destroys the relevance of the education effort.

This is our situation today—only it is we, ironically, not some distant strangers—who are building the dam that will annihilate the culture of the present. Never before has any culture subjected itself to so intense and prolonged a bombardment of technological, social, and info-psychological change. This change is accelerating and we witness everywhere in the high-technology societies evidence that the old industrial-era structures can no longer carry out their functions.

Yet our political leaders for the most part propagate (and believe) the myth that industrial society is destined to perpetuate itself indefinitely. Like the elders of the tribe living on the riverbank, they blindly assume that the main features of the present social system will extend indefinitely into the future. And most educators, including most of those who regard themselves as agents of change, unthinkingly accept this myth.

They fail to recognize that the acceleration of change—in technology, in family structure, marriage and divorce patterns, mobility rates, division of labor, in urbanization, ethnic and subcultural conflict and international relations—means, by definition, the swift arrival of a future that is radically different from the present. They have never tried to imagine what a super-industrial civilization might look like, and what this might mean for their students. And so, most schools, colleges and universities base their teaching on the usually tacit notion that tomorrow's world will be basically familiar; the present writ large. Nothing, I believe, could be more profoundly deceptive.

I would contend, in fact, that no educational institution today can set sensible goals or do an effective job until its members—from chancellor or principal down to the newest faculty recruit, not to mention its students—subject their own assumptions about tomorrow to critical analysis. For their shared or collective image of the future dominates the decisions made in the institution.

The primitive father teaching his son how to carve a canoe had in mind an image of the future his son would inhabit. Since he assumed that the future would replicate the present, just as the present replicated the past, his image of the future was just as rich, detailed, comprehensive and structured as his image of the present. It *was* his image of the present. Yet when change struck, his imagery proved not merely obsolete but antiadaptive because it left out the possibility of radical change.

Like our distant ancestor, educators, too, need an image of tomorrow's society. But this image must include the possibility—indeed, the high likelihood—of radical change. This image need not be "correct" or "final"; it cannot be. There are no certainties, and any picture of a foreseeable society that depicts it as static or stable is probably delusory. Thus, to design educational systems for tomorrow (or even for today) we need not images of a future frozen in amber, as it were, but something far more complicated: sets of images of successive and alternative futures, each one tentative and different from the next.

What applies to the educator and the institution applies even more strongly to the learner. Just as all social groups and institutions have, in effect, collectively shared images of the future, each individual also has, in his or her cranium, a set of assumptions, an architecture of premises, about events to come. The child, almost from birth, begins to build up a set of expectations from its daily experience. Later these expectations become more complexly organized, and they begin to encompass more and more distant reaches of future time. Each person's private image of the future shapes his or her decision-making m crucial ways.

Students today receive a vast amount of undigested information and misinformation from newspapers, records, TV, movies, radio and other sources. As a result, they are aware of the rapidity with which the world is changing. But if many young people are prepared to contemplate the idea of radical change in the real world, this does not mean that they have the slightest idea about the implications of high-speed change for their own lives.

Some time ago I performed an unusual and confusedly nonscientific experiment with thirty three high-school students, mainly fifteen- and sixteen-year-olds. I asked each of them to help formulate a collective image of the future by writing down on a slip of paper seven events he or she thought likely to occur in the future, and to then date these events. I avoided saying anything that would restrict the kind of events or their *distance* into the future. The class threw itself enthusiastically into the exercise, and in a few minutes I had collected from them 193 forecast events, each of them duly dated. The results indicated that these urban, middle-class, rather sophisticated teenagers had accumulated many notions about the world of tomorrow.

From their forecasts there emerged, for example, a terrifying future for the United States in which, presumably, they would live out at least a part of their lives. The class scenario begins peacefully enough with predictions that the Vietnam War would end and United States relations with China would improve, both in 1972. (The exercise was run a year earlier, in 1971.) But soon events become more turbulent. New York City breaks away to become a state in 1973, and 1974 is a bad year characterized by race riots in June and a United States pullout from the United Nations. While both marijuana and prostitution are legalized, internal political events must be bleak because 1975 sees a political revolution in the United States.

In 1976 the value of the dollar declines, other nations ostracize the United States, and gas masks are distributed, presumably because of pollution. By 1977 the space program has ended and United States citizens are under constant surveillance in streets and homes. Senator Kennedy emerges somehow as President in 1978 (a special election?), but a major financial crisis occurs, and the following year, 1979, we break off relations with Europe. We learn to cure cancer, but by then pollution has become irreversible and we are highly dependent upon the oceans for food. All this, however, is merely a prelude to a cataclysmic year, 1980. That year can be described in a burst of screaming headlines:

AMERICAN REVOLUTION OVERTHROWS PRESENT GOVERNMENT
CULTURAL AND POLITICAL REVOLUTION BREAKS OUT IN U.S.
MAJOR RIVERS AND STREAMS DIE
NATURAL DISASTER WIPES OUT MANY PEOPLE
FAMILY SIZE LIMITED
MARS LANDING
COLONY PLANTED ON MARS
NUCLEAR WAR BREAKS OUT!

America's time of troubles is far from over. In 1981, Richard Nixon is assassinated, and while race relations take a turn for the better, and the renewed space program results in new missions to the planets, by 1983 we have a military dictatorship ruling the nation. Now the Soviet Union joins with the United States in a war against China (this is, after all, 1984 by now). Scientific progress continues and the rate of change accelerates further—indeed, embryos now take only six hours, instead of nine months, to gestate. But science is of no help when

California, hit, one assumes, by an earthquake, slips into the Pacific Ocean in 1986. We are beginning to colonize the moon, while population on earth reaches a crisis point, and the dollar is now worth only 25 percent of its 1971 value.

As the 1990s open, the Russo-Chinese War is still on, but things begin to improve. Peace among the great powers becomes more likely. Nuclear energy, especially in the form of fusion reactors, is widely in use, and a three-day work week is initiated. Our ecological problems are still extremely pressing, but solutions are at least in sight. In fact, 1995 looks like a good year. The government changes, the space effort expands once more, we finally develop a "more organized system" of education, and, apparently, young people are making their political weight felt, for we elect a new President who is only twenty years old. (Scoffers might note that William Pitt became prime minister of Britain at twenty four.) We are now also experiencing zero population growth.

I will not go on to describe their forecasts after 2000 A.D., but there is enough here presumably to suggest that at least this group of teenagers do not look forward to a stable world, or one progressing smoothly along well-worn grooves. They look forward to high turbulence for at least the next two decades.

The Impersonal Future

Perhaps the most striking fact about these forecasts has to do with the role of the student, his or her self-image as seen in relationship to the outside world. Indeed, in asking the students for their images of the future, I was less interested in the future, as such, or in their attitudes toward it, than I was in their attitudes toward *change*.

I was, therefore, fascinated and troubled to discover that for this class, while the future was clearly exciting as subject matter, it was distinctly impersonal. Thus, of the 193 responses, fully 177 referred to events that would occur "out there" somewhere in the world or the universe. Only sixteen events made any reference to "I"—the student making the forecast. Of the thirty-three students in the class who submitted usable responses, only six saw themselves as part of the picture.

One student, along with such forecasts as antigravity cars (1984) and destruction of the earth (2050–2100), scheduled his or her own life as follows:

Graduation	1976
Working	1977
Marriage	?
Success	1984
Death	2030–2040

Another forecast marriage in 1980 and concluded "I will be a great lawyer" by 1988. He, too (a boy, I would guess from his prediction that the football Giants would win the 1974 Super Bowl), slated himself to die in 2040. One respondent foresaw his or her own death by 1996—i.e., at about age forty.

Having tried a similar experiment with another much smaller group earlier, I was not surprised by the lopsided emphasis on the impersonal or nonpersonal in thinking about the future. In general, at least for the teenagers I have experimented with, the future is something that happens to somebody else.

I must emphasize that the teenagers making these forecasts were incontestably bright, lively, and probably more sophisticated than their counterparts in smaller cities. Yet no matter how turbulent a world they pictured, no matter how many new technologies might appear or what political revolutions might take place, the way of life foreseen for themselves as individuals seldom differed from the way of life possible in the present and actually lived by many today. It is as though they believed that everything happening outside one's life simply by-passes the individual. The respondents, in short, made no provision for change in themselves, no provision for adaptation to a world exploding with change.

I pursue this not because I think these experiments are anything more than suggestive; I would expect different groups to formulate quite different images of tomorrow and to reflect different degrees of connectedness with the racing pulse of change. Rather, I raise it because I believe that the schools and universities, with their heavy emphasis on the past, not only implicitly convey a false message about the future—the idea that it will resemble the present—but also that they create millions of candidates for future shock by encouraging the divorce between the individual's self-image and his or her expectations with regard to social change. More deeply, they encourage the student to think of his or her "self" not as subject to change, growth or adaptation, but as something static.

Action and Imagery

Education is not just something that happens in the head. It involves our muscles, our senses, our hormonal defenses, our total biochemistry. Nor does it occur solely *within* the individual. Education springs from the interplay between the individual and a changing environment. The movement to heighten future-consciousness in education, therefore, must be seen as one step toward a deep restructuring of the links between schools, colleges, universities and the communities that surround them.

When we introduce change and, therefore, higher levels of novelty into the environment, we create a totally new relationship between the limited reality of the classroom and the larger reality of life. Abstractions are symbolic reflections of aspects of reality. As the rate of change alters technological, social and moral realities, we are compelled to do more than revise our abstractions: we are also forced to test them more frequently against the realities they are supposed to represent or explain.

But the university and the lower schools, as organized today, are designed to construct or transmit abstractions, not to test them. This is why we need to accelerate the trend in many colleges and universities to offer credit for action-learning done off-campus through participation in real work, in business, in community political organizing, in pollution-control projects, or other activities. Many of these efforts today are badly organized, ill-thought-through, and regarded by the university as basically insignificant—concessions to the restlessness of students who no longer want to remain cooped up in the classroom. I would argue that such efforts not only must be continued, but must be radically expanded, must be linked more imaginatively to the formal learning process, must be extended downward to younger and younger students in the secondary schools and even, through adaptation of the idea, to primary-school children. Indeed, for older students, this action-learning ought to become the dominant form of learning, with classroom learning seen as a support rather than as the central element in education.

In the United States we herd 8,000,000 university students and some 51,000,000 younger children into educational institutions, assuring them all the while that it is for their own future benefit. It is all done with the best of intentions. It keeps them out of the labor force and, for a while, off the streets.

This policy, however, is based on a perilously faulty image of the future. By maintaining the false distinction between work and learning, and between school and community, we not only divorce theory from practice and deprive ourselves of enormous energies that might be channeled into socially useful action, we also infantalize the young and rob them of the motivation to learn.

On the other hand, by linking learning to action—whether that takes the form of constructing buildings on campus, or measuring traffic flow at an intersection and designing an overpass, or campaigning for environmental legislation, or interning at city hall, or helping to police a high-crime area, or serving as sanitation and health aides, or building a stage set, or doing research for a trade union, or working out a marketing problem for a corporation—we change the source of motivation.

The motive to learn is no longer the fear of a teacher's power to grade or the displeasure of the parent, but the desire to do something useful, productive and respected—to change the community, to make a dent, if even a small one, on reality. This desire to leave a dent, to make an impact, today fuels a wide range of antisocial activity from spray-painting graffiti on a public wall or vandalizing a school building to committing murder. It is not unrelated to the fact that most crime is the work of the young.

Today, unfortunately, most action-learning programs scarcely begin to take advantage of their full potentials. For example, most are seen as forms of independent study. For many students, they might be far more effective as group ventures. The organization of groups of students (self-organization would be better) into problem-solving or work teams makes it possible to design additional learning—learning about organization and group dynamics—into the situation. By consciously including people of varied ages in such teams, it becomes possible to provide "generational bridges"—a way of breaking down some of the trained incapacity of different age groups to talk to one another.

Through focusing on some sharply defined external objective or desired change, the group develops a degree of shared intimacy and attacks the prevailing sense of loneliness and isolation felt by so many students even on small campuses. Most important, however, the motivation for learning changes. The group itself generates internal social reinforcements for learning, and the nature of the problem being attacked defines the nature of the learning required, so that the definition of relevance is created by the real situation rather than by the say-so of a teacher.

In the meantime, decision-making, so crucial to coping with change, becomes, itself, a subject of the learning process. Most students in most schools and universities seldom participate in group decision-making. While they may be asked to make decisions about themselves—such as which courses to take (and even this is restricted at the lower levels)—they are seldom called upon to make personal decisions *that affect the work or performance of others.* The decisions they are characteristically called upon to make have little or no impact on anyone's life but their own. In this sense, they "don't count." They are isolates. Attempting to solve real-life problems, action-learning done in the context of a goalsharing group, trains the participants in decisional skills and begins to develop an understanding that their decisions do count—that personal decisions can have important consequences.

It is precisely at this point that action-learning converges with future-consciousness. For, when we speak of an image of the future, we are speaking of the ram)fied consequences of present-day decisions, whether public or personal. Action-learning, particularly when carried out by groups, is a useful tool for demonstrating the necessity for a future-orientation—the need to study alternatives, to develop long-range plans, to think in terms of contingencies—and especially to think through the *consequences,* including second- and third-order consequences, of action.

In short, the combination of action-learning with academic work, and both of these with a future orientation, creates a powerfully motivating and powerfully personal learning situation. It helps close the gap between change occurring "out there" and change occurring within the individual, so that learners no longer regard the world as divorced from themselves, and themselves as immune to (and perhaps incapable of) change. In a turbulent, high-change environment, it is only through the development of a "psychology of the future" that education can come to terms with learning.

Smokers' Space

Student

Closing the door on my car, I stop, glance up, in the direction of the educational institution that I call home. I start to move toward the school. I notice an immense group of students that lurk around the outside entrance, like a pack of wolves hovering over their freshly killed prey. Instead of devouring some half dead bloody carcass however, they group together not to hunt their prey but to be preyed upon by the addictive predator known as the cigarette. Moving through the pack and into the school is a little like trying to navigate your way through the Kansas City Chief's defensive line on a foggy day.

Not every student and teacher feels the same way I do about the smokers who linger outside the school. However, there are several people who must move in and out of the building on a daily basis who do find the smokers around the entrances fairly inconvenient. This is a problem that really doesn't plague other higher learning institutions to the extent that it does DeVry. This is probably due to the fact that DeVry is centered around only one building and does not have a traditional distributed campus. This greatly reduces places for people to smoke so they huddle around what little area is left, the entrances to the school.

A solution to this problem is to designate an area for smoking. Fourteen of the twenty-seven people surveyed agree with this solution. I also asked a question of those people who agreed that there should be a designated place for smoking where this area should be. I received numerous responses to this question but the main ones were a room inside the school and various places outside the school. Some of the ideas for places outside of the school included the north and south areas away from the entrances and the parking lot. Another more drastic suggestion that was made was to ban smoking from the campus altogether.

In the questionnaire I circulated I also found that thirty-seven percent of people who were surveyed smoke while at school. If this questionnaire is fairly representative of the overall number of students then there is a good collection of smokers that attend DeVry. Most of these students would tend to disagree with having a designated place for smoking. Students that smoke would be inconvenienced by having to walk a greater distance to the designated smoking area and perhaps they wouldn't even like the area that was specified. Although, there were a few smokers who liked the idea of having a room inside the school for the designated area. Student and faculty smokers would be heavily against the ban on smoking as smokers might feel that they were losing their freedom of choice.

This is an issue that most people feel strongly about whether they are smokers or non-smokers. I am not any different, I don't believe in an over all ban on smoking at school but I do think that having an area for smokers might be helpful to those on both sides of the fence. Neither smoker nor student would have to spin, hurdle, dodge, twist, and turn to avoid each other as people make their way in and out of the school. Having easier access to the school would be a benefit to everyone.

Smokers Questionnaire

Tabulations

1. Do you currently smoke?

> Yes   12   No   15

2. If so, do you smoke while you're at school?

> Yes   10   No   2

3. Do you feel that there should be a designated area for smoking?

> Yes   14   No   13

4. If so, where would you place the designated smoking area?

   A room inside the school.

   A designated area outside the school.

   An overall ban on smoking.

5. If you are a non-smoker do you find it inconvenient to have to pass through a large group of smokers to gain entry into the building?

> Yes   10   No   5

6. Do you feel that smoking should be prohibited all together on campus?

> Yes   12   No   15

No Smoking Section

Student

The issue of smoking in public places has become a real war zone between smokers and non-smokers. Naturally, smokers feel they have the right to smoke anytime, anywhere they want. Just the same, non-smokers feel they have the right to breathe clean, fresh air anywhere they happen to be, at any time. I agree with the second argument, and feel that the first literally stinks! One of the most recent and heated discussions concerns enclosed public smoking in restaurants.

When I am eating, there is one thing that I cannot stand, cigarette smoke. Most people that I have talked to who have never smoked, and even some who have, feel the same way. I have never been able to understand why smokers think they have the right to make other people inhale their nasty habit. This has always reminded me of an old saying that I was told when I was younger: "You are free to swing your arms any direction you want, as long as they do not make contact with another person's face." I feel the same way about smoking. Whether a person smokes or not is their own business, but when they begin to ruin an expensive dinner of mine, it quickly becomes my business.

Within the last five years, managers and owners of restaurants have created "no smoking" sections. This was a very nice gesture, but what about the person who has to sit right next to the smoking section? The smoke doesn't know that there is a non-smoking area nearby. Even if there is a definite boundary between the smoking and non-smoking sections, there are always those few who think it is not good enough to sit in a designated area for them, and they come over and sit where they are not supposed to. When a person does this and I am around, I immediately tell the manager. The manager always tells the smoker to quit smoking or move. The smoker always does, but it still ruins my dinner, because I always feel badly about doing that.

Last Saturday night I decided to take my mom, dad, and my girlfriend out to dinner for Mother's Day. I took them to the Olive Garden because I like the atmosphere of the place. After one and a half hours of waiting, we were finally seated in a non-smoking section. Shortly after we received our pre-dinner drinks, I began to smell a familiarly nasty odor. I turned around to see three people sitting at a table of four with lit cigarettes. I checked around to make sure they really did put us in a non-smoking section. Sure enough, they did. Soon two of the women smokers got up and passed by us to the restroom. My dad, in a polite manner of course, said, "Hey, lady, do you know this is a non-smoking section?" The lady quickly answered by informing us that "they" told us we could smoke here. I got up, went to the manager and informed him of our situation. Within five minutes, the smokers were gone.

Just recently, the Surgeon General has pronounced that secondary cigarette smoke is a known carcinogen. This simply means that the smoke that non-smokers have to breathe as a result of smokers smoking causes cancer. I think that people who choose to not smoke and, hopefully live a cancer-free life should not be endangered by inconsiderate people who think they have to smoke in public restaurants. Therefore, I believe that smoking should be banned completely from these places.

Ch. 9: Argument and persuasion

Suggestions for writing:

1. Choose one of the essays from this chapter and find three or four weaknesses. They could be as broad as an unsupported major point in the writer's argument and as specific as a choice of an individual word that you think is biased. You don't necessarily have to disagree with the overall essay; you could, for example, envision yourself as a friend of the writer, giving advice on how to make the essay stronger.

2. Do you have some original thoughts on the gun-control issue? On drug testing? Civil rights? Affirmative action? Write a paragraph or essay using one of the essays in this chapter as a source of disagreement or a source of support, expressing your own personal thoughts on the topic. Do not simply echo the sentiments of bumper-sticker messages or talk-show hosts. Think it over objectively and say something original.

3. Choose a specific problem or shortcoming in your school environment and propose a solution for it. First, persuasively illustrate the problem, and then offer an effective, agreeable, workable solution to it. Consider writing a questionnaire about the problem and circulating it among a representative sampling of students.

4. Write a paragraph or essay on one of the following topics or a similar controversial topic. Consider the following approach to really test your ability to be objectively persuasive: pick one of the topics that you have strong feelings about and argue against your own viewpoint.

    the welfare system   the legalization of drugs
    adoptions by unmarried people   chemical/biological warfare
    manned exploration of space   capital punishment

Checklist for argument and persuasion:

1. Have you picked a worthwhile topic? Is it controversial? Is it meaningful?

2. Have you examined both sides of the argument before beginning to write?

3. Have you aimed your paper at a specific audience?

4. Do you effectively support your major points with logical arguments and sound, adequate, and appropriate evidence?

5. If authorities are used, are they qualified and valid?

6. Have you been sure to eliminate any logical fallacies from your arguments?

7. Have you anticipated objections to your arguments and addressed them?

8. If you have used an emotional appeal, does it center on those emotions most likely to sway your targeted audience?

9. Have you varied your vocabulary and sentence structure?

10. Did you check for accuracy in grammar, punctuation, and spelling?

CHAPTER 10

Documented Essays

Reading and Writing from Sources

Using Sources

We use sources every day in both informal and formal situations. We explain the source of a phone message, for example, or we refer to an instructor's comments in class. We use someone else's opinion in an essay, or we quote an expert to prove a point. We cite sources both in speaking and in writing through summary, paraphrase, and direct quotation. Most of your college instructors will ask you to write papers using sources so they can see how well you understand the course material. The use of sources in academic papers requires you to process what you have read and integrate this reading material with your own opinions and observations—a process that requires a high level of skill in thinking, reading, and writing.

Defining Documented Essays

Documented essays provide you with the opportunity to perform sophisticated and exciting exercises in critical thinking; they draw on the thinking, reading, and writing abilities you have built up over the course of your academic career, and they often require you to put all the rhetorical modes to work at their most analytical level. Documented essays demonstrate the process of analytical thinking at its best in different disciplines.

In the academic world, documented essays are also called "research papers," "library papers," and "term papers." Documented essays are generally written for one of three reasons: (1) to **report,** (2) to **interpret,** or (3) to **analyze.**

The most straightforward, uncomplicated type of documented essay **reports** information, as in a survey of problems children have in preschool. The second type of documented essay both presents and **interprets** its findings. It will examine a number of different views on a specific issue and weigh these views as it draws its own conclusions. A topic that falls into this category would be whether children who have attended preschool are more sociable than those who have not. After considering evidence on both sides, the writer would draw his or her own conclusions on this topic. A documented essay that **analyzes** a subject presents a hypothesis, tests the hypothesis, and analyzes or evaluates its conclusions. This type of essay calls for the most advanced form of critical thinking. It might look, for example, at the reasons preschool children are more or less socially flexible than non-preschool children. At its most proficient, this type of writing requires a sophisticated degree of evaluation that forces you to judge your reading, evaluate your sources, and ultimately scrutinize your own reasoning ability as the essay takes shape.

Each of these types of documented essays calls for a higher level of thinking, and each evolves from the previous category. In other words, interpreting requires some reporting, whereas analyzing draws on both reporting and interpreting.

In the following paragraph, a student reports, interprets, analyzes, and uses sources to document the problem of solid waste in America. Notice how the student writer draws her readers into the essay with a commonly used phrase about America and then questions the validity of its meaning. The student's opinions give shape to the paragraph, while her use of sources helps identify the problem and support her contentions.

> *"America the Beautiful" is a phrase used to describe the many wonders of nature found throughout our country. American's natural beauty will fade, however, if solutions to our solid waste problems are not found. America is a rich nation socially, economically, and politically. But these very elements may be the cause of Americans' wastefulness. Americans now generate approximately 160 million tons of solid waste a year— 3 1/2 pounds per person per day. We live in a consumer society where "convenience," "ready to use," and "throwaway" are words that spark the consumer's attention (Cook 60). However, many of the products associated with these words create a large part of our problem with solid waste (Grossman 39). We are running out of space for our garbage. The people of America are beginning to produce responses to this problem. Are we too late? A joint effort between individuals, businesses, government industries, and local,*

state, and federal governments is necessary to estab-
lish policies and procedures to combat this waste war.
The problem requires not one solution, but a combi-
nation of solutions involving technologies and people
working together to provide a safe and healthy envi-
ronment for themselves and future generations.

How to Write Documented Essays

Preparing to Write. Just as with any writing assignment, you should begin the task of writing a documented essay by exploring and limiting your topic. In this case, however, you draw on other sources to help you with this process. You should seek out both primary and secondary sources related to your topic. Primary sources are works of literature, historical documents, letters, diaries, speeches, eyewitness accounts, and your own experiments, observations, and conclusions; secondary sources explain and analyze information from other sources. Any librarian can help you search for both types of sources related to your topic.

After you have found a few sources on your general topic, you should scan and evaluate what you have discovered so you can limit your topic further. Depending on the required length of your essay, you want to find a topic broad enough to be researched, established enough that you can find sources on it in the library, and significant enough to demonstrate your abilities to grapple with ideas and draw conclusions.

Once you have established these limitations, you might try writing a tentative thesis. At this point, asking a question and attempting to find an answer is productive. But you should keep in mind that your thesis is likely to be revised several times as the range of your knowledge changes and as your paper takes different turns while you write. Then, decide on a purpose and audience for your essay.

Once your tentative thesis is formed, you should read your sources for ideas and take detailed notes on your reading. These notes will probably fall into one of four categories: (1) summary—a condensed statement of someone else's thoughts or observations; (2) paraphrase—a restatement in your own words of someone else's ideas or observations; (3) direct quotations from sources; or (4) a combination of these forms. As you gather information, you should consider keeping a "research journal" where you can record your own opinions, interpretations, and analyses in response to your reading. This journal should be separate from your notes on sources and is the place where you can make your own discoveries in relation to your topic by jotting down thoughts and relationships among ideas you are exposed to, by keeping a record of sources you read and others you want to pursue, by tracking and developing your own ideas and theories, and by clarifying your thinking on an issue.

Finally, before you write your first draft, you might want to write an informal working outline for your own information. Such an exercise can help you check the range of your coverage and the order and development of your ideas. With an outline, you can readily see where you need more information, less information, or more solid sources. Try to be flexible, however. This outline might change dramatically as your essay develops.

Writing. Writing the first draft of a documented essay is your chance to discover new insights and see important connections between ideas that you might not be aware of yet. This draft is your opportunity to demonstrate that you understand the issue at hand and your sources on three increasingly difficult levels—literal, interpretive, and analytical; that you can organize your material effectively; that you can integrate your sources (in the form of summaries, paraphrases, or quotations) with your opinions; and that you can document your sources.

To begin this process, look again at your thesis statement and your working outline, and adjust them to represent any new discoveries you have made as you read your sources and wrote in your research journal. Then, organize your research notes and information in some logical fashion.

When you begin to draft your paper, write the sections of the essay that you feel most comfortable about first. Throughout the essay, feature your own point of view and integrate summaries, paraphrases, and quotations from other sources into your own analysis. Each point you make should be a section of your paper consisting of your own conclusion and your support for that conclusion (in the form of facts, examples, summaries, paraphrases, and quotations). Remember that the primary reason for doing such an assignment is to let you demonstrate your ability to synthesize material, draw your own conclusions, and analyze your sources and your own reasoning.

A documented paper usually blends three types of material:

1. *Common knowledge, such as the places and dates of events (even if you have to look them up).*

    EXAMPLE: Neil Armstrong and Edwin Aldrin first walked on the moon on July 20, 1969.

2. *Your own thoughts and observations.*

    EXAMPLE: Armstrong and Aldrin's brief walk on the moon's surface was the beginning of a new era in the U.S. space program.

3. *Someone else's thoughts and observations.*

    EXAMPLE: President Richard Nixon reacted to the moon-walk in a telephone call to the astronauts: "For one priceless moment in the history of man all the people on this earth are truly one—one in their pride in what you have done and one in our prayers that you will return safely to earth."

Of these three types of information, you must document or cite your exact source only for the third type. Negligence in citing your sources, whether purposeful or accidental, is called *plagiarism*, which comes from a Latin word meaning "kidnapper." Among student writers, it usually takes one of three forms: (1) using words from another source without quotation marks; (2) using someone else's ideas in the form of a summary or paraphrase without citing your source; and (3) using someone else's term paper as your own.

Avoiding plagiarism is quite simple: You just need to remember to acknowledge the sources of ideas or words that you are using to support your own contentions. Acknowledging your sources also gives you credit for the reading you have done and for the ability you have developed to use sources to support your observations and conclusions.

Documentation styles vary from discipline to discipline. Ask your instructor about the particular documentation style he or she wants you to follow. The most common styles are the Modern Language Association (MLA) style, used in humanities courses, and the American Psychological Association (APA) style, used in behavioral sciences and science courses. (See any writing handbook for more details on documentation formats.)

Even though documentation styles vary somewhat from one discipline to another, the basic concept behind documentation is the same in all disciplines: You must give proper credit to other writers by acknowledging the sources of the summaries, paraphrases, and quotations that you use to support the topics in your documented paper. Once you grasp this basic concept and accept it, you will have no trouble avoiding plagiarism.

Rewriting. To rewrite your documented essay, you should play the role of your readers and impartially evaluate your argument and the sources you have used as evidence in that argument. To begin with, revise your thesis to represent all the discoveries you made as you wrote your first draft. Then, look for problems in logic throughout the essay: Are the essay's assertions clear? Are they adequately supported? Does your argument flow smoothly? Are other points of view recognized and examined? Does the organization of your paper further your assertions/argument? Are all explanations in your paper clear? Have you removed irrelevant material? Have you added information to underdeveloped portions of your paper? Next, look carefully at specific words and sentences: Do the words say what you mean? Do your supporting sentences clearly amplify your main ideas? Then, check your documentation style: Is your source material (either summarized, paraphrased, or quoted) presented fairly and accurately? Have you rechecked the citations for all the sources in your paper? Do you introduce the sources in your paper when appropriate? Are your sources in the proper format according to your instructor's guidelines (MLA, APA, or another)? Then, proofread carefully. Finally, prepare your paper to be submitted to your instructor: Does your title page follow the assignment's regulations? Have you prepared your paper with the proper margins? Are your page numbers in the proper place? If you have tables and abstracts in your paper, have you consulted the instructor and followed the appropriate rules? Have you prepared an alphabetical list of your sources for the end of your paper? Have you followed all your instructor's directions?

Student Essay: Documentation at Work

The following student essay uses documented sources to support its conclusions and observations about our eating habits today. First, the writer creates a profile of carnivorous species in contrast to human beings. She then goes on to discuss the harsh realities connected with eating meat. After recognizing and refuting some opposing views, this student writer ends her paper with her own evaluation of the situation and a list of some famous vegetarians. Throughout the essay, the student writer carefully supports her principal points with summaries, paraphrases, and quotations from other sources. Notice that she uses the MLA documentation style and closes the paper with an alphabetical list of "Works Cited."

Food for Thought

The next time you sit down to a nice steak dinner, pause for a moment to consider whether you are bio-logically programmed to eat meat. Unlike carnivores,

Background informa-tion such as lions and tigers, with claws and sharp front teeth allowing them to tear and eat raw flesh, humans are omnivores, with fingers that can pluck fruits and grains and flat teeth that can grind these vegetable Common knowledge foods. To digest their meals, carnivores have an acidic saliva and a very strong hydrochloric acid digestive fluid. In contrast, we humans have an alkaline saliva, and our digestive fluids are only one-tenth as potent as Common knowledge those of carnivores. Moreover, carnivores have an intestinal tract barely three times their body length, which allows for faster elimination of rotting flesh; humans have an intestinal tract eight to twelve times our body length, better enabling us to digest plant Paraphrase of sec-ondary source nutrients. These marked physiological distinctions clearly suggest that carnivorous animals and humans are adapted to very different kinds of foods (Diamond and Diamond, <u>Fit for Life II</u> 239). What happens, Citation (MLA form) Thesis then, when we eat flesh? <u>The effects of a meat-based diet are far-reaching: massive suffering of the animals killed and eaten, a myriad of diseases in humans, and a devastating effect on world ecology.</u>

Student's first conclusion <u>The atrocities committed daily to provide meat should be enough to make a meat-based diet completely unconscionable.</u> According to Peter Singer, of People for the Ethical Treatment of Animals (PETA), every year several hundred million cattle, pigs, and sheep and three billion chickens are slaughtered to provide food for humans (92). That is equal to 6,278 animals every minute of every day—and those are just the ones that make it to the slaughterhouse. Over 500,000 animals die in transit each year (Singer 150). *Summary of secondary source* *Support for conclusion #1*

Paraphrase of secondary source (fact) A slaughterhouse is not a pretty sight. Anywhere from 50 to 90 percent of the cattle are slaughtered in a "kosher" manner (Robbins 142). "Kosher" sounds innocent enough, but what it actually means is that the animal must be "healthy and moving" at the time of death. This requires the animals to be fully conscious as "a heavy chain is clamped around one of their rear legs; then they are jerked off their feet and hang upside down" for anywhere from two to five minutes, usually twisting in agony with a broken leg, while they are moved down the conveyer belt to be slaughtered (Robbins 140–1). *Summary of secondary source*

Student's opinion The pain doesn't start at the time of slaughter, however, for most of these animals, but rather at birth. An in-depth look at the animal most slaughtered by people, the chicken, reveals particularly horrendous treatment. Chickens are used in two ways—for their flesh as well as their eggs. For egg manufacturers, the one-half million male chicks born every day are useless, so they are immediately thrown into garbage bags and left to suffocate. When you consider the life of their female counterparts, however, perhaps such brutal treatment is a blessing (Robbins 54). *Examples to support opinion* *Opinion from secondary source*

Paraphrase of secondary source (facts) Chickens naturally belong to a flock with a specific pecking order. They seem to enjoy open spaces to stretch their wings as they scratch around, dust-bathe, and build nests for their eggs (Singer 109). Today, however, chickens are housed in wiremesh cages suspended over a trench to collect droppings. The typical cage is 12- by 18-inches holding four or five hens for their entire productive lives, which is at least a year or more (Mason in Singer, Defense 91). This overcrowding results in such high levels of stress that the hens resort to pecking each other's feathers out and to cannibalism (Singer 98). Rather than incur the expense of increasing space to alleviate these conditions, chicken farmers have routinely adopted the practice of debeaking the hens by slicing a hot knife through their *Paraphrase of secondary source (facts)* *Analysis from secondary source* highly sensitive beak tissue (Singer 99). Another result ^{Paraphrase} of this overcrowding is that the hens' toenails get tan- ^{of sec-}^{ondary} gled in the bottom wires of the cages; after some time ^{sources} the flesh grows onto the wire. The solution to this ^(facts)

^{Opinion} ^{from} problem has become to cut off the chick's toes within a ^{secondary} day or two of birth (Robbins 61). Conditions for other ^{source} farm animals are equally despicable (Singer, Defense). ^{Student's}

While we would like to assume the animals we eat ^{opinion} are healthy at the time of butchering, this is often not the case. Most veal calves, for example, are near death from anemia when sent to the butcher (Diamond and ^{Examples} Diamond, Fit for Life II 238). Inspections have ^{from sec-}^{ondary} revealed leukosis (cancer) in 90% of the chickens ^{sources} (Robbins 67), pneumonia rates of 80%, and stomach ulcers of 53% in pigs (Robbins 94). Salmonellosis is found in 90% of the chickens dressed and ready to be purchased (Robbins 303).

^{Student's} How can the factory farming industry justify its ^{opinion} behavior? The answer boils down to money, for facto-ry farming has become an incredibly huge business, and meat producers can't afford to be sentimental. As shown by USDA Economic Indicators for the Farm Sector, in 1988 the United States had cash receipts totaling over $150 billion from farm marketing ^{Paraphrase} Financial Summary 151) and nearly $80 billion from ^{of sec-}^{ondary} livestock and livestock products (153). As Fred Haley, ^{sources} head of a poultry farm with nearly 250,000 hens, has ^{Quotation} ^(fact) stated, "The object of producing eggs is to make ^{from}^{secondary} money. When we forget this objective, we have forgot- ^{source} ten what it is all about" (qtd. in Robbins 67). Cattle ^{Quotation} auctioneer Henry Pace has a similar comment about ^{from} the treatment of cattle: "We believe we can be most ^{secondary}^{source} efficient by not being emotional. We are a business, not a humane society, and our job is to sell merchan-dise at a profit. It's no different from selling paper clips or refrigerators" (qtd. in Robbins 104).

^{Student's} <u>Even if we, like the industry leaders, could turn a</u> ^{second}^{conclusion} <u>cold heart to the plight of our fellow creatures, we</u> <u>would still find many reasons to warrant a vegetarian</u> <u>diet, beginning with our own health</u>. Recapping just a few hundred of the hundreds of studies that link diet to disease, we might consider the following:

^{Paraphrase} —A study of nearly 90,000 American women pub- ^{Support for} ^{of sec-} lished in the <u>New England Journal of Medicine</u> reports that ^{conclusion} ^{ondary} daily pork, lamb, or beef eaters have a 250 percent greater ^{#2} ^{sources} ^(facts) likelihood of developing colon cancer than people who con-sume these foods once a month or less ("Red Meat Alert").

—The Journal of the American Medical Association stated that a vegetarian diet could prevent 97 percent of coronary occlusions (Robbins 247).

—Scientists now routinely screen cattle workers for BIV, a disease that "shares about 35 percent of its genetic makeup with HIV," the human AIDS retrovirus ("Cattle's Link with AIDS" 19).

Other equally shocking residual health problems associated with a meat diet are also being documented. For instance, people tend to think that vegetarians are at high risk for pesticide poisoning, but according Summary of to the EPA's Pesticides Monitoring Journal, most pestisecondary cides in the American diet come from foods originatsource ing from animals. Studies have shown that 95 to 99 percent of toxic chemicals in the American diet come from meat, fish, and animal products (Robbins 315). These same pesticides are ending up in the milk of lactating mothers. A similar study in the New England Paraphrase Journal of Medicine showed that the breast milk of of secondary vegetarian mothers has contamination levels only 1 to sources 2 percent of the average (Robbins 345). Not only does (facts) vegetarian breast milk have strikingly lower levels of contamination, it also has higher levels of essential ele-
Student's ments, such as selenium (Debski et al. 215).
question But don't we need a lot of protein to be strong and healthy? The RDA for protein is 56 grams (just under two ounces) per day (Diamond and Diamond, Fit for Life 88). People seem to think that meat is the best (or Paraphrase the only) way to get protein, but think about this: Some of secondary Paraphrase of the world's strongest animals—elephants, horses, sources of gorillas—eat principally fruits, grain, or grass (facts) secondary (Diamond, Fit for Life 89–90). Lest you believe that source (fact) humans must eat meat to be strong and healthy, consider the following: Edwin Moses, undefeated in the 400-meter hurdles for eight years, is a vegetarian; Andreas Cahling, 1980 Mr. Intentional Body Builder, is a vegetarian (Robbins 160–1); and Dave Scott, Ironman Examples Triathlon winner four times (no one else has won it to answer
Examples to more than once), is a vegetarian (Robbins 158). In study question answer pro- protein tein question after study, the consumption of protein is linked not with health but with such diseases as heart disease, hypertension, various forms of cancer, arthritis, and
Student's osteoporosis (Diamond and Diamond, Fit for life 87).
third conclu- The effects of meat diets go beyond causing sion human disease and death. Perhaps the most frightening legacy being left by America's dietary ritual is just now being realized, and that is the profound ecological

<u>impact factory farming is having on our planet</u>. Every Support for conclusion #3 five seconds, one acre of forest is cleared in America, and one estimate is that 87 percent is cleared for either livestock grazing or growing livestock feed (Robbins 361). According to Christopher Uhl of the Paraphrase of secondary sources (facts) Pennsylvania State University Department of Biology and Geoffrey Parker of the Institute of Ecosystem Studies, 55 square feet of forest in Central America is lost for each hamburger eaten (642).

Student's opinion Forests are not all that we are sacrificing. Local governments are constantly calling for water conservation, yet over 50 percent of all water used in America goes into grain production for livestock (Robbins 367). According to one study, the water Paraphrase of secondary sources (facts) required to feed a meat eater for one day is 4,000 gallons, but it is only 1,200 gallons for a lacto-ovo (dairy and egg eating) vegetarian and 300 gallons for a vegan (one who consumes no animal-derived products) (Robbins 367). Not only is the vast amount of water wasted through a meat-based diet outrageous, but the added cost of controlling animal waste must also be taken into account. One cow produces sixteen times as much waste as one human (Robbins 372), and cattle waste produces ten times the water pollution that human waste does (Robbins 373).

Student's opinion A third loss is even more serious than the losses of forests and water. This year, 60 million people will die of starvation, yet in America, we feed 80 percent of our corn and 95 percent of our oats to farm animals. The feed given to cattle alone, excluding pigs and chickens, would feed double the population of humans worldwide (Robbins 352). Three and one-quarter acres of farmland are needed to provide meat for one person per year. A lacto-ovo Vegetarian can be fed from just one-half acre per year; a vegan needs only one-sixth of an acre. This means twenty vegans can eat a healthy diet for the same acreage needed to feed just one meat eater. Cutting our meat habit by only 10 percent would provide enough food for all of the 60 million people worldwide who will starve this year (Robbins 352–3).

As John Robbins, who relinquished his inheritance of the largest ice cream company in America, Baskin- Quotation from secondary source Robbins, said, "We live in a crazy time, when people who make food choices that are healthy and compassionate are often considered weird, while people are considered normal whose eating habits promote disease and are dependent on enormous suffering" (305).

Student's final remarks   With all the devastation the average American diet is creating, we must begin to take responsibility for the consequences of our actions. Let us follow in the footsteps of such famous vegetarians as Charles Darwin, Leonardo da Vinci, Albert Einstein, Sir Isaac Newton, Plato, Pythagoras, Socrates, and Tolstoy (Parham 185). Every time we sit down to eat, we can choose either to contribute to or to help put an end to this suffering and destruction. Only one vote matters, and that is the one we make with our forks.

Works Cited

Alphabetical list of sources "Cattle's Link with AIDS." <u>New Scientist</u> 8 Oct. 1987: 19. *Modern Language Association form*

Debski, Bogdan, et al. "Selenium Content and Glutathione Peroxidase Activity of Milk from Vegetarian and Nonvegetarian Women." <u>Journal of Nutrition</u> 119 (1989): 215–20.

Diamond, Harvey, and Marilyn Diamond. <u>Fit for Life</u>. New York: Warner, 1985.

————. <u>Fit for Life II</u>, <u>Living Health</u>. New York: Warner, 1987.

Parham, Barbara. <u>What's Wrong with Eating Meat</u>? Denver: Ananda Marga, 1981.

"Red Meat Alert." <u>New Scientist</u> 22/29 Dec. 1990.

Robbins, John. <u>Diet for a New America</u>. Walpole: Stillpoint, 1987.

Singer, Peter. <u>Animal Liberation: A New Ethics for Our Treatment of Animals</u>. New York: Hearst, 1975.

Singer, Peter, ed. <u>In Defense of Animals</u>. New York: Basil Blackwell, 1985.

Snowdon, David A., and Roland L. Phillips. "Does a Vegetarian Diet Reduce the Occurrence of Diabetes?" <u>Journal of Public Health</u> 75 (1985): 507–11.

<u>State Financial Summary, 1988</u>. Washington: Economic Indicators for the Farm Sector, 1988.

Uhl, Christopher, and Geoffrey Parker. "Our Steak in the Jungle." <u>Bio Science</u> 36 (1986): 642.

Student Writer's Comments

From the moment this essay was assigned, I knew my topic would be vegetarianism, because I felt the key to a convincing argument was to select a topic I was passionate about. I was undertaking the task of speaking out against an American way of life, so I needed to approach the topic in as nonthreatening a manner as possible. I wanted to be graphic as I appealed to the emotions, concerns, and ethics of my audience so my message would not easily be forgotten, yet I had to strike a careful balance so I would not alienate my readers by appearing preachy or accusatory while I wrote, I kept in mind that I would be successful only if my words caused my readers to make a change, however small, in their behavior. The only frustration was my difficulty in tracking down a number of key sources. Otherwise, writing this essay was a pleasure.

Some Final Thoughts on Documented Essays

The essays that follow are vigorous exercises in critical thinking. They use a combination of different types of persuasive appeals (logical, emotional, and ethical) and draw on a wealth of rhetorical modes that we have studied throughout the book. As you read these essays, be aware of the combination of appeals at work, the various rhetorical modes each author uses to further his or her argument, and the way each author uses sources to support the topics within the argument.

Cheops: The Great Pyramid

Student

Rising into the clear blue skies of Egypt, made of two-and-a-half million rocks weighing anywhere from two to seventy tons apiece, is the Great Pyramid of Egypt. The Great Pyramid is called Cheops or Khufu after the pharaoh that built it around the year 2560 B.C. This structure, now about 450 feet high, was 481 feet tall when first built (Casson 118; Ashmawy 1; Budge 407). Thirty feet have been lost as the Egyptians stripped away some of the capstone and outer covering for use in other constructions (Casson 118). For over forty-three centuries the Great Pyramid was the tallest man-made structure on earth and not surpassed until the 1800s. Today, the Pyramid is as tall as a forty-story building. The building of Cheops astounds modern engineers. The task of building the mammoth construction and the precision used to build it are baffling problems an ancient civilization solved (Tompkins 1). Why did the ancient Egyptians build the pyramids? How did they achieve such seemingly impossible feats of architecture and engineering? These are questions experts are still trying to answer.

The Great Pyramid is located on a rocky, mile square, man-leveled plateau called Giza by the Arabs, formerly called Memphis (Ashmawy 1). Giza is located ten miles west of Cairo, Egypt. Surrounding Cheops are a total of eight other smaller pyramids. Two of these pyramids are thought to be built by Cheops' successors and the six smallest pyramids for Cheops' wives and daughters (Tompkins 1).

The Great Pyramid covers about twelve acres at its base. The Great Pyramid's sides are all at an angle of 54 degrees 54 minutes and each side lines up directly with the cardinal north, south, east, and west points of a compass. The ancient Egyptians did not have compasses so this accuracy is difficult to explain (Ashmawy 1). The entrance to Cheops is forty-three feet from the ground facing north (Budge 407). Upon entering, there is a passage three and a quarter feet high and four feet wide that inclines 320 feet. At the bottom of the Descending Passage, well under ground, is the King's Chamber. This chamber still contains the red granite sarcophagus of Cheops, although the sarcophagus is broken and coverless (Budge 408). Interestingly, the sarcophagus measurements are larger than that of the entrance to the chamber (Ashmawy 2). The floor of this chamber is over 140 feet below the base of the pyramid. Also from the original passageway, halfway down before arriving at the King's Chamber, there is the Ascending Passage leading up to the Queen's Chamber. The only other chambers located within the pyramid are hollow and located high above the King's chamber to relieve the pressure bearing down on the King's Chamber from the Pyramid above (Budge 408).

The limestone that was used to build Cheops seems to have been quarried in layers from the top down at the Giza plateau, or in the Mokattam hills located twenty miles away across the Nile (Tompkins 221). The casing stones that lined the outside of the Pyramid are believed to come from these same areas. The granite blocks used in the construction of the King's Chamber could only have been found 500 miles up the Nile. Archeologists believe these must have been transported by the ancient Egyptians on barges made of reed, although the granite blocks weighed up to 70 tons apiece (Tompkins 220). Herodotus, a scholar who saw the Pyramid in 440 B.C., claims that he was told that a hundred thousand men, working for three months at a time, moved the stone from the quarries. A causeway three-thousand feet long, sixty feet wide, made of polished stone, taking ten years to build was used to transport the rocks from the Nile up to the Giza plateau according to Herodotus (Tompkins 220). These stones were then placed on sleds and pulled up the causeway. A generally accepted theory of how this was accomplished was put forth by Commander F. M. Barber, an American naval attaché stationed in Egypt in the 1800s. He estimated that 900 men, trained to pull together, could have pulled these sleds up the causeway by greasing the stoneway. Ancient Egyptian pictures exist depicting people hauling stones in this way (Tompkins 223). The difficulties of transporting these massive stones were somehow solved by the ancient Egyptians. However, the tools used to quarry the stones must have been made of bronze and tempered in a way unknown in modern time (Tompkins 222).

The Herculean task of getting the rocks to the construction site was only the beginning. The ancient Egyptians had to devise a way to raise these stones to the height of a 40 story building. They also had to devise a way to place these stones in very exact positions and craft these stones so they fit together smoothly and perfectly. Egyptologist and archeologists have many different theories on how these pyramids were actually constructed, but no one really knows how they were built.

Possibly of more concern than how the Great Pyramid was built, is why the Great Pyramid was built. The ancient Egyptians strongly believed in an afterlife because of their religious beliefs. Because the Egyptians believed that their souls returned to their bodies after death, great care was taken in burial (Casson 76–77). Archeologists know that early Egyptian graves were covered with stones and loose sand to protect the deceased. However, because of the animals and wind in the desert, the ancient Egyptians were driven to find a more secure way of burying their dead. These grave mounds evolved into mastabas. These were made of mud, had sloping sides, and were flat on top (Casson 117). Contained below this mud construction were chambers to hold the items the deceased would need in the afterlife, as well as the body (Casson 118). To decorate these tombs, mud bricks were placed on the outside of the mastaba in geometric patterns (Casson 117). As the ancient Egyptians evolved, so did the mastabas. Some of the later mastabas had 30 chambers and some grew to a height of seventeen feet. The

Egyptians also started incorporating limestone into these constructions (Casson 118).

The first pyramid-like structure actually built entirely of stone was the Step Pyramid at Sakkarah. Built by Imhotep during the Third Dynasty, it was actually six mastabas layered one upon another. The Step Pyramid was 200 feet high and built almost two centuries before the Great Pyramid. Therefore, archeologists can trace the evolution of the ancient Egyptian's tombs from a mound of rocks to the Great Pyramid (Casson 118).

Besides the obvious use of the Great Pyramid as a tomb, astronomers have long thought that Cheops was used as an astronomical observatory. Translated inscriptions from the time of the pyramids mention a ceremony that took place before the building of important structures called "stretching of the cord." The royal ceremony is described as "Looking up at the sky at the course of the rising stars, recognizing the *ak* of the Bull's Thigh Constellation (our Great Bear), I establish the corners of the temple," Johannes Dumichen translates ak as "the star's culmination as it passes the meridian" (Tompkins 150).

British astronomer Richard A. Proctor claims that the Descending Passage in the Great Pyramid is inclined at an angle that represents the rays of the ancient Egyptian's polar star (Tompkins 150). This may also account for the exact straightness of the passageway walls. By using a star's meridian, the ancient Egyptians were able to dig a tunnel so exact that the 350 feet of the passageway never varies more than 1/4 of an inch (Tompkins 151). The Descending Passage, leading to the King's Chamber, may have been used with the stars overhead, to plot the exact positioning and construction of the Great Pyramid built above it. Once the Pyramid reached a high enough level, the Descending Passage would no longer have been useful. That's when the Ascending Passage, leading to the Queen's Chamber, may have been designed. Proctor believes the ancient Egyptians may have filled the Descending Passage with water, reflecting the polar star up to get the angle of the Ascending Passage. This may explain why the joint where these two passageways meet is constructed from harder, smoother stones than anywhere else in the Pyramid. This improved joint would have been required for the Descending Passageway to hold water (Tompkins 151).

Not only does it appear that astronomy was used in the construction of the Pyramid, the Pyramid may have been built to be used as an observatory as well. The Ascending Passage changes into a gallery that is twenty-eight feet high at the top. Architecturally there appears to be no reason for this. Astronomers can see a reason for this gallery. The top of this gallery is open and the opening slot is exactly bisected by a true meridian (Tompkins 152). Proctor believes "Such a Grand Gallery might well be described as the only very accurate method available for preparing an accurate map of the sky and of the zodiacal cyclorama— before the invention of the telescope in the seventeenth century of our era" (Tompkins 152).

The mysteries of the Great Pyramid are endless. Unfortunately, we may never know how the ancient Egyptians accomplished the construction of such an extraordinary building. We may never know all the reasons the ancient Egyptians may have had for building such a wondrous tomb. But as long as the Pyramid stands, people will search for answers. An Arab proverb may explain some of the ongoing wonder, "Man fears time, yet time fears the Pyramids" (Ashmawy 1).

Works Cited

Ashmawy, Alaa K. "The Great Pyramid of Giza." *The Seven Wonders.* http://Pharos.bu.edu/Egypt/Wonders/pyramid.html (5 Feb. 1996).

Budge, E.A. Wallis. *A Handbook of Egyptian Funerary Archaeology.* New York: Dover Publications, Inc., 1925.

Casson, Lionel. *Great Ages of Man: Ancient Egypt.* New York: Time Inc., 1965.

Tompkins, Peter. *Secrets of the Great Pyramid.* New York: Harper & Row, 1971.

Java: A Revolutionary Programming Language for the Internet

Student

During the winter of 1990, Sun Microsystems, a manufacturer of high-end computer workstations, organized a group of engineers to study and evaluate business opportunities in the general consumer electronics market. Their market research showed that consumers did not really care what components were inside electronic devices. Instead, consumers were buying electronic devices that were simple to use, had familiar interfaces, and were relatively cheap. Personal computer purchasing was not an exception to this research. The average consumer did not care what type of processor was installed in his computer. Consumers purchased computers that they considered to be reliable and easy to use. In response to this market, Sun's group of engineers, led by James Gosling, set out to create a platform independent computer language that would enable electronic devices composed of widely dissimilar elements to talk to one another. In other words, an application written in this new language would be able to run on an IBM personal computer or clone, an Apple Macintosh, a Sun workstation, or any platform capable of hooking into a distributed client-server environment (Gosling and McGilton 5; Nelson 1). After 18 months of work, the group had developed an operating system and a language that were both named "Oak." However, "Oak" was later changed to "Java" because "Oak" did not pass a trademark search (O'Connell 7). By March of 1993, Sun was attempting to subcontract its development team and new technology to Time Warner for use in an interactive cable TV trial. Unfortunately, the Time Warner deal fell through leaving Sun with a great deal of new technology and virtually no marketing strategy (O'Connell 8). Sun's engineers did not realize at this time that the language they had created would be perfectly suited for bringing multi-media capability to the Internet.

Until the early 1990s, most computers connecting to the Internet had been running some version of the UNIX operating system. UNIX provides a command line interface much like the DOS command line interface familiar to PC users. In April of 1993, this non-intuitive interface was swept away by NCSA Mosaic, the first graphical browser for the Internet. Mosaic changed a large part of the Internet landscape from a dry, stark, text-driven UNIX interface to the colorful world of pictures and graphics (van Hoff 1; O'Connell 7).

During this same time period, non-UNIX computers connected to the Internet more than ever before. The Internet rapidly evolved into a huge heterogeneous network of disparate machines (van Hoff 1). Sun, realizing that Java would enable developers to write applications that could run on the many different types of computers connecting to the Internet, refocused its engineers on the development of on-line services (O'Connell 2). On May 23, 1995, Sun announced to the world that it had created a prototype of a World Wide Web Browser, called HotJava, that would bring animation and interactively to the Internet's diverse community of computers (O'Connell 9).

What special quality of the Java language enables developers to write one application that will run on many different platforms? The answer is that Java was designed to be architecturally neutral from the ground up (Gosling and McGilton 27). Unlike Java, most symbolic languages are translated into machine code by compilers that are specifically designed to produce code that will only run on a particular platform. For instance, a program written in C that is intended to be run on both a PC and a Macintosh would have to be compiled once with a compiler specifically designed to produce machine code that a PC understands, and compiled again by a compiler specifically designed to produce machine code that a Macintosh understands (van Hoff 1). Java, on the other hand, is truly revolutionary. When Java is compiled, it is changed to a special code called a byte code that is further interpreted at run time by another program called a run time module. A run time module is simply a program that translates Java's byte codes into machine language that a computer's hardware can understand. In this way, given that a run time module exists for a target platform, Java code can be executed on any computer (van Hoff 1).

Because Java is architecturally neutral, interactivity and animation can now be added to the Internet. A World Wide Web site is a location on the Internet that looks much like a document created in a Microsoft Windows application because the site is capable of displaying pages containing different size fonts and color graphics. Positioning the mouse cursor on displayed icons or highlighted text and then clicking the left mouse button can cause a new page from a different location on the Internet to display itself. World Wide Web site creators write and then embed tiny Java applications called applets into their web pages. The Java applets then execute seamlessly whenever a user enters the site with a Java aware browser. In this manner, video, sound, animation, and a host of interactive applets appear in an otherwise static World Wide Web site (Leonard 1).

Many new and exciting applications of Java technology are beginning to appear on the Internet. Teachers are designing virtual classrooms that employ Java animations to demonstrate complex processes such as chemical reactions (Schmitz 4). Stock brokers will soon provide on-line stock tickers. Advertisers on the Internet are adding background music to their advertisements as well as animated cartoons that hawk their wares (Trager 1).

The ability to add multi-media applications to the Internet may revolutionize the way consumers use software. Currently, consumers purchase the software they need from retailers and install the software on their personal computers. But what if this same software was available on the Internet? Written in Java, the software could run on any desktop computer. Software vendors might be able to rent software over the Internet to users on an as-needed basis (Trager 2; Alsop 2).

Another ramification of using a language that can run on any platform is that the differences between the operating systems of Microsoft and Apple may become meaningless. If consumers can all run the same software on any computer, the problem of whether to buy a computer that runs Microsoft Windows or a computer that runs Macintosh software will no longer exist (Trager 1).

A major concern of Internet users is the detection and handling of computer viruses. How does the Java language safeguard against computer viruses being transported along with Java applets? Virus protection is built into Java. The correctness of the intermediate code created where Java is compiled is verified by the run time module each time the apples is run. In other words, a computer virus is not able to enter a system disguised as a Java apples because the run time module will detect a problem with the byte codes and halt the execution of the offending apples (van Hoff 4).

Java was designed to look much like the C++ language. In this way a very large base, of C++ programmers would be able to more quickly traverse the learning curve and begin producing Java applications. At the same time, most of the complexity inherent to the C++ language has been removed from Java. For instance, in C++ a pointer is a variable that holds the address of another variable. This particular variable type has been isolated as the source of many program bugs. Therefore, pointers have been removed from the Java language. Pointers are just one of the many complexities that have been stripped away in the design of Java. By making Java look like C++ and by making Java simple, Sun Microsystems hopes to create an army of Java programmers (Gossling and McGilton 13).

The World Wide Web already has many sites that are incorporating Java technology. Major software companies are licensing Java from Sun. Even Microsoft licensed Java rather than spend the two man-years of work it would take to develop the same technology (Tennant 2). Borland International plans to release a Java development environment in the near future. Natural Intelligence Inc. has nearly completed a Java development environment for the Macintosh (SunWorld Online 2). According to Sun Microsystems, Lotus International will be licensing Java for use with its widely used money management software, Quicken (SunWorld Online 3). Sun Microsystems hopes that Java will eventually replace the C++ language in major applications development (SunWorld Online 4). Considering all of the above developments, the future looks very bright for this innovative technology.

Robert A. Heinlein wrote in his novel, *The Rolling Stones*:

> *Every technology goes through three stages: first a crudely simple and quite unsatisfactory gadget; second, an enormously complicated group of gadgets designed to overcome the original and achieving*

> *thereby somewhat satisfactory performance through
> extremely complex compromise; third, a final proper
> design therefrom. (Heinlein qtd. in Gossling and
> McGilton 13)*

Java promises to be the introduction to stage three of the technology needed to run applications over a diverse network of different computers. Over the next several years as the World Wide Web portion of the Internet becomes fully interactive, Java will lead the way as the premier development tool for cross-platform applications.

Works Cited

Alsop, Stewart. "DistributedThinking." *Info World Electric.* http://www. infoworld.com/pageone/opinions/sal2l 8.htm (3 Jan. 1996).

Gosling, James and McGilton, Henry. "The Java(tm) Language Environment: A White Paper." http://www.sun.com/whitePaper/java-whitepaper-(1-11).html (16 Dec. 1995).

"Java Proliferates Through Licensing Deals." *Sun World Online.* http://www.Sun.COM:80/sunworldonline/swol-12-1995/swol-12javadeal.html (13 Dec. 1995).

Leonard, Andrew. "Java Java Java: Is It the Future or the End?" *Web Review.* http://www.gnn.com/wr/ nov22/features/java/index.html (5 Jan. 1996).

Nelson, Brian. "World Wide Web Gets Jolt from Java and Shockwave." *CNN Interactive.* http:// www.cnn.com/TECH/9512/java/index.html (4 Jan. 1996).

O'Connell, Michael. "Java: The Inside Story." *Sunworld Online.* http://www.Sun.COM:80/ sunworldonline/swol-07-1995/swol-07-java.html (4 Jan. 1996).

Schmitz, John. "JAVA, Super Browsers, and the Virtual Classroom." http://w3.ag.uiuc.edu/AIM/2.0/ overview.html (4 Jan. 1996).

Tennant, Don. "The World According to Gates." *Info World Electric.* http://www.inforworld.com/cgibin/displayStory.pl ?79gates.htm (3 Jan. 1996).

Trager, Louis. "Java Computer Language Brings Gee-Whiz Futurism (10/31)." *The New York Times Syndicate.* http:Hnytsyn.com/live/features/304-103195-083533-21012.html (5 Jan. 1996).

van Hoff, Arthur. "Java and Internet Programming." *Dr. Dobb's Journal.* http://www.ddj.com/ddj/ 1995/1995.08/hoff.htm (5 Jan. 1996).

On-line Outlaws

Student

The first thing *Time* Senior editor Phillip Elmer-DeWitt noticed was awry was that he had somehow been registered for over one hundred different E-mail sources in less than one day's time. Yet, almost as soon as he had unsubscribed himself from every last one of them, he discovered that he had been enrolled in over 1,500 more. Elmer-DeWitt states that his "file of unread E-mail had swelled to 16 megabytes, and was growing by the minute" (77). With the help of his on-line service provider, Phillip Elmer-Dewitt was able to reduce the flow of messages from a gargantuan two hundred forty per hour to almost fifty per hour. What caused this phenomenon? Elmer-Dewitt was unfortunately the target of an E-mail bomb, an attempt by an anonymous person to flood another computer's system with garbage mail (Elmer-DeWitt 77). Even though events like this cause no real damage they are annoying and are considered serious crimes. In fact, many new crimes have been introduced to the world because of the rapid growth and expansion of the computer industry. The creation and release of destructive viruses, tampering with cellular phone networks, and a sundry of other crimes cause much chaos in the computer world.

One illustration of a computer crime is the creation and release of destructive computer viruses. Some viruses are destructive and lethal to the computer's system and others are used only as bothersome pranks. One recent example of a destructive virus is the well-publicized Michelangelo virus. It was designated the Michelangelo virus because it becomes operational only on March 6, the birthday of the famous artist, Michelangelo. This virus posed a threat to computer users because it had the ability to actually destroy data on computer disks which could cause computers world-wide to collapse.

Fortunately, the Michelangelo virus wasn't allowed to cause much damage largely because of the extensive publicity and widespread detection efforts (Jenish 49). Where did the program originate? Most evidence seems to point towards a programmer in the Netherlands or Sweden. The virus became widely circulated when "an unidentified Taiwanese software company unwittingly began distributing infected programs" (Jernish 49). Even though Michelangelo had infected many computers world-wide, it, however, did not have the distinction of being the most widespread virus. This honor belongs to the Stoned virus, which when the computer is booted up will clear the screen and produce "one of several variations of the message 'Your PC now is stoned'" (Jenish 49). A second virus becomes operational at 5 o'clock on predetermined days and plays the tune "Yankee Doodle" through the computer's PC speaker (Jenish 49). These viruses are contracted by sharing computer disks or running infected programs acquired online. To prevent the viruses, the computer must have a virus detection program (Booth 12e). This program can be arranged to automatically scan any incoming data before it is executed. In this manner, a computer can remain virus free (Booth 52).

A second type of computer crime involves cellular phone networks. Two methods of cheating this system are in known existence today. The first method, cloning, requires altering the computer chip inside the phone to match that of a legitimate cellular phone. Many times, the legitimate customer doesn't know what is happening until the bill arrives. Such is the case when "one U S West Cellular customer in Albuquerque recently received a hefty phone bill. Total: $20,000" (Flanagan and McMenamin, "Why Cybercrooks" 189). Fortunately, the cellular customer is not held responsible for such a bill, but it costs cellular phone companies approximately $300 million a year in illegitimate services. The second method, tumbling, makes use of the fact that cellular carriers allow customers to call outside of the home area. When the phone is used away from its home base, the verification process takes so long that the connection is completed before it is verified. If the call is found to be invalid, that office will not allow any more calls by the verification number. That doesn't matter to the phone, for it changes numbers every time a call is placed, therefore bypassing the confirmation check. Although the gamble of using chipped-up phones may be high, it is worth the risk, especially for immigrants and drug dealers who make frequent international calls (Flanagan and McMenamin, "Why Cybercrooks" 189).

Many amazing computer related crimes have been accomplished in the past. In addition, there are several kinds of computer hackers which commit these crimes. Computer stunt hackers are small time offenders who are merely out for an intellectual joyride while trashing someone else's computer system. For example, take the 1988 case of Robert Morris, who launched an attack on the world-wide Internet. He developed and unleashed a "worm" program which "jammed an estimated 6,000 computers tied into Internet, including those of several universities, NASA, and the Air Force, before it was stopped" (Flanagan and McMenamin, "The Playground Bullies" 187). Even though the aftermath cost at least $15 million to clean up, Robert Morris only received a sentence of three year's probation, community service of 400 hours, and a $109,000 penalty. The penalty was not as stiff as it could have been, for Morris's defense argued "that the worm did not actually delete or modify any files"; it only duplicated itself ceaselessly on every computer system ("Noted and Notorious" 152). Secondly, there are the hardcore hackers. These programmers are only out for their own gain. They cheat and scam their way into bank accounts, telephone companies, and government agencies, tricking people into giving away passwords, credit card numbers, and other personal information. For example, researchers have discovered a new kind of computer fraud on the Internet. In this scheme, the computer hacker creates a webpage that is similar to a legitimate page on the web, such as microsoft.com. Instead of microsoft.com, the page is saved as microsOft.com, a close match. Once a victim has stumbled upon this site, the hacker can monitor any activity. If the user attempts to purchase something using a credit card or completes an application on-line, the hacker instantly takes a victim (Young A25). "A lot of this technology is being put out there without thinking of the consequences of what can be done to the Web users" says Eugene H. Spafford, a computer science professor at Purdue University (Young A25). Many times the computer user doesn't know what has happened until it is too late.

Finally, from the virus creators to the stunt hackers to the hardcore hackers, the world of computer miscreants is growing every year. Law enforcement considers computer crimes to be more of a threat than ever. As we face the 21st century, the frequency of these crimes increases, while the fines and prison terms lengthen. We only hope our law enforcement can remain one step ahead of tomorrow's cybercriminal.

Works Cited

Booth, Stephen A. "Doom Virus." *Popular Mechanics* June 1995: 51-54+.

Elmer-DeWitt, Phillip. "I've Been Spammed!" *Time* 8 March 1996: 77.

Flanagan, William G. and Brigid McMenamin. "The Playground Bullies Are Learning How to Type." *Forbes* Dec. 1992: 184–189.

——"Why Cybercrooks Love Cellular." *Forbes* Dec. 1992: 189.

Jenish, D'Arcy. "A 'Terrorist' Virus." *Byte* Sept. 1995: 48+.

"Noted and Notorious Hacker Feats." *Byte* Sept. 1995: 151–162.

Young, Jeffrey R. and David L. Wilson. "Researchers Warn of the Ease With Which Fake Web Pages Can Fool Internet Users." *Chronicle of Higher Education* 10 Jan. 1997: A25.

Software Piracy

Student

"Global losses caused by software piracy totaled $13.2 billion in 1995, an amount that exceeded the combined revenues of the 10 largest PC software companies" (Anthes 24). Today, computer software, ranging from video games and educational programs to word processors and database managers, continue to be illegally copied. Crime occupies every facet of life, but computer crimes, like software piracy, are unique because of the wide ranged age groups, gender, races, life-styles and geographical locations. Anyone is capable of software piracy: "surveys indicate that the demographics of the people browsing the Web has shifted to more closely reflect those observed in the general population . . . ("Who's Using" 46). With the vastness of the Internet, software piracy continues to escalate despite the prevention tactics and the threat of punishment.

The Internet, also known as the World Wide Web, the Information Superhighway, cyberspace, and others, has gained enormous popularity, which has provided a rising ocean, full of ships, for the software pirate. "The fast-growing 'network of networks,' with some 30 million users around the globe" is only the beginning ("Piracy on the" 9). This increasing demand for service has spawned commercial and private network servers, expanding accessibility to the work place, to educational institutions, and even to your own home. With this growth and ease of accessibility, "software piracy, the illegal copying of computer software, . . . has become a widespread problem in university, government and business environments" (Sims, Cheng, Teegen 839). All types of information including pictures, sounds, videos, games, mail, shopping, newspapers, magazines, pornography, and pirated software are transferred on a daily basis through cyberspace. Subsequently, the web has become a hacker's playground, a virtually clueless crime scene in virtual space. For example, a continuous movement of illegal activity would be laborious to track in any environment. "Monitoring ever-changing Web pages for content is difficult" (Deck 6). Hackers, software pirates, use the Internet to acquire, distribute, and display their conquered victims, copyrighted software. Mostly due to the size and population of the World Wide Web, software piracy is incredibly difficult to trace.

Equally important, anti-piracy (the prevention tactics of copying software illegally) is continually revised and revisited by industry, and supported by the government. "Software producers have tried just about everything to protect themselves from losses due to unauthorized copying" (Sims, Cheng, Teegen 839). Recently, one such method, "'cryptolope,' . . . cryptographic envelope," is software designed to house encrypted information allowing a prospective customer to sample a small portion by viewports displayed on the video screen (Ross 137). After purchasing the information, a key is obtained from "on-line or from a disk" to gain access (Ross 137). Other tactics include disk copy prevention techniques, which consist of using non-standard disk formats, creating burn marks and holes in the disk made with lasers, and unique coding (Sims, Cheng, Teegen 839). Since breaking the copyright law is a federal offense, the government is forced to take action, as well as expected to become involved. "Software piracy directly affects over 1,000 U.S. companies engaged in computer programming and software development" (Sims, Cheng, Teegen 839), which significantly affects profits of individual companies as well as tax revenue to the United States government.

The government is a major player in the litigation of anti-piracy concerns; "publishers of software, . . . said the bill, which is before the Senate, must protect them from electronic piracy" (Anthes 28). These bills were proposed to include the information superhighway in the legality of copyrights that are currently used for tangible media (Anthes 28). Despite the many bills passed and anti-piracy organizations formed, some consumers are unaware that they have committed software piracy.

Furthermore, the threat and severity of punishment for software piracy does not seem to deter the crime. Lawsuits are common throughout the software industry whenever there's a case of copyright infringement. "The Software Publishers Association (SPA) filed lawsuits. . . that charge two Internet service providers and a World Wide Web-hosting service with software piracy" (Deck 6). These suits accused three Internet providers of consenting to their customers intrusion of copyright laws by allowing users to post pirated software, to publish illegal identification numbers, and to display software hacking tools or to allow customers to upkeep addresses to "file transfer protocol sites" which contain unauthorized software (Deck 6). Until there's an understanding and an agreement of who is responsible for enforcing the copyright laws, many companies will continue to suffer a profit loss. Sometimes, the threat of a lawsuit is replaced by a fine.

For example, "'they want to fine us $5,000 per computer. If we pay, they won't sue'. . . said the . . . chief executive" (Garber 214). During a "surprise audit" by inspectors, 19 computers at the main company office had illegal copies of software (Garber 214). For this new company, $95,000 in fines was steep, since profits were at least 18 months in the future (Garber 214). Besides lawsuits and fines, the act of property seizure is another form of punishment against software pirates. For instance, "FBI officials seized computer hardware and documents as part of an . . . investigation, code-named 'Cyber Strike'" (Wong 24). Although this provides hard evidence against the criminal and will most likely lead to prosecution, the government can not knock on every door in the United States, or the world for that matter.

In conclusion, the Internet presents major problems with the issue of software piracy, due to ease of accessibility and lack of security. Meanwhile, the future, creative prevention methods introduced by the software industry, along with progressive government support look promising, but there are no guarantees of resolution. Although punishment is severe and well publicized, the number of offenders continues to increase. Finally, while ignorance of the law is no excuse, the true criminals are not always punished, because they are rarely caught, but you know where they have been by the tagged code-names left behind in pirated software.

Works Cited

Anthes, Gary. "Software pirates' booty topped $13B, study finds." *Computerworld* 6 Jan. 1997: 24.

——. "Cyber copyright issue sparks fierce debate." *Computerworld* 20 May 1996: 28.

Deck, Stewart. "Internet providers sued for software piracy." *Computerworld* 14 Oct. 1994: 6.

Garber, Joseph. "Piracy." *Forbes* 22 Apr. 1996: 214.

"Piracy on the Electronic Seas." *World Press Review.* Apr. 1995: 9.

Ross, Philip. "Cops versus robbers in cyberspace." *Forbes* 9 Sep. 1996: 134–39.

Sims, Ronald R., Hsing K. Cheng and Hildy Teegen. "Toward a Profile of Student Software Piraters." *Journal of Business Ethics* 15 (1996): 839–49.

"Who's Using the World Wide Web?" *The Futurist.* Jan./Feb. 1996: 46.

Wong, Wylie. "FBI targets BBS operators, seizes hardware in software piracy sting." *Computerworld* 3 Feb. 1997: 24.

Ch. 10: Documented Essays

———————

Suggestions for writing:

1. Who is your favorite writer? Write a research paper about him or her, recounting major life events along with a publishing history. Find a biography of the writer in the library (a good biography will probably have a useful bibliography at the end of the book), locate recent articles about the writer's work in academic journal indices, and search the Internet for very up-to-date information.

2. What is your favorite book? Write a paper in which you establish the exact day that the book was published and give a survey of what was happening in the world from five days before until five days after that day.

3. Write a research paper on one of the following topics or a similar topic:

    how robotics is affecting industry   the history of the Internet
    software piracy   computer viruses
    telecommunications in the 21 st century   virtual reality
    how computers are changing medicine   the future of the space program
    your favorite movie director   the career field you hope to enter

Checklist for research papers:

1. Does your introduction attract the reader's interest and present a thesis that clearly establishes what you will accomplish in your paper?

2. Does each body paragraph begin with a good transition? Does each body paragraph contain a topic sentence that relates back to your thesis?

3. Have you developed each body paragraph with quotations, paraphrases, or summaries?

4. Did you lead into each quote clearly and effectively?

5. Did you develop an effective conclusion?

6. Did you strictly adhere to the rules of whatever documentation system you are using? Did you cite all information that came from outside sources, even if you didn't present it as a direct quotation? Did you compile a "works cited" or a "bibliography" listing that contains all of the sources that you used?

7. Did you vary your vocabulary and sentence structure?

8. Did you check for correctness of grammar, punctuation, spelling, and format?

Student Rating Form

To the Student: Your ratings of the reading selections will help us to plan future editions of *The Red Bridge Reader*.

Selection	Interesting	Not Interesting	Too Difficult	Readable	Too Easy	Didn't Read
Description						
A Guard's First Night on the Job						
Take This Fish and Look at It						
Graduation						
Summer Rituals						
Marrying Absurd						
An Athlete's Locker Room						
My Grandma						
An Urban Legend						
Learning Experience						
Narration						
Mind Your Tongue, Young Man						
A Total Eclipse						
Passport to Knowledge						
The Perfect Picture						
My Experience with Hunting						
An Eventful Flight						
Example						
Civil Rites						
What the Nose Knows						
Idiosyncrasies, Anyone?						
Were Dinosaurs Dumb?						
Writing with a Word Processor						
Bike Wear						
How to Save Fuel and Money						
How to Be a Successful Basketball Player						
Process Analysis						
A Hairy Experience						
Foundation Waterproofing						
On Keeping a Notebook						
How to Say Nothing in Five Hundred Words						
How to Write with Style						
Let's Get Vertical						
Collecting Stamps						
Division / Classification						
The Big Five Fears of Our Time						
The Plot Against People						
Why I Want a Wife						
It's Only a Paper World						
Predictable Crises of Adulthood						
DeVry Students and Financial Aid						
Spare Time at DeVry						

Selection	Interesting	Not Interesting	Too Difficult	Readable	Too Easy	Didn't Read
Comparison / Contrast						
Neat People vs. Sloppy People						
Nursing Practices—England and America						
Grant and Lee: A Study in Contrasts						
Second Thoughts on the Information Highway						
Get a Life?						
Kansas vs. Hawaii						
A Comparison Between Business and the Life of the Non-Traditional Student						
Cause / Effect						
Children and Violence in America						
The Agony Must End						
My Wood						
Why We Crave Horror Movies						
Fear of Dearth						
My Decision to Attend DeVry						
This Is Not a Tall Person's World						
Definition						
Barrier Signals						
Baseball's Hot Dogs						
The Bureaucrat						
The Sweet Smell of Success Isn't All That Sweet						
Television Addiction						
The Right Stuff						
What Is a Lamer?						
Failure						
Success						
Argument and Persuasion						
Get a Knife, Get a Dog, but Get Rid of Guns						
Putting in a Good Word for Guilt						
I Have a Dream						
Gettysburg Address						
Drug Testing Violates Workers' Rights						
Affirmative Action: It's Not Progress						
Affirmative Action: The Price of Preference						
The Psychology of the Future						
Smokers' Space						
No Smoking Section						
Documented Essays						
Cheops: The Great Pyramid						
Java: A Revolutionary Programming Language for the Internet						
On-line Outlaws						
Software Piracy						